REVISED EDITION

Indiana
Gardener's Guide

Published by Cool Springs Press, a Division of Thomas Nelson, Inc., P. O. Box 141000, Nashville, Tennessee, 37214.

Sharp, Jo Ellen Meyers.
    Indiana gardener's guide / Jo Ellen Meyers Sharp, Tom Tyler—Rev. ed.
        p. cm.
    Rev. ed. of: Indiana gardener's guide / Tom Tyler, Jo Ellen Meyers Sharp. c1997.
    Includes bibliographical references (p.   ).
    ISBN 1-59186-068-7 (pbk.)
    1. Landscape plants—Indiana. 2. Landscape gardening—Indiana. 3. Gardening—Indiana.
    I. Tyler, Tom. II. Tyler, Tom. Indiana gardener's guide. III. Title.
SB407.T95 2004
635.9'09772—dc22
                                    2003021255

First Printing 2004
Printed in the United States of America
10 9 8 7 6 5 4 3 2 1

Managing Editor: Ramona D. Wilkes
Horticulture Editor: Mark Zelonis
Copyeditor: Sally Graham
Production Design: S.E. Anderson
Cover Designer: Sheri Ferguson Kimbrough

'Nicole' and 'Jean Keneally' rose photos were provided courtesy of Heirloom Roses, Inc. (www.heirloomroses.com)

On the cover: Purple Coneflower, photographed by Dency Kane

Visit the Thomas Nelson website at www.ThomasNelson.com

REVISED EDITION

Indiana
Gardener's Guide

Jo Ellen Meyers Sharp
Tom Tyler

COOL
SPRINGS
PRESS

Nashville, Tennessee
A Division of Thomas Nelson, Inc.
www.ThomasNelson.com

Dedication

In honor of my great-grandparents, John and Anna Kempe Heidenreich, and grandparents, Arthur and Helen Staub Heidenreich, who made their living in the nursery, greenhouse, and florist business; my uncle, Bill Heidenreich, who taught me the basics; my parents, Frank and Joann Heidenreich Meyers, who taught me about nurturing all living things; and my son, Benjamin, a gardener in the making. —*J.E.M.S*

For my mother, Pat, whose garden grows lush in heaven, and my father, Art, who always encouraged me to follow my heart. For my partner Chris, the best coach and cheerleader ever—my everyday inspiration, friend, and companion. With love and gratitude. —*T.T.*

Acknowledgments

We wish to thank all who shared with us their knowledge of gardening and horticulture as well as their technical assistance on the first edition including Doug Akers, Russ Anger, Bill Brink, Dick Crum, Mike Dana, Mike Griffith, Wayne Kreuscher, Ruth Krulce, Rosie Lerner, Steve Mayer, and Sarah Palmatier. For this revised edition, we wish to thank:

Chris Bobowski, for his editorial assistance and support throughout the writing process; Hilary Cox, Master Gardener and owner of Leescape Garden Design, Avon, IN, who reviewed annuals and perennials for native status; Dick Crum, retired Extension Agent, Marion County, who taught us a great deal about garden communications; Katy J. Copsey, a Master Gardener and owner of Betony Herbs, Brownsburg, IN, who reviewed the herb chapter; Cindy Games, The Waynick Group, who gets us good gigs to help sell our book; Susan Gilmer, an editor and gardener—a great sounding board who supported writing efforts and answered questions about grammar; Bill and William Heidenreich, Heidenreich Greenhouses, Indianapolis, Jo Ellen's uncle and cousin who grow plants for a living and who provide a forum for learning and teaching; The Indianapolis Museum of Art's Mark Zelonis and his staff, who helped with the horticulture editing and who freely share their knowledge and enthusiasm for gardening, including Sue Nord Peiffer, Lynne Steinhour Habig, Katie Booth, Irvin Etienne, Chad Franer, Kevin Harmon, and Geoff VonBurg; Lynn Jenkins, Master Gardener and owner of Nature's Garden, Zionsville, IN, who reviewed annuals and perennials for wildlife attractions; Linda Kimmel, Indianapolis Rosarian, who cheerfully reviewed the roses chapter in the second edition and who gave invaluable advice; Hank McBride, Cool Springs Press, for giving us this opportunity to help Hoosiers succeed in gardening; Steve Mayer, Marion County Horticulture Extension Agent, Indianapolis, who reviewed shrubs and who readily shares his knowledge and research skills—one of the most helpful people we know; readers of *The Indianapolis Star*, with whom Jo Ellen shares a special relationship; Dave Rudat (Koffee), who helped spread the word about good gardening practices over the airwaves at the former WMYS in Indianapolis; Greg and Sue Speichert, owners of Crystal Palace Perennials, St. John, IN, and publishers of *Water Gardening* magazine, who reviewed the water gardens chapter; Ramona Wilkes, Cool Springs Press editor, Nashville, Tennessee, who has been wonderful to work with.

Table of Contents

Featured Plants *for Indiana*

Welcome to Gardening
in Indiana

Gardening is America's most popular outdoor activity, so Indiana gardeners are in good company. The majority of us spend several hours a week fertilizing a houseplant, cutting the lawn, weeding, watering, or picking the fruits of our labor. Gardening is a dynamic process, influenced by the changing forces of nature and by the plants we use. One of Indiana's blessings is its long growing season. There is usually enough natural rainfall to guarantee that a wide variety of plants will do well in our state. In this book, we provide gardeners with information on more than 180 ornamental plants. These are not all of the plants that thrive in the Hoosier landscape, but these are ones that we know will do well. We talk about the basics: how to grow, use, and maintain the plants, as well as how to enjoy them for a lifetime full of seasonal pleasures.

The *Indiana Gardener's Guide* includes both native and adaptive plants in twelve chapters by type: annuals, bulbs, ground covers, herbs, lawns, ornamental grasses, perennials, roses, shrubs, trees, vines, and water garden plants. The plants are listed by common name, which is the name they are usually called here in Indiana. The Latin, scientific, or botanical name of each plant follows its common name. Botanists have assigned a scientific name to each plant for the purpose of universal identification. This prevents confusion when identifying plants, since different regions or countries often use different common names for the same plant. For instance, some people call the August-blooming resurrection lily (*Lycoris squamigera*) a "surprise lily." Others refer to it as a "naked lady." Using a plant's Latin or botanical name will ensure that you purchase the plant you want.

Indiana gardening also means contending with hot, dry, humid summers and the fluctuating temperatures of winter and spring that seem to freeze and thaw the ground every other day. Another factor is the ground itself, which is often hard-packed clay or a wet boggy site with poor drainage. Though Indiana is well known for its rich and productive farmland, the same soil for gardens often proves to be a challenge. While there's little we can do about the weather, we can make the best of what we have by knowing our sites, carefully choosing our plants, and improving our soil.

Getting Started

You will get much better results if you pick the right plant for the right place, which means researching light, soil, moisture, and other requirements. For instance, pay attention to how much sun or shade a particular area of the yard gets or which sites stay wet longer than others.

Full-sun plants need at least six hours of direct sunlight a day; part-sun plants should receive about four hours of sunlight a day, and they prefer light that is filtered through the canopies of tall trees. Part-shade means the plants should get direct sun only in the early morning or very late afternoon. They must get shade in the hottest time of the day, whereas a "shade" plant can live with little or no sunlight. Reflective light and general brightness are also factors to consider.

Don't be afraid to try new plants. Check with neighbors, relatives, and friends about what has worked well in their yards. Visit public gardens and parks to see what the experts grow. Along with commercial sites, these gardens and parks are often the first places to use new plants in the landscape. An example of this is the popular red fountain grass (*Pennisetum setaceum* 'Rubrum'). The annual ornamental grass was used in public and commercially planted settings for several years before homeowners started planting it in their yards.

The ideal time to plant permanent plants such as trees, shrubs, ground covers, and perennials is usually in the spring or fall. Transplanting may also be performed in summer if the gardener is vigilant about keeping the new plants well watered. Spring-flowering bulbs are planted in fall; summer-flowering bulbs may be planted in the spring or fall; annuals are usually planted in the spring after the last frost. Though the gardening bug bites most of us in the spring, the fall is actually the best time to prepare the landscape. In the fall, the soil is more evenly moist, and the temperature is more consistent. Organic matter incorporated into the soil has a chance to break down and improve the drainage.

Beds prepared in the fall may be planted in the fall, or they may be allowed to settle for spring planting. Fall-prepared beds usually warm up and dry out sooner than those prepared in spring. This is important, especially because spring rains frequently limit our chances to get outside and garden.

Before understaking major landscape projects, digging new beds, or installing a water garden, find out where your underground utilities are on your property. With two days notice, Indiana Underground Plant Protection Service, Inc. will locate the underground utilities for you at no charge. For this service, call (800) 382-5544.

Know Your Soil

Improving the soil is a never-ending task in the Indiana landscape. When we talk about digging up soil and mixing in organic matter, we recommend you use compost, finely chopped leaves, leaf mold, well-aged manure, or dried grass clippings. The *Indiana Gardener's Guide* gives specific how-to's for amending soil in each chapter according to plant type. Soil testing is another important step in gardening. Gather samples of the soil every three to five years in the spring, summer, or fall. Take samples throughout the yard, or from specific beds, and send them to a soil testing lab. Contact your County Extension office for a lab near you. Among other things, the results of the test will reveal the pH and fertility of the soil. As basic as blood pressure and heart rate, soil test results serve as guides for determining fertilizer rates. They also give an idea as to the overall health of the soil, such as the content of minerals and organic matter. A soil test really helps gardeners begin to understand what is happening under ground.

A Recipe for Gardener's Gold

The best way to enrich the soil and improve its drainage and consistency is to add compost. No backyard should be without a compost pile. Most landfills in Indiana have banned plant debris, so composts are the perfect place to dispose of what we glean from the yard. Plant debris can be mixed with biodegradable trash from the house, such as lint, carpet and floor sweepings, kitchen scraps (such as vegetable peelings, coffee grounds and filters, and egg shells), pet and human hair (burying hair like you would food scraps), and paper towels. Kitchen scraps may attract rodents, so bury them deep inside the pile. Some communities have forbidden the construction of compost heaps. This seems odd since compost makes plants thrive, making their neighborhoods more beautiful.

Don't add cat or dog waste, grease, fat, meat products, coal, coal dust or ashes, charcoal briquettes, synthetics, street sweepings, bulky materials that are slow to decompose, or sewer sludge to a compost.

Grass clippings and other plant material that have been treated with pesticides and/or herbicides should be set aside to allow the chemicals to break down before they are mixed into the pile.

The ideal size for a compost pile is about three feet wide, deep, and tall. Build a compost pile in the sun or shade. Enclose the pile in a bin that you construct yourself or purchase a bin from retailers, garden centers, or mail-order catalogs. Making a compost pile is a lot like making lasagna. Add layers of ingredients and when it is cooked, the result is a nutritious food: "gardener's gold." At the base of the compost pile, place about three inches of coarse material like twigs, small branches, or stalks.

Hardy Geraniums Brighten a Border

Serene Landscape with Japanese Iris

Add a six-inch layer of dry plant material such as chopped leaves. Add a two-inch layer of green material such as grass clippings, kitchen scraps, or fresh livestock manure. Add a thin layer of soil, composted manure, or compost. Water the layers as you go and repeat with layers of brown material, green material, and soil until the pile reaches the desired height. Fertilizers high in nitrogen can be used in place of grass clippings or livestock manure. Use about one-quarter to one-half cup for each layer. For the best and fastest compost, grind or chop the ingredients before adding, keep the pile in the sun, turn it at least once a month, and keep the materials moist but not soggy.

Enriching the Soil

When the compost is finished, add it to your garden. If you can't make enough from your own pile, purchase some from a local garden center or landscape supplier. Retailers sell it in bags as well as in bulk. Spread the compost about one inch thick around plants in spring and fall. It will work its way down into the soil, improving it along the way. You can also mix it in beds when preparing for planting. Spread a two- to four-inch layer over the soil and mix it into the top six to twelve inches of soil as you dig. Pile it two to three inches around shrubs and trees to provide a nutritious mulch that moderates soil temperatures and helps retain moisture.

Another good additive is a natural, slow-release nitrogen fertilizer or an all-purpose synthetically derived fertilizer. These are good products to mix in the soil when preparing a bed for the first time. They can also be sprinkled around plants or in flower beds. Always follow soil test results and label directions when using any product.

Watering and Fertilizing

It is impossible to give a regular watering schedule for plants. That's because each garden is different and rainfall is highly variable. Some parts of the yard may be wetter than others, and one side of town may get rain while other neighborhoods do not. Almost always, it's better to err on the dry side. In this book, if plants have specific moisture requirements, they are noted under the Growing Tips. As a general guideline, water plants when the top inch of soil feels dry to the touch.

Well-prepared planting beds and the year-long use of compost or other organic matter as soil amendments or as mulch drastically reduces the need for fertilizing most plants. Only annuals would likely need supplemental doses of a water-soluble fertilizer throughout the growing season.

Learning to Live with Pests

In this book, we have taken a natural approach to gardening when it comes to bugs and diseases. That doesn't mean we garden *au natural*. Rather, we accept that insects and diseases are as much a part of gardening as are flowers and foliage.

Gardening is an up-close and personal experience with nature in your own backyard. Before long, you'll notice that goldfinches eat the seedheads of purple coneflowers and that butterflies flock to zinnias. Those who pay even closer attention may see that lady beetles are dining on the aphids and that lightning bugs zap slugs.

Many insects and diseases are opportunistic, which means the conditions have to be just right for them to cause a problem. Some years, fungus may be a problem on plants because the weather has been cool and wet. Or one year the Japanese beetles will be more numerous and voracious than other years.

A "pest" can be an insect or a disease. Rather than prescribe pesticides for these individual problems, we prefer to recommend good overall cultural or environmental practices, and we encourage gardeners to be more tolerant of plant damage.

Cultural and environmental controls are easy. Keeping plants healthy is probably the best defense from occasional insect or disease damage. That starts with good soil preparation and selecting the right plant for the right place. And it means patience. Most of the time, untreated disease and insect damage will not cause a plant to die, but sometimes it does. That, too, is a part of nature. Selecting plants that are resistant to insects or diseases also helps reduce or eliminate the need for pesticides.

In nature there are good and bad bugs. Natural gardening presumes that Mother Nature will take care of herself if we let her. An infestation of aphids on honeysuckle may look disturbing and cause a few distorted leaves, but if left alone, lady beetles (good bugs) will devour the aphids (bad bugs), one of their favorite snacks.

In this case if you use an insecticide for the aphids, you run the risk of killing the beetles, bees, and butterflies, too. This may be one of the ways gardening teaches us patience. We just have to wait for the beetles to arrive for their aphid dinner.

Gardening is a lifelong learning opportunity. Learn to identify signs and symptoms of good and bad bugs or disease. Always identify the pest before you decide what to do about it. For instance, it is a waste of money to use an insecticide to treat a fungus. There are often pest "diagnosticians" right in your local community through the County Extension Master Gardener programs and your local County Extension Office. The Internet and your local library also have resources to help you figure out your pest problem. Correctly identifying the problem before treating it also saves money.

If you decide you need to control a pest, choose the least toxic method first. For insects, the first line of attack may be a strong spray from the garden hose to knock the critters off the plant. For a plant disease such as a fungus, consider moving the plant to a different site or try pruning the inner branches to improve air circulation. The next step would probably be natural controls, such as insecticidal soaps for bugs or sulphur mixes for fungus. *Whatever product you choose, make sure it is the right one for the job, and always read and follow label directions.*

Reducing or eliminating the use of pesticides may also increase the number of flowers, fruits, and vegetables in the garden. Butterfly and hummingbird gardeners particularly should refrain from spraying pesticides.

Natural gardening means we may have to get used to a holey or half-eaten leaf here and there, just like we find in nature.

Understanding Hardiness Zones

Indiana's challenging weather requires us to use those plants that do well in the Hoosier climate. We make reference to plant hardiness throughout the *Indiana Gardener's Guide.* Hardiness refers to a plant's useful range and is determined by its ability to survive low temperatures in the winter months and grow satisfactorily the following spring.

Daily high and low temperatures have been recorded across the continent for many years. The average of these temperatures was used to build a hardiness zone map. The map referred to in this book is the USDA Hardiness Map published by the U.S. Department of Agriculture (see page 19). All of Indiana lies in Hardiness Zones 5 and 6. There is a ten degree difference between these zones and the next warmer or colder zones.

For the most part, the plants selected for this book are adapted for both Zones 5 and 6, but there are a few exceptions. While a species may be adapted to your zone, a favorite variety or cultivar may not. Be sure to choose plants that are adapted to the hardiness zone you live in when planning your landscape. Otherwise, they may not survive the winter. In central Indiana, for instance, plants that may be winter hardy in Johnson County may not be winter hardy in Hamilton County.

There's also a movement in the horticultural community to identify a plant's heat tolerance. Some plants, such as pansies, decline in hot weather. In some publications and on plant tags, gardeners may see reference to the American Horticultural Society's Heat Zone Map. The AHS's map is designed to help in selecting plants that tolerate heat. The map breaks the United States into twelve zones, depending on the average number of "heat" days. Heat days are those when the temperature is 86 degrees Fahrenheit or above. Heat-zone 1 has no days of 86-degree Fahrenheit weather, while Heat-zone 12 has at least 210 days.

Indiana has four heat zones. Even though these numbers are similar to cold hardiness, they refer to heat.

- Northeast Indiana is Zone 4, which has 15 to 30 heat days. This includes Steuben and LaGrange counties.
- Northern Indiana is Zone 5, which has 31 to 45 heat days. The area is north of a line drawn across Lake, Jasper, White, Tippecanoe, Clinton, Tipton, Madison, Rush, and Wayne counties.
- Central Indiana is Zone 6, which has 46 to 60 heat days. It includes Vigo, Marion, Monroe, Bartholomew, and Dearborn counties.
- Southern Indiana is Zone 7, which has 61 to 90 heat days. It includes an area south of a line drawn across Knox, Davies, Martin, Orange, Harrison, Floyd, Scott, Jefferson, and Ohio counties. This area also has scattered spots of Zone 8, which has 91 to 120 heat days.

Hardiness is affected by other factors as well. If they are not watered well and mulched in the late fall, the leaves of evergreens like boxwood or leatherleaf viburnum may dry out when winter temperatures fluctuate.

Dazzling Row of Maples

Plants that get stressed from summer drought, flooding, or other disturbance to their roots may not tolerate as low a temperature as those that are healthy. Protection from prevailing winds will improve winter hardiness to a limited extent, as will a plant's exposure to sun or shade.

Soil type and planting time also influence plant hardiness. For example, hardy mums purchased in full bloom and planted in the fall have limited chances for survival since the plants will not have sufficient time to establish a good root system before the onset of winter's killing cold.

Hoosier Gardening Heritage

Native Americans were Indiana's first gardeners, growing many of the staple crops of today—corn, beans, squash, and sunflowers. They used the barks, branches, berries, and seeds of trees and shrubs for food,

medicine, and household items. Their woods and fields were rich with purple coneflowers, black-eyed Susans, serviceberries, bluebells, redbuds, birches, and maples. Today we rely on many of these plants or their close relatives (mixed with some friendly exotics) to beautify our own landscapes.

Hoosiers have been working the soil for generations. Over the years, immigrants added to the existing variety of plants. Wine grapes were grown along the Ohio River as early as 1802 by Swiss settlers in Vevay; German immigrants moved here in great numbers during the mid- to late 1800s, establishing nurseries and greenhouses all over the state.

The northern part of the state was once filled with blueberry and

The Intriguing Ginkgo

cranberry fields that were eventually drained to make farmland. Northern Indiana celebrates the state's blueberry history with annual festivals.

Johnny Appleseed (born Jonathan Chapman in 1774) took on the role of missionary nurseryman and spent a great deal of time in Indiana. He was quite a sight traveling the frontier with bare feet, tattered clothing, and a pan turned upside down to protect his long hair from the rain. Appleseed gave seeds to everyone he met, stressing the importance of growing one's own food. When the plantsman died in the 1840s, he was buried in what is now Appleseed Park in Fort Wayne. Every year Fort Wayne celebrates his work with a festival that keeps his legendary legacy alive.

The "grandfather" of Indiana plants, Charles C. Deam, was born in 1865. He cataloged trees, shrubs, grasses, and other plants and wrote *Shrubs of Indiana* in 1924, *Grasses of Indiana* in 1929, *Trees of Indiana* in 1931, and *Flora of Indiana* in 1940. Deam spent his career with the Indiana Division of Forestry, where he was a state forester and a research forester. After a long life of service to horticulture, this esteemed researcher died in 1953.

In 1931, the Garden Club of Indiana was formed. It had its first meeting at the John Herron Art Museum in Indianapolis. Garden Club members promoted victory gardens during World War II and continue their education efforts today by working with fifteen junior garden clubs, or children's groups, throughout Indiana. The Garden Club now has more than 3,000 members in more than 300 clubs across the state.

A recent trend has been the growth of the state's Master Gardener Program, where participants are trained in gardening basics and given a certificate after completing a set number of hours volunteering to help others learn about horticulture. Several counties have Master Gardener Programs through their local offices of the Purdue Cooperative Extension Service. Look in the blue government pages of the telephone book for your local number.

Helping others is as much a part of gardening as growing the plants. We've learned about gardening by doing it ourselves and from others who have shared their growing experiences. We hope that through this book you will come to enjoy getting your hands dirty as much as we do—and that your life will be filled with earthly delights.

How to Use the *Indiana Gardener's Guide*

Each entry in this guide provides you with information about a plant's particular characteristics, its habits, and its basic requirements for vigorous growth, as well as our personal experience and knowledge of it. We have tried to include the information you need to help you realize each plant's potential. Only when a plant performs at its best can one appreciate it fully. You will find such pertinent information as mature height and spread, bloom period and seasonal interest (if any), sun and soil preferences, planting tips, water requirements, fertilizing needs, pruning and care. Each section is clearly marked for easy reference.

Sun Preferences

For quick reference, we have included symbols representing the range of sunlight suitable for each plant. "Full Sun" means a site receiving at least six to eight hours of direct sun daily. "Part Sun" means a site that receives at least six hours of direct sun daily. "Part Shade" means a site that receives about 4 or less hours of direct sun daily. "Shade" means a site that is protected from direct sun. Some plants grow successfully in more than one range of sun, which will be indicated by more than one sun symbol.

Full Sun   **Part Sun**   **Part Shade**   **Shade**

Additional Benefits

Many plants offer benefits that further enhance their appeal. The following symbols indicate some of the more notable additional benefits:

Attracts Butterflies or Caterpillars

Attracts Hummingbirds

Produces Edible Parts

Has Fragrance

Produces Food for Birds and Wildlife

Drought Resistant

Suitable for Cut Flowers or Arrangements

Long Bloom Period

Native to North America

Supports Bees

Provides Shelter for Birds

Colorful Fall Foliage or Winter Interest

Companion Planting and Design

In this section, we suggest companion plantings and different ways to showcase your plants. Experimenting with plants is where many people find the most enjoyment from gardening.

We Recommend

This section describes those specific species, cultivars, or varieties that we have found to be particularly noteworthy. Give them a try—many times we mention favorite plants we just couldn't bear to leave out of the book.

USDA Cold Hardiness Zones

ZONE	Average Annual Min. Temperature (°F)
5A	-15 to -20
5B	-10 to -15
6A	-5 to -10
6B	0 to -5

Hardiness Zones

Cold-hardiness zone designations were developed by the United States Department of Agriculture (USDA) to indicate the minimum average temperature for an area. A zone assigned to an individual plant indicates the lowest temperature at which the plant can be expected to survive over the winter.

Annuals *for Indiana*

Annuals are plants that sprout from seed, mature, flower, set seed, and die all within one growing season. They are programmed to grow and are valued for their sustained flowers and color. Many are low maintenance and require little care once planted. Many make wonderful cut flowers or are seasonal food sources for bees, butterflies, and birds. Annuals also are the number one choice for windowboxes, pots, and other containers.

Plants grown as summer annuals here in Indiana are often perennials (geranium, or *Pelargonium*, is one such plant), but they usually are too tender to survive our winter cold or the heat of Hoosier summers. The plants in this chapter are a good representation of those that grow well here.

Gardeners can purchase annuals either as seeds or as bedding plants from nurseries, garden centers, and mail-order catalogs. Self-sowing annuals such as flowering tobacco or gloriosa daisies are easily acquired from friends and neighbors.

Bedding plants are sold in plastic packs, peat pots, or other containers. Look for full squatty plants with good foliage color. Plants are usually in bloom so that the buyer will know what color the flowers are. However, some annuals, such as spider flower, won't be in bloom when purchased.

Annuals in Planter

Pansies

Growing from Seeds and Transplants

Whether you are growing from seeds or transplants, it is important to pick the right site for your plants. Shade-loving plants will probably not do well when planted in full sun, and plants that require full sun will not survive if planted in shade. You should also consider the condition of the soil. Is it well drained or does it retain water? Paying attention to these factors will help you select the right plant for the right place. Finally, all plants do better when planted in a site where the soil has been well prepared. Dig the soil eight to twelve inches deep. Add two to four inches of organic matter, such as compost, finely chopped leaves or well-rotted manure, on top of the bed and mix it into the top few inches of soil.

Many annuals are easy to grow from seeds. Some can be sown directly in the garden. Others may need more time to grow before flowering, so starting seeds indoors is sometimes a better option. Most packets and catalogs offer precise information about sowing seed, so follow those directions. We give some basic instructions in this chapter, but space limits us when discussing each plant. Since soil and seeds are inexpensive, growing plants from seed is less costly than buying bedding plants. But seeds need a controlled environment to grow successfully; some require cool temperatures while others need warmth. Some seeds need light to germinate, and others sprout in the dark. If you purchase lights or plant-heating pads, for example, creating that special environment can be costly, but the results can be rewarding. However, the cost of sowing seeds indoors should be tallied against the convenience of and better chance for success with bedding plants.

It is essential that you use moistened soilless potting mix or sterilized soil to start seeds. Don't use soil taken from the garden as it is too heavy and may harbor diseases or insects that could kill seedlings. The second most important factor in growing annuals from seeds is the light source. Rather than starting seeds on a windowsill, use fluorescent lighting such as shop lights; these are available at hardware stores, home centers, and other retailers. Use one forty-watt warm fluorescent and one forty-watt cool fluorescent light bulb in each two-lamp holder to give the best spectrum of light. Grow lights are also

Walkway Bordered by Annuals

recommended. Lights should always be about two inches above the seedlings. Raise the lights as the plants grow.

When you remove a seedling from its container, be sure the soil is moist. Force the plant from its pack by gently pushing from the bottom. Gently grasp the leaves and wiggle the plant loose. Sometimes you may have to cut or tear away the plastic pack if the plant doesn't come out easily. If the seedling is growing in a peat pot or other biodegradable organic fiber, plant it pot and all. Break off any material that sticks above the soil surface, as this material could act as a wick, drawing necessary moisture away from the soil and into the atmosphere. Plant seedlings the same depth they were growing previously. Water freshly sown seeds and seedlings at the base of the plant; splashing water on the leaves can make plants more susceptible to disease. Plants in containers usually need to be watered and fertilized more frequently than those grown in the ground. Check the pots daily to determine watering needs. Apply a bloom-booster, water-soluble fertilizer every two weeks or use a compost tea.

If you're planting transplants and they are tall and leggy, cut them back to encourage branching and new growth. It doesn't hurt to pinch off the flowers, but it is not necessary except to shape the plant and

to encourage branching. Roots on healthy transplants should be white or light brown. If the roots are wrapped around the soil or are encircled and very tight, you can tease them loose or, better still, use a sharp knife to slice them lengthwise in two or three places before planting. Space according to label instructions.

Designing with Annuals

Annuals are the mainstay for ornamental containers, including decorative pots, hanging baskets, and windowboxes. Plant the annuals close together in containers to give a full, lush look. Container plantings can be used for spot color in the landscape or on porches, decks, and patios. Select plants that are appropriate for the size of the pot and its location, such as full sun or shade.

Many annuals mix well in perennial flower beds and offer color when other plants are resting or still preparing to bloom. They are an easy

Coleus 'Rusty'

and inexpensive way to try new colors, textures, or looks in the landscape before investing in the more permanent perennials. Unless otherwise noted, most of the plants listed here are relatively pest free.

Ageratum

Ageratum houstonianum

Ageratum makes an excellent edging plant in the front of the flower bed, or you can plant it in a cluster for a fuzzy patch of blue. Ageratum also does well in window-boxes or containers. The most common varieties are compact types that rarely get taller than eight to ten inches. There are taller varieties that make excellent cut flowers, but those are not always available at garden centers. They can, however, be started from seed. The taller varieties also can be dried for floral arrangements. Don't confuse this plant with the perennial ageratum (Conoclinium coelestinum—formerly Eupatorium coelestinum), a native which spreads by rhizomes and can be very aggressive.

Other Common Name
Floss Flower

Bloom Period and Seasonal Color
Blue, white, or pink flowers in summer.

Mature Height × Spread
6 to 30 in. × 8 in.

When, Where, and How to Plant
Ageratum is a warm-weather annual. Plant ageratum in containers, windowboxes, or in the front of the flower garden. It is easy to grow in average soil. If using seeds, sow indoors about eight weeks before the last frost. Gently press the seeds into the soil surface, but don't cover them with soil; they need light to germinate. Place them in a bright area out of direct sunlight where the temperature is about 70 degrees Fahrenheit. Germination may take up to two weeks. Transplant seedlings outdoors when all danger of frost has passed. For a nice, full look within a few weeks, space the compact varieties about 8 inches apart. Transplants often wait for warmer weather to get started, so be patient.

Growing Tips
Fertilize regularly throughout the growing season with a water-soluble mixture or compost tea. Water plants if the top 2 inches of soil feels dry to the touch.

Care and Maintenance
You may pinch ageratum to make the plants bushier, but this is not required. They are easy to grow and not bothered much by pests or disease.

Companion Planting and Design
A great combination for beginners is ageratum with pink or peach geraniums and yellow marigolds. The plants are compatible for water and fertilizer requirements, and the colors are complimentary. Ageratum is frequently planted in the front of the flower bed as a seasonal border.

We Recommend
There are several compact varieties that are readily available. 'Blue Blazer' is 8 inches tall and has blue-mauve flowers. 'Blue Danube' is 6 inches tall and has lavender-blue flowers. 'Blue Mink' grows 8 to 10 inches tall, also with lavender-blue flowers. 'Pink Powderpuffs' grows about 9 inches tall and has rosy-pink blooms. 'Summer Snow' is about 6 inches tall with white blooms. 'White Cushion' is about 12 inches tall with white flowers. 'Bavaria' has 18- to 20-inch-tall, light-blue flowers tipped in dark blue. 'Blue Horizon' grows to 30 inches tall and has lavender-blue flowers that are frequently dried for arrangements. Both 'Bavaria' and 'Blue Horizon' make excellent cut flowers.

Begonia
Begonia × Semperflorens-Cultorum

When, Where, and How to Plant
Plant container-grown transplants in the spring, after all danger of frost has passed. Sow seeds indoors at least twelve weeks before the last frost. Wax-leaf begonia does best in partial shade, but it will tolerate full sun as long as it receives adequate moisture. It will also tolerate full shade, but this may make it a little leggy. Begonia does best in moist, well-drained, organically rich soil. It will tolerate a wide range of conditions but does not do well in soil that is constantly wet. Space plants 8 to 10 inches apart. Starting seeds indoors can be difficult; transplants or bedding plants are recommended.

Growing Tips
Begonia benefits greatly from both regular watering and applications of a water-soluble fertilizer or compost tea.

Care and Maintenance
Begonia has a compact growing habit that requires no deadheading or pinching, except for a rare errant stem. If begonia is kept too wet, it will rot. Begonia may be wintered over by taking a cutting from a growing tip and rooting it in a soilless potting medium. The easiest way, however, is to dig the plant up, trim it back, pot it, and place it in a bright window. Begonia is easy to grow and not bothered much by pests or disease.

Companion Planting and Design
Wax-leaf begonia is a very adaptable plant, working well as an edger for a flower bed or as a ball of color in a container. Plant begonia under trees, in the front of flower beds, in windowboxes, or in other containers.

We Recommend
The 'Cocktail Mix' series has white-flowered 'Whiskey', red-flowered 'Vodka', and rose-pink-flowered 'Gin'. All have bronze leaves that make an excellent contrast to the flowers. 'Wings' is a hybrid with larger flowers and green leaves. 'Olympia Salmon Orange' is a relatively new introduction, as is the Prima Donna™ series of picotee colors, which has white flowers edged in pink.

Begonia leaves are waxy, and they have slightly fringed, or ragged, edges that are frequently tinged in red or bronze. Some varieties have green leaves; others have reddish-bronze leaves, a color that intensifies in sunlight. The prolific flowers have disk-like petals and fuzzy yellow centers. Flowers are single or double. Don't confuse this plant with the perennial begonia (Begonia grandis), a spectacular, late-bloomer for shade with pink flowers and pale green foliage with red veins that is hardy in all but the coldest regions of Indiana. The wax leaf and B. grandis are different still from the tuberous begonia (B. tuberhybrida), a tender, shade-loving plant that grows from a tuber.

Other Common Names
Wax-leaf Begonia, Fibrous Root Begonia

Bloom Period and Seasonal Color
Pink, white, or red flowers in summer.

Mature Height × Spread
6 to 10 in. × 6 in.

Browallia
Browallia speciosa

Linneas, the scientist who developed plant nomenclature, named browallia to honor Bishop Browall, who was a good plant breeder. Browallia is one of those plants that is not used nearly enough, probably because people don't know what it is. A native of South America, browallia is a low growing, rounded, bushy plant with profuse, one-inch-wide, blue-violet, trumpet-shaped flowers, and oval green leaves. It is very easy to grow and works well in the front of a semi-shady bed, in windowboxes, or in other containers. In the fall, you can also cut the plant back to about four inches tall, pot it up, and bring it indoors to a sunny window to enjoy during the winter as a houseplant.

Other Common Name
Bush Violet

Bloom Period and Seasonal Color
Blue or white flowers in summer.

Mature Height × Spread
15 in. × 6 in.

When, Where, and How to Plant
Plant browallia in the spring after all danger of frost has passed. Browallia does best in a partially shaded spot with well-drained soil. The soil can be average. Sow seeds indoors six to eight weeks before the last frost. Browallia seeds are very small; sow them on the surface of pots or seedling trays filled with a moistened, soilless mix. Place them in a bright, warm area out of direct sunlight and keep them moist. Germination may take up to two weeks. As they grow, transplant them to larger pots or thin the seedlings out so there is enough space for individual plants. Transplant seedlings outdoors after the last frost. Space them 10 to 12 inches apart, water well, and mulch lightly if you wish.

Growing Tips
Browallia will develop a lot of green growth if you water or fertilize it too much. Follow fertilizer label directions.

Care and Maintenance
Pinch the plant back when it is small to encourage bushiness. Pests are not a problem with browallia.

Companion Planting and Design
Because browallia is such a profuse bloomer, it mixes very well with many shade loving perennials including hosta, pulmonaria, and ferns, all of which are appreciated for their foliage. Browallia combined with salmon-colored impatiens is a show stopper. Browallia comes in many shades of blue and in various heights, though none is too tall.

We Recommend
'Major' grows up to 14 inches and has 2-inch lavender flowers. 'Marine Bells' grows 10 inches and has 1 1/2-inch indigo-blue flowers. 'Sky Bells' grows up to 10 inches and has 1 1/2-inch sky-blue flowers. 'Vanja' reaches 14 inches and has 2-inch blue flowers with white centers. 'Blue Troll' grows up to 10 inches and has 1 1/2-inch violet-blue flowers. 'Jingle Bells' hybrids range from 9 to 14 inches tall, with 1 1/2-inch blue, white, or lavender flowers. 'Silver Bells' and 'White Troll' are white varieties.

Cape Daisy
Osteospermum spp. and hybrids

When, Where, and How to Plant

Choose a location where cape daisy will get partial shade to full sun. Plant container-grown plants in spring, at the same depth they were growing. Space according to label instructions. (See chapter introduction for more detailed planting instructions.) Cape daisy is fairly cold tolerant, which makes it great for early and late season color in windowboxes or other containers.

Growing Tips

This plant is a heavy feeder needs a fair amount of water. Water regularly to keep the plant from drying out, especially the first two weeks after planting. It benefits from heavy doses of fertilizer. Use a slow-release granular fertilizer in containers and apply a bloom-booster water soluble fertilizer or compost tea every ten days during the growing season.

Care and Maintenance

Removing the spent flowers, called deadheading, will keep the plant blooming strong. In really hot weather, the plant may slow down and produce smaller flowers. Shear off a couple of inches, give it a dose of water-soluble fertilizer, and it should revive to provide many more weeks of flowers once the temperatures drop. It is easy to grow and not bothered much by pests or disease.

Companion Planting and Design

The flowers are upright, but the plant has a bit of a trailing habit, which makes it perfect for containers, including windowboxes and hanging baskets. It does better in containers than in the ground. It looks great all by itself or planted with annuals, such as trailing petunias, annual ornamental grasses, or lantana. Another great long bloomer in summer is Marguerite daisy (*Argyranthemum frutescens*), which comes in white, pink, or yellow flowers. It gets about 20 inches tall and takes full sun. It also is a heavy feeder but tolerates soil a bit drier than *Ostersopermum*. Its foliage is more fern-like.

We Recommend

'Symphony' cultivars come in peach, vanilla, lemon, cream, and orange; all of them are yummy. 'Soprano' comes in pink, purple, and white. For a Marguerite daisy, consider 'Butterfly', a butter yellow form, which lives up to its name.

The first year I tried Osteospermum, I was really disappointed. The gorgeous daisy-like flowers just whimped out in the Hoosier heat and looked awful for most of the summer. Fortunately, hybridizers have greatly improved this plant and bolstered its ability to withstand Hoosier summers. However, even with improvements, Osterspermum may slow down in really hot weather. It bounces back once temperatures drop, blooming well into fall, making it worth a little fussing. Cape daisy is native to the Cape of South Africa. The leaves are green and fleshy. The giveaway sign for the lovely plant is a purple or bluish center and a slight purple cast to the undersides of the petals. —J.E.M.S

Bloom Period and Seasonal Color

Yellow, orange, pink, white, and various colors in summer.

Mature Height × Spread

12 to 15 in. × 12 to 15 in.

Cockscomb
Celosia argentea

One variety of Celosia looks like the lead in a movie called The Plant with Big Brains. *The crested flowers take on a rounded shape with ridges; the result resembles more closely a colorful velvety brain than it does a cockscomb, its common name. Celosia argentea var.* cristata *is divided into three subgroups:* cristata, *or crested flowers,* plumosa *(pictured above), which has feathery, plume-like, flowers; and* spicata, *which has spikes. Each variety does well in containers and window-boxes. You can also cut the flowers for indoor bouquets or dry them for arrangements. Some of the new varieties have attractive red and purple foliage as well as long-blooming flowers. 'Prestige Scarlet', an All-America Selection in 1997, has a large, central, red flower and smaller combs along its branches; it grows about 20 inches tall and wide.*

Bloom Period and Seasonal Color
Various colors from midsummer to frost.

Mature Height × Spread
6 to 36 in. × 8 to 12 in.

When, Where, and How to Plant
Plant transplants in the spring in well-drained, average soil after the danger of frost has passed. Try not to disturb the roots when transplanting seedlings or transplants. Sow seeds indoors about six to eight weeks before the last frost. If you are starting from seed, sow the seeds in individual pots or six-packs that have been filled with a moistened, soilless mix. Barely cover the seeds and place them in a warm, bright location out of direct sunlight. Germination may take up to two weeks. Transplant seedlings outdoors when the danger of frost has passed.

Growing Tips
Cockscomb is drought tolerant, so grow it in a drier environment once it's established. Use a water-soluble, all-purpose, or bloom-booster fertilizer, or compost tea about once a month.

Care and Maintenance
Since it thrives in hot weather, cockscomb is apt to be a fairly slow grower when you first plant it in the spring. Don't worry—it's a late bloomer. Cockscomb may self-sow, but it usually isn't a problem. Remove unwanted seedlings as soon as they sprout. It is not bothered much by pests or disease.

Companion Planting and Design
The taller varieties we recommend below are good for the middle of a border. The brainy *Celosia* is an acquired taste, but it makes a strong color statement in the flower bed when planted en masse.

We Recommend
'Chief' hybrids grow to 40 inches tall; the combs may grow to 8 inches across and will produce red, scarlet, rose, pink, or yellow flowers. 'Empress' grows 12 inches tall with reddish-green foliage and deep-red combs that grow 10 inches wide. 'Fireglow' grows about 2 feet tall and has 6-inch reddish-orange combs. The recommended feather, or plume, Cockscomb cultivars are 'Apricot Brandy', which grows about 15 inches tall; the 'Castle' series, which reaches 12 inches and has yellow or pink flowers; and 'Century', which has 6-inch plumes on 20-inch plants. Try the spike 'Flamingo Feather', which is about 40 inches tall with flowers in shades of pastel pink.

When, Where, and How to Plant

Plant transplants in the spring, after all danger of frost has passed. Plant coleus in a well-drained, moist spot. Space plants about 12 inches apart, water them well, and add mulch. If starting from seeds, sow them eight to twelve weeks before the last frost in pots filled with a moistened, soilless potting mix. Do not cover seeds with soil. Instead, place them in a bright, warm area out of direct sun. It may take three weeks for seeds to germinate. Seedlings will start out green. Transplant them outdoors when the danger of frost has passed. Although some coleus tolerates full sun, it does best in part shade to shade where the colors remain more vibrant and intense. However, there are some new coleus developed for sun now available.

Growing Tips

Water coleus regularly so that it does not dry out. If the plant gets too large or leggy pinch it back to improve its bushiness. Apply an all-purpose water-soluble fertilizer or compost tea every two weeks to coleus in windowboxes or other containers.

Care and Maintenance

Many gardeners pinch off the coleus flowers, but you may leave them on the plants if you wish. Some plants are marketed as "sun-loving coleus," but these will need more water than those grown in shade. You can take cuttings in the fall, or you can dig coleus up for an indoor houseplant. Coleus is fairly pest and disease free.

Companion Planting and Design

Coleus is wonderful in a container or when planted en masse in the landscape. Its colorful foliage mixes well with perennials or other annuals, usually in the front of the border.

We Recommend

'Rainbow Mix' grows about 15 inches tall and has medium-sized leaves. 'Wizard Mixed' grows 10 to 12 inches tall and has large leaves. 'Dragon Sunset' has deeply carved leaves. 'The Line' has chartreus leaves with a purple vein. 'Inky Fingers' is almost black, with light green, and is one of the best. 'Solar Sunrise' is a sun-loving variety that's hard to beat.

Coleus is prized for its leaves, which come in a rainbow of colors and a variety of textures. It is slow to grow from seed but not too difficult; it is frequently used for children's gardening projects. Most people think the spiky blue flowers are unattractive and remove them; however, bees, butterflies, and hummingbirds like them. Coleus is equally at home as a bedding plant or in flower boxes and other containers. It comes in creamy white to almost black, and the foliage may be solid-colored, mottled, banded, puckered, highly scalloped, or serrated. Coleus is easy to grow and requires little maintenance. Don't hesitate to cut a branch for a striking addition to an indoor flower arrangement. Coleus also used to be this plant's botanical name.

Bloom Period and Seasonal Color
Various colored foliage in summer.

Mature Height × Spread
6 to 36 in. × 12 to 18 in.

Cosmos

Cosmos bipinnatus

Depending on the reference, kosmos is a Greek word for universe, harmony, or ornament. Whichever you prefer, the name is apt, because cosmos indeed brings harmony to the garden and it is a very ornamental flower, too. All summer long, cosmos produces colorful, daisy-like flowers and fern-like leaves on spindly, branched stems. Cosmos is a native wildflower. Birds, especially goldfinches, eat the seeds. Use it as a staple in the cutting garden or to attract butterflies and hummingbirds. It is very easy to grow and readily self-sows. Cosmos is a great plant anywhere in the garden. Because its foliage is airy and flowers light, cosmos dangles above and amid companion plants without overwhelming them.

Bloom Period and Seasonal Color
Pink, maroon, white, and yellow flowers in summer.

Mature Height × Spread
12 to 36 in. × 18 in.

When, Where, and How to Plant
Plant transplants in spring in average soil, after the danger of frost has passed. Space about about 12 to 18 inches apart, water well, and mulch lightly if you wish. Start seeds indoors about four weeks before the last frost. Plant $1/8$ inch deep in pots filled with a moistened, soilless potting mix. Place them in a bright, warm area out of direct sunlight. Germination may take up to ten days. After the last frost, transplant seedlings outdoors or sow seeds directly. Use planting instructions in the chapter introduction or those on your cosmos seed packet.

Growing Tips
Apply a bloom-booster, water-soluble fertilizer or use a compost tea. Too much fertilizer, especially that with high nitrogen, causes cosmos to develop more leaves and delay flowering. Follow fertilizer label instructions. Water occasionally during long periods of drought.

Care and Maintenance
Grow taller varieties of cosmos in the middle of the bed so they can brace themselves on nearby plants. Otherwise, taller varieties may need to be staked. The more you cut cosmos, the more flowers you'll get. Cosmos is easy to grow and not bothered much by pests or disease.

Companion Planting and Design
The flowers float above and blend with companion plants, including other annuals such as zinnias and snapdragons, or perennials such as coneflowers, black-eyed Susans, and yarrow.

We Recommend
'Sensations' hybrids grow about 3 feet tall with 3-inch-wide red, pink, or white flowers. 'Sonata' grows about 3 feet tall with 3-inch-wide red, pink, or white flowers that bloom earlier than other varieties. 'Sea Shells' grows 6 feet tall; it has 4-inch-wide pink or white flowers with tubes that flare red or white. 'Early Wonder' grows about 4 feet tall, with $3^1/2$-inch-wide red, pink, or white flowers. 'Hot Chocolate' has a chocolate color and scent. *Cosmos sulphureus* hybrids are shorter, with 2-inch-wide red, yellow, or orange flowers. 'Bright Lights' grows about 3 feet tall and has 2-inch-wide orange, yellow, gold, and red-orange flowers. 'Ladybird' grows about 1 foot tall with 2-inch-wide semi-double orange or yellow flowers.

Dusty Miller
Senicio cineraria

When, Where, and How to Plant

Plant container-grown plants in the spring after all danger of frost has passed. Dusty miller does best in full sun but is tolerant of shadier locations with well-drained, ordinary soil. Water well and mulch. If starting with seed, sow them indoors about ten weeks before the last frost. Place them on the surface of moistened, soilless potting mix in pots or seedling trays. Place pots and trays in a warm, bright area out of direct sun. Water seedling trays from below the plants to avoid fungus diseases. Germination can take three weeks. Transplant seedlings outdoors when the danger of frost has passed. Space dusty miller 8 to 10 inches apart. (See chapter introduction for more about planting.)

Growing Tips

Apply an all-purpose water-soluble fertilizer or compost tea about every two weeks if dusty miller is in a container or windowbox. Dusty miller grown in the ground usually doesn't need fertilizers. It tolerates heat and drought well but may wilt in prolonged dry spells. It usually recovers well with a good soaking.

Care and Maintenance

Dusty miller is very easy to grow and is remarkably free of pest and disease. Plants may be pinched to improve bushiness, but this is not required.

Companion Planting and Design

Dusty miller's light color and interesting texture make a nice relief in a mass of colorful flowers; its dusty-white appearance cools down the scene or provides a complementary contrast to bold colors.

We Recommend

'Silver Feather' and 'Silver Dust' have lacy or deeply cut foliage. 'Cirrus' has oval, slightly serrated leaves. 'White Diamond' grows about 15 inches tall and is less silvery than the others.

Dusty miller is a name given to a group of annuals and perennials that are grown for their silvery-green foliage, which can be bold and deeply cut or lacy like snowflakes. Most have a mounding habit and grow 10 to 15 inches tall; a few may reach a height of 2 feet. Dusty miller may winter over, especially if the season is not too severe, blooming the second year. The daisy-like flowers are yellow, which seems odd for a plant with gray foliage. Although some varieties have been known to winter over, you should probably not count on this. Similar-leaved species, sometimes called dusty miller, include Cineraria maritima, Senecio maritima, Senecio cineraria, Centaurea cineraria, Pyrethrum ptarmiciflorum, and Chrysanthemum ptarmiciflorum.

Other Common Names

Silverdust, Ragwort

Bloom Period and Seasonal Color

Yellow, with silver-green foliage in summer.

Mature Height × Spread

12 in. × 12 in.

Flowering Tobacco
Nicotiana spp.

Hummingbirds flock to this plant at dawn and at dusk, so plant it where you can enjoy the show. Some varieties will knock your socks off with fragrance, especially at night. In fact, some flowering tobacco varieties close their flowers during the day and open up at night. White ones are showy and smell spectacular in the night garden. Most flowering tobacco are a food source for the tobacco hornworm, the caterpillar of a large moth, which is drawn to the plant at night for nectar. Flowering tobacco does well in the landscape, in windowboxes, or in other containers. It may self-sow a bit, but that usually isn't a problem. Transplant the seedlings where you want them or toss them in the compost pile.

Other Common Name
Jasmine Tobacco

Bloom Period and Seasonal Color
Pink, white, or red flowers in midsummer to fall.

Mature Height × Spread
12 to 48 in. × 12 to 20 in.

When, Where, and How to Plant
Sow flowering tobacco's very small seeds indoors on the surface of moistened soilless potting mix about six weeks before the last frost. Place them in a warm, bright area out of direct sunlight. Germination may take up to twenty days. Plant transplants or sow seeds directly in spring after the danger of frost has passed, in well-drained ordinary soil. (See chapter introduction for more about planting.) These begin to bloom late in the season.

Growing Tips
Flowering tobacco requires almost no maintenance. Water occasionally during long dry periods. Deadheading encourages blooming and cuts down on self-sowing but is optional. Apply an all-purpose water-soluble fertilizer or compost tea. Too much nitrogen fertilizer will result in more foliage than flowers; follow label directions.

Care and Maintenance
Flowering tobacco self-sows easily. Flowering tobacco shares the same family as the smoking types, so the bottom leaves can get fairly large. Shorter varieties are usually less fragrant than taller ones. It is fairly cold tolerant, frequently lasting well into fall and early winter. It is easy to grow and relatively pest free.

Companion Planting and Design
Plant fragrant varieties where you will be able to smell them at night, such as by a bedroom window, porch, patio, or deck. You may need to stake very tall varieties, or plant them far enough back in the flower beds that shorter plants can help prop them up. Plant it with other annuals such as cosmos and snapdragons or with perennials like black-eyed Susans, coneflowers, or yarrow.

We Recommend
'Sensation Mixed' has fragrant, white, pink, and rose flowers that stay open during the day. 'Nicki Mix' has scented 18-inch-tall bright- and dusty-pink, rose, white, and lime-green flowers. 'Lumina' grows 3 to 4 feet tall with white, jasmine-scented flowers. 'Heaven Scent' reaches 2 feet and has fragrant flowers ranging from crimson to white. 'Domino' hybrids are compact and heat tolerant. *Nicotiana sylvestris* can grow 6 feet tall and has 3- to 4-inch-long fragrant white trumpet-like flowers that grow about 1 1/2 inches wide.

Geranium

Pelargonium × *hortorum*

When, Where, and How to Plant

Sow seeds indoors twelve to fourteen weeks before the last frost in moistened, soilless potting mix in pots or seedling trays. Barely cover the seeds. Place the tray in a light, warm area out of direct sunlight. Germination may take three weeks. Give seedlings as much light as possible, or they will get leggy. Pinch plants when they are small to encourage bushiness. Transplant seedlings or container-grown transplants outdoors in spring when the danger of frost has passed. Geraniums do best in well-drained soil. Ivy-leaved geraniums do better with protection from afternoon sun. (See chapter introduction for more on planting.)

Growing Tips

Geraniums are fairly drought tolerant, so water only when they are dry. Ivy-leafed geranium tends to need a little more water, especially if you plant it in full sun. Don't overfertilize; too much fertilizer will cause geraniums to produce more foliage than flowers. Follow fertilizer label directions.

Care and Maintenance

Geraniums require little care. Pinch off dead flowers to keep them blooming. To winter them over, dig up the plants before a frost. Plant in pots and cut back the tops to about 6 inches. Place in a sunny window, water and fertilize as needed, and the geraniums will bloom. They are easy to grow and not bothered much by pests or disease.

Companion Planting and Design

Geraniums are great in pots or in the ground. Consider planting geraniums in clusters or en masse for the most dramatic and showy look. Vining geraniums can be used as a summer ground cover.

We Recommend

There are dozens of selections. Make choices based on color, size, and use. *Pelargonium domesticum* are called "show geraniums," and these include the 'Martha Washington' varieties, which have azalea- or pansy-like flowers. They prefer a growing season with cool nights. Several geraniums are prized for their scented leaves rather than for their flowers, which are not usually showy. There are rose-, peppermint-, lemon-, apple-, and nutmeg-scented plants, just to name a few.

A geranium is one of those plants that just says "summer." These tender perennials are grown as summer annuals. Native to South Africa, geraniums are among the best-known flowers in the world. Pelargonium × hortorum is sometimes identified by zones, or rings, of color on its leaves. Pelargonium peltatum is the "ivy-leaved" or "vining" geranium and is distinguished by its glossy, waxy leaves. It used to be that geraniums were grown only by cuttings, but new seed-grown hybrids are less expensive and are becoming much more common. However, many gardeners think seed geraniums don't bloom as profusely as those grown from cuttings. There is a hardy geranium which is discussed in the chapter on perennials. Pelargonium is Greek for "stork" and describes the shape of the seed.

Other Common Name
Scented Geranium

Bloom Period and Seasonal Color
Various colors, including white, pink, red, violet, lavender, and magenta in summer.

Mature Height × Spread
12 to 36 in. × 12 to 36 in.

Globe Amaranth
Gomphrena globosa

Globe amaranth looks like clover and lasts a very long time on and off the plant. The one- to two-inch rounded flowers can be white, pink, red, orange, or purple; they are actually modified leaves, or bracts, which grow at the tips of the stalks that rise above the plant. Globe amaranth holds its color for a long time and does especially well in hot, dry locations. "Amaranth" is probably derived from the Greek word "amarantos," which means "everlasting," or the Greek "amaranton," which means "unfading flower." It is part of the Amaranthaceae family, as is Amaranthus, another group of ornamental annuals, which includes love-lies-bleeding and summer poinsettia. There is also a group of amaranths made up of grain plants.

Bloom Period and Seasonal Color
Various colors, including pink, red, white, purple, and orange in summer.

Mature Height × Spread
6 to 24 in. × 12 in.

When, Where, and How to Plant
Plant transplants in the spring after all danger of frost has passed. Plant in well-drained soil in a sunny location. Globe amaranth also does very well in hot, dry spots with ordinary soil. Space plants 8 to 10 inches apart and water well. If you are starting from seeds, do so about six weeks before the last spring frost. Soak them in warm water overnight then sow in containers filled with a moistened soil-less potting mix. Barely cover the seeds with the mix and place them in a warm, dark location until they sprout. Germination takes one to two weeks. Move seedlings to a bright location out of direct sunlight. You can also sow seeds directly in the garden after the last frost. Remember to first soak them in water overnight.

Growing Tips
Because globe amaranth is drought tolerant, it will require watering only during long dry periods. Apply an all-purpose granular fertilizer or compost on the soil surface at planting and again in the middle of summer.

Care and Maintenance
You can pinch out the centers of the plants to encourage bushiness. Globe amaranth is easy to grow and not bothered much by pests or disease.

Companion Planting and Design
Globe amaranth is a staple in the cutting garden for indoor bouquets or for dried flower arrangements. It should be planted with other drought-tolerant annuals, such as cockscomb or cosmos. Cluster plants in groups of three or more. Globe amaranth also does well in containers.

We Recommend
Shorter varieties of globe amaranth for the front of the border include 'Buddy', which grows 6 to 8 inches tall and has purple flowers. 'Gnome' hybrids grow 6 inches tall and have pink, purple, or white flowers. 'Lavender Lady', 'Strawberry Fields', 'Bicolor Rose', 'Blushing Bride' (pink), 'Professor Plum', and 'Innocence' (white) are taller, ranging from 15 to 24 inches. *Gomphrena haageana* has $1^1/2$-inch reddish-orange flowers and grows about 18 inches tall.

When, Where, and How to Plant
Rudbeckia hirta prefers well-drained, average soil. Sow seeds directly in the garden or plant transplants in the spring as soon as you can work the soil. Sow seeds in the garden by scattering them on the surface of the soil and covering them lightly. (See chapter introduction for more planting information.)

Growing Tips
Apply a water-soluble bloom-booster fertilizer. Choose one where the middle number is highest, such as a 10-20-10, and follow label directions. You can also apply a ring or light layer of compost around the plant. Gloriosa daisy is fairly drought tolerant.

Care and Maintenance
Since you can easily sow these seeds directly in the garden, starting them indoors is unnecessary work. *Rudbeckia hirta* frequently self-sows, coming back year after year, which explains why it is sometimes mistaken for *Rudbeckia fulgida*. Pull up unwanted plants or dig them when they are small to transplant elsewhere. It is easy to grow and not bothered much by pests or disease.

Companion Planting and Design
The shorter varieties mix well in containers or windowboxes. Gloriosa daisy looks nice with ornamental grasses and sedum as a backdrop. Because it blooms a bit later in the season, it prolongs color in the perennial border and cutflower garden.

We Recommend
'Prairie Sun' and 'Cherokee Sunset', recent All-America Selections winners, are very long blooming. 'Gloriosa' has 2- to 3-foot-tall, 5-inch-wide flowers; the flowers are usually yellow but may sometimes have rays of red or brown at the center. 'Goldilocks' has 2- to 3-foot-tall, 2- to 4-inch-wide, double or semi-double flowers. 'Marmalade' is 18 to 24 inches tall and has 3- to 4-inch-wide orange flowers with a purple-black cone. 'Irish Eyes' or 'Green Eyes' has a green center, or cone, but reaches the same height as the more traditional *Rudbeckia hirta*. 'Toto', 'Becky', and 'Sonora' are dwarf varieties, ranging from 8 to 12 inches tall.

If ever there was a confusing annual it's Rudbeckia hirta, or the black-eyed Susan. It is frequently thought to be the same as Rudbeckia fulgida, a perennial cousin that is also known as black-eyed Susan. To make things even more complicated, Rudbeckia hirta and Rudbeckia fulgida are sometimes referred to as yellow coneflowers! This North American wildflower has been hybridized into various cultivars, such as 'Gloriosa' and 'Goldilocks'. Their daisy-like flowers are wonderful additions to the landscape because they bloom late when there isn't a lot of other color. The single or double flowers range from yellow to mahogany. Most have dark eyes, or centers, but a few have green centers. Goldfinches like to sit on the cones and eat the seeds.

Other Common Name
Black-eyed Susan

Bloom Period and Seasonal Color
Yellow, orange, and mahogany in mid- to late summer.

Mature Height × Spread
2 to 3 ft. × 2 to 3 ft.

Impatiens
Impatiens walleriana

Impatiens walleriana is one of the top-selling annual bedding plants in America. From tender perennials in its native Tanzania and Mozambique, hybridizers developed dozens of varieties that thrive in shade, making impatiens a much-sought-after plant for the landscape where few things bloom. They grow naturally in mounds and rarely need pinching. Impatiens blooms constantly. Some varieties have shimmering flowers, while others are picotee (possessing contrasting color on the edge of the petals). The doubles resemble tiny roses. Impatiens may self-sow, but it is never a problem. The plants also have very fleshy stems, which may break easily. If that happens, stick the broken stem in a glass of water on a bright windowsill out of direct sun and within a few weeks, voila!, a blooming plant.

Other Common Name
Busy Lizzie

Bloom Period and Seasonal Color
Various colors, including red, white, pink, lavender, rose, and purple in summer.

Mature Height × Spread
8 to 24 in. × 10 to 12 in.

When, Where, and How to Plant
Plant container-grown bedding plants in the spring after all danger of frost has passed. Impatiens prefer a well-drained, moist location. Space 8 to 12 inches apart. Water well and mulch 3 or 4 inches away from the plant's stem. If starting from seed, sow seeds indoors eight to ten weeks before the last frost, on the surface of pots filled with moistened soilless potting mix. For best results grow them under fluorescent light. Germination takes two to three weeks. Transplant when the danger of frost has passed. (See chapter introduction for more on planting.)

Growing Tips
Impatiens does not require regular fertilizing if it is planted in good soil. However, container-grown plants will require monthly feeding. Too much nitrogen fertilizer may halt flowering. Follow fertilizer label directions. Water when the soil surface feels dry.

Care and Maintenance
These flowering jewels are shallow-rooted plants that lose moisture quickly and wilt in the sun. They do better shaded by larger plants and protected from west or south exposure. Impatiens planted in full sun may not flower as prolifically as those planted in some shade.

Companion Planting and Design
Gardeners should select *Impatiens walleriana* according to particular colors, styles, and uses. Impatiens mixes nicely with ferns, hostas, pulmonaria, and other plants grown for their foliage in the shade garden. It also does great in windowboxes or containers.

We Recommend
'Super Elfin' has large flowers but is a very compact grower. *Impatiens balsamina* is taller and more upright. The flowers are borne along succulent stems or clustered at the top; they are not particularly showy. New Guinea impatiens tolerates more sun than *I. walleriana* but still grows better in shade. New Guinea impatiens' leaves may be green, variegated, bronze, or have red veins. Its flowers are frequently larger and it colors more intense.

Lobelia
Lobelia erinus

When, Where, and How to Plant
Plant lobelia in a well-drained spot with average soil and partial shade. Plant container-grown transplants or seedlings in the spring after all danger of frost has passed. Space 4 to 6 inches apart at the same depth they were growing previously, water well, and mulch lightly if you wish. Sow seeds indoors eight to twelve weeks before the last frost on the surface of pots filled with moistened soilless potting mix. Prevent them from drying out by keeping them in a clear plastic bag or under clear glass or plastic until the seeds sprout. Germination may take three weeks. For best results indoors, grow seedlings under fluorescent lights. Thin or transplant them to individual containers if necessary.

Growing Tips
Give lobelia a shot of water-soluble, bloom-booster fertilizer or a drenching of compost tea every week or ten days, and keep it well watered. Lobelia does not like hot, dry weather.

Care and Maintenance
Lobelia may stop blooming in really hot weather. Cut lobelia back about halfway if it starts to look dry or leggy. The plant usually responds with new, better-looking growth when the temperature cools down. Pests are not a problem.

Companion Planting and Design
This is an excellent edging plant for the front of the flower bed, especially where protected from afternoon sun. It does well in containers and will trail over the sides of windowboxes. Lobelia mixes well with impatiens, narrow-leaf zinnia, and many other annuals.

We Recommend
'Crystal Palace' is 4 to 6 inches tall with dark-blue flowers and bronze leaves; 'Mrs. Clibran Improved' is 6 inches tall with dark-blue flowers and white centers; 'Blue Stone' grows up to 9 inches tall with sky-blue flowers; 'Rosamund' is 6 inches tall with carmine-red flowers, white "eyes," and bronze foliage; 'White Lady' is 6 inches tall with white flowers; and 'Riviera' hybrids are also good choices. Trailing hybrids include 'Cascade', light blue to ruby; 'Sapphire', dark-blue flowers, white eyes, and bronze foliage; and 'Regatta', a range of blues.

The intense blue of Lobelia *or 'Crystal Palace' lobelia is hard to beat in the annual garden or windowbox.* Lobelia *grows in clumps or as trailing plants. It has one-half-inch-wide tubular flowers on spindly stems. The ferny, narrow leaves are sometimes bronzy-purple. There also are perennial lobelias, including the native* Lobelia cardinalis, *or cardinal flower, a great, late-season bloomer that prefers a shady, moist location. It also attracts hummingbirds and butterflies. Another native perennial,* Lobelia siphilitica, *or the great blue lobelia, is also a late bloomer that likes wet areas and attracts hummingbirds and butterflies.* Lobelia *contains a poisonous alkaloid, so don't eat the plant.*

Other Common Name
Edging Lobelia

Bloom Period and Seasonal Color
Blue, white, and pink in summer.

Mature Height × Spread
4 to 12 in. × 6 in.

Marigold

Tagetes spp.

Marigolds may be labeled as French or African, but they originated in Mexico. In fact, the plant's history dates back to the time of the Aztecs. This easy-to-grow summer staple is equally at home in the landscape, in window-boxes, or in other containers. Most marigolds are compact growers, but African and American varieties can reach heights of up to 3 feet. The leaves are deeply cut and fern-like. Marigold flowers are usually in the yellow to orange range, but a white variety was introduced a few years ago that is a standout when planted en masse and resembles a carnation in cutflower arrangements. Marigolds are solid color, bicolor, or picotee in dozens of variations; flowers may be single or double.

Other Common Names
French Marigold, African Marigold

Bloom Period and Seasonal Color
Yellow, orange, mahogany, and white blooms in summer.

Mature Height × Spread
6 to 36 in. × 8 to 15 in.

When, Where, and How to Plant
Plant bedding plants in the spring after all danger of frost has passed. Space them 6 to 24 inches apart depending on the variety. Water well. Sow seeds in pots indoors six to eight weeks before the last frost in moistened soilless potting mix. Barely cover them and place in a warm, bright area out of direct sunlight until they germinate. For best results, grow them under fluorescent lights until they are large enough to transplant outdoors. Water at the base of the plants as marigolds are sometimes susceptible to disease. Transplant seedlings outdoors when the danger of frost has passed. Taller varieties prefer full sun. (See chapter introduction for more on planting.)

Growing Tips
Apply an all-purpose water-soluble fertilizer throughout the growing season, or drench marigolds with compost tea. Remove dead flowers to keep the plant blooming. Water when soil is dry. Marigolds have a distinct odor that some people like but others don't. It has the reputation of keeping bugs away from people and gardens, but that trait actually belongs to the native species, which has a very pungent odor.

Care and Maintenance
Pinch plants to promote more branches and flowers. Marigold is easy to grow and not bothered much by pests or disease.

Companion Planting and Design
Marigolds mix well with annuals in containers or windowboxes and work well in the perennial border as an edging plant. Taller varieties look good with perennials and can be cut for indoor enjoyment.

We Recommend
Select varieties according to color and height requirements. *Tagetes erecta* is the African, Aztec, or American marigold. It is more upright than the others, and the flowers are double or semi-double, more like a pompom. *T. patula* is the French marigold, which grows 6 to 18 inches tall; its flowers are anemone-like, single, double, or carnation-like. *T. tenuifolia* is short with single flowers that only grow 6 to 8 inches tall.

Mexican Sunflower
Tithonia rotundifolia

When, Where, and How to Plant

Bedding plants may not be available, but tithonia is very easy to start from seed. Sow seeds directly in the garden in the spring when all danger of frost has passed. They are so easy to sow outdoors that there's no reason to start them indoors. Give this bushy, quick growing plant plenty of room. Deadheading will keep it blooming. Cutting the blooms for indoor arrangements will also boost flower production and branching for more cutting.

Growing Tips

Tithonia is very tolerant of hot, dry conditions but will benefit from watering if drought is extended. It will not start flowering in earnest until the weather gets hot. Apply an all-purpose granular fertilizer or a thin layer of compost at planting and again in midsummer.

Care and Maintenance

Tithonia is pretty much pest free. Even deer don't eat this plant.

Companion Planting and Design

Tithonia's two- to three-inch-wide flowers and dark-green spear-shaped leaves compliment other late-summer plants, including black-eyed Susans. It looks best in the back of the flower garden and makes an excellent cut flower. A group planting will make a good summer screen or hedge. Smaller varieties can be grown in pots for the patio or balcony.

We Recommend

'Fiesta Del Sol', the first dwarf tithonia, was an All-America Selection in 2000. The single, orange daisy flowers are 2 to 3 inches across on 2- to 3-foot tall plants. 'Torch', another All-America Selection, has fiery, bright-orange flowers about 3 inches wide on 4- to 6-foot-tall plants. 'Goldfinger' grows 3 to 4 feet tall. 'Sundance' has 3-inch-wide scarlet-orange flowers on plants that grow 4 to 6 feet tall.

Mexican sunflower loves hot and dry conditions. It comes into its own when the temperature is similar to that of its native Mexico and Central America, where tithonia grows as a perennial. It is easy to grow in Indiana as an annual and is not too fussy about location. It has several benefits, including attracting butterflies and humming-birds. The botanical name Tithonia is from Tithonus, a character of Greek myth who was loved by the goddess Eos. Eos appealed to Zeus to make Tithonus immortal but forgot to ask that her lover not age. Zeus eventually turned Tithonus into a grasshopper as a reminder to all mortals that their time is limited and should be put to good use.

Other Common Names
Mexican Hat, Tithonia

Bloom Period and Seasonal Color
Orange flowers from mid- to late summer.

Mature Height × Spread
3 to 6 ft. × 3 to 5 ft.

Moss Rose
Portulaca grandiflora

Moss rose is an easy-to-grow plant that makes an excellent addition to a rock garden or any hot, dry location with poor soil. Moss rose is a Brazilian native with succulent, reddish-green stems and narrow, pointed leaves. Its sprawling habit keeps it low to the ground. The single, semi-double, or double bright or pastel flowers resemble one- to two-inch-wide roses as they unfurl. The flowers open in sun and close in late afternoon or in shade, although some of the newer cultivars will stay open on cloudy days. Moss rose is a member of the purslane family, which includes an obnoxious weed, Portulaca oleracea (sometimes called pigweed), that is edible.

Other Common Name
Rose Moss

Bloom Period and Seasonal Color
Red, yellow, orange, rose, purple, pink, bi-color, or white flowers in summer.

Mature Height × Spread
6 in. × 6 in. or more

When, Where, and How to Plant
Transplant bedding plants in late spring. Moss rose won't bloom unless it is in the sun. It also does well in windowboxes or containers. Moss rose is a bit finicky about being transplanted, so the less disruption the better. Space 6 to 12 inches apart; the closer you plant them the more mat-like the planting will be. Sow seeds directly in the garden after the last frost. Keep seedbeds moist until the seedlings appear, then allow the soil to become a little dry; moss rose seedlings may be susceptible to root rot if they are kept too wet. Start seeds indoors in pots filled with a moistened soilless potting mix six to eight weeks before the last frost. Place the pots in a warm, bright location out of direct sunlight. Germination may take two weeks. Transplant seedlings outdoors when the danger of frost has passed.

Growing Tips
Moss rose does not like wet soil. Water only during extended dry periods. Cutting moss rose back about halfway at midsummer and fertilizing with an all-purpose water-soluble fertilizer or compost tea will renew growth and thicken the plant.

Care and Maintenance
Moss rose requires almost no maintenance and is relatively free of pests. It frequently self-sows but is not considered invasive.

Companion Planting and Design
Grow it in full sun as an edging plant or in clusters to form a mat of color or summer ground cover. The needle-like foliage and reddish stems also work well in rock gardens and other well-drained areas.

We Recommend
'Sundial' hybrids are 5 inches tall with a 1-foot spread; they have more succulent foliage and tend to stay open on cloudy days. The 'Sundial Peppermint' hybrid has light-pink flowers with fuschia specks. 'Calypso' hybrids grow 6 to 8 inches tall, and their double flowers spread about 1 foot wide. 'Double Mix' has double flowers, and 'Sunnyside Mix' or 'All Double Mix' has semi-double or double flowers. 'Sundance' and 'Cloud-beater' are said to bloom more readily on cloudy days. 'Minilaca' grows only about 4 inches tall.

When, Where, and How to Plant

Plant bedding plants a few weeks before the last frost in the spring. Like many tropical natives, nierembergia loses its vigor in hot, dry weather. It prefers well-drained, moist (but not wet) soil. Plant transplants the same depth they were growing previously. Space 6 to 8 inches apart and water well. Sow seeds indoors eight to ten weeks before the last frost in pots filled with moistened soilless potting mix. Barely cover them and place them in a warm, bright area out of direct sunlight. Germination takes two to four weeks. Transplant seedlings outdoors a few weeks before the last frost. (See chapter introduction for more on planting.)

Growing Tips

Apply a compost tea or an all-purpose water-soluble fertilizer throughout the growing season; follow label directions. Do not let nierembergia dry out. Water when the soil surface is dry to the touch.

Care and Maintenance

Some gardeners shear nierembergia back 1/3 to 1/2 after the first flush of flowers to encourage new growth, but this is optional. Nierembergia is very easy to grow and is relatively free of pests and disease.

Companion Planting and Design

Nierembergia mixes well with annuals, especially those with bold or large leaves. The plant trails gently over the side of pots or windowboxes, and the flowers will pop up among companion plants for added charm. You can enjoy a long bloom period with nierembergia. Be sure to cut some of the flowers for use with indoor arrangements.

We Recommend

'Mont Blanc', a recent All-America Selection, has pure-white flowers with yellow eyes. *N. frutescens* 'Purple Robe' has violet-blue flowers. *Nierembergia hippomanica* var. *violacea* or *N. caerulea* grows up to 15 inches tall with purple flowers; it is considered the hardiest of these plants but may be hard to find except in seed catalogs. The same goes for *N. repens*, a low-grower with white flowers.

This under-used, charming plant has 1-inch cup-like flowers on stems with fern-like leaves. The plant has a mounding, sprawling habit, which makes it a good annual for windowboxes, hanging baskets, or other containers. It also makes a good edging plant in the front of a flower bed. Named for Father J.E. Nieremberg, a Jesuit from Madrid, nierembergia is a perennial in its native Argentina. For decades, it was a popular greenhouse or indoor plant, but it has slowly been gaining popularity as a garden plant. Nierembergia is fairly frost tolerant and frequently keeps blooming into fall. It may survive mild winters in Zone 6 but is not reliable. Nierembergia's flowers and fern-like leaves are attractive in floral arrangements.

Other Common Name
Cupflower

Bloom Period and Seasonal Color
Blue or white flowers in summer.

Mature Height × Spread
6 to 12 in. × 10 in.

Pansy

Viola × wittrockiana

The pansy has about as many names as it has faces and color combinations. Viola × wittrockiana is a hybrid of several Viola species. Its leaves are oval with scalloped edges. The five-petaled flowers are large. Pansies are mildly fragrant, short-lived perennials that are usually treated as annuals in our Indiana climate. Hoosier winters may be too severe for pansies and summers too hot. Pansies' preference for cool weather makes them difficult to grow from seed; most gardeners cannot produce the particular growing conditions that are required. Pansies' popularity has expanded to fall, where they have begun to rival chrysanthemums for autumn color. They are great cut for petite arrangements. The flowers are edible and dress up salad mixes.

Other Common Names
Viola, Johnny Jump-Up

Bloom Period and Seasonal Color
Blue, purple, yellow, white, pink, and various mixed colors in spring and fall.

Mature Height × Spread
4 to 12 in. × 6 to 12 in.

When, Where, and How to Plant

Plant transplants in the spring as soon as you can work the soil or in late summer and early fall when temperatures begin to cool. Pansies do best in well-drained soil where they are protected from hot afternoon sun. Pansies are excellent plants for windowboxes or other containers.

Growing Tips

Apply an all-purpose water-soluble fertilizer according to label directions (throughout the growing season) or use a compost tea. Dead-heading keeps pansies blooming. You can also pinch them to encourage bushiness. Pansies will lose vigor when it gets hot; water them when the soil feels dry.

Care and Maintenance

In mild winters in Zone 6, or on the south side of the house with a nice straw mulch, pansies may winter over. The leaves turn purple, and the plants flatten. If it gets warm enough, a flower or two may blossom throughout the winter. When spring arrives, pansies come out of their semi-dormant stage ready for the season. You can cut pansies back to about 4 inches tall in summer to help them withstand the hot temperatures. Keep them well watered. Plants will sometimes bloom again in the fall and may self-sow. Pansies are easy to grow and are not bothered much by pests or disease.

Companion Planting and Design

In spring, plant pansies in containers or mix them with spring-flowering bulbs. Because they are lightly scented, plant them where passersby can enjoy the fragrance. Pansies last longer than mums, holding their color well into late fall and early winter. In some protected locations, especially in Zone 6, pansies may flower off and on throughout winter and make a spectacular comeback in the spring.

We Recommend

There are dozens of color combinations to choose from including solid, bicolors, and tricolors. Select according to your color preferences. There are several All-America Selections, including 'Imperial Blue', 'Maxim Marina', and 'Padparadja'. Some heat-resistant hybrids include 'Imperial', 'Flame Princess', 'Maxim', and 'Viking'. *Viola tricolor*, or Johnny-jump-up, is a smaller plant that self-sows freely. Flowers may be solid or bicolor.

Periwinkle

Catharanthus roseus

When, Where, and How to Plant

Plant bedding plants in the spring after all danger of frost has passed. Periwinkle does best in a well-drained, loamy location but tolerates ordinary soil. It is one of the best annuals for hot and dry locations. Space 10 to 12 inches apart, planting at the same depth they were growing in their containers. Water them well. Starting from seed can be a bit tricky and is best left to experienced gardeners. (See chapter introduction for more on planting.)

Growing Tips

Apply an all-purpose granular or water-soluble fertilizer according to label directions or ring the plants with compost when you plant them. Water as needed throughout the growing season, but this plant prefers it more dry than wet. If the soil is kept too wet, the stems will rot.

Care and Maintenance

This plant requires little care and maintains an attractive look throughout the growing season. Deadheading periwinkle is not necessary. It may self-seed and return in the spring but is not reliable. It is relatively free of pests and diseases.

Companion Planting and Design

Vinca's long bloom period makes it an ideal plant for summer enjoyment. It works well in a perennial flower bed, as a mass planting in the landscape, or in windowboxes and other containers.

We Recommend

In the last few years, several members of the 'Jaio' series have been named All-America Selections winners, so any of those would work great. 'Pretty In . . .' pink, rose, white, etc., hybrids are another All-America Selections series. Select for color, paying attention to the contrasting eyes that are an attribute on many cultivars.

Periwinkle is a workhorse in sunny locations, much as impatiens is in the shade. Sometimes called vinca, periwinkle requires little or no care and will bloom continuously throughout the summer. The small, oval leaves are glossy and dark green with light-colored veins. The one-inch-wide flowers have five petals and open flat; some varieties have contrasting centers, or eyes. Sometimes this plant is listed as Vinca rosea and should not be confused with the perennial woody ground covers, Vinca minor or Vinca major, both of which also are called periwinkle and vinca. Periwinkle can be cut for indoor enjoyment, but it has a little bit of an off smell that some people may not like. Periwinkle also may self-sow, but it usually is not a problem.

Other Common Name
Vinca

Bloom Period and Seasonal Color
White, pink, lavender, peach, and red flowers in summer.

Mature Height × Spread
12 in. × 12 in.

Petunia

Petunia × hybrida

The petunia is one of nature's most rewarding and easy-to-grow annuals. It is among the top three bedding plants, probably because it requires little care and thrives in full sun from late spring until a hard freeze. Scientists have developed an incredible palette of color and an impressive array of styles to suit a variety of uses. There have been great improvements to these plants, including eliminating their need for deadheading, reducing their desire to get leggy, boosting the number of flowers, and reintroducing scent—an attribute missing from hybrids for many years. One of the new plants marketed as "Million Bells" petunia is really not a petunia at all but rather Calibrachoa hybrids. These vining, spreading plants are loaded with 1-inch blooms all summer long.

Bloom Period and Seasonal Color
Various colors including white, purple, red, variegated, picotee, blue, and yellow in summer.

Mature Height × Spread
6 to 18 in. × 6 to 48 in.

When, Where, and How to Plant
Transplant bedding plants or seedlings in the spring after all danger of frost has passed. Petunias prefer well-drained soil. They also grow extremely well in containers, such as hanging baskets or windowboxes. If the site is too shady, they will get leggy and produce few flowers. Space them 8 to 10 inches apart at the same depth they were growing in their containers. If starting from seeds, plant them indoors in pots, eight to ten weeks before the last frost. Place seeds on the surface of moistened soilless potting mix and put the pots in a bright, warm area. Germination may take three weeks. Keep seedlings a bit on the cool side.

Growing Tips
Water petunias at the soil level to avoid weighing the leaves down with moisture. Though they are somewhat drought tolerant, you should water petunias during long dry spells. Apply a granular all-purpose fertilizer or compost on the soil surface at planting time and again in midsummer.

Care and Maintenance
Sticky leaves and stems are natural for petunias and do not indicate insects or disease. If petunias get leggy, cut them back about halfway in mid- to late summer. This will stimulate new growth and flowers that will last well into fall. Pinch them to keep them bushy. Petunias are easy to grow and not bothered much by pests or disease.

Companion Planting and Design
Many petunias are pleasantly scented, especially when planted en masse, so put them where you can enjoy the fragrance, such as near a bedroom window or around a deck, patio, or porch. They work extremely well in the front of the flower garden, where they form a nice floral base for taller annuals and perennials.

We Recommend
'Madness' series are particularly fragrant. Almost any of the improved varieties, such as the Supertunia and Wave® series, would be great. Select for color and growth habit. Some are much more trailing than others.

Pot Marigold

Calendula officinalis

When, Where, and How to Plant

Sow seeds directly outdoors in spring as soon as you can work the soil, or plant bedding plants in the spring after all danger of frost has passed. Though pot marigold prefers well-drained, organically rich soil, it tolerates ordinary soil. Space 12 to 18 inches apart, depending on the variety. Mulch to retain moisture and to keep the roots cool. Sow seeds indoors six to eight weeks before the last frost. Plant in individual pots or packs filled with moistened, soilless potting mix. Barely cover seeds, and water seedlings at their base to avoid fungus diseases. Place them in a warm, bright area. Germination may take up to two weeks. Transplant outdoors when the danger of frost has passed. You can also sow them directly outdoors in midsummer for fall-flowering plants.

Growing Tips

Pot marigold loses vigor when the weather turns really hot. If the plant is in a pot, move it to a cooler location. Mulch the plant to keep the roots cool and moist. Apply an all-purpose water-soluble fertilizer according to label directions, or use a compost tea two or three times during the growing season. Water when the soil feels dry.

Care and Maintenance

Deadheading prolongs the flowering period. Pinch plants to encourage bushiness. Pot marigold frequently self-sows in the garden and sometimes becomes a nuisance. It is easy to grow and not bothered much by pests or disease.

Companion Planting and Design

This plant prefers cooler temperatures, and it makes a nice companion plant for pansies in the spring and fall. This plant does well in a cutting or butterfly garden mixed with perennials or other annuals.

We Recommend

'Bon Bon', 'Coronet', 'Dwarf Gem', 'Fiesta Gitana', and 'Sunglow' are dwarfs, growing 10 to 12 inches tall. 'Pacific Giant Mix' grows up to 2 feet tall and has 2¹/₂-inch-wide, yellow, semi-double flowers. 'Prince Mix' has stems up to 2¹/₂ feet tall with 3-inch double orange-and-yellow blooms. 'Touch of Red' is about 18 inches tall; its flowers are tinged with red. *Calendula muselli* has lemon-yellow, 2-inch flowers with silver-green foliage.

If you need a quick spot of color in your flower bed, this easy-to-grow annual makes a great fill-in. It is also an excellent cut flower. A native of the Mediterranean, it was once thought to have tremendous medicinal powers for stomach ailments and liver disfunction and was a staple in everyone's garden. At home in the herb or flower garden, pot marigold is not picky about the soil, although well-drained is best. It can be grown in pots, windowboxes, or other containers. The 2- to 4-inch-wide, daisy-like flowers may be single or double. This is an easy plant for children to grow from seed for a classroom project or in the home garden. The seeds resemble dried, comma-shaped worms. The flowers are edible in salads, soups, and other dishes.

Other Common Name
English Marigold

Bloom Period and Seasonal Color
Orange, gold, and cream flowers in summer.

Mature Height × Spread
10 to 24 in. × 18 in.

Salvia
Salvia spp.

There are two common salvias we use in the annual garden. Scarlet sage, Salvia splendens *(pictured above), has been a staple for years.* Salvia farinacea *is newer to Midwestern gardens but has fast become a regular. It has spikes of small blue or white cuplike flowers. The plant gets its common name, "mealycup," from the stems which seem to be dusted with a whitish powder. In late summer and fall, goldfinches sit on the flower stems to eat the seeds, creating a colorful picture. The tubular flowers of scarlet sage are red, coral, white, orchid, salmon, burgundy, or purple.* Salvia officinalis *is garden sage, an herb that also does well in the perennial flower bed (See the Herb chapter). There are also perennial salvias, discussed in the Perennials chapter.*

Other Common Names
Mealycup, Scarlet Sage

Bloom Period and Seasonal Color
Various colors in summer.

Mature Height × Spread
10 to 36 in. × 10 to 24 in.

When, Where, and How to Plant
Plant bedding plants in the spring after all danger of frost has passed. Both salvias tolerate ordinary soil and somewhat dry conditions. Space them 10 to 12 inches apart and water well. Sow seeds indoors on the surface of pots or seed packs filled with moistened soilless potting mix eight to ten weeks before the last frost. Place in a warm, bright location out of direct sunlight. Germination takes two to three weeks. Water at the base of the plants. Transplant seedlings outdoors when the danger of frost has passed. (See chapter introduction for more planting details.)

Growing Tips
Deadheading is not necessary. Pinch to encourage bushiness. A periodic dose of water-soluble fertilizer or compost tea throughout the growing season is all right, but don't overfertilize. Follow label directions. If grown in container with other annuals, fertilizer about every two weeks. Salvia prefers it more dry than wet.

Care and Maintenance
Both types do well in hot, dry conditions and also tolerate cool temperatures. *Salvia farinacea* is more cold tolerant. These plants may make it through a mild winter in Zone 6 if you plant them in a protected area and give them a little mulch. Their seedheads silver out, adding winter interest. Salvia is easy to grow and not bothered much by pests or disease.

Companion Planting and Design
Salvias look great en masse or clustered in a perennial bed. *Salvia splendens* and *S. coccinea* are musts in the hummingbird or butterfly garden. *Salvia farinacea* makes a good cut flower for indoor arrangements, or you can dry the flowers for everlastings.

We Recommend
Salvia farinacea 'Victoria Blue' has dark-blue, 8-inch-tall flower spikes; 'Argent White' has white spikes; and 'Strata', a recent All-America Selection, has spikes of white and dark-blue flowers. *Salvia splendens* 'Sizzler' hybrids are about 12 inches tall and come in a variety of colors. *Salvia coccinea* 'Lady in Red' is another recent All-America Selection. It grows about 24 to 30 inches tall. Its bright red flowers have a whorled appearance.

Snapdragon
Antirrhinum majus

When, Where, and How to Plant

Plant bedding plants or transplant seedlings a few weeks before the last frost in the spring. Snapdragons prefer rich, moist, loamy, well-drained soil for best flowering. They do not do well in wet soil. Provide snapdragons with good air circulation. Space plants at least 6 inches apart, farther if the varieties are intermediate or tall. Sow seeds indoors about eight weeks before the last frost. Sow in pots on the surface of moistened soil-less potting mix. Place seeds in a warm, bright area out of direct sunlight. Germination may take up to two weeks. Pinch plants when they are 3 to 4 inches tall to encourage bushiness.

Growing Tips

Tall varieties will probably need to be staked. Deadheading or cutting keeps snapdragons blooming. In hot weather, snapdragons sometimes stop flowering or slow down drastically. Cut them back and feed them with a water-soluble fertilizer or compost tea. They should recover when temperatures cool. Water when the soil feels dry.

Care and Maintenance

Snapdragons are susceptible to rust and other fungal diseases, so try to plant resistant varieties. Snapdragons frequently self-sow, but this is usually not a problem. They do better when the weather is cool and moist, and they frequently make a strong comeback late in the season.

Companion Planting and Design

Snapdragons are a wonderful addition to the cut flower garden mixed with perennials or other annuals. The taller varieties can be planted in the middle of the bed to show off the spikes. If you are planting snapdragons for a cutting garden, select intermediate or tall varieties.

We Recommend

'Floral Carpet', 'Magic Carpet', 'Bells', 'Floral Showers', and 'Tahiti' are dwarf varieties. Smaller snapdragons make excellent summer ground covers. They are also great for containers and windowboxes. 'Coronette' hybrids, 'Sprite', 'Liberty', 'Cinderella', 'Sonnet' hybrids, 'Monarch', 'Popette', 'Rainbow', and 'Lipstick' are intermediates; they are a good size for containers. 'Rocket', 'Black Prince', 'Giant Ruffled Tetra', and 'Double Madam Butterfly' are tall varieties.

Snapdragons are reliable bloomers in a wide range of colors. They are equally at home in the perennial border, in the cutting garden, or in mass plantings in the landscape. They also do well in windowboxes and other containers. Newer varieties are resistant to many of the mildew problems that sometimes plague snaps. Snapdragon gets its name from its flowers, or florets, which resemble miniature dragon heads. If you gently squeeze the throat or sides of a floret, it snaps open and shut. Children get a big kick out of this trick! Snapdragons tolerate cool weather better than most annuals, so they can be planted in spring as soon as the ground can be worked or in late summer for fall enjoyment.

Other Common Name
Snaps

Bloom Period and Seasonal Color
Various flower colors in late spring through fall.

Mature Height × Spread
8 to 48 in. × 12 in.

Spider Flower
Cleome hassleriana

British resources sometimes refer to spider flowers as Cleome spinosa. This tall, unusual-looking plant can be used as a summer shrub or hedge if you cluster it in the back of the flower border, or you can plant it in a bare spot in the landscape. It gets its name from the stamens, which look like spider legs dangling from the flowers. The ball-type blooms appear at the ends of leafy, thorny stems. They are airy and open, and they look exotic bobbing above the plants. The seedheads also are attractive; however, if there's a drawback to this plant, it is that it self-sows like crazy. Spider flower has a distinctive scent that some people dislike. When it's hot, the flowers close up a bit during the day; they open later in the afternoon and through the night.

Bloom Period and Seasonal Color
Pink, white, and rose flowers in summer.

Mature Height × Spread
5 ft. × 5 ft.

When, Where, and How to Plant
Plant outdoors after the danger of frost has passed. Give spider flower a lot of room; it easily can have a 5-foot spread. It does best in a rich, well-drained spot but will tolerate ordinary soil and dry conditions. Space transplants 2 to 3 feet apart; if you plant them too close together, they will get leggy. You can sow seeds indoors six to eight weeks before the last frost. First, chill seeds overnight in the refrigerator. Then sow them in pots on the surface of moistened, soilless potting mix. Place the seeds in a warm, bright location out of direct sun, and keep them moist. Germination takes one to two weeks.

Growing Tips
Apply a granular, all-purpose fertilizer or a layer of compost when planting transplants. Water during long dry spells.

Care and Maintenance
Bedding plants may not show color at the garden center, but they are usually in full flower by midsummer. Cutting the flowers encourages branching, but watch out for thorny stems. Spider flower tends to lose vigor in late summer; you can pull it out when it does. It self-sows with abandon, but its hairy, palm-like leaves make it easy to recognize. Pull out seedlings and dump them in the compost pile or transplant them to a desirable location in spring. This plant is easy to grow and mostly pest free.

Companion Planting and Design
Spider flower looks ratty at the base of the plant once it begins to bloom, so plant shorter plants around it or plant it at the back of the flower bed. Because the ball-type flowers bob above the plant, mix it with spikey flowers, such as salvias and nicotiana. If the scent doesn't bother you, cut spider flower for indoor floral arrangements; they continue to open for at least a week.

We Recommend
The 'Queen' series has rose, pink, white, and violet flowers. 'Helen Campbell' is white. *Cleome lutea*, or yellow bee plant, is an annual wildflower in the western United States.

Sunflower

Helianthus annuus

When, Where, and How to Plant

Sunflowers do best in average, well-drained soil. They resent being transplanted, so leave them undisturbed. Sow seeds directly outdoors in the soil when all danger of frost has passed. Sow 3 or 4 seeds to a small hill, or mound of soil. Cut off the weakest seedlings, leaving one to grow. Mound soil up around the base of the taller varieties to help keep them upright; you may also have to stake them. Space the plants 12 to 36 inches apart depending on the variety. (See chapter introduction for more on planting.)

Growing Tips

Apply a water-soluble bloom-booster fertilizer or compost tea when sunflowers first begin to bloom. Too much fertilizer weakens plants, causing them to flop over. Follow label directions. Water during long dry spells.

Care and Maintenance

Cutting the smaller-flowered cultivars encourages branching and more flowers. Sunflowers are relatively pest and disease free. Birds find the seeds as edible as humans do, so many gardeners who plan to harvest the seedheads cover the heads with netting to keep birds out.

Companion Planting and Design

Sunflower heads turn to stay with the sun; north-facing sites may not be the best location as the heads would always be turned away. Shorter or dwarf varieties such as 'Teddy Bear' (2 feet tall), 'Big Smile' (12 to 14 inches), or 'Music Box' (24 to 30 inches) do well in containers and windowboxes.

We Recommend

'Russian', 'Tall Single', 'Giant Yellow', 'Giant Single', 'Giganteus', and 'D131' are tall varieties with large heads. Intermediate-sized varieties include 'Autumn Beauty' (6 to 7 feet tall with a mix of yellow, bronze, and red flowers); 'Italian White' (4 to 5 feet tall with creamy white flowers with black centers); 'Valentine' (5 feet tall with pale lemon-yellow flowers with black centers); 'Moonwalker' (up to 6 feet tall with pale-yellow flowers); and 'Sunbeam' (5 feet tall with 4-inch yellow flowers with green centers).

The common sunflower has been refined from a too-tall annual with a too-heavy flower head to shorter, more manageable varieties that are standouts in the perennial bed or cutting garden. The new varieties have tremendous branching characteristics, which make them ideal for a cutting garden. You can still choose the 18-foot varieties with its 12-inch-wide heads, but now there are smaller plants that grow only 18 to 24 inches tall. Sunflowers are easy to grow from seeds. You can sow them directly outdoors after the last frost; starting seeds indoors is not necessary. Plants are also readily available at garden centers. Some varieties are bicolor, and some have the traditional "sunflower" seedhead while others do not. Children love to grow this friendly plant.

Bloom Period and Seasonal Color
Various colors including yellow, orange, red, and mahogany from mid- to late summer.

Mature Height × Spread
1¹/₂ to 18 ft. × 3 to 5 ft.

Sweet Alyssum
Lobularia maritima

Sweet alyssum is one of those indispensable edging plants that help define flower beds or other landscape characteristics. It is easy to grow and flowers throughout the growing season. A compact low-grower, it makes a colorful, fragrant summer ground cover. The flowers are clustered in a globe atop weak stems, and the leaves are small. The flowers have a faint honey scent most noticeable when planted en masse or in a confined area where people sit or walk. Sweet alyssum has a charming trailing habit that softens the edges of containers and windowboxes. It sometimes slows down when it gets really hot, but it picks up and starts producing dense flushes of flowers in late summer or early fall.

Bloom Period and Seasonal Color
Soft yellow, apricot, white, rose, or purple flowers in summer.

Mature Height × Spread
6 in. × 12 in.

When, Where, and How to Plant
Plant bedding plants after the last frost in the spring. Sweet alyssum takes full sun to light shade and will tolerate average soil and dry conditions, but it performs best in well-drained, moist, loose soil. Space about 6 inches apart. If you are starting with seeds, sow indoors six to eight weeks before the last frost. Sow them on the surface of pots filled with moistened soilless potting mix. Place in a bright, warm area out of direct sunlight and keep them moist. Germination may take up to two weeks. Transplant seedlings outdoors in late spring. You can also sow seeds directly outdoors in early spring in a site prepared in fall. (See chapter introduction for more on planting.)

Growing Tips
Water sweet alyssum regularly. It sometimes loses its vigor when the weather gets very hot. Cut plants back about halfway, water well, and apply an all-purpose or bloom-booster, water-soluble fertilizer or a compost tea. They should come back in full force when the weather cools down.

Care and Maintenance
Sweet alyssum frequently self-sows, coming back year after year with little effort on the gardener's part. You can cut sweet alyssum for small indoor floral arrangements. It is fairly free from insects and diseases.

Companion Planting and Design
Sweet alyssum forms a mat as it ambles along the ground or rock garden. Plant it where the wonderful scent can be most enjoyed, such as an outdoor sitting area. For a simple planting, mix white sweet alyssum with a blue lobelia in a hanging basket or windowbox.

We Recommend
'Carpet' hybrids grow about 4 inches tall. 'Rosie O'Day' has rose-colored flowers on plants that spread about 10 inches wide but get only about 3 inches tall. 'Oriental Night' is about 4 inches tall with very fragrant purple flowers. 'Wonderland' hybrids grow 3 to 4 inches tall and have purple, rose, red, yellow, apricot, or white flowers. 'Carpet of Snow' grows up to 6 inches tall with white flowers. 'Royal Carpet' is violet purple.

When, Where, and How to Plant

Plant bedding plants or seedlings after the last frost in the spring. Soil should be fertile and well drained. *Zinnia angustifolia* tolerates light shade and prefers a moist soil until it is established. Space dwarf varieties 6 inches apart and taller ones 10 to 12 inches apart. If you are starting seeds indoors, sow them six to eight weeks before the last frost, in pots filled with moistened potting mix. Barely cover them with soil and place them in a warm, bright location. Germination may take up to three weeks. You can also sow seeds directly, after all danger of frost has passed.

Growing Tips

Apply a bloom-booster fertilizer or compost tea when you are transplanting zinnias outdoors, again when bloom begins, and every few weeks during the growing season. Watering when the soil feels dry will encourage more blooms.

Care and Maintenance

Deadheading and cutting *Zinnia elegans* keeps it flowering. If you avoid wetting the leaves when you water, especially with *Zinnia elegans*, you will cut down on mildew problems.

Companion Planting and Design

Zinnias look great when planted en masse or clustered in beds with perennials or other annuals. Shorter varieties do well in containers or windowboxes. *Zinnia angustifolia*, which comes in white or gold, has a sprawling, slightly trailing habit that makes it indispensible in containers or as a fill in the flower bed.

We Recommend

For cutting, you can't beat *Zinnia elegans*. Select for color and height. Popular tall (24 to 40 inches) varieties include 'California Giants' and 'State Fair'. Intermediate sizes (18 to 24 inches) include 'Whirligig', 'Cut and Come Again', and 'Lilliput'. Shorter varieties (6 to 18 inches) include 'Pulcino Double', 'Peter Pan', and 'Thumbelina'. The 'Profusion' series is resistant to powdery mildew but not suitable for cutting. *Zinnia angustifolia* varieties include 'Classic', 'Crystal White' (a recent All-America Selection), and 'Star'. *Zinnia haageana*, or Mexican zinnia, is bicolor and thrives in hot, dry locations. Varieties to look for include 'Persian Carpet' and 'Old Mexico'.

With its wide variety of shapes, colors, and textures, Zinnia elegans says summer garden. These annuals are native to Mexico and produce flowers all season long. Zinnias are easy to grow. Seeds planted outdoors in late May and early June will be in flower by late July. It is a must in the cutting garden. Flowers are solid, bicolor, or tricolor; they may be cactus-like, ruffled, or resemble pompons. Zinnia seeds started in late June bloom a little later but are less susceptible to powdery mildew (one of their few drawbacks). However, Zinnia angustifolia does not seem to be bothered by this problem. Zinnia attracts butterflies and hummingbirds and is another annual that children love to grow.

Bloom Period and Seasonal Color
Various colors in summer.

Mature Height × Spread
6 to 36 in. × 6 to 12 in.

Bulbs *for Indiana*

Bulbs come programmed to perform. Just add water, and, as if by magic, their fleshy layers transform into leaves and flowers that delight the senses. In late winter and early spring, scilla, snowdrops, crocus, and daffodils affirm another growing season while they warm the heart and brighten the landscape with color and fragrance. By midsummer, lilies, dahlias, and cannas are holding court. They are followed by fall-blooming crocus just before the weather chills, and the process begins all over again.

The term "bulb" commonly refers to a group of bulbous plants including bulbs, corms, tubers, and rhizomes. Lilies, daffodils, and onions are true bulbs. Crocuses and gladioli are examples of corms. Begonias, anemones, and potatoes are tubers.

The Many Faces of Bulbs

True bulbs have fleshy leaves attached to a short stem, called a basal plate. Leaves and stems grow from the top of the plate; roots grow from the bottom. A scaly bulb, such as lily or garlic, has fleshy leaves attached to a base. A tunicated bulb, such as hyacinth, daffodil, or onion, wears tunic-like fleshy layers or rings. When selecting bulbs, the bigger the better. Bulbs should be firm and without bruises, cuts, or mushy spots. It's okay if the outside, paper-thin layer is loose or peels away. Bulbs frequently have pointed tops (which you should plant facing up) and small, dry roots at the base.

Corms are squat stems covered by a layer of leaves that tend to be thin and scaly. Corms are flatter than bulbs. They frequently have a sunken place at the top; you should plant them with this sunken spot face up. The flatter side is the bottom, or basal plate, which is where roots form. Some corms benefit from an overnight soaking in water before you plant them. Corms should be firm and without bruises or cuts.

Tubers are swollen, irregularly shaped stems that grow underground. Like above-ground stems, tubers have nodes.

Fringed Tulip

Cactus-Flowered Dahlias

Growth points, or "eyes," are the flower buds. These are planted at or near the surface. Look for firm, healthy tubers with two or more eyes. Many tubers should be soaked in room-temperature water overnight or for a few hours before planting. Tubers frequently are meant to be planted horizontally with their eyes facing up.

Rhizomes are fleshy stems that creep underground or near the surface. The stems store food and produce leaves. Select rhizomes that are firm and without bruises. Soak rhizomes in room-temperature water for a few hours to overnight before planting.

Basic Bulb Planting

Bulbs are hardy or tender. Tender bulbs, while they may be perennial, are not winter hardy in Indiana and must be dug in fall, stored during winter, and replanted in spring. Hardy bulbs may be left where they are for winter.

Most bulbs follow the same planting guidelines. After you've chosen the proper location with well-drained soil and proper sunlight (according to the needs of the plant), dig a hole about three times deeper than the circumference of the bulb. For example, if you have a two-inch bulb, plant it six inches deep, or plant a three-inch bulb eight to nine inches deep. Too deep is better than not deep enough. Always water a newly planted patch of bulbs. During dry periods in the fall and winter, continue to supplement rainfall for bulbs and other plants. Plants will be better prepared for their winter survival if you give them several good soakings before the ground freezes. Although bulbs produce their own food, it doesn't hurt to give them a helping hand. Do this by applying a thin layer of compost around the plants when new growth emerges and again at the end of the growing season.

Each season, bulbs process and store nutrients that will help them perform again the following year. Be sure to allow the foliage to remain on the plant until it ripens, turns yellow or brown, and falls to the ground.

Daffodils, tulips, and ornamental onions will survive the winter outdoors, as they are hardy bulbs. Tender bulbs, like dahlias, must be lifted and stored indoors for the winter, then replanted outside in late spring as stated previously.

Get the Most "Bang" for Your Bulbs

Plant different species of bulbs in the same planting bed to get more "bang" for your bulbs. Mix bulbs with different sizes, heights, or bloom times by planting them at different depths.

- Dig a hole ten to twelve inches deep and as wide as you wish. Work the soil to break up dirt clumps and remove roots, rocks, and other debris. Return two to three inches of soil to the bottom of the hole and amend it by mixing in an inch or two of compost, finely chopped leaves, or dried grass clippings. Fertilizer is not needed when planting bulbs.

- Place the largest bulbs (such as daffodils and tulips) in the hole so that they are six to eight inches deep; adjust the amount of soil in the hole to get the correct depth. In general, plant bulbs approximately two to three times deeper than they are in diameter. Cover with just enough soil to plant the next layer of bulbs. Plant medium-sized bulbs (such as hyacinth, crocus, and smaller

daffodils) in the second layer, placing them around the larger bulbs. The second layer should be about four to six inches below ground level. Cover with just enough soil to plant the third layer. Scatter the smaller bulbs (such as Dutch iris, scilla, and snow drops) around the larger ones you have already planted so that they are about two to four inches below ground level. With many spring-flowering bulbs, it is better to plant them more deeply than to err by planting them too close to ground level.

Tulips and Grape Hyacinths

Ornamental Onion

Bulb Care

The best time to divide or transplant spring-flowering bulbs is in early summer, after the foliage has died. Carefully dig with a garden fork or spade, beginning some distance from the clump so that the bulbs don't get speared. Gently raise the clump and remove it from the hole. Separate the bulbs, keeping as many of their roots intact as possible. Trim off foliage and replant the bulbs, using the directions given above, as soon as possible, preferably in a bed you have already prepared. Water well. The bulbs may also be separated, dried, and stored in a cool, dry place where they won't sprout until fall. Then plant them as soon as possible.

You also can divide and move bulbs in the fall, but finding them can be a challenge. Be sure to mark the clumps you wish to divide in the spring by outlining them with short twigs, wooden ice cream sticks, metal stakes, a ring of jute, or twine, or the bamboo sticks that are sold at many garden centers as plant stakes.

Some bulbs, particularly summer-flowering lilies and surprise lilies, have long stems and bloom well above their foliage, leaving a large gap. You may wish to use companion plants to help fill that space. Think about the foliage that must remain on the bulbs when you are deciding where to plant them. Daylilies, chrysanthemums, and several other perennials make good companion plants because, as they grow, they hide the bulbs' ripening foliage.

You can force hardy, spring-flowering bulbs to bloom indoors. Tender bulbs, such as freesias, can also be forced to bloom indoors. For the best and most satisfying results, select bulbs that say "ideal for forcing" or "ready for forcing." These have gone through a necessary cold, dormant period and can be potted up or placed on water and pebbles for a wonderful indoor display. After the bloom is finished, discard hardy, spring-flowering bulbs forced to bloom indoors.

Bulbs bring tremendous interest to the garden throughout the growing season, from the early spring bloomers to the dramatic foliage and spectacular flowers of the late-summer cannas. They are well worth their time and space in the garden.

Allium
Allium spp.

Ornamental alliums are in the same family as garlic, onions, and chives, which is why they smell like their flavorful cousins if you crush or cut them. Alliums are easy to grow, and there are nearly 400 species from which to choose. Many have long-lasting, fragrant flowers; you can use them in floral bouquets or dry them for arrangements. Allium flowers form atop leafless stalks that shoot up from the base of the plant. Alliums have two types of flower heads: ball-type and tufted. Allium giganteum is an example of the ball-type flower; it is a dramatic, purple-headed, early summer bloomer that looks like a giant drumstick. Allium moly (called golden garlic or lily leek) is an example of the tufted flower; it has loose upright or drooping clusters.

Other Common Name
Ornamental Onion

Bloom Period and Seasonal Color
Purple, white, yellow, and pink blooms in spring and summer.

Mature Height × Spread
12 to 36 in. × spread depending on variety

When, Where, and How to Plant
Plant allium in the fall with spring-flowering bulbs. The larger alliums bloom in early summer, however. When you are making your selections, be sure to check blooming times as well as height and color. Plant bulbs 4 to 12 inches apart; smaller bulbs should be closer together. Water well.

Growing Tips
Mulch lightly with compost or wood chips. Apply a granular, all-purpose fertilizer after blooming and until the foliage dies back, or ring the emerging clump with compost. Supplemental watering usually isn't necessary.

Care and Maintenance
It is fine to cut the flowers for arrangements or remove them as the blossoms die, but about half the foliage must remain on the plant after the flowers have gone. Foliage helps to store food the bulb needs to flower again next year. Wait until foliage turns yellow or brown, then remove it by cutting it at ground level. Pests are not a problem with allium.

Companion Planting and Design
Alliums that grow three feet tall or more are good center-of-the-bed plants, where other perennials or annuals soften the look of the stems. The companion plants will also camouflage the allium foliage as it ripens and turns yellow and brown. Shorter allium can be planted in clusters toward the front of the flower bed or as companions to late blooming tulips.

We Recommend
A. cernuum, or the nodding onion, is native to Indiana. It has umbrella-like, or umbel, flowers in white, pink, or lavender atop 18- to 24-inch stems in midsummer. It also tolerates deep shade. *A. christophii*, or star of Persia, blooms in late spring or early summer; it grows about 3 feet tall and has 10-inch-wide lavender flowers. Chives, *A. schoenoprasum*, make a lovely, edible, low-growing allium for the front of the flower border. (See the Herbs chapter for more about chives.)

Canna
Canna × generalis

When, Where, and How to Plant

Plant container-grown transplants in the spring after the last frost (see chapter introduction). Canna rhizomes should be started indoors in March or April because they are very slow to grow. If you are planting rhizomes in containers, fill 6-inch clay or plastic pots $2/3$ to $3/4$ full with a moistened, soilless mix. Place the rhizomes horizontally in the pots, covering with 2 inches of mix. Put them in a warm bright area and keep them moist. Transplant when cannas are at least 6 or 8 inches tall. You can start cannas from seed, but it takes a long time for them to germinate. Notch or nick seeds before planting and follow planting instructions on the seed packet.

Growing Tips

Cannas don't like to dry out, so keep the soil moist. Cannas do well in boggy areas around ponds. Apply a water-soluble fertilizer or compost tea every two weeks during the growing season.

Care and Maintenance

You can divide rhizomes in the spring; cut them into sections that have two or more "eyes," or growth points. To winter over the rhizomes for transplanting next year, allow frost to kill the foliage. Remove all but 4 to 6 inches of the foliage and dig up the rhizome. Rinse the rhizome, let it dry for a few days, and store in a cool, dry place through the winter. Or, you can allow the canna to go dormant indoors in its pot for the winter. Cannas are relatively free of pests and disease.

Companion Planting and Design

Cannas are appreciated as much for their foliage as their flowers. Foliage with tints of yellow or red look especially nice when backlit by the sun. Dwarf varieties do well in containers, too.

We Recommend

'King Humbert' is 6 feet tall with red flowers and bronze foliage; 'Pretoria' is 4 feet tall, with creamy yellow and green zebra-striped foliage and melon-orange flowers. 'Tropicana' has stunning red/pink/gold leaves with stripes and grows 5 to 7 feet. Dwarf varieties, including 'Pfitzer' and 'Futurity' do well in containers. *Canna indica* is native to Central America and the West Indies and grows up to 6 feet tall with small, bright-red flowers. Its seed was used with sling shots, thus the name Indian Shot.

Cannas are considered old-fashioned flowers, but they are hard to beat in mid- to lat late summer when most other plants have stopped blooming. These easy-to-grow plants are dramatic in the landscape, adding stately structure and exotic foliage. Cannas are native to Central and South America, South Africa, and a few other tropical climates. Their rhizomes are tender in Indiana, so dig cannas for winter storage when the tops are killed by frost. They were a staple in the Victorian garden and are enjoying a revival. Because cannas bloom late, their foliage is as important a design element as the flowers. Some leaves are a solid green, while others have stripes of red or yellow or are reddish with bronze and yellow stripes.

Other Common Names
Indian Shot, Canna Lily

Bloom Period and Seasonal Color
A range of colors including red, pink, yellow, and orange in mid- to late summer.

Mature Height × Spread
$1^{1}/2$ to 6 ft. × 2 to 3 ft.

Crocus

Crocus spp. and hybrids

With purple, white, blue, yellow, or variegated flowers, these harbingers of spring harken another growing season and tell us all is right with the gardening world. Crocus grow from corms, and although they're hardy enough to withstand the coldest Indiana winter, they are treated like annuals in many yards because squirrels will gobble them up. Squirrels often will eat them as fast as you plant them, or as they bloom, so plant a lot. The seasoning saffron comes from the orange stamens of Crocus sativus, or saffron crocus, one of several varieties that bloom in the fall. Another fall blooming plant called autumn crocus is Colchicum, or meadow saffron, although it's not a Crocus species.

Bloom Period and Seasonal Color
Various colors from February to April.

Mature Height × Spread
2 to 6 in. × 2 in.

When, Where, and How to Plant
Plant crocus after the middle of September until the ground freezes. Corms may be moved or divided in early summer after the foliage has died back. Those in the sun will probably bloom earlier than the ones in the shade. Amend the soil well with compost for good drainage. Plant corms flat side down about 3 or 4 inches deep. Rather than dig individual holes for each corm, consider digging one larger hole and cluster the corms 2 to 3 inches apart. Water them well.

Growing Tips
Apply a granular all-purpose fertilizer or a layer of compost in spring when crocus leaves break ground. Mulch lightly with compost or wood chips, if desired. They will not need additional moisture.

Care and Maintenance
Remove foliage to ground level when it is ripe. Fall-blooming crocus are ordered in spring and should be planted as soon as they arrive. They start blooming in September and last for several weeks. The foliage also needs to remain on the plant until it turns yellow or brown.

Companion Planting and Design
Because crocus are small, plant them where they can be seen, such as in a patch by the mailbox, along the walk from the house to the garage, or at the very front of a flower bed. Underplant crocus in groundcover that is not too dense, such as *Epimedium*, *Tiarella*, or *Pachysandra*. They also mix well with *Iris reticulata* and early blooming daffodils.

We Recommend
Crocus flavus (sometimes called *Crocus aureus*) is called Dutch crocus or Dutch yellow crocus and is among the earliest, sometimes breaking ground in January; *Crocus vernus* also is called Dutch or common crocus. Dutch crocus tends to have large flowers. Select based on color, height, and blooming period. *Crocus speciosus* is an easy-to-grow fall-blooming type. *Crocus tomasinianus* is a very early, small-flowered crocus that multiplies rapidly. In shades of light blue to lavender, it looks wonderful naturalized in a lawn.

Daffodil
Narcissus spp. and hybrids

When, Where, and How to Plant

Plant *Narcissus* bulbs from mid-September until the ground is frozen (the earlier you plant the better). They grow in sun or shade. Choose a well-drained spot and amend it with compost or other organic material. Avoid planting bulbs in areas that stay wet because they will rot. Water well and mulch lightly.

Growing Tips

Fertilize in spring when its leaves break ground with an all-purpose granular product or add a layer of compost around the bulbs. Many varieties are good for naturalizing in the landscape, especially 'February Gold', 'King Alfred', 'Mount Hood', 'Barrett Browning', and 'Ice Follies'. Watering should not be necessary.

Care and Maintenance

You can move or divide bulbs in early summer, after the foliage has died back. Don't cut back foliage until it turns yellow or brown. When cutting for indoor use, avoid mixing *Narcissus* with other flowers. They emit a substance that clogs the stems of other types of flowers and causes them to wilt. Daily water changes reduce this. Daffodils come back year after year with little or no fuss. Daffodils are relatively pest and disease free.

Companion Planting and Design

Daffodils mix well with many ground covers and perennials, including daylilies (*Hemerocallis*), which grow to camouflage the ripening foliage of *Narcissus*. When making selections, consider the twelve divisions, some of which describe generally the shape of the daffodil's flower: Trumpet, Large-Cupped, Small-Cupped, Double-Flowering, Triandrus, Jonquilla, Tazetta, Cyclamineus, Poeticus, Species, Narcissus with Split Coronas (Butterfly), and Miscellaneous.

We Recommend

Try 'Dutch Master', 'Peaches and Cream', 'Salome', 'Cheerfulness', 'Hawara', 'Jack Snipe', 'Tete-a-Tete', and 'Actaea'. Make selections based on color, blooming times, and height. It's hard to make a bad choice.

If you can have only one type of spring-flowering bulb, make it daffodils. They can be intoxicatingly fragrant and are an excellent value for your money. The botanical name Narcissus *comes from Greek mythology. Narcissus was cursed to fall in love with himself, which he did when he saw his image in a pool. He drowned trying to reach the person he loved. The names narcissus, daffodil, and jonquil are frequently used interchangeably, but experts classify this bulb into twelve divisions. Early-blooming daffodils often flower before trees or large shrubs get leaves, so you can plant them in very shady locations. Although the yellow daffodil is most common, hybrids come in many colors, including gold, white, cream, peach, or pale pink. You can find daffodils with single or double flowers, or even multiple flowers on the same stem.*

Other Common Name
Jonquil

Bloom Period and Seasonal Color
Various colors from February to April.

Mature Height × Spread
4 to 20 in. × 3 in.

Dahlia
Dahlia hybrids

Dahlias are native to Mexico and South America, where they grow wild at altitudes of 5,000 and 10,000 feet. In the eighteenth century, the tuber was named after Andreas Dahl, a Swedish botanist and student of Carolus Linnaeus, the Swede credited with devising the modern system of naming plants. By the 1830s, Europe raged with "dahliamania." Countries fought over the plant, and the gardening elite experimented with growing it. Marie Antoinette hoarded her supply behind a fence and reportedly told those who asked for cuttings, "Let them grow roses!" There are some excellent, bedding-type dahlias that are grown from seed; these require less care, and they also develop tubers. Dahlia aficionados pride themselves on growing dinner-plate-sized flowers on stalks that must be staked. Dahlia colors are brilliant.

Bloom Period and Seasonal Color
Red, purple, pink, lavender, white, yellow, and variegated from mid- to late summer.

Mature Height × Spread
1 to 5 ft. × 3 ft.

When, Where, and How to Plant
Transplant bedding plants in the spring after the danger of frost has passed. Plant tubers or clumps in a prepared bed a week or two before the last frost in the spring. Dahlias prefer full sun and well-drained soil that has been amended with compost or other organic material. Protect them from southern or western sun. Bedding types do well in containers and flower boxes. Plant tubers or clumps 4 to 6 inches deep in a wide hole that allows roots to spread out (see chapter introduction). If you are planting a tall variety, place the stakes at this time to avoid injuring the plant later.

Growing Tips
Apply a water-soluble bloom-booster fertilize or compost tea every two weeks throughout the growing season. Water when the top inch of soil feels dry.

Care and Maintenance
Pinch plants when young for bushier growth and remove side shoots to make the flowers larger. Tall varieties will need to be staked. Dahlia tubers and clumps can be lifted to winter over. After frost has killed the top foliage, cut the stems to about 6 inches and gently lift the rootball. Trim back the roots and allow the plant to dry slightly. Store in a bin of peat moss; choose a cool, dry place with protection from freezing and rodents. Divide clumps in spring by cutting them into sections with at least one "eye," or growth spot. Good drainage is the most important maintenance issue.

Companion Planting and Design
Dahlias have many different flower types. These include single, anemone, collarette, waterlily, decorative, ball, pompon, cactus, semi-cactus, and Lilliput (a bedding variety). They are indispensible in the cutting garden and are fine additions with other mid- to late summer blooming annuals or perennials.

We Recommend
There are hundreds of varieties. Select the color and flower style that best suits your garden. Smaller varieties, such as 'Rigolletto', are great in containers. 'Bishop of Llandaff' has red flowers and purple foliage. 'Winsome' has a deep rose with a flush of yellow-orange.

Dutch Iris
Iris reticulata

When, Where, and How to Plant
Plant *Iris reticulata* bulbs through the fall, up until the ground is frozen. *Iris reticulata* is not fussy about soil quality but prefers a well-drained spot. Plant along the edges of walkways or flower beds. The bulbs are small, so plant them about an inch apart. Water well and mulch lightly with compost or shredded bark.

Growing Tips
Apply an all-purpose granular fertilizer after the flowers fade and until the foliage dies back or dust some compost around the plants as they emerge in spring. You may cut the flowers for arrangements or remove them as the blossoms die. Watering should not be necessary.

Care and Maintenance
Dutch iris send up grasslike foliage in fall as part of their natural growing process. The foliage should be left alone until it dies, then remove it by cutting it at ground level. Although they rarely need dividing, clumps can be split in fall, or they can be divided in late spring or early summer after the foliage has died back. These irises are relatively free of disease and pests.

Companion Planting and Design
Iris reticulata makes a good companion plant for crocus and early-flowering short narcissus. They will spread rapidly without becoming invasive. They also adapt well with many ground covers. Because they bloom early, their foliage is usually camouflaged as companion plants grow.

We Recommend
I. reticulata 'Harmony' has deep-blue flowers and flecked throats. 'Cantab' has light-blue flowers, and 'Joyce' has sky-blue flowers and red markings. Another species, also called Dutch iris (*Iris xiphium*), is usually 16 to 18 inches tall, flowers in May and June, and is grown as an annual in Indiana. You can frequently find it in bouquets of cut flowers at florist shops. Good varieties include: 'Blue Ribbon', purple-blue flowers with yellow throats; 'Romano', light-blue flowers with white-and-yellow falls; 'White Perfection', white with a touch of yellow in the throat; 'Oriental Beauty', lavender flowers with white and pale-yellow falls; and 'Purple Sensation', dark-purple flowers with yellow throats.

These miniature irises bloom in February and March, and the flowers last several weeks. It's always a contest in the garden to see which blooms first—Iris reticulata or crocus. Because these iris are small, plant them close together in drifts or large clusters to ensure a good show. The flowers come in purple, blue, yellow, and white. Some are solid colored; others have throats with attractive contrasting colors or tiny flecks on the petals. Don't confuse Iris reticulata and other Dutch, English, or Spanish irises with bearded irises, which are sometimes called "old-fashioned iris" or "flags." The former grow from bulbs while the latter grow from rhizomes, as do Siberian and Japanese irises. (See the Perennials chapter for more about irises.)

Other Common Name
Netted Iris

Bloom Period and Seasonal Color
Various colors in early spring.

Mature Height × Spread
3 to 6 in. × 2 in.

Grape Hyacinth
Muscari spp.

Grape hyacinth is a very reliable bloomer—once you plant it, you can pretty much leave it alone. The flowers are fragrant spikes of ball- or grape-like flowers. They make a sweet, cut-flower bouquet. Because of their telltale foliage, they also make excellent markers for perennials and other bulbs that may be hard to locate in the garden. If these lovely blue or purple flowers have a drawback, it is that some varieties may self-sow, sending new plants to other parts of the landscape where you don't want their grass-like fall foliage. M. botryoides is the common, blue-flowering grape hyacinth. It is the hardiest and is also most likely to send up fall foliage. 'Album' is an interesting white cultivar.

Bloom Period and Seasonal Color
Blue, purple, and white blooms in spring.

Mature Height × Spread
6 to 10 in. × 4 in.

When, Where, and How to Plant
Plant bulbs in the fall as early as possible, before the ground freezes. You can divide plants in early summer, when the foliage has died back. They tolerate shade, especially in areas where they can flower before deciduous trees and shrubs leaf out. Plant about 3 inches apart with their pointed ends up. Instead of individual holes, dig several large ones to plant muscari in drifts or clusters. This ensures the best show. Cover and water well. Mulching isn't necessary, but a light layer of shredded bark, compost, or chopped leaves is okay.

Growing Tips
Apply an all-purpose granular fertilizer in the fall or spring when foliage appears, or spread a thin layer of compost over the clumps in the spring and fall. If *Muscari* is naturalizing in the lawn, do not cut your grass until the foliage has ripened. Watering is not necessary.

Care and Maintenance
Grape hyacinth can have a very long foliage period, sending up leaves in fall. The flowers rise from these grassy clumps in the spring. Don't remove the foliage. Grape hyacinths are relatively free of pests or diseases.

Companion Planting and Design
Muscari does well under trees and shrubs. Try to plant grape hyacinth where the flowers can be seen easily. They look and smell best when densely planted. They are also very attractive growing naturally in a lawn. For a traditional spring-flower combination, plant muscari with yellow daffodils and red tulips. Grape hyacinth should not be confused with *Hyacinthus orientalis* (commonly referred to as Dutch hyacinth or hyacinth), which is discussed on the next page.

We Recommend
M. armeniacum blooms in April with a white edge on dark-purple flowers. 'Blue Spike' produces double, blue flowers, 4 to 6 inches tall in early spring. *M. azureum* has bright-blue, low-growing flowers. *M. latifolium* has 10-inch-tall spikes with shades of grape-hyacinth blue in the top third of the flower to a deep purple or blue on the bottom two-thirds. It blooms in April or May.

Hyacinth
Hyacinthus orientalis

When, Where, and How to Plant
Plant hyacinth bulbs as early as possible in the fall or up until about a month before the ground freezes. Choose a well-drained spot and amend the soil with organic material. Plant 6 to 8 inches apart. Instead of digging several holes, dig one larger hole and place hyacinths, tulips, and daffodils several inches apart in the bottom. Be sure to plant the bulbs with the pointed ends up. Cover, water well, and mulch with shredded bark or a thick layer of chopped leaves.

Growing Tips
Apply an all-purpose granular fertilizer in the spring when leaves break ground, or spread a thin layer of compost around and over the clump. You can help the bulb replenish itself for next year's growth by removing the hyacinth flower after it fades but before seeds are formed. Watering shouldn't be necessary.

Care and Maintenance
Be aware that hyacinths are not as long-lived as other bulbs. Winter cycles of freezing and thawing may push newly planted bulbs out of the soil. If that happens, gently press the bulb back in the ground.

Companion Planting and Design
Plant hyacinths where you can enjoy their beauty and fragrance. To intensify their scent, plant hyacinths in large clusters or drifts. These fat bulbs can also be potted in a container and forced to bloom indoors.

We Recommend
Plant 'Delft Blue', 'Ostara', and 'Blue Jacket' for shades of blue and purple; 'City of Haarlem' for yellow, 'Gipsy Queen' for peach, and 'Carnegie' for white. Another species known as "hyacinth" includes Indian hyacinth (*Camassia leichtlinii*) which has starlike flowers on stalks up to 3 feet tall. *Endymion hispanicus*, *Scilla hispanicus*, and *S. campanulata* are known as wood hyacinths or Spanish bluebells. These are excellent plants for naturalizing, growing well in the partial shade of a woodland.

Everyone should have a cluster of hyacinths somewhere in the landscape, if only to provide cut flowers to perfume a room. Hyacinths are easy to grow, and they will produce large, tightly packed flowers the first year. In subsequent seasons, they will produce looser, more airy blossoms. Hyacinths sometimes seem a bit stiff and formal, but they do well mixed with plants that soften their shape. They work particularly well with ground covers like Pachysandra, *which also help hide hyacinth's foliage as it dies back. Grape hyacinths* (Muscari) *are a different species and are covered on the previous page. Be careful not to confuse them!*

Bloom Period and Seasonal Color
Blue, pink, white, and yellow blooms in spring.

Mature Height × Spread
10 to 12 in. × 4 in.

Lily

Lilium spp. and hybrids

Lilies look delicate with their tall stalks and large flowers, but they are fairly easy to grow. Many lilies are intoxicatingly fragrant. Lilies add drama and elegance to the garden, frequently towering over companion plants to herald their presence. Lilies are classified in six categories, depending on the shape of their flowers: trumpet, chalice, pendant, reflexed, bowl, and sunburst. They are also sorted into ten divisions, including Oriental, Asiatic, Candidum, American, and Longiflorum hybrids. The lilies sold at Easter are Lilium longiflorum; *they may not be winter hardy in Indiana. North America natives include* Lilium canadense *which blooms in the summer and has red or yellow flowers on 5-foot-tall stalks. Tall varieties frequently need to be staked.*

Bloom Period and Seasonal Color
Various colors including pink, yellow, orange, red, purple, white, and peach in summer.

Mature Height × Spread
18 to 48 in. × 6 in.

When, Where, and How to Plant
Plant lilies, or divide clumps in the fall or early spring in a spot with good drainage—lilies will rot if the soil stays too wet, especially in winter. Amend the soil with compost or other organic material. Try not to bruise or break any of the scales, or layers, that form on the outside of the bulb. Plant the bulbs with the pointed sides turned up. Cover, water well, and mulch lightly.

Growing Tips
Fertilize in spring when the foliage breaks ground. Use an all-purpose granular fertilizer or apply a layer of compost to the clump. Too much fertilizer may weaken the stems. Lilies don't like competition for nutrients, so avoid places too close to large plants. Many prefer to have hot heads and cool feet—with full sun exposure for the tops of plants and shaded, well-mulched soil for the roots. Water only if it is extremely dry.

Care and Maintenance
Tall varieties often need staking. When cutting lilies for indoor use, leave about half of the stem on the plant. The stem and foliage are needed to replenish the bulb for next year's flowers. Cut to the ground when the foliage ripens to a brown or yellow color. Mulch them for winter, and remove mulch in spring when new growth appears.

Companion Planting and Design
Because lilies bloom at the top of the plant, they mix nicely with lower-growing herbaceous perennials, annuals, or small shrubs at the base. Smaller varieties are great in containers during the summer. Transplant these to the ground in fall if desired.

We Recommend
Lilium philadelphicum, or wood lily, grows about 3 feet tall and has orange flowers; *Lilium superbum*, or native Turk's cap, grows approximately 10 feet tall. Also, Asiatic lilies 'Turk's Cap', 'Connecticut King', and 'Enchantment' bloom in early summer. Oriental lilies, 'Star Gazer', 'Casa Blanca', and 'Mona Lisa', bloom later and are the most fragrant. *Lilium tigrinum*, the freckled, orange-flowered tiger lily, is a Hoosier mainstay. At 2 to 4 inches tall, it boasts from 8 to 20 flowers per stem.

Siberian Squill

Scilla siberica

When, Where, and How to Plant
Plant *Scilla* bulbs as early as possible in the fall but before the ground freezes. *Scilla* prefers full sun or partial shade, but avoid hot, dry places. If you are trying to naturalize the lawn, cut and lift sections of sod, plant several of the bulbs, replace the sod, and water. Naturalize *Scilla* by planting in clumps or drifts.

Growing Tips
Apply an all-purpose granular fertilizer or a thin layer of compost around the plants in late winter or early spring when new growth breaks ground. Keep the bulbs well watered as winter approaches.

Care and Maintenance
The foliage is unobtrusive. Siberian squill blooms so early that the foliage is usually gone or easily camouflaged as companion plants begin to grow.

Companion Planting and Design
Squill looks great under both deciduous and evergreen trees and shrubs. Siberian squill sometimes is confused with glory-of-the-snow (*Chionodoxa*), which blooms a little later but has the same great naturalizing habit for lawns. Do not confuse *Scilla siberica* with *Scilla hispanicus* (known as wood hyacinth or Spanish bluebell) or with *Scilla nonscriptus*, (known as English bluebell). Both of these are excellent bulbs for naturalizing but are much larger plants.

We Recommend
Grow the species for blue flowers or 'Alba' for a white variety, which might be hard to find. *S. bifolia* has 6-inch stalks of blue, starlike flowers. *S. mischtschenkoana* has several 4-inch spikes of light-blue flowers with dark-blue stripes. *Puschkinia scilloides*, sometimes called striped squill, has clusters of fragrant pale-blue or almost-white flowers.

This is probably one of the best spring-flowering bulbs to naturalize in the lawn. The bell-shaped flowers hang from stems, and they create a sea of blue, white, or pink against the grassy green of the lawn. The bulbs' ripening foliage is easily camouflaged by the lawn well before it needs its first cutting. Both Siberian squill and snowdrops (Galanthus nivalis) bloom in February, creating an attractive show. Scilla siberica 'Spring Beauty' readily self-sows, but the plants are unobtrusive and have no nuisance qualities; you can leave them to grow where they land. For the fastest show, plant Scilla in large masses. The flowers may be cut for sweet little arrangements indoors.

Other Common Name
Squill

Bloom Period and Seasonal Color
Blue, pink, or white from late winter to early spring.

Mature Height × Spread
4 to 8 in. × 2 in.

Snowdrop
Galanthus nivalis

Galanthus means "milk-white flowers," and that's what we get with snowdrops at a time when we really need some encouragement that spring will soon be here. Snowdrops bloom while there is still snow on the ground, hence their name. These bulbs may be small, but with their long-lasting, white, bell-shaped flowers, they produce a lovely show in late winter and early spring. Some snowdrop flowers may have tiny green dots at the tips or base of their petals. If you plant them in a sunny spot, they may bloom in late January or early February; in a shadier spot, they will bloom later. Snowdrops are great naturalizers.

Bloom Period and Seasonal Color
White blooms in late winter and early spring.

Mature Height × Spread
2 to 6 in. × 2 in.

When, Where, and How to Plant
Plant bulbs as soon as possible in the fall, but before the ground freezes. They can grow in sun or shade. Snowdrops will grow almost in any kind of soil except very wet. Cluster them where you can see them or where their white flowers can brighten a distant spot. They naturalize nicely under both deciduous and evergreen trees and shrubs.

Growing Tips
Apply an all-purpose granular fertilizer in late winter or early spring when new growth breaks ground, or spread a layer of compost in the area. Watering is not necessary.

Care and Maintenance
Leave the foliage on the plant until it turns yellow or brown; it is usually unobtrusive and decomposes very quickly without having to be trimmed. Because snowdrops bloom so early in the season, the foliage disappears by March. Mark them with a stake so that you don't lose track of them when you are digging in the beds for other plantings.

Companion Planting and Design
Snowdrops are most attractive if you plant them in large clusters or drifts for a fuller look and bigger impact. Instead of digging dozens of small holes, dig larger ones and cluster the bulbs. Snowdrops mix well with the ground cover epimedium, the early-flowering blue *Iris reticulata* and yellow winter aconite (*Eranthis hyemalis*). Their short stature makes them excellent rock garden plants.

We Recommend
Galanthus nivalis 'Flore Pleno' blooms very early in the spring; it is a 4-inch-tall double white. *G. nivalis* 'Viridapicis' has green-edged outer petals. Giant snowdrop (*G. elwesii*) has larger flowers with stems that reach 8 inches. It may bloom a little earlier than *G. nivalis*.

Surprise Lily
Lycoris squamigera

When, Where, and How to Plant
Plant in early spring or in the fall in a well-drained spot. Surprise lily can be grown in sun or shade. Plant bulbs in clusters or clumps about 6 inches apart with their tops about 6 inches below the soil surface. Cover, water well, and mulch lightly.

Growing Tips
Apply an all-purpose granular fertilizer in spring when foliage breaks ground and in late summer when the flowers begin to fade, or add a layer of compost around the clump at the same time. Watering usually is not necessary.

Care and Maintenance
These are delightful plants that are showing off at a time when there are few flowers blooming in the landscape. They naturalize nicely, too. Their foliage is sometimes confused with daffodil leaves, which begin their growth at the same time. When cutting for indoor use, leave half of the stem on the plant so it can help provide the food necessary for next year's growth. *Lycoris* is relatively free of pests and disease.

Companion Planting and Design
Because surprise lilies bloom late, they bring color and elegance to the garden when there is not a lot else going on. Plant *Lycoris* among ground covers, in the middle of the flower bed, between shrubs, or mixed with daylilies to enhance the element of surprise in the garden.

We Recommend
Only the species is available. *L. radiata* is known as red spider lily and is hardy in Zone 6. In Zone 5, plant it about 6 inches deep in the spring if you want summer flowers. The flowers resemble pink, red, or white spiders; they hover over narrow leaves on 15-inch stalks. *L. albiflora* is a white spider lily, and *L. africana* is gold. *L. chinensis*, *L. sanguinea*, *L. longituba*, and *L. incarta* are hardy to Zone 6.

Lycoris squamigera, native to Asia, is named for Lycoris, a Roman actress who reportedly had an affair with Marc Antony. It sends up strap-like leaves early in the growing season, then the leaves disappear. In August, as if by magic, lovely fragrant lilac-pink, trumpet-like flowers rise from the ground on slender stalks with no foliage. Over time, surprise lily develops clumps with several stalks, each one loaded with many flowers. Even though lily is part of the common name, Lycoris is really part of the amaryllis family. Only L. squamigera is winter hardy in Indiana.

Other Common Names
Resurrection Lily, Naked Lady

Bloom Period and Seasonal Color
Pink blooms in mid- to late summer.

Mature Height × Spread
30 in. × 4 in.

Tulip

Tulipa spp. and hybrids

Tulips are like dots of color on a stick. Once sold as a high-priced commodity during Tulipmania in Holland in the 1630s, these lovely flowers originated in Turkey. They can have single, double, frilly, fringed, lily-, parrot-, or star-like flowers. Many are fragrant. Tulips are classified and sold as hardy bulbs, but they are short-lived in most Indiana landscapes. Hoosier summers are too warm for them to retain their vigor, and most of the soil is too heavy and compacted. Even in Holland, the tulip capital of the world, the bulbs are dug in the spring, summered over in a controlled environment, and planted again in the fall. After their first flowering, tulips seem to decline about 33 to 50 percent each year. Plan to replant most garden tulips every two or three years.

Bloom Period and Seasonal Color
Various colors including red, pink, yellow, purple, white, and variegated in early spring to early summer.

Mature Height × Spread
4 to 24 in. × 6 in.

When, Where, and How to Plant
Plant bulbs in the fall, before the ground freezes. Tulips prefer well-drained, loamy soil. Avoid planting tulips where the soil stays wet. Early tulips will bloom in partial shade before the trees leaf out. Some gardeners believe that tulips are longer-lived when they are planted more deeply. Consider digging large holes and placing tulips and daffodils about 4 inches apart in a suitable arrangement, allowing for your height and color preferences. Cover and water well. Mulch lightly with shredded bark, compost, or chopped leaves.

Growing Tips
Apply an all-purpose granular fertilizer when the flowers fade and until the foliage dies back, or spread a layer of compost over the clump in the spring and fall. Watering is not necessary. Garden tulips, or hybrids, will produce fewer flowers in the second year than they did in the first; fewer flowers in the third year than they did in the second; and so on. Early-flowering tulips, or species tulips, are much longer-lived, returning year after year with little effort.

Care and Maintenance
You must leave the foliage on the plant until it turns yellow or brown; this can take quite a while. After it turns yellow, remove the foliage at ground level.

Companion Planting and Design
Plant different cultivars of tulips according to color preference and timing of flowers (such as early, mid-, or late season bloomers). Tulips combine wonderfully with other spring-flowering bulbs, including daffodils and hyacinths. They also blend nicely with spring blooming perennials, such as columbine and coral bells.

We Recommend
Tulipa greigii, T. kaufmanniana, T. tarda, T. praestans, and *T. fosteriana* are good selections for early-flowering tulips. Darwin hybrid tulips are midseason bloomers. 'Apeldoorn' varieties, which produce a number of colors, are included in this group. Midseason tulips last for quite a while in the garden; many range from 20 to 30 inches tall. Darwin tulips, (different from Darwin hybrids), are single late bloomers. *T. viridiflora* 'Greenland' is fragrant and has staying power. 'Angelique' is another late bloomer; it has a pink, peony-like flower.

Virginia Bluebell
Mertensia virginica

When, Where, and How to Plant
Plant tubers in fall until the ground freezes. They do best in a moist area in part sun to full shade. They prefer a well-drained, loamy area, so prepare the soil by mixing with organic material. Plant container-grown stock in spring as soon as the soil can be worked. Virginia bluebells are a woodland plant, thriving in the shafts of light or fringes of woods.

Growing Tips
These are so easy to grow that they don't even need fertilizer, especially if planted in a woodsy area. Watering is not usually needed.

Care and Maintenance
Try not to cut all of the flowers for indoor use. The spent flowers and seedheads left on the plants will spread to naturalize an area. Virginia bluebells are remarkably pest and disease free.

Companion Planting and Design
After blooming, Virginia bluebells completely disappear without any work on the gardener's part, which makes them ideal in any garden, including perennial beds. However, don't forget where you planted them! Plant with yellow, midseason blooming daffodils and red tulips for a tremendous show of traditional spring color.

We Recommend
Only the species is available. Make sure this and any other native plant you buy is marked "nursery propogated." Unethical plant sellers sometimes illegally dig these natural beauties from their native habitat.

This is a true native ephemeral, coming and going from dormancy without a trace. In early spring, Virginia bluebell sends up small purple leaves. These grow into large oval green leaves, followed by 15- to 18-inch-tall stems loaded with blue, bell-shaped flowers. Then, as if by magic, the foliage disappears. There's no clean up on these plants. Virginia bluebells sometimes can be found in pots at garden centers in spring, but most get their start in our gardens as a tuber, ordered from a seed or bulb catalog, and planted in fall. Once the plants bloom, they naturalize by seed. The flowers start out as a pale purple and age to a bluish-pink, attracting hummingbirds as an added bonus.

Other Common Name
Virginia Cowslip

Bloom Period and Seasonal Color
Blue flowers in mid-spring.

Mature Height × Spread
20 in. × 12 in.

Ground Covers *for Indiana*

Whether you choose a creeping vine, low-growing shrub, or solid stand of perennials, ground covers add definition, color, and texture to the landscape. They moderate soil temperature and moisture, reduce weeds, and provide shelter and food for birds and wildlife. Some of them form carpets of flowers, making them even more valuable. They can unify and frame the landscape—coordinating trees, shrubs, and the borders of perennial beds. Ivies, vines, clump-growers, and ground-hugging shrubs are the most common types. Some scamper across the soil sending down roots, while others form underground runners that sprout shoots above ground, sometimes a few feet from the mother plant.

There are deciduous ground covers, which drop their leaves in winter, and evergreen ground covers, which do not. There are also semi-evergreen ground covers, which—depending on the weather—may retain their leaves in winter. Daylilies (*Hemerocallis*) can be used as a ground cover and so can clematis (*Clematis*), thyme (*Thymus*), shrub roses (*Rosa rugosa*), and climbing hydrangea (*Hydrangea anomala* spp. *petiolaris*). These are discussed in other chapters within this book.

A perfect place for ground covers is where grass won't grow, such as the shady, root-bound, nutrient-competitive areas under trees and shrubs. Ground covers do well on difficult-to-mow hills or slopes, where they also prevent soil erosion.

Planting Ground Covers

The best way to ensure success is to plant ground covers in a well-prepared bed. Dig the soil to a depth of at least twelve inches. Break up clods of dirt and remove rocks, roots, and other debris. Mix two to four inches of high quality compost into the top six to eight inches of soil and smooth out the bed. Rake a slow-release nitrogen fertilizer into the top two to three inches of soil and smooth out again. In most cases, ground cover transplants should be planted the same depth they are growing in their plastic packs or peat pots. If the transplant is in a peat pot, break off any part of the container that shows above the soil line, then plant the ground cover, pot and all. If it is in a plastic pack, remove the transplant from the cell before planting. Try not to disturb the rootball. Backfill with the soil removed from the hole.

When planting bare-root plants, such as those that come from many mail-order

Christmas Fern

Pachysandra by Walkway

companies, soak the roots in water overnight before transplanting. Prepare the soil in the same manner as described above. Form small mounds of soil in the center of the planting hole to get the correct height. Gently spread the roots over the top of the mound and backfill the hole.

Digging deeply to prepare beds is not always possible, especially under well-rooted trees and shrubs. Dig as deeply as possible, even if it is only a couple of inches. However, be gentle with tree roots. If roots are too thick, add one or two inches of topsoil mixed with compost to the root zone. Adding any more than this may suffocate the tree roots. Never cover the root flare with added soil or mulch. After planting your ground cover, bulbs, or other plants, mulch to two or three inches deep. Instead of planting in rows, consider staggering the plants by placing them in triangles with equal spacing between for a better, more uniform look. Water deeply after transplanting.

The ground covers in this chapter are readily available and easy to grow. While good for starters, they are part of a plant list limited only by a gardener's imagination. Consider several factors when you choose ground covers, including the look you want and the amount of time you have to maintain the plants.

Bearberry
Arctostaphylos uva-ursi

Bearberry's awkward botanical name is a good disguise for this simple and beautiful native ground cover. In Indiana, it is a niche plant that favors poor, sandy, acid soils. It is very salt tolerant which makes it suitable for roadside plantings where spray from ice melt may damage other plants. Bearberry creeps along slowly when young, forming a dense mat as it goes. Its branches hug the ground and root at the nodes. The branch tips turn up and show the small but thick, glossy green leaves. In late spring, its white flowers open from clusters at the tips. Bright red lustrous "bearberries" follow suit from July through September and provide food for wildlife. They frequently last until the following March. In the fall, leaves turn a reddish bronze and last all winter.

Other Common Names
Kinnikinick, Hog Cranberry, Sandberry

Bloom Period and Seasonal Color
White to pink flowers in April through June; bright red berries July through winter; leaves turn bronzish red in fall and last all winter.

Mature Height × Spread
6 to 12 in. × 2 to 4 ft.

When, Where, and How to Plant
Plant bearberry in well-drained soil. It likes poor, sandy, gravely sites so don't bother amending with compost unless drainage is especially bad. Even though bearberry requires acidic soil, it also appears to grow in limestone rock which is usually alkaline. We suggest you get the soil tested if needed first, and lower the pH with sulfur as needed. Alternatively, try a small amount and see how it fares. (See book introduction for more on soil testing.) In the spring, dig and pulverize the soil to a depth of 8 to 12 inches and then plant. Transplant from large containers or remove it in mats from an existing planting for best results. In all cases, handle the roots carefully. Plant to the same depth they were growing, then tamp the soil lightly and water deeply.

Growing Tips
Keep 2 to 3 inches of mulch over the roots during the establishment period. Water during the heat of summer especially in the first season after planting. There is no need to fertilize or baby this plant after it establishes itself.

Care and Maintenance
Use a rotary mower or pruning shears to trim back right after flowering in early summer. Mildew and galls occasionally disfigure the leaves, but controls are not necessary. Otherwise, bearberry is bothered by few pests.

Companion Planting and Design
Plant on protected slopes along the highway. Use as an excellent ground cover around bayberry, ornamental grasses, rugosa roses, and evergreens such as yew and arborvitae. To add variety, underplant with spring or fall blooming bulbs.

We Recommend
'Emerald Carpet' grows to 18 inches tall and has pink flowers. It tolerates shady areas better than others. 'Massachusetts' hugs the ground closely and bears many flowers and fruit. It resists disease and insects well. 'Point Reyes' has dense leaves and tolerates heat and drought but may have fewer berries. 'Wood's Red' has large pink flowers followed by large red fruit on smaller, compact plants.

English Ivy
Hedera helix

When, Where, and How to Plant

Plant container-grown ivy plants any time during the growing season. Cuttings with at least three aerial roots will root quickly when planted directly in loamy, moist soil. English ivy can be planted in sun or dense shade. If planted in full sun, remember that the leaves may burn from the winter sun and winds. For best results, prepare the soil by amending with organic matter. Gently remove an ivy plant from its container, trying not to disturb the rootball. Don't plant it any deeper than it was already growing in the pot. Plants spaced about 12 to 18 inches apart should fill in and form a solid mass in about two years. Water deeply and mulch lightly to retain moisture.

Growing Tips

Always make sure newly planted material receives an inch of rain or water every seven to ten days. Apply a slow-release high-nitrogen fertilizer or compost tea in early spring as new growth appears. Mulch is not needed once plants are established.

Care and Maintenance

Spread a thin layer of compost over the ivy bed in early spring and late fall. Use hedge trimmers to shear English ivy two to three times a year to keep it neat and tidy, to thicken growth, and to remove leaves browned from winter winds. English ivy may be affected by fungus, especially leaf spot and canker. Avoid overhead watering or check with the local office of Purdue Cooperative Extension Service for control options.

Companion Planting and Design

Plant English ivy on the north side of house under trees and shrubs, around the foundation of a home, or on hills or banks. Allowing the ivy to climb houses or other structures is usually not recommended because the aerial roots may damage wood, brick, stone, stucco, and other materials. Underplant the ivy with bulbs such as crocus, daffodils, alliums, and surprise lilies.

We Recommend

'Thorndale' and 'Baltica' are more resistant to cold weather and are readily available in Indiana. These varieties are recommended in more exposed planting sites.

English ivy is a woody, evergreen vine that can reach a length of 50 feet or more. It spreads quickly once established, setting down shallow roots as it creeps along the ground or up a house or tree. As English ivy establishes itself, the roots get more woody and can reach a depth of 3 feet. Leaves are dark green, glossy, and veined. Young leaves have three points; mature leaves have five. It is the perfect ground cover for the shade of large maples or pines. Its shiny leaves also make great additions to flower arrangements at any time of year—simply snip the tips of the vines and put in water. English ivy can be aggressive, so trim it back regularly; otherwise, it is a very low-maintenance plant.

Bloom Period and Seasonal Color
Dark evergreen leaves all year.

Mature Height × Spread
6 to 8 in. × up to 90 ft.

Epimedium

Epimedium spp.

Epimedium may be slow to take hold, but it is well worth the wait. It holds its own against roots and shade, which makes it an excellent choice for planting in small masses at the base of trees and shrubs. Its thin panicles of flowers appear above heart-shaped, leathery, dark-green leaves. The tiny, waxy flowers have spurs and resemble columbine. As an added bonus, it also makse good cut flowers. Depending on the cultivar or species, epimedium comes in several colors. Leaf color also varies from lime green to copper. It usually blooms from early April to early May. Epimedium is a wonderful plant for dry shade.

Other Common Names
Barrenwort, Bishop's Cap

Bloom Period and Seasonal Color
Yellow, white, or pink flowers in April to May; green leaves turning bronze red in fall; semi-evergreen.

Mature Height × Spread
8 to 12 in. × 12 in.

When, Where, and How to Plant
Plant container-grown plants in spring or early fall. Epimedium is a woodland plant, so it does best in a shady or partially shady spot with rich, organic, moist soil. It will also do well in the dry, moisture-competitive area under trees. The better the soil, however, the faster it will grow. Don't plant them any deeper than they were growing in the containers. Space plants about 12 inches apart. Tamp the soil lightly and water deeply.

Growing Tips
Epimedium may need extra moisture until it gets established—especially if it is planted at the base of trees and shrubs where there is a lot of competition for moisture and nutrients. Continue to water every seven to ten days with the equivalent of 1 inch of rain until it is established. Spread 2 to 3 inches of mulch to help retain moisture and to keep the weeds down. Sprinkle with an all-purpose fertilizer in early spring when new growth appears.

Care and Maintenance
Divide epimedium clumps in early spring, as soon as the soil can be worked and new growth appears on the plants. Slice through clumps with a sharp spade and gently lift them from the soil. Leave the foliage on through the winter, but for the best flower show, cut it back in late February or early March before new growth begins. Epimedium is usually free of pests and diseases.

Companion Planting and Design
Depending on the variety, its foliage changes color in fall, making it interesting even as it dies back. Plant under coarse textured shade-loving shrubs such as leatherleaf viburnum or bottlebrush buckeye. Its heart-shaped leaves stand out against a neatly trimmed yew.

We Recommend
Epimedium grandiflorum is the most common species. It has rose, lavender, or white flowers. 'Rose Queen' and 'White Queen' are recommended named cultivars. *E. pinnatum* grows about 15 inches tall; it has red and yellow flowers. *E. rubrum* grows about 12 inches tall. Its leaves have red edges and veins, and its flowers are yellow, red, or white.

Fern

Athyrium nipponicum 'Pictum'

When, Where, and How to Plant

Plant ferns in late fall after the first frost, in moist and well-drained soil amended with an abundance of compost. All ferns prefer shady sites though some may tolerate slightly more sun than others. In that case, make sure they only get morning sun since later afternoon sun is too hot. They don't seem to be picky about pH. Incorporate 2 to 4 inches of compost into the soil and then plant at the same depth they were growing in the pot. Cover with 2 inches of leaf mulch to protect for winter. Tamp the soil lightly and water deeply when finished.

Growing Tips

Water regularly to make sure ferns stay moist. Their fronds usually turn brown if they get too dry. Keep 2 to 3 inches of rotted bark mulch or chopped leaves over the fern bed. Ferns seem to thrive with little to no fertilizer.

Care and Maintenance

Sprinkle an inch of compost over the soil each year to improve fertility and moisture retention. Fronds will turn black after the first frost. Cut them back and add mulch to protect the crowns in winter. To divide, dig up runner plants in large clumps in early spring. Don't slice through the center of the plant or it may die. Ferns are mostly low maintenance and free from pests.

Companion Planting and Design

Plant the metallic leaved Japanese painted fern in nooks and crannies in the shady garden. It looks good near a pond or water feature or peeking out from behind woodland stones and rocks. Mix with the bold-leaved hostas for textural contrasts. Use low-growing ground covers like epimedium under tall ferns like ostrich and cinnamon.

We Recommend

Japanese painted fern is a prized fern by gardeners. It grows well as a ground cover or in a shady garden. Experiment with other fast growing ferns like *Osmunda cinnamomea* (Cinnamon Fern), *Athyrium filix-femina* (Lady Fern), *Onoclea sensibilis* (Sensitive Fern), or *Polystichum acrostichoides* (Christmas Fern).

Represented in the photo by Japanese painted fern, landscape ferns are a unique group of plants unlike any others in this book. Though ferns are among the oldest plants on earth, many have evolved into wonderful plants for the modern landscape. Their light, feathery leaves (called "fronds" by fern-o-philes) can be short or long and soft- or coarse-textured. Some have colorful fronds, like Japanese painted fern, though most are shades of green. In early spring, the fronds unfurl in a fuzzy whitish curly-cue that is fun to watch. The young, unfurling leaves are known as fiddleheads. Some are edible and considered "gourmet" by culinary types. Most ferns die back in the fall, but most spread quickly enough to be considered ground covers if planted in the right place. Some are evergreen.

Other Common Names

Cinnamon Fern, Christmas Fern, Sensitive Fern, Lady Fern, Maidenhair Fern, Ostrich Fern.

Bloom Period and Seasonal Color

Rust-colored spots of spores on the undersides of the leaves; cinnamon fern and its relatives produce spores on a rusty orange spike in the plant's center.

Mature Height × Spread

12 to 18 in. × 12 to 18 in., up to 3 ft. × 5 ft. depending on the species

Hellebore

Helleborus spp. and hybrids

Aptly nicknamed Christmas or Lenten rose for its ability to flower as early as Christmas or Lent, hellebore is one of our earliest blooming plants. Growing from 1 to 2 feet tall or higher, its dark green buckeye-like leaves last all year, finally looking tired by late winter. The cup-shaped and nodding flowers hide behind the leaves until warmer temperatures arrive, as early as January or February. Flowers range from dusty rose to deep purple to white and green and shades in between, including some with "freckled" petals. It is well suited to late winter snows and cold temperatures. It multiplies quickly in moist shady areas, making a wonderful ground cover. Among gardeners, hellebore is en vogue. Hybridizers develop new types so regularly it is hard to keep up with all the varieties.

Other Common Names
Lenten Rose, Christmas Rose

Bloom Period and Seasonal Color
Dusty rose, purple, white, or green flowers from February through May depending on the type; evergreen leaves.

Mature Height × Spread
1 to 2 ft. × 2 ft. or more

When, Where, and How to Plant
Plant hellebore in mid- to late spring in moist soils amended with plenty of compost. Hellebore prefers shady sites but is not fussy about soil acidity. Gently remove the pot to loosen the roots and plant into soils that were dug to 12 inches, as recommended in the introduction. Tamp the soil lightly and water deeply after planting.

Growing Tips
Hellebore likes water, so be sure to irrigate if it doesn't rain, especially during dry periods in summer. Keep 2 to 3 inches of organic mulch around the roots at all times to conserve moisture and to keep the weeds down. Apply a high nitrogen slow-release fertilizer or compost tea. Be sure to follow soil test recommendations.

Care and Maintenance
Use hand pruners or shears to remove dead leaves in late winter. Sprinkle an inch of compost over the planting bed once or twice a year. Certain types of hellebores may be hard to transplant or recover slowly. Dig carefully and handle the roots gently. Some species self-sow easily, so share the seedlings with friends. It takes two to three years for hellebore to bloom from seeds. It has few insect or disease problems.

Companion Planting and Design
Plant in groups or clumps in shaded areas under trees or in woodland gardens. Plant along pathways or next to rocks or water features. Underplant with late blooming bulbs like alliums or leucojums. Plant as ground cover under deciduous shrubs such as fothergillas and viburnums. The coarse foliage contrasts well with the finer texture of yews and boxwood.

We Recommend
Lenten rose has many cultivars boasting big and colorful flowers. 'Dusk' and 'Dark Burgundy' resemble their names. The 'Party Dress' series has frilly, double flowers. 'Red Hybrid' and 'Red Mountain' are also good selections. *Helleborus foetidus* is a related species that grows taller with narrow finger-like leaves. Blooms are mostly green to white and sometimes have an unpleasant smell—so much so that they've been nicknamed stinking hellebore, stinkwort, or dungwort.

Juniper
Juniperus spp.

When, Where, and How to Plant

Plant juniper in full sun and well-drained soil any time the soil can be worked in spring or fall. Dig a planting hole three times the width of the pot or rootball. Dig so that the top of the rootball is level with the surrounding ground after planting. For container-grown junipers, gently tap the sides of the pot to loosen the rootball. Carefully remove the plant and tease out any roots that appear to be growing in a circular pattern. Finally, backfill the hole with the original soil and water deeply.

Growing Tips

Spread 2 to 3 inches of organic mulch around new and mature plantings to retain moisture. Water deeply during dry periods in summer. Sprinkle an all-purpose granular fertilizer in early spring or apply a thin layer of compost around the plant in spring and fall.

Care and Maintenance

Prune occasional errant branches to contain them in a planting bed. Junipers succumb to *Phomopsis* and *Kabatina*, two fungi which cause the branch tips to dieback. Cut off tips infected with blight with sharp hand pruners. In large commercial plantings, fungicide sprays may be warranted. Pick off any bagworms or spray with *Bacillus thurengiensis* var. *kurstaki* (Bt) in June when bagworms are small.

Companion Planting and Design

Combine with plants with coarse texture or colorful bark and leaves such as red twig dogwood or river birch. The low growing junipers help provide a strong foundation that complements other plants.

We Recommend

J. horizontalis 'Wiltoni' or 'Blue Rug' grows 4 to 6 inches tall with a 6-foot spread and bears silvery blue cones. It is one of the most widely grown ground cover junipers. 'Blue Mat' grows 6 inches tall with blue-green foliage that turns purple in winter. 'Bar Harbor' grows 1 foot by 8 feet, with rich blue-green foliage that turns purple in winter. *J. procumbens* 'Greenmound' grows only 8 inches tall with an 8-foot spread, a mounded center, and light-green foliage. 'Nana' grows up to 2 1/2 feet tall with a 12-foot spread and light blue-green foliage that turns purple in winter.

Creeping "rug" and other low-growing Juniperus are very adaptable and versatile in the landscape, providing year-round color, texture, and structure. Low-growing juniper forms a rug, or carpet, of greens or blues that makes an excellent ground cover for shrubs and trees in full sun. It is ideal on sunny slopes with good drainage. In summer, it blends into the landscape, whereas in winter its evergreen branches help frame the plants around it. Like many evergreens, certain cultivars will turn a purple-bronze color in winter. Its colors and textures help show off the bark on neighboring trees and shrubs. Usually the mats are so dense that other plants won't grow through them, which makes juniper an excellent weed barrier. Its blue-green berries provide additional interest.

Other Common Name
Rug Juniper

Bloom Period and Seasonal Color
Dark green or blue-green all year, turning bronze in winter, depending on cultivar.

Mature Height × Spread
1 to 2 ft. × 10 to 15 ft.

Leadwort
Ceratostigma plumbaginoides

This low-growing perennial spreads aggressively enough to be classified as a ground cover. Its underground rhizomes and trailing stems help make a dense, wiry mat of small glossy green leaves. From August through the first frost, the leaves are topped with deep blue flowers that are reminiscent of myrtle or woodland phlox. In fall, the leaves turn a beautiful orange red. Growing to a height of 8 to 12 inches, it is a real sleeper, only getting its leaves in May then dying back to the ground after a hard freeze. It is a wonderful plant for sun or part shade and well-drained soil. It may be marginally hardy in extreme northern Indiana.

Bloom Period and Seasonal Color
Deep blue phlox-like flowers from August through frost; coppery red leaves in fall.

Mature Height × Spread
8 to 12 in. × 18 in.

When, Where, and How to Plant
Transplant leadwort in spring into moist but well-drained soils. Amend the soil with 2 to 4 inches of high quality compost mixed to a depth of 8 to 12 inches before planting. Gently remove the plant from its pot and plant to the same depth it was growing. Space plants about 12 inches apart. They will fill in within one to two years to form a dense carpet. Tamp the soil lightly and water deeply.

Growing Tips
Keep 2 to 3 inches of mulch over the roots before it completely fills its growing space. Make sure the soil drains well since leadwort will languish, if not die, in soggy soils and cold weather. Follow spring shearing with a light sprinkling of balanced fertilizer and compost.

Care and Maintenance
Lightly shear dead stems from the tops of the plants in spring to encourage new growth. Divide in early spring by slicing through the mat with a sharp spade and gently lifting the divisions. Share them with friends and family.

Companion Planting and Design
Use leadwort underneath shrubs and trees for color, especially late in the summer after the garden peaks. Underplant with spring bulbs. Plant beneath yew to contrast colors and textures. Edge walls and rock gardens with leadwort. It forms a nice border when clipped and sprawls nicely over edges of rock walls as well. Combine with Russian sage, switchgrass, and purple coneflower for an interesting and long-blooming mixture with contrasting textures and similar colors. In 2003, this particular combination was named Artful Garden™ Design Selection by The Horticultural Society of the Indianapolis Museum of Art (www.artfulgarden.org). In full sun and good drainage, it will turn heads in your garden, also.

We Recommend
There are no improved cultivars of leadwort, so plant the species.

Lily Turf

Liriope spp.

When, Where, and How to Plant

Transplant container-grown plants in spring or fall in any moist but well-drained soil. Lily turf tolerates dry, shady places under trees and shrubs like few other ground covers. The clump variety can take more sun, making it useful in the front border of a perennial bed. Plant transplants at the same depth they were growing in their pots. Tamp the soil lightly and water deeply.

Growing Tips

Lightly fertilize by sprinkling slow-release forms of nitrogen fertilizer around the roots when still young. Liriope withstands dry conditions but will benefit from occasional watering during drought.

Care and Maintenance

Keep 2 to 3 inches of mulch over the roots when young. Liriope won't need mulch after establishing itself. Cut brown and winterburned leaves back in the early spring with a lawn mower or weed whacker. Divide in the spring or fall. If needed, slice through drifts or clumps with a sharp spade. Repot and share with neighbors, friends, and family.

Companion Planting and Design

Lily turf grows well and helps to stablilize banks and hillsides. Plant under deciduous shrubs in part sun to part shade. Plant with fothergilla, viburnums, and other low growing shrubs. It makes a nice carpet planted around Japanese maples. It thrives in dry shade, a normally difficult planting situation.

We Recommend

L. spicata 'Silver Dragon' has white and green variegated leaves and is hardy in Zone 6. *L. muscari* cultivars include 'Big Blue', about 12 inches tall with green foliage and dark violet flowers in July and August; 'Majestic', slightly shorter with green leaves and violet flowers; and 'Variegata', which has yellow-striped, green leaves and lilac flowers in early to midsummer.

Liriope spicata has $1/4$ to $1/2$-inch-wide, straplike, evergreen leaves that resemble coarse grass. It is sometimes called creeping lily turf, reflecting its tendency to spread rapidly by underground rhizomes. As a result, some gardeners consider it invasive. Liriope muscari is not considered invasive. It grows in clumps with $1/2$- to $3/4$-inch-wide, strap-like leaves. They both bloom in late summer through early fall. L. muscari is reliably hardy in Zone 6 but may survive in Zone 5. L. muscari has violet-blue spiked flowers that resemble grape hyacinths; L. spicata has pale lavender to nearly white flowers. The latter is considered less showy. Both tolerate poor soil and dry conditions. They are tough and sturdy and easily fill in voids. Liriope makes an excellent evergreen ground cover.

Other Common Name

Creeping Lily Turf

Bloom Period and Seasonal Color

Lavender flowers in August to September; shiny black fruit through fall and winter; evergreen leaves stay green all year.

Mature Height × Spread

1 to 2 ft. × variable

Pachysandra
Pachysandra terminalis

Like its counterparts English ivy and sweet woodruff, pachysandra is an excellent choice for shady areas that are difficult to mow. Of the three, pachysandra takes the longest to get established, but once it does, it forms a delightful, non-invasive evergreen mat. Pachysandra has dark-green, glossy leaves with scalloped or jagged edges clustered at the top of wiry stems. The leaves cup down slightly, like two tiny green umbrellas on top of each other. It has a trailing growth habit, sending new stems out from under the mulch. In the spring, it sports white, slightly fragrant, fuzzy flowers at the tops of the plants that last for several weeks.

Bloom Period and Seasonal Color
White blooms in late spring; evergreen.

Mature Height × Spread
9 to 12 in. × 18 in.

When, Where, and How to Plant
Plant pachysandra any time the soil is workable in spring or fall. It does well under trees and shrubs or in other shady areas, in moist but well-drained soil. If planted in full sun, the leaves will yellow or get winter-burned. Before planting, thoroughly mix 2 to 4 inches of high quality compost into the top 6 inches of soil. Plant pachysandra slightly deeper than it was growing in the pot. Space the plants 6 to 8 inches apart so they fill in more quickly. Tamp the soil lightly and water deeply.

Growing Tips
Keep 2 to 3 inches of mulch or compost around the roots to encourage faster growth, especially during the first few years after planting. Water deeply every week, particularly during dry periods in summer. Apply an all-purpose fertilizer in early spring or add a thin layer of compost in spring and fall.

Care and Maintenance
Cut off leaves that were damaged by winter weather. Pachysandra may get leaf blight and stem canker. Remove and discard diseased plants and reduce any heavy mulch buildup. Thin the planting to improve air circulation and reduce stress from sun or over-watering. Fungicides may also help prevent the spread of disease. If the plants get spindly, shear them off and they will grow denser. Divide in spring or early fall by cutting through clumps with a sharp spade.

Companion Planting and Design
Plant under large shade trees where tree roots grow on the surface of the ground. It is compatible with spring-flowering bulbs and shade-loving perennials such as hostas, ferns, and pulmonaria.

We Recommend
Pachysandra terminalis cultivars include 'Green Carpet', which grows about 8 inches tall, and 'Variegata', which has white-edged leaves. 'Green Sheen' has extraordinarily glossy deep green leaves. Allegheny spurge, *Pachysandra procumbens*, is a deciduous native of similar character. However, it is taller with pinkish-purple, fragrant flowers in early spring, and its leaves are also more blue-gray than dark green.

Sweet Woodruff
Galium odoratum

When, Where, and How to Plant
Plant container-grown transplants any time the soil can be worked in early spring or early fall. Sweet woodruff grows best in moist, shady areas. If grown in too much sun without enough water, it may go dormant in summer. It prefers slightly acidic soil. Amend with 2 to 4 inches of high quality compost. Mix with soil to 6 or 8 inches deep. Space plants 10 to 12 inches apart and plant them at the same level they were growing in their pot. Water well and mulch lightly to help it retain soil moisture.

Growing Tips
Always make sure newly planted material receives 1 inch of rain or water every seven days. Water weekly with 1 to 1^1/$_2$ inches per week throughout the summer for best results. Apply an all-purpose granular fertilizer in early spring as new growth begins or spread a thin layer of compost around the plants in spring and fall. Mulching is not necessary once plants are established.

Care and Maintenance
Divide in spring by slicing through clumps with a sharp spade and gently lifting from the ground. Sweet woodruff forms low growing mats in organic soils with ample moisture. It will also generously reseed itself in moist shade but not invasively so. Pests are not a problem.

Companion Planting and Design
Sweet woodruff does well in cracks and crevices, and around stones, walkways, and other areas where brushing the leaves releases their fragrant scent. Underplant with spring bulbs. Plant it near bold-leaved shade plants, like hostas, to contrast leaf textures. Use the dried leaves in herbal mixtures of potpourri, and sachets.

We Recommend
There are no improved varieties of sweet woodruff; however, there are other deciduous ground covers that grow very similarly to sweet woodruff. Spotted Nettle, *Lamium maculatum* 'White Nancy', and Yellow Archangel, *Lamium galeobdolon* 'Herman's Pride', have early spring flowers. 'White Nancy' has silver-white leaves with white flowers for moist, partial shade. 'Herman's Pride' grows in deep shade with green and silver leaves that look webbed. Yellow flowers emerge in spring.

References to sweet woodruff can be found in Shakespeare. In Germany, it is a prime ingredient in May wine. A delicate-looking plant with starlike whorls of pointy green leaves, it dies back in winter but quickly recovers with a carpet of leaves and flowers in early spring. It forms a dense cover under trees and shrubs or throughout a flower bed. Though it may look delicate, sweet woodruff will take moderate foot traffic, giving off its fragrant sweet smell when the leaves are crushed. The white, four-petaled flowers are fragrant, too. It mixes well with spring-flowering bulbs, summer perennials, and other ground covers. You can remove it easily if it travels where it isn't wanted.

Other Common Name
Bedstraw

Bloom Period and Seasonal Color
Deciduous green leaves producing delicate white flowers in April to May; turns yellow in fall before dying back completely.

Mature Height × Spread
6 to 8 in. × 1 to 2 ft.

Herbs *for Indiana*

Most herbs are easy to grow and not demanding at all. You can plant them with your annuals and perennials, in containers, in their own garden, or on a sunny windowsill.

Herbs have many different uses. The leaves are easy to dry and store in the pantry, or many can be frozen for later use. They may also be used fresh; many are particularly good in summer salads. In addition, many herbs will provide beautiful cut flowers. Herbs may be annuals, perennials, or biennials. Annuals go from seed to flower in one growing season; perennials come back every year. Biennials usually develop foliage the first year but bloom the second. Some herbs may be tender perennials, but we treat them as annuals because they are not winter hardy in Indiana gardens. Herbs may be hardy evergreens or semi-evergreens that retain most of their foliage through the winter, or they may be tender and herbaceous and lose leaves or top growth when cold weather hits. Some herbs can be aggressive, but many are worth growing anyway because of their flowers, foliage, or fragrance. For the best taste, harvest herbs before they flower. Cut off the flowers before the seeds form to keep volunteers at a minimum. Herbs that spread into unwanted territory can be pulled up as soon as they appear.

Bed Preparation Basics

As with any planting, the best results come from a good base, and that means adequate soil preparation, especially when you are planting perennials. Herbs last several growing seasons, so they need a good bed

Lavender 'Hidcote'

Thyme

in which to start. The best way to ensure you have good quality soil is to have it tested for nutrient content and pH level and to adjust according to test recommendations. Dig a bed that is twelve to eighteen inches deep. Break up clumps of dirt and remove stones, roots, sticks, or other debris. Smooth out the bed. Amend the top two to three inches of soil by mixing in compost, peat moss, rotted manure, or other organic material. You can add a granular all-purpose fertilizer as well.

Planting

It is possible to sow seeds directly in the prepared bed. Follow seed packet instructions on when to sow, sowing depth, and watering. Starting seeds indoors can be fun, but it is very challenging. It is hard to duplicate ideal growing conditions by controlling light, heat, humidity, and other factors indoors. Seedlings generally need very good light to keep from getting scrawny or leggy; place them directly under grow lights, keeping them two inches from the bulbs at all times. This can be as easy as using shop lites equipped with one cool and one warm, forty-watt fluorescent tube, or "grow bulbs." These items are available at your local garden center or hardware store. Herbs grow best in a greenhouse or in a room nearly surrounded with light. Some seeds need light to germinate while others require darkness, so be sure to follow label directions or instructions in this book.

It is possible to have more herbs by dividing plants or by taking cuttings, rooting them, and transplanting them. Spring is usually the best time to divide herbs. Dig up the plant you want to divide and separate portions by hand; you can also cut sections with a sharp knife or spade. To get the best idea of where to make a cut, look at the plant to see how it is growing. Some plants grow in such a way that it is easy to see where to divide them. Plant divisions immediately so the roots will not dry out and water well.

To root a cutting, cut off a three- to four-inch-long stem or soft wood branch early in the growing season. Strip off the lower leaves and dip the cut end in a hormone-rooting powder or liquid. Allow the cutting to root in a growing medium such as vermiculite or a soilless potting mix. Once the plant has rooted, you can transplant it to a larger container or into the ground, depending on its size and hardiness. Plant at the same depth it was growing. Most herbs do not need a lot of fertilizer or rich soil. Soil that is too rich may inhibit growth and result in less flavor.

Basil

Ocimum basilicum

Basil is as much a staple for the gardener as it is for the gourmet cook. This square-stemmed annual dresses up the front of the ornamental garden with as much ease as it spices up a dish. Basil is strongly associated with the Mediterranean but is a native plant of the Pacific islands and also is at home in Asian cuisine. In various cultures, basil was a sacred plant, a symbol of love, a sign of witchcraft, or a great healing agent. People thought the seed needed to be planted with a curse in order to ward off evil and ensure healthy plants. The idea was so prevalent that the French developed a phrase, semer le basilic ("seeding the basil"), to mean ranting and raving. Fortunately, ranting and raving are not required to produce the lusciously aromatic plants.

Bloom Period and Seasonal Color
Pink or white flowers in summer.

Mature Height × Spread
2 ft. × 2 ft.

When, Where, and How to Plant
Plant container-grown transplants in the spring, after the danger of frost has passed. Basil also is easy to start from seed. Sow seeds in pots indoors about a month before the last frost. You can also sow seeds directly outdoors in spring, again after the risk of frost. The warmer the soil the better; it should be at least 50 degrees Fahrenheit. Seeds may not germinate in cold, wet soil. Depending on the variety, plant basil in the front or middle of a flower garden. Basil also does very well in flower boxes or pots. (See chapter introduction for more planting information.)

Growing Tips
Keep soil moist but not wet. If growing in a window box or other container, apply a water-soluble, all-purpose fertilizer every two weeks or use a compost tea.

Care and Maintenance
Pinch back or harvest basil regularly to keep plants bushy and productive. Store harvested basil leaves above 40 degrees Fahrenheit. The sweetest leaves are usually the smaller ones at the top of the plant. Basil is one of the first plants to be killed by frost, which turns it black and renders it useless.

Companion Planting and Design
Basil leaves can be smooth, puckered, or ruffled. It mixes very nicely in an herb bed or as an ornamental in containers with petunias, coleus, and salvias.

We Recommend
All-America Selections named a Thai basil, 'Siam Queen', an award winner in 1997, and it is a standout in a container. Purple basil ('Purpureum', 'Dark Opal', or 'Purple Ruffles') has purple leaves and pink flowers. Miniature bush, or French basil, 'Minimum', is very compact with tiny green leaves and white flowers.

When, Where, and How to Plant

Plant container-grown transplants from early spring through the growing season. You can sow seeds directly outdoors when all danger of frost has passed. Plants may also be divided in the spring. Chives do best in well-drained soil, but they will tolerate poor soil, dry conditions, and a little shade. About six weeks before the last frost in spring, sow seeds $1/2$ inch deep in small pots indoors, growing them until they are ready to be transplanted. If you purchase small plants, remove them from their plastic packs to plant. Space plants about 10 inches apart. (See chapter introduction for more planting information.)

Growing Tips

Chives require little or no care. When you harvest the leaves, cut them off close to the base to keep the plant looking tidy and to keep it growing. You may also cut chives back to the ground throughout the growing season; this will encourage new growth. Cut dried or spent flowers when they start to look ratty. Apply an all-purpose fertilizer in early spring when new growth appears or spread a thin layer of compost in the bed in spring and fall. Divide clumps every three or four years to keep growth vigorous. Chives are drought tolerant, so supplemental watering usually isn't necessary.

Care and Maintenance

Chive leaves should die back in winter and can be cut off and tossed in the compost pile. New growth appears in early spring. Chive flowers form black seeds which easily self-sow. To prevent this, remove the flowers before seeds are formed. If you keep them too wet, chives may develop root or crown rot. Otherwise chives are relatively pest and disease free.

Companion Planting and Design

You can grow chives in containers for outdoor enjoyment in summer or in small pots for a windowsill garden in winter. They mix nicely in the herb garden or in the front of a perennial border.

We Recommend

Usually only the species is available; however, one cultivar, 'Ruby Gem', is different from the species with its red flowers and gray foliage.

Chives belong to the same family as onions, garlic, and several other spring- and summer-flowering ornamental bulbs. This easy-to-grow perennial herb works well in the front border of the flower garden because its smaller, drumstick-like flowers mix well with other plants that bloom in early summer. You can use the hollow leaves as a mild-tasting garnish for dozens of dishes, and the flowers are as decorative and edible as they are attractive. You can dry or freeze the leaves and flowers for later use. Be sure to wash leaves and flower heads well to remove any insects or grit. And even though the stems smell like a mild onion, the flowers are wonderfully fragrant.

Bloom Period and Seasonal Color
Purple flowers in late spring.

Mature Height × Spread
10 in. × 12 in.

Dill
Anethum graveolens

There's nothing like a dill dip for vegetables, especially when the herb or veggies come from your garden. The word dill comes from the Norse dilla, which means lull to sleep. Dill seeds are known to induce a mild sleep, but its wonders don't end there. Nicholas Culpeper, the great herbalist from the seventeenth century, said a tea made of dill seeds "stayeth the hiccough." A native of the Mediterranean, dill has been cultivated in Britain since the Roman occupation. In the Hoosier garden, dill's ferny, bluish-gray-green foliage and frothy, yellow Queen Anne's lace-like flowers bring a light, airy look in the bed. Butterflies and bees flock to this plant, which also serves as a food source for swallowtail caterpillars. Humans eat the foliage in salads and dozens of other food dishes.

Bloom Period and Seasonal Color
Yellow flowers in mid- to late summer.

Mature Height × Spread
3 ft. × 3 ft.

When, Where, and How to Plant
Dill prefers a rich, moist soil in full sun. It resents being transplanted, so sow seeds directly in the soil in spring after all danger of frost has passed or start them indoors about a month before the last frost in biodegradable pots. Follow seed packet instructions on depth to sow and spacing. (See chapter introduction for more planting information.)

Growing Tips
Do not let plants dry out. Water when the soil's top two inches feels dry, especially until plants get established. Once established, dill roots will be shaded by companion plants, reducing the need for supplemental watering. Sow seeds every four to six weeks through the summer for a succession of plants. Fertilizer usually isn't necessary if dill is planted in soil that has been amended with organic matter as described in the chapter introduction.

Care and Maintenance
Dill will self-sow after the first year. To keep in check, deadhead before the seeds are formed. Unwanted seedlings can easily be removed with a hoe. Dill is relatively pest and disease free. Swallowtail caterpillars use it as a source of food, however.

Companion Planting and Design
George Washington made a good choice when he used dill as a backdrop behind chives and beans at his farm in Mount Vernon. Dill looks best in the middle or back of the garden bed. There, its yellow flowers seem to hang like clouds above the other plants, bringing a lightness to the garden. It also blends nicely with shrub roses.

We Recommend
Try growing the species, or the cultivar 'Fernleaf', which is shorter and has more flowers.

Fennel
Foeniculum vulgare

When, Where, and How to Plant

Plant in average soil that has not been amended with a lot of organic matter. If the soil is too rich in organic matter, the plant may get floppy. Sow seeds directly in spring after all danger of frost has passed. Sometimes fennel can be found already growing in pots in garden centers in spring. Transplant when there's no danger of frost. (See introduction for more planting information.)

Growing Tips

Do not let fennel dry out. New plants need about an inch of water every week or ten days. Once established, their roots will be shaded by companion plants and will not need as much supplemental watering. Water when the top 2 inches of soil feels dry to the touch. Be careful when handling fennel stems and foliage. Some people may develop a light-sensitive dermatitis.

Care and Maintenance

Remove the spent flowers before seeds develop to keep fennel from self-sowing all over the landscape. Cut it back to the ground when killed by the frost. Fennel is relatively pest and disease free; however, swallowtail caterpillars use fennel as a food source. Fennel also attracts many beneficial insects – those that kill bad bugs.

Companion Planting and Design

Fennel is like dill in that it does best in the middle or back of the perennial or annual border or included in the herb or vegetable garden. The airy foliage and flowers of fennel also make a good companion to shrub roses.

We Recommend

Try the cultivar 'Purpurascens', or bronze fennel, which has purple or bronze-colored foliage.

Written references of fennel date to the Egyptians, who used the herb much like we do today—to flavor food. Fennel has a distinct anise aroma and taste. In Indiana, fennel may be marginally hardy in Zone 5, where it will be a short-lived perennial, usually dying out after two or three years. However, it does self-sow, which means new plants can take the place of those that die. The common fennel, which is green, and copper fennel, which is bronze, are grown for their foliage and stems. Florence fennel (F. var. azoricum) is a biennial grown for its edible bulb, which has a licorice or anise flavor and is frequently used in salads.

Other Common Name
Copper Fennel

Bloom Period and Seasonal Color
Yellow flowers in early to midsummer.

Mature Height × Spread
3 ft. × 2 ft.

Lavender
Lavandula angustifolia

Lavender leaves, flowers, and stems are very aromatic. Lavender derives its name from lavare which is Latin for "to wash." (Incidentally, the word lavatory has the same origin.) It has also been suggested that the word comes from the Medieval Latin livere which means "to make bluish." For centuries, people have used lavender to make perfumes, scent linens and bath water, and make the air smell wonderful. Flowers can be sprinkled on salads, frozen in ice to add a blue tint to drinks, or used as a flavor for ice cream. You can also dry the flowers and leaves for a sachet or potpourri. Most of the flowers arrive in early summer, but it blooms intermittently throughout the season. Lavender is supposed to be hardy to Zone 5, but it may freeze in severe winters.

Other Common Name
English Lavender

Bloom Period and Seasonal Color
Lavender-blue flowers in summer.

Mature Height × **Spread**
2 ft. × 2 ft.

When, Where, and How to Plant
Plant container-grown transplants from spring through the growing season. Seeds may be sown in pots indoors about ten weeks before the last frost in spring. Lavender needs well-drained, average soil. Choose a spot with good air circulation that isn't too wet, especially in winter. Seeds may be difficult to germinate, and seed-grown plants take about two years to reach maturity. Space plants about 2 feet apart. (See introduction for more planting information.)

Growing Tips
Water new transplants well. Once established, they usually don't have to be watered. Apply an all-purpose fertilizer in early spring when new growth appears or spread a thin layer of compost in spring and fall.

Care and Maintenance
Organic mulch is not recommended because it might invite fungus disease that will rot the plant. Keeping lavender too wet will cause fungus problems, too. Do not cut English lavender back in the fall; last year's flowers and foliage act as buffers or insulation against winter winds and temperatures. Wait until spring, when new growth appears as fresher and greener growth down the stem. Then cut back to the new growth.

Companion Planting and Design
The silvery green leaves on this shrubby evergreen make a nice contrast for other plants, especially in the front of the perennial garden. Lavender should be planted in clusters or drifts of three of more plants so that the fragrance can be enjoyed. It's a good companion to roses.

We Recommend
'Lavender Lady', a recent All-America Selection that was developed for northern climates, grows the first year from seed and has a nice scent. 'Hidcote' grows about 18 inches tall and has dark-purple flowers and silver-gray leaves. 'Jean Davis' also grows about 18 inches tall but has pale pink flowers. 'Alba' has white flowers, grows about 10 inches tall, and may not be winter hardy. 'Munstead' is 18 inches tall with dark-lavender flowers. *Lavandula dentata* and *Lavandula stoechas* (French and Spanish lavenders) have greener leaves, very ornamental dark-purple flowers, and are not hardy in Indiana.

Oregano
Origanum spp.

When, Where, and How to Plant

For best results, buy transplants of oregano and marjoram at local garden centers. Plant container-grown transplants in spring after the danger of frost has passed. Plant in full sun with well-drained soil. Once established, oregano and marjoram do well in dry soil. Space either species 12 to 24 inches apart. Keep newly planted transplants well watered. (See introduction for more planting information)

Growing Tips

For oregano, apply an all-purpose granular fertilizer in spring and again during the growing season or dust the bed with a layer of compost in spring and fall. It is fairly drought tolerant and needs watering only during very dry periods. Marjoram is an annual and would benefit from a feeding of water-soluble fertilizer about once a month. It, too, is drought tolerant. Oregano and marjoram are best if harvested before they flower. *Origanum vulgare* has pink flowers and is a hardy perennial in Zone 5.

Care and Maintenance

Oregano may be divided in spring. Heavy frost will kill the tops of *Origanum vulgare;* cut away the dead foliage and add it to compost along with any marjoram that is dead from frost. Oregano and marjoram are relatively free of pests and disease.

Companion Planting and Design

You can use the flowers of either species for floral arrangements or potpourri. Oregano and marjoram are at home in an herb bed or in a mixed border of perennials and annuals. They also can be grown in containers on decks, patios, balconies, or porches.

We Recommend

O. vulgare 'Compactum' is a shorter variety that has dark-green leaves and dark-pink flowers. The best flavor comes from a Greek oregano, *O. vulgare* ssp. *hirtum*, which has white flowers. 'Variegatum' is a gold marjoram with a mild flavor, yellow-and-green leaves, and pink or white flowers.

Oregano grows wild in Greece, and it perfumes the summer air throughout the Mediterranean region. In fact, the word oregano *comes from Greek words meaning "joy of the mountains." The Greek goddess Aphrodite is supposed to have created the plant as a symbol for happiness. There are two common types, oregano and marjoram. Oregano, O.* vulgare, *is a perennial with a slightly sprawling growth habit and dark-pink or white flowers. The dark-green, oval leaves are a pungent staple of Italian, Greek, and Mexican dishes. Its flowers are also edible. Marjoram, O.* majorana, *is an annual with pale-green leaves; it has white or purple flowers that form fragrant, edible clusters, or knots, at the tips of its stems. Its flavor is sweeter and milder than its perennial cousin.*

Other Common Name
Sweet Marjoram

Bloom Period and Seasonal Color
Pink, purple or white flowers in mid- to late summer.

Mature Height × Spread
1 ft. × 2 ft.

Parsley
Petroselinum crispum

This is the one herb most people recognize, since it comes with almost every plate of food served in restaurants. Parsley has been used for many things other than as a garnish. The Greeks used it to decorate tombs and fed it to their horses in the belief that it would make them run faster. The Romans believed that it enabled them to consume more wine without drunken after-effects. Curly leaf parsley is the most popular variety sold in the United States, although it has less flavor than the flat-leaved varieties. Parsley is rich in minerals and vitamins. Parsley does well in flowerpots or containers, outdoors in summer, or in a small pot for a windowsill garden in winter. Swallowtail caterpillars use parsley as a food source.

Bloom Period and Seasonal Color
Green foliage in summer.

Mature Height × Spread
1 ft. × 1 ft.

When, Where, and How to Plant
Plant container-grown transplants in spring after the danger of frost has passed. You can sow seeds directly in the ground about a month before the last frost or indoors about eight weeks before the last frost. Parsley seeds need darkness to sprout; germination takes three weeks or longer. You can speed up germination by soaking seeds in warm water for a day or two or by freezing them overnight before planting. Parsley prefers a well-drained spot that is rich in organic material. Add a layer of compost after planting. (See chapter introduction for more planting information.)

Growing Tips
Don't allow parsley to dry out. Water when the top 2 inches of soil feels dry to the touch. Maintain a layer of compost around parsley, adding it in the spring and in the fall.

Care and Maintenance
When you harvest parsley, snip stems close to the base of the plant. It is a biennial in Zone 6, which means that it grows foliage the first year and flowers the second. It is marginally hardy in Zone 5, overwintering when the season is mild. Parsley tends to lose its flavor once it starts to flower, so plan on replanting every year. Frost causes the top part of the plant to die; if this occurs, cut the top off and compost it.

Companion Planting and Design
The curly leaf parsley makes a nice border of dark-green clumps when planted in the front of the flower garden. The curly leaf varieties also can be used to define lines or borders in places such as a parterre, a garden, or along a walkway.

We Recommend
Try curly leaf varieties of 'Moss Curled', 'Forest Green', 'Rina', and 'Krausa'. For flat leaf varieties (*Petroselinum crispum* var. *neapolitanum*), consider 'Gianti d' Italia', 'Gepetto', 'Dark Green Italian', or 'Catalogno'. Hamburg parsley (*Petroselinum crispum* var. *tuberosum*) also has edible leaves but is prized for its root, which is used to flavor stews and soups.

When, Where, and How to Plant

Plant container-grown transplants any time during the growing season (spring through fall), but spring is best. They can be planted in full sun to partial shade. Start seeds indoors eight to ten weeks before the last spring frost. Seeds are picky about temperatures; keep them at 55 degrees Fahrenheit. They may take thirty days to germinate. Thyme forms its own mat, so mulching won't be necessary.

Growing Tips

Thyme needs good drainage. It will be attacked by fungus diseases and rot if it sits in soggy soil. Supplemental watering is needed only in times of drought. Apply an all-purpose granular fertilizer in early spring when new growth appears or spread a thin layer of compost around the plant in spring and fall.

Care and Maintenance

Thyme may be sheared or cut back in spring to shape it up or remove winter damage. Rust fungus disease may cause brown, red, or tan spots on the leaves. Remove infected leaves or branches and avoid watering the plant from above. Thyme may be divided every two to three years in the spring; this will ensure that it looks healthy and grows vigorously.

Companion Planting and Design

Thyme grows well under roses or in the front of the flower garden. Stuff it in the cracks and crevices of steps, walkways, and rock gardens. Thyme's fragrance is released as passersby brush against it. In summer, thyme does well mixed in containers with other flowers where it trails gently over the side.

We Recommend

Try 'Thyme de Provence' or the species thyme. *Thymus serpyllum* is a woody shrub-like plant called mother-of-thyme; it only grows 1 to 3 inches tall and has purple or rose-colored flowers from June through September. Lemon thyme comes two ways: *Thymus × citriodorus* 'Citriodorus' is upright, grows about 1 inch tall, and has a lemony scent; *Thymus* ssp. is a ground cover. *T. pseudolanuginosus* is called woolly thyme.

The word "thyme" is another herb name that can be traced to the Greeks. Thuo is Greek for "perfume," which certainly describes the wonderful scent this common herb gives off. Thyme is an herb that doubles as an aromatic, flowering ground cover. This herb is tough, withstanding a little wear from a swinging driveway gate or even foot traffic. It is a multi-stemmed, woody plant with small, oval leaves and flowers that cover the low-growing plant in late spring or early summer. Thyme is nearly ever-green. Depending on conditions, some varieties hold their leaves well into winter, but don't be concerned if the plant loses its foliage. It also grows in pots for a windowsill garden in winter.

Other Common Names

French Thyme, English Thyme, Mother of Thyme

Bloom Period and Seasonal Color

Pink, mauve, or white flowers in spring and summer.

Mature Height × Spread

4 to 12 in. × 12 in.

Lawns *for Indiana*

We have a love/hate relationship with our lawns in Indiana. We *love* expansive, weed-free, green carpets leading up to the front door. Unfortunately, most of us *hate* spending the time it takes to maintain that kind of lawn. We may try to do it all by ourselves, or we may hire lawn care companies. Either way, we are bound to the lawn by our wallets or by the weekends we lose to mowing, raking, and speculating with the neighbors about the grub or weed problem. Of course, there are also passive lawn lovers who sleep in and don't miss a sporting event over the weekend. For them, a lawn may be pure dandelions, but at least it's something green.

The Dirt on Lawns

The keys to a good lawn are good cultural practices and good timing. With a few routine chores done at the right time of the year there is hope for even the worst lawn. One of the best ways to start your lawn improvement program is to measure the turf area in your yard. Research shows that the average homeowner overestimates the area of their lawn and consequently over-applies fertilizers and pesticides.

Grass grows best in slightly acidic, loamy, and moist but well-drained soils. Poor lawns might be a result of soils that are too acidic or too alkaline. Test the soil and adjust the pH to between 6.0 and 7.0 as needed. Most soils in Indiana are naturally alkaline. Adding lime to already alkaline soils is futile and could ultimately harm the turf.

Fine-leaf Fescue

What Type of Grass Seed?

Cool season grasses including tall and fine-leaf fescues, bluegrass, and ryegrass provide the best green color year-round. Warm season grasses like zoysia turn brown for seven months of the year and are best grown in warmer climates. Grass grows best in full sun. Some species of fescues have adapted to shadier sites; however, no species thrives in deep shade.

Bluegrass

When it comes to grass, bluegrass is royalty. Its soft, lush, blue-green blades and fine texture make the picture-perfect lawn. In good soils, it spreads easily by underground runners, filling in blank spots as it goes. It grows best in spring and fall when temperatures are cool. It slows down when it gets hot and dry in summer. Bluegrass is a higher maintenance grass. It likes full sun and well-drained loamy soil. Some cultivars of bluegrass tolerate shade better than others. In sunny areas, sow a mixture of 100 percent bluegrass or 80 percent bluegrass and 20 percent perennial turf-type ryegrass. Good mixtures use three to five improved varieties of each grass type. For lawns that get a mixture of sun and partial shade, sow a mixture of 50 to 70 percent Kentucky bluegrass and 50 to 30 percent fine-leaf fescue. Always select cultivars labeled for shade tolerance if planting in part shade.

Turf-type Perennial Ryegrass

Like bluegrass, perennial rye has fine-textured leaves and dark green color. It grows in clumps and does not send out runners. It also likes cool weather and goes dormant in summer. Ryegrass is higher maintenance and prefers medium to highly fertile soils. Ryegrass is more tolerant of drought than bluegrass. It is rarely used as the sole species because it is prone to disease. It grows the quickest of any of the grasses. Use no more than 20 percent in a mixture to help the lawn establish itself. Use shade tolerant cultivars in partly shaded areas.

Fine-leaf Fescue

In part to full shade, fine fescues such as chewings or creeping red will dominate. Both grow short and have fine, wiry, medium-green leaves. Creeping red fescue spreads by underground rhizomes and forms a dense mat similar to bluegrass. Chewings fescue is a bunch-type grass with more shade tolerance than the creeping type. The fine-leaf fescues tolerate hot, dry summer conditions as easily as they do the extreme cold of winter. For shady sites, mix 30 to 50 percent shade tolerant bluegrass with 30 to 60 percent fine fescue and a smaller portion of shade tolerant perennial ryegrass. Creeping red and chewings fescues are low maintenance grasses always sold in mixtures with Kentucky bluegrass and perennial ryegrass. Over time, the bluegrass varieties will dominate in full sun while the fescues will dominate in shadier places.

Turf-type Tall Fescue

Most Hoosiers living in the country are familiar with "Kentucky 31." The name is synonymous with the tall coarse-bladed fescue sown around homes and farmsteads. Today there are numerous improved new varieties with shorter, softer, greener leaves that make wonderful lawn grasses. Tall fescue is hardy, deep rooted, and somewhat drought tolerant. A low maintenance grass, it thrives in full sun but tolerates more shade like the fine fescues. It is considered a lower maintenance grass. Because of its coarse blades, don't mix it with finer types like bluegrass and ryegrass. It will stand out like a weed.

Seeding New Lawns

Growing grass from seed is cost effective and easy if done in late August or early September. At this time of year the soil is warm and the grass grows quickly, squeezing out potential weeds. Start by adding two inches of improved topsoil and one inch of high quality compost and tilling it into the top four inches of soil. When finished, add another inch of compost and rake into the top layer of soil. Adjust pH according to soil test results if necessary. Break apart any clumps and rake smooth with a metal garden rake. Choose the appropriate grass species or mixture and use a drop spreader to apply it at the rates listed in the chart below. For a more even distribution, split the seed in two and apply half in a north-south direction and the other half going east-west. Use a metal leaf or garden rake and lightly rake the soil to ensure good seed-to-soil contact. Add starter fertilizer then spread straw mulch over the newly seeded area. Use enough to cover about 50 percent of exposed soil. Water lightly three to four times a day to make sure the seedbed stays moist. Mow when grass gets tall enough.

Below is a table of recommended seeding rates for lawns in Indiana, according to the experts at the Purdue Cooperative Extension Service:

	Seeding Rate	
Seed Mix	lbs./1000 ft.	lbs./acre
100% Kentucky bluegrass	1.5-2.0	65-87
80-90% Kentucky bluegrass + 10-20% perennial rye	3.0-4.0	130-175
50-70% Kentucky bluegrass + 30-50% fine fescue	4.0-5.0	175-220
100% tall fescue	6.0-8.0	261-348

Repair Those Bare Spots

If you have to fix bare patches in the spring, remove the dead grass and weeds with a de-thatching rake. Use a hoe to scratch the surface of the soil down to one inch deep. Mix one inch of fine grade compost in with the loose soil. Spread the seed by hand following the directions above. For best results, try to fix bare patches before the new leaves emerge on the trees, or in late August and September.

Mowing

Mowing the grass seems like an ordinary and routine chore, and it is. Mowing it improperly, however, can result in serious problems. Grass roots grow in proportion to the leaf blades—the longer the blades the deeper the roots. Mow between $2^1/2$ and 3 inches tall to encourage a deep and healthy root system. Long grass blades also help shade out weeds like crabgrass and ground ivy.

As rule-of-thumb, mow often enough that you never remove more than one-third of the grass blade at one time. If you like the grass at 3 inches long, let it grow an inch or slightly more over that, then cut it again. An exception to this rule is the first cut in spring. Make the first cut at $1^1/2$ inches in early spring to remove the dry, dead tips from winter. Leave the grass clippings on the lawn after mowing, except when they grow so long that they leave clumps behind the mower. Clippings return valuable nutrients and organic matter to the soil and help cut down on fertilizer costs. Mow often enough so that the clippings stay short. Surprisingly, mowing more often saves time overall. Studies show that even though you mow more often, you do it in less time than if you had to stop and empty a catch bag. Sharpen the mower blade regularly. Dull mower blades fray the edges instead of leaving a sharp cut. As a result, the tips turn brown and the lawn loses its lush green color.

Fertilizing

Homeowners have to decide for themselves how much time and resources to invest in their lawn. The most important nutrient to add to a lawn is nitrogen. A *high maintenance* lawn needs three to four pounds of actual nitrogen per thousand square feet of lawn area, per year. With proper irrigation and cultural practices, the result should be a lush, green lawn. A *low maintenance* lawn only needs one to two pounds of fertilizer per thousand square feet, per year. The end result should be a reasonably acceptable green lawn. Whether you choose a high or low maintenance program, you should apply the majority of the nutrients in smaller doses in the fall. This schedule helps the grass develop extensive root systems that store nutrients to use later. As a result, the grass stays lush and green late in the year and greens-up early in the spring.

Use fertilizers with at least 50 percent "slow-release" nitrogen. This dissolves small amounts of nitrogen over long periods of time and allows the grass to absorb the nutrients slowly and when needed.

It also reduces the chance that the nitrogen may dissolve in runoff and pollute local waterways. Organic fertilizers also release nitrogen slowly, but the nitrogen is less concentrated and may need to be added at a higher rate. Fertilize once in mid-September for a low-maintenance lawn. For a moderately green lawn, fertilize in mid-September and in early November. For higher maintenance lawns, fertilize again in May to help it stay green through the summer. Spread a fourth but lighter application of fertilizer in July. High maintenance lawns need irrigation. Fertilizing in the heat of summer may burn the turf unless there is rain or supplemental watering. There are many options available when purchasing fertilizer. We suggest you consult your local office of the Purdue Cooperative Extension Service to discuss fertilizer programs and application rates.

Wicked Weeds

There are millions of weed seeds lying dormant in your lawn, waiting for the right time to sprout and wreak havoc on the lawn. Annual weeds like crabgrass sprout from seeds each year in the spring. Perennial weeds go dormant in winter but grow again the following spring. The best way to control weeds is to encourage lush and healthy turf that will crowd out undesirable weeds. In the absence of a lush, dense turf, pesticides can also help. Control annual weeds with pre-emergent type pesticides applied in early spring. Control perennial weeds like dandelions with broadleaf weed killers in the fall. Identify the weeds to control first then choose the appropriate pesticide. Consult your local extension office for help identifying and controlling weeds.

What Else Should I Do?

Annual core aeration is one of the only alternatives for improving heavy and compacted soil. It also helps prevent the development of a harmful thatch layer. When they pass over the grass, core aerating machines remove cylindrical plugs of soil from the turf and leave them on the surface of the lawn. This allows air to reach the roots more quickly. After aerating, apply high quality compost to the surface of the lawn. Called topdressing, the compost should be fine enough to pass through a screen with holes that are $3/8$ of an inch square. Use a leaf rake to help it blend into the turf and to break apart soil cores. The best time to core aerate is in late summer or early fall.

Lawns need the equivalent of 1 to $1 1/2$ inches of rainwater per week. Infrequent but deep watering encourages deeper roots. Water all at the same time or split in half and water $1/2$ inch, twice per week. During extended dry periods, reduce the watering and allow the lawn to turn brown and go dormant. This is considered environmentally friendly and is better than wasting water. Most lawns can fully recover from as much as six weeks without rain or supplemental watering.

Kentucky Bluegrass

Troubleshooting

Moss can be a nice feature that adds character with little or no effort. Some people grow gardens filled with hundreds of different types of moss; however, most people want to get rid of it. Moss thrives in shady areas with compact, infertile but slightly acidic soil. If you want to discourage moss from growing, prune lightly any tree limbs that create the shade. Fertilize according to soil test results to improve fertility and core aerate to relieve soil compaction.

Insect populations vary from year to year according to weather patterns and other environmental factors. You can reduce the number of pests with good cultural practices such as core aeration, proper mowing techniques, and fertilizing in the fall. This gives the lawn an advantage over troublesome white grubs and other insects. From time to time, you may need to use pesticides to control outbreaks of one insect or another. Please consult your local extension office or a garden center professional for recommended treatments.

Disease abounds in Indiana lawns. Fertilizing heavily in the spring and frequent shallow watering in summer encourage turf diseases. Follow good cultural practices like fall fertilizing, infrequent but deep watering in the morning, and core aeration to reduce or eliminate disease problems.

Our Top Ten Turf Tips for a Healthy Indiana Lawn

1. Measure the entire lawn area and apply amendments accordingly.

2. Test the soil and adjust pH if necessary.

3. Plant improved varieties of favorite grasses.

4. Mow $2^{1}/_{2}$ to 3 inches tall.

5. Mow frequently with a sharp blade.

6. Return clippings to the lawn.

7. Water deeply on a weekly basis.

8. Aerate annually in fall.

9. Topdress with high quality finely ground compost.

10. Fertilize in the fall.

Ornamental Grasses *for Indiana*

The term "ornamental grass" may seem redundant—most of us spend a good part of our leisure time manicuring acres of lawn grasses around our homes, schools, businesses, and public institutions, all for ornamental effect. In this section, however, ornamental grass describes a group of plants in the grass family that are useful in gardens and landscapes or for conservation purposes. They are diverse in size, color, texture, and hardiness. Grasses are the second largest plant family in the world—one fifth of the earth's total vegetation is grasses! Familiar grasses include the palms, bamboos, major food crops (such as rice, corn, wheat, millet, and sorghum) along with the bluegrass, ryegrass, and fescue we sow for lawns.

Ornamental grasses are a unique group of plants grown for their year-round ornamental effects and freedom from pests. An integral element in "The New American Garden" style (an idea started by Wolfgang Oehme and James van Sweden in the 1970s), they exemplify the term *low maintenance*. The preponderance of grasses in the New American Garden is the result of a shift in landscape design toward plants that require less maintenance, as well as those that are indigenous or easily adapted to the region they are grown in.

Grasses come in all shapes and sizes, from a very short six inches to plumes more than fifteen feet tall. Most have fine textures, an upright and arching growth habit, and leaves that shimmer, billow, and sway in the breeze. They add movement and sound to the garden and help soothe the soul. They offer varying shades of green, yellow, and variegated leaves as well as plume-like blooms. Many turn scarlet or straw-colored in cold weather, and the best varieties, like maiden grass or bluestem, stay showy through most of winter. If planted next to the right selection of broadleaf plants, the effect can be dazzling at any time of the year. Ornamental grass plumes glisten when backlit by the sun, especially in the winter landscape.

Ornamental grasses have either a clumping or running growth habit and

Japanese Blood Grass

Northern Sea Oats

they establish quickly, as a rule. Clumpers spread more slowly than runners, some of which (like ribbon grass) can be invasive. Most have extensive root systems, especially those that are native to the tall grass prairies. Their deep roots help to them find the moisture they need to withstand drought as well as to pull up extra nutrients that might be lacking in the topsoil.

Most nurseries and garden centers sell grasses in gallon-size containers. Most grasses prefer full sun, but a few (like northern sea oats or garden sedges) will grow in the shade. The soil should be light and well drained. Some grasses will tolerate moisture better than others. Know your planting site first, then choose an appropriate grass for the conditions.

To transplant the selected grass, dig a hole up to three times the width and only slightly deeper than the container. Mix compost with the displaced soil and return enough of it to the hole so that the top of the rootball will be even with the ground around it after planting. Tap the container on a hard surface to loosen the roots from the sides of the pot. Gently tease the roots apart from the root mass after removing the pot and spread them out in the hole. Backfill with the remaining soil and water deeply. Though most grasses are drought tolerant, keep two to three inches of mulch around the roots, especially in the first few years after planting.

Enjoy the plants as they grow and change throughout the year. Don't be tempted to cut back the straw-colored leaves and flowers in the fall. Some show their greatest features in winter. Instead, wait until early spring and cut them to within four to six inches of the ground. Divide ornamental grass in spring when the center of the plant looks bare or dead and all of the new growth is in a ring. To divide, slice through the crown and root mass with a sharp shovel or spade. Transplant the divisions as described above and water them deeply every few days. Ornamental grasses have no regular insect or disease problems. The little maintenance they require will free up time for other gardening endeavors.

Dwarf Fountain Grass

Pennisetum alopecuroides 'Hameln'

Fountain grass is a popular ornamental grass throughout Indiana—and rightly so. Its fine-textured, glossy, narrow leaves have an upright, arching habit that bend and sway in a summer breeze. The exquisite and fuzzy, foxtail-like flowers start to open in July. They cascade outward from the plant, opening just barely above the leaves. When in bloom, the plant looks like a water fountain. The flowers are almond-colored but fade to pinkish brown as fall approaches. With the onset of frost, the leaves streak yellow then bleach to a straw-yellow by November. There are annual and perennial fountain grasses, so choose accordingly. 'Hameln' is a short perennial whose leaves and flowers stay upright through winter, even after snowfall. They have no pests to speak of and are simple to care for. They may qualify as "indestructible."

Other Common Name
Fountain Grass

Bloom Period and Seasonal Color
July through frost; almond-colored flowers fade to pinkish brown with onset of fall. Green leaves in summer turning tawny yellow after frost; some cultivars stay showy all winter.

Mature Height × Spread
Generally 1 to 4 ft. × 1 to 4 ft; 'Hameln' 3 ft. × 3 ft.

When, Where, and How to Plant
Fountain grass prefers spring planting in any moist, well-drained soil enriched with compost. Dig planting holes to appropriate size (see chapter introduction). Return enough soil to the hole so that, after planting, the top of the rootball will be even with the ground around it. Lightly tap the side of the container to loosen the roots from the pot. Tease out any roots growing in concentric circles or slice the root mass vertically in four or five places if the roots look potbound. Cut off any roots that form a mat in the bottom of the pot. Place the plant, backfill the hole with the original soil, and water deeply.

Growing Tips
Keep 2 to 3 inches of bark mulch around the root zone at all times. Water deeply during dry periods in summer. Dwarf fountain grass doesn't require fertilizer.

Care and Maintenance
Fountain grass is a maintenance-free plant. It is a perfect choice for gardeners who have little time to invest. In the late winter or very early spring, cut the foliage back to 3 to 4 inches with hedge shears.

Companion Planting and Design
Plant this beautiful grass along a walkway, and the flowers will "bow" to the passersby. It looks natural planted on the edge of a water garden. Plant it with chokeberry or winterberry holly for a fantastic winter combination. Mix purple cultivars with lavender and pink annuals like nicotiana or vinca, or yellow sun coleus for contrast. Annual fountain grasses grow wonderfully in well-watered containers.

We Recommend
'Little Bunny' is cute and shorter, growing 1 foot tall. *Pennisetum setaceum* is an annual fountain grass with long, thin, bottlebrush-type blooms. *P. setaceum* 'Rubrum' grows to 3 feet while 'Rubrum Compactum' and 'Red Riding Hood' grow 1 to 2 feet. They both have burgundy-red leaves. *Pennisetum glaucum* 'Purple Majesty', the ornamental millet and a recent All-America Selection, is a breeding breakthrough. It is an annual that grows to 5 feet with wide, purple leaves and erect, candle-like blooms.

Feather Reed Grass
Calamagrostis × acutiflora 'Karl Foerster'

When, Where, and How to Plant

Transplant feather reed grass in early spring into moist, well-drained soil. It tolerates clay if kept moist but not wet. Dig the planting hole to the appropriate size (see chapter introduction). Return enough soil to the hole so that, after planting, the top of the rootball is even with the ground around it. Lightly tap the side of the container on a hard surface to loosen the roots from the pot. Tease out any roots growing in concentric circles or slice the root mass vertically in four or five places if it looks potbound. Cut off any roots that form a mat in the bottom of the pot then place in the hole. Backfill the hole with the original soil, and water deeply.

Growing Tips

Keep 2 to 3 inches of organic mulch around the roots to keep them moist and to prevent weeds. Water deeply during dry spells in summer. The more moisture feather reed grass receives, the taller it will grow. Fertilize lightly in barren soils.

Care and Maintenance

Cut it back with hedge shears to 6 to 8 inches in the late winter. Feather reed grass starts spring growth earlier than most other ornamental grasses, so cut it soon enough that the tips of the new leaves won't be injured. This is a pest and maintenance free plant.

Companion Planting and Design

Feather reed grass makes a powerful vertical accent in the garden. Plant it in large groups to create a sea of golden flowers that wave during summer breezes. It looks especially good with a dark evergreen background or planted near water. The tawny flowers tinged in pink mix well with lavender or blue flowers such as blue salvia or Russian sage. Like many grasses, feather reed grass holds its upright character throughout winter. It may lean under heavy snow, but it will spring back to its upright habit.

We Recommend

'Overdam' has variegated foliage with a cream-colored stripe running the length of its leaves.

Many of us anxiously await the end of summer when most tall grasses send up their cottony flower plumes. Feather reed grass is the perfect ornamental grass for gardeners who can't wait that long! Its clumps of slender, spike-like flowers open in June, making it one of our earliest blooming grasses. The fine textured blooms are thin and wispy, with a rosy pink tinge that fades to golden tan. The flower stalks rise 2 to 3 feet above their glossy green leaves in an upright, stiff habit that gives the entire plant a strong vertical effect in the garden. The flower spikes last throughout the rest of the summer. 'Karl Foerster' is sterile and will not reseed like other grasses. After the first hard frost, both leaves and the flower spikes bleach to a straw color.

Bloom Period and Seasonal Color

Flower spikes in June; green leaves all season, turning straw-colored in frost.

Mature Height × Spread

4 to 6 ft. × 3 to 4 ft.

Fiber Optic Grass
Isolepis cernua

Though native to the British Isles, southern Europe, and north Africa, fiber optic grass is so new and unusual for Indiana that we had to include it. It looks like a cross between fiber optic cables, tinged green, and a large, green "stress ball." Its long, stringy, green leaves spill over the sides of containers or walls like dripping water. The ends of the leaves are tipped with small brown beads. Fiber optic grass has a high-tech look, as its name suggests. It feels at home in containers where it best shows off its unique character. Used in this way, it will soon be a favorite among our younger generation of gardeners living in apartments and small spaces. It isn't hardy in Indiana, but it's so unusual that you'll be willing to treat it as an annual, replacing it yearly. It can also be found with the botanical name Scirpus cernuus.

Bloom Period and Seasonal Color
Filamentous green leaves with flowers at the tips, from June through frost.

Mature Height × Spread
1 ft. × 1 ft. globe

When, Where, and How to Plant
Plant after the last frost in containers filled with soilless mix. Plastic pots with drain holes in the bottom work well. Use commercially available mixtures of peat, perlite, vermiculite, and finely shredded bark. Avoid using garden soil in containers since it gets too hard and is too heavy. With your bare hand, dig a planting hole that is slightly larger than the pot the plant is currently in. Tap the pot to loosen the roots and gently remove the plant. Pull encircling roots away from the root ball or slice through potbound roots with a sharp knife. Plant so that the top of the rootball is at the same soil mixture level that it was in the pot. Water heavily, moistening all of the soil mix so that water runs from the bottom of the pot.

Growing Tips
Fiber optic grass is native to boggy areas so water the pot freely. Fertilize with liquid plant food such as 15-30-15, diluted according to package instructions.

Care and Maintenance
Prune dead leaves as needed. When the season is over, add the dead plants and soilless mix to a compost pile. Replace soilless mix in this or any container each year for best results. This grass is generally pest free.

Companion Planting and Design
Grow it as single specimens where they can really show their true character, or plant as accents in large containers mixed with annuals grown for foliage or flowers. Charteuse, purple coleus (for leaves), osteospermums, along with blue salvia make nice companions. Fiber optic grass can grow in the garden but starts to look unkempt after a lot of rain.

We Recommend
Grow it separately or in mixed containers. There are no other cultivars. Mexican feather grass, *Nasella tenuissima*, formerly *Stipa tenuissima*, is a light, feathery, silver- green grass that turns tawny yellow by mid-summer. It is one of the finest textured grasses, arching over the sides of walkways or pots. It nods and sways in gentle breezes. Except for extreme southern Indiana, it isn't hardy and grows as an annual in most of the state.

Garden Sedge

Carex spp.

When, Where, and How to Plant

Plant sedges in early spring in acidic or alkaline, moist but well-drained soil amended with compost. Prepare a planting hole that is the appropriate size (see chapter introduction). Mix the displaced soil with compost and backfill the hole high enough so that, after planting, the top of the rootball will be even with the ground. Tap the side of the pot to loosen the roots. Remove the plant and tease out any roots growing in concentric circles around the bottom. Spread the roots out and finish backfilling with the amended soil. Tamp lightly and water deeply.

Growing Tips

Keep 2 to 3 inches of mulch around the roots to conserve moisture and keep the weeds down. Water generously, especially during dry periods in summer. Fertilizer isn't necessary.

Care and Maintenance

Sedges are mostly carefree. Cut dead leaves back to 3 or 4 inches tall in late winter. To propagate, divide by slicing through the clump with a sharp spade. Sedges have few to no known pests.

Companion Planting and Design

Plant sedges near water gardens and ponds amidst rocks and stones. Mix brown-leaved cultivars with purple-leaved perennials like coral bells or annual coleus. Edge perennial gardens with fine-leaved clumping types; use spreaders as ground covers in shadier spots. Some sedges make good water garden plants.

We Recommend

Carex buchananii, leatherleaf sedge, and *Carex comans*, New Zealand hairy sedge, are native to New Zealand. They have unique brown leaves that make it look dead! Plant them as annuals in Indiana since they aren't hardy here. *Carex flagellifera* 'Toffee Twist' is a short new cultivar good for accents and containers. Most cultivars of *Carex morrowii*, Morrow's sedge, have flat leaves that resemble lilyturf. Many are variegated such as 'Ice Dance' and 'Variegata'; however, 'Silk Tassel' has fountain-like hairy leaves. *Carex albula* 'Frosty Curls' is a one-of-a-kind plant. Its silverly green and filamentous leaves burst from the ground like a low fountain. Use it as an annual since it isn't hardy.

There are several thousand sedges that grow naturally around the world. Botanically speaking, they are not grasses, even though there is a strong resemblance. For gardening purposes, however, we use them in the same way. They usually have fine, hair-like leaves and come in shades of green, pink, red, purple, or brown. Some have variegated leaves. Others have leaves that look like hairy mops growing on top of the soil. Some grow in tight clumps while others spread by underground stems called rhizomes. Others form fleshy tubers. This is why nutsedge, one of the all-time annoying weeds, is so hard to control. Luckily, garden sedges are much more submissive. Though some like more sun, most will thrive in hard-to-grow places such as damp shade. Whether evergreen or deciduous, all sedges make wonderful additions to water and woodland gardens.

Other Common Names
Morrow's Sedge, Kan Sedge, Blonde Sedge, Frosty Curls Sedge

Bloom Period and Seasonal Color
Usually insignificant flowers in summer or early fall, with burgundy or yellowish brown fall color, depending on the species.

Mature Height × Spread
1 to 2 ft. × 1 to 2 ft., depending on species

Golden Japanese Forest Grass

Hakonechloa macra 'Aureola'

Among the most elegant, refined, and soothing of all grasses, Japanese forest grass is a must for shady gardens. Native to the moist, rocky cliffs of Mt. Hakone on Japan's main island of Honshu, it is a staple in Japanese style gardens. Fortunately, this grass is making a name for itself in America. Its soft, pointed leaves cascade over themselves, resembling fast flowing water or a gurgling fountain. It spreads by underground stems called rhizomes, eventually losing its individual character by forming a mass. Though it is a slow spreader, it will fill in empty spaces and function as a ground cover. 'Aureola' has light yellow to white stripes which vary based on its exposure to sun. Give it ample shade, especially in midday. The species, which is green, will tolerate more light. It turns golden red in fall.

Other Common Name
Hakone Grass

Bloom Period and Seasonal Color
Insignificant flowers in August; bright yellow-white variegated leaves all season, turning coppery in the fall.

Mature Height × Spread
2 ft. × variable

When, Where, and How to Plant
Plant in the spring in slightly acidic or alkaline, moist, well-drained soil. 'Aureola' grows more slowly than the solid green species but quickens the pace when ample compost is mixed with the soil. Add 2 to 4 inches when preparing the bed. Dig a planting hole up to three times the width of the container. Gently tap the container on a hard surface to loosen the root mass from the sides of the pot. Remove the plant from the pot and tease out any roots growing in concentric circles. Slice the root mass vertically in four or five places if it looks potbound. Space plants 6 inches apart and plant level with the ground around them. Tamp the soil lightly and water deeply when finished.

Growing Tips
Keep partially shaded as Japanese forest grass dislikes sun. Add 2 inches of compost to the garden each spring. Keep 2 to 3 inches of bark mulch around the roots at all times to conserve moisture and prevent weeds. Water deeply on a weekly basis, especially during dry periods in summer. Unlike other grasses, Japanese forest grass may benefit from fertilization. Add fertilizer in mid-spring as the grass begins to wake up from its winter sleep.

Care and Maintenance
Cut leaves back to 4 inches in early spring or allow new leaves to blend in with old leaves. Dig root pieces in early spring after cutting back and share them with friends or transplant them to other shady locations. There are no known pest problems.

Companion Planting and Design
The fine-textured leaves of Japanese Forest Grass contrast well with coarse-leaved hostas or chocolatey purple coral bells. They go perfectly along a slate or stone path, paying homage to passersby. Plant near ponds and streams. They are popular container plants, but the roots need protection in winter.

We Recommend
'Albovariegata' has white stripes and is more vigorous growing than 'Aureola'. The species is solid green and more subtle in the garden. 'All Gold' has lime green to gold leaves with no stripes.

Japanese Blood Grass
Imperata cylindrica 'Red Baron'

When, Where, and How to Plant
Plant in the early spring in full sun after the soil dries, in any moist but well-drained soil amended with compost. Prepare a planting hole to the appropriate size (see chapter introduction). Mix the displaced soil with compost and backfill the hole so that, after planting, the top of the rootball will be even with the ground around it. Tap the side of the pot to loosen the roots. Remove the plant and tease out any roots growing in concentric circles around the bottom. Spread out the roots and finish backfilling with the amended soil. Tamp lightly and water deeply.

Growing Tips
It spreads faster in moist soil but grows poorly in overly wet or dry situations. To keep it from spreading too aggressively, plant in a large pot and bury it in the soil. The leaves turn deeper red with more sun. Keep 2 to 3 inches of organic mulch around the roots at all times. Water it deeply during dry periods in summer. Fertilizing is not necessary.

Care and Maintenance
Cut the foliage down to 3 or 4 inches in the late winter. Sometimes a part of the plant will revert to a green form. These green "mutants" are usually very aggressive and may take over the rest of the clump. Prune them out with a shovel or spade. Japanese blood grass has few known pests.

Companion Planting and Design
Plant it as a border plant around yellow-blooming flowers such as zinnia, coreopsis, or black-eyed Susans. Use as a ground cover under red-leaved shrubs such as fothergilla or viburnum. It is a perfect companion to winterberry holly which also likes moist soil. Japanese blood grass grows well in a pot or other large container or on the edge of a water garden.

We Recommend
Unlike other ornamental grasses, Japanese blood grass does not produce appreciable flowers. We base its ornamental character solely on its leaves. 'Red Baron' has good red leaf coloration and is our favorite.

The name "Japanese blood grass" sounds dramatic, and for good reason. This grass appears as if the leaves were dipped in blood! From the time they emerge, the new leaves are tinged with red from the tip to halfway down the 18-inch blade. The color intensifies throughout the summer and is especially spectacular in the fall. After the first hard frost, the leaves turn a tawny brown and stay that way until the following spring. You can appreciate Japanese blood grass best when it is backlit by early morning or late afternoon sunlight. At those times of day, it appears as if the leaves are glowing red. Japanese blood grass spreads by rhizomes. With ample water, it will spread aggressively in large clumps, filling in empty spaces if you give it free rein. It may not be reliably hardy in Zone 5.

Bloom Period and Seasonal Color
Red-tipped leaves all season, intensifying in fall; yellow-brown in winter.

Mature Height × Spread
12 to 18 in. × variable

Little Bluestem
Schizachyrium scoparium

When the pioneers first settled the prairie states, they made their way through meadows of bluestem. This native was the backbone of the tall grass prairie that covered the Midwest and Plains states, including parts of northern Indiana. Most of the tall grass prairie has since disappeared. The bluestems and other native prairie plants were conserved and recently reintroduced to Hoosier gardeners. Little bluestem grows to 4 feet, shorter than its larger 6- to 8-foot cousin, big bluestem (Andropogon gerardii). Its thin, wispy stems are a silvery blue-green at the base, which helps give the grass its name. Its clumping leaves and branches grow straight up then arch slightly toward the tip, especially in a breeze. The leaves turn light bronze with the onset of frost. The plant stays upright all winter, providing food and shelter for wildlife.

Bloom Period and Seasonal Color
Blue-green leaves in spring and summer, turning light bronze in fall and winter; insignificant bloom in late summer.

Mature Height × Spread
3 ft. × 4 ft.

When, Where, and How to Plant
Transplant bluestems in spring into moist but well-drained soil. They tolerate tough growing conditions, especially dry soils. Dig a planting hole up to three times the width of the container. Gently tap the container on a hard surface to loosen the root mass from the sides of the pot. Remove the pot and tease out any roots growing in concentric circles. Slice the root mass vertically in four or five places if they look potbound. Cut off any roots that form a mat in the bottom of the pot. Transplant to the same level it was growing in the pot. Backfill the hole with the original soil, and water deeply.

Growing Tips
Avoid planting in heavy clay or wet soils. Mulch with 2 to 3 inches of shredded bark to keep weeds down, but keep the mulch away from the crown. Water during times of drought but don't overwater, as bluestems like it dry. Avoid fertilizing since bluestems do not thrive in rich soils.

Care and Maintenance
Bluestems are pest and maintenance free. Cut the leaves back in late winter with hedge shears before growth begins again.

Companion Planting and Design
Its deep root system makes it good for naturalizing and for erosion control on banks, hillsides, or open fields. Plant in masses with other tall prairie plants such as coneflowers, rattlesnake master, or asters. Use small starter plants, or "plugs," or a customized seed mix if planting a large area for naturalizing. Dried bluestem plumes make nice additions to everlasting flower arrangements.

We Recommend
'Aldous' is a tall blue cultivar. 'Blaze' turns deeper red than others in fall. Plant them both from seeds. 'The Blues' is a vivid light blue that has to be propagated by division. Big Bluestem, *Andropogon gerardii*, is also known as turkey foot. Combine both grasses and native wildflowers for a meadow. 'Champ' is a shorter cultivar, and 'Pawnee' is taller and more arching.

Maiden Grass

Miscanthus sinensis 'Morning Light'

When, Where, and How to Plant

Plant in early spring in full sun after the soil dries. It is flexible but prefers moist, slightly acidic or alkaline, well-drained areas enriched with compost. Dig a planting hole up to three times the width of the container. Gently tap the container on a hard surface to loosen the root mass. Remove the pot and tease out any roots growing in concentric circles. Slice the root mass vertically in four or five places if potbound. Cut off any roots that form a mat in the bottom of the pot. Transplant to the same level it was growing in the pot. Backfill the hole with the original soil, and water deeply.

Growing Tips

Keep 2 to 3 inches of mulch around the roots at all times. Water deeply during dry periods in summer. Maiden grass cultivars may flop over in too much shade. No fertilizer is needed.

Care and Maintenance

Cut maiden grass back to a height of 6 to 8 inches in late winter or early spring with a weeder or sharp pruning shears. To re-invigorate or share with friends, divide every few years by removing the entire clump and slicing it with a spade. Don't be afraid to use an axe to cut through the rootball if you have to. There are no regular pest problems.

Companion Planting and Design

Use in dried arrangements or leave them in the garden to collect frost and snow. They look superb planted near small ponds and water gardens or combined with American beautyberry and high bush cranberry. They also make a fast growing screen.

We Recommend

'Gracillimus' is a common cultivar with glossy green leaves. 'Zebrinus', also called zebra grass, has long, arching green leaves with small yellow bands or hash marks down the length of the blade. It is tall and tends to flop. Try 'Hinjo', a smaller and more compact version. 'Variegatus' has wider leaves. Overall this one is whiter and more coarse than 'Morning Light'. *Miscanthus* 'Purpurescens' is a hybrid that turns scarlet purple in fall.

Of all the ornamental grasses, there are probably more types of maiden grass than any other. This genus includes grasses such as flame grass, zebra grass, Japanese silver grass, porcupine grass, and many others. It is one of the oldest ornamental grasses used today. It is often confused with "pampas grass" because of its tall stems with plume-type flowers, but true pampas grass is not hardy in Indiana. 'Morning Light' is arguably among the best maiden grass cultivars, with thin, wispy, fine-textured leaves edged in white. A clump grower, maiden grass is like fountain grass, only taller and more robust. Its leaves grow dense and upright but sprawl outward in a classic vase shape, dancing in the wind. It reaches a height of 4 to 8 feet when its fluffy flowers mature. After the first frost, it turns a straw color that lasts through the winter.

Other Common Names

Japanese Silver Grass, Eulalia Grass

Bloom Period and Seasonal Color

Long, narrow grassy-green leaves through late summer, turning straw-colored after frost and lasting all winter; plume-like flowers in early fall.

Mature Height × Spread

4 to 6 ft. × 5 to 8 ft.

Northern Sea Oats
Chasmanthium latifolium

If you don't look too closely, northern sea oats looks a little like bamboo. It has short, wide leaves that come to a sharp point and are attached at right angles to the upright stems. In midsummer, it sends up flower stalks that droop with light-green, flat seedheads which hang like spangles and shimmer in the breeze. The seedheads turn tawny yellow in the fall and persist well into winter. They make wonderful additions to dried flower arrangements and are much sought after in the florist trade. Northern sea oats has the unusual ability to grow both in sun and in shade, making it ideal for just about any garden. It is a generous plant and reseeds readily. Share the new starts with friends and neighbors.

Other Common Names
Wild Oats, River Oats

Bloom Period and Seasonal Color
Blue-green leaves in spring and summer, turning tawny yellow in fall; flowers in midsummer that last all winter.

Mature Height × Spread
2 to 3 ft. × 2 to 3 ft.

When, Where, and How to Plant
Transplant northern sea oats when the ground dries in the early spring. Plant in deep, moist, well-drained soil enriched with organic matter. These are versatile plants that grow well in full sun or partial to full shade. They even grow in creek bottoms in their native habitats. Dig a planting hole that is the appropriate size (see chapter introduction). Mix the displaced soil with compost and backfill the hole so that, after planting, the top of the rootball is even with the ground around it. Tap the side of the pot to loosen the roots. Remove the plant and tease out any roots growing in concentric circles around the bottom. Spread the roots out and finish backfilling with the amended soil. Tamp lightly and water deeply.

Growing Tips
Keep 2 to 3 inches of organic mulch over the roots. Water deeply during dry periods in summer. In full sun, the leaves will be a lighter green; shadier sites produce a darker-green leaf. Broadcast a tablespoon of balanced fertilizer around the root zone each spring as growth begins.

Care and Maintenance
Like other ornamental grasses, sea oats requires very little care. Cut the foliage back to 3 inches in late winter, before new growth begins. To divide, cut through clumps in spring with a sharp spade. It has few to no known pests.

Companion Planting and Design
Plant sea oats in masses or as an accent against a dark evergreen background like yew or boxwood, where it will stand out. It is also wonderful as an edging or as container plants around a water garden. It is a native woodland grass in the southern and eastern United States. Use it in shade or woods near streams or ponds. It is highly prized for its ornamental flowers and seedheads.

We Recommend
Plant the species.

Prairie Dropseed
Sporobolus heterolepis

When, Where and How to Plant

Transplant prairie dropseed in the early spring after the soil dries. Plant in well-drained soil, including clay, in sun to part sun. Avoid overly wet sites. Dig a planting hole the appropriate size (see chapter introduction). Mix the displaced soil with compost and backfill the hole so that the top of the rootball will be even with the ground. Tap the side of the pot to loosen the roots. Remove the plant and tease out any roots growing in concentric circles around the bottom. Make four or five vertical slices in the root ball if potbound. Cut away roots growing in a mat at the bottom. Spread remaining roots and finish backfilling with the amended soil. Tamp lightly and water deeply.

Growing Tips

Maintain 2 to 3 inches of organic mulch around the roots. Water deeply during dry periods when the grass is young. Prairie dropseed has deep roots and is considered drought tolerant once established. After three or four years it won't require additional water. No fertilizer is needed.

Care and Maintenance

Prairie dropseed is virtually maintenance and pest free. Cut the foliage back to a height of 4 inches in late winter or early spring, just before new growth begins. Divide in early spring after cutting the leaves back. Use a sharp spade and slice through the center of the clump. Continue dividing in half until you obtain root divisions 4 inches square. Water the divisions deeply after you transplant them. Prairie dropseed is slow to establish itself. It may not bloom until the second or third year. Patience will eventually reward you with permanent satisfaction.

Companion Planting and Design

Plant it in groups or masses for a sunny ground cover, or as a specimen or accent in the perennial border. Its clumping, hair-like growth makes a nice edging around the garden. Mix with other native prairie grasses and wildflowers like coneflowers, rudbeckias, and bluestems to provide excellent food and cover for wildlife, and for meadow-restoration projects.

We Recommend

Plant the species for good results.

At one time, fields of prairie dropseed covered the Midwest and Plains states, but this grass has since been greatly reduced because of development. At one time, Native Americans ground the seeds into flour for baking. An important component of the original tall and short grass prairies, it is native to northwest Indiana, where prairie was common. Prairie dropseed is an elegant grass that grows in clumps of fine, hair-like leaves up to 3 feet long. The leaves sprawl readily and are topped with airy, light-green wispy blooms. The flowers rise 2 or 3 feet above the leaves and make a fine accent in the garden. Seeds mature in early fall and are an excellent food source for birds. The first hard frosts will give the leaves their orange-brown "winter coat" until early spring, when the cycle begins again.

Bloom Period and Seasonal Color

Fine, thread-like green leaves through October, turning coppery after frost; open and tawny erect panicles of flowers in August.

Mature Height × Spread

1 to 3 ft. × 1 to 3 ft.

Switch Grass
Panicum virgatum 'Heavy Metal'

Combined with other grasses and native wildflowers, switch grass was an important part of the tall grass prairie in the Midwest and Plains states. Both annual and perennial in nature, these natives helped form the thick sod that created the deep soils which gave rise to the Corn Belt. Switch grass is loved for its blue-green leaves, clouds of light and airy seedheads, and upright habit through winter. 'Heavy Metal' has among the bluest-green leaves of all. They grow to 3 feet and have a mostly upright habit, arching only slightly toward the tips. The wispy blooms open in mid- to late summer tinged in pink. They mature to golden tan with hard burgundy seeds that provide food for birds and other wildlife. The leaves turn a dull straw color in winter and make a nice show when massed.

Other Common Name
Panic Grass

Bloom Period and Seasonal Color
Blue-green leaves all season turning light brown or straw-colored after frost; flowers open light brown tinged with pink in August.

Mature Height × Spread
2 to 4 ft. × 4 to 8 ft.

When, Where, and How to Plant
Plant switch grass in early spring after the ground dries, in slightly acid or alkaline, well-drained soils. It grows well in sand or clay and even withstands wet areas after it's established. Dig a planting hole up to three times the width of the container. Gently tap the container on a hard surface to loosen the root mass. Remove the pot and tease out roots growing in concentric circles. Slice the root mass vertically in four or five places if pot-bound. Cut off roots that form a mat in the bottom of the pot. Transplant to the same level it was growing in the pot. Backfill the hole with the original soil, tamp lightly and water deeply.

Growing Tips
Keep 2 to 3 inches of organic mulch around the roots. Water deeply during dry periods in summer, especially in the first few years after planting. Switch grass is drought tolerant after a few years. Fertilizer is not needed.

Care and Maintenance
Switch grass is mostly low maintenance and pest free. For faster growth, water deeply once a week throughout the growing season. Cut leaves back to a height of 6 to 8 inches in early spring, before new leaves emerge. Plants can be divided in spring by slicing through the root ball with a sharp spade.

Companion Planting and Design
Plant around ponds, streams, and water gardens. Combine with other prairie wildflowers like asters and rudbeckias. Switch grass makes a nice specimen or accent in a mixed perennial border. Plant it for conservation purposes in fields and wildflower meadows.

We Recommend
Red switch grass, *Panicum virgatum* 'Haense Herms', grows 3 feet tall and has wine-red to purple-tipped leaves all season. The red deepens through the summer, and the fall color is an intense orange-red. 'Shenandoah' is taller and has the best wine-red leaves of all red-leaved types. 'Cloud Nine' grows to 8 feet with warm gold color through winter.

Tufted Hairgrass
Deschampsia caespitosa

When, Where, and How to Plant
Set out container-grown plants in spring after the soil dries. Plant in slightly acidic or alkaline, moist but well-drained soils. Don't be afraid to put it near poorly drained spots. Provide light shade in mid- to late afternoon to help prevent the leaves from drying around the edge, especially in dry areas. Dig a planting hole up to three times the width of the container. Gently tap the container on a hard surface to loosen the root mass. Remove the pot and tease out roots growing in concentric circles. Slice the root mass vertically in four or five places if potbound. Cut off roots that form a mat in the bottom of the pot. Transplant to the same level it was growing in the pot. Backfill the hole with the original soil, tamp lightly, and water deeply.

Growing Tips
Keep 2 to 3 inches of organic mulch around the roots. Water deeply during dry periods in summer. No fertilizer is needed.

Care and Maintenance
Trim flowers back to foliage height when it starts to look ragged in the late summer or fall. The new growth of this species is some of the earliest in spring. Use sharp pruning shears to trim dead leaves in very early spring. To divide, slice through the middle of the plant with a sharp spade or shovel. Rabbits are its only real "pest."

Companion Planting and Design
Tufted hairgrass flowers are good additions to dried arrangements; cut them shortly after they open. Plant as an accent or specimen near a water garden. The billowy tufts of the flowers make a nice background for periwinkle, shasta daisies, or *Agastache* 'Blue Fortune'. Plant in masses in partly shaded gardens and with shade-loving companions such as foam flower and coral bells.

We Recommend
'Bronzeschleier', also called 'Bronze Veil', has bronze-colored flowers that have a drooping growth habit. 'Fairy's Joke' produces new plantlets at the flower tips. 'Schottland' has fine leaves and light green flowers that finally turn golden yellow. 'Goldgehaenge' produces mounds of bright, golden flowers in June.

Tufted hairgrass is a shorter native grass with dark green leaves that look like they are plugged into an electric outlet. They stick out more than they arch and grow in low, tight clumps to 2 feet tall. It's a cool-season grass, so it blooms earlier in the season—in late June or July in Indiana. Billowy clouds of creamy-white seedheads tower over the short, slender leaves and appear almost top-heavy. Unlike most grasses, tufted hairgrass likes wet and boggy sites and is tolerant of part shade. The flowers and stalks will brighten darker more wooded gardens when in bloom. By fall, the flowers begin to break apart. Cut them back so they won't detract from other garden plants.

Bloom Period and Seasonal Color
Glossy green leaves from spring to frost; light tan to yellow flowers and stalks from late June through fall.

Mature Height × Spread
1 to 2 ft. × 3 to 4 ft., in bloom

Perennials *for Indiana*

Perennials are tempting plants. The more you have, the more you want. By definition, a "perennial" is a plant that lives for two years or more. Some perennials (such as daylilies) last for many years, while others (columbine, for example) have short, spectacular lives. Most perennials are grown for their flowers (such as salvia), while others (hosta, for example) are grown for their foliage. Many (like sedum) are grown for both foliage and flowers; some (coneflowers, for example) are valued for the dried flower heads that provide food for birds or decorate the winter landscape.

In theory, it all seems easy. Buy plants that come back each year, put them in the ground, then stand back and watch them grow! It is that easy for some plants, especially the native varieties that thrive in Indiana. Purple coneflowers (*Echinacea purpurea*) and black-eyed Susans (*Rudbeckia fulgida*) are two natives that "strut their stuff" with little help from the gardener. Other perennials, like phlox, may require more effort on your part. As with anything worthwhile, perennials take time, from planning the beds to selecting and maintaining the plants. Before a spade turns soil, pencil should hit paper to sketch out a plan. One might say "plan" is a root word of "plant."

Here are some basics for growing perennials successfully:

- Measure and make a sketch of the area to be planted. Show existing plants, shrubs, and trees; structures, such as a fence, air conditioner, driveway, or sidewalk; and other permanent objects in the landscape, like stumps or boulders.
- Indicate what sizes, colors, and textures you want in the garden. Research and make a list of plants that bloom in the color and at the time of the year you desire. Do you want an all-season garden, a summer cutting garden, or something more formal? You can create a cottage, English, or wildflower garden, or

Asters

simple islands of plants that bring personal pleasure. Your perennial garden may be monochromatic, blooming all in one color; or it may be an evening garden, with plants that come into their full glory at night; or you may choose to grow flowers that fill the air with their fragrant scents. Depending on your ideas and budget, a perennial border can be created in one season, or it can be an ongoing multi-year project.

- Prepare the bed by digging at least twelve inches deep. If planting large or deep-rooted perennials such as peonies and roses, dig eighteen to twenty-four inches deep. Perennials are considered permanent plantings, and their beds should be well prepared for the long stay. The deeper the bed is dug, the better.

- Mix organic material such as compost or finely chopped leaves with the soil in the hole to improve drainage and add nutrients. Work the soil until it is so loose that it can be dug by hand.

- If you don't want to dig because of hard, compacted soil, consider making raised beds. Mound additional soil up to twelve inches above the level of the ground and plant your plants there. Eventually the beds will settle closer to ground level.

- One of the easiest ways to grow perennials is to buy them already growing in containers at garden centers, retail shops, or through mail-order catalogs. You can also get transplants from neighbors, friends, or plant sales. Plant perennials in holes dug three times as wide as the rootball or container they came in. Plant them the same depth they were growing in the container, or slightly higher.

Phlox

- Another easy way to acquire plants is by dividing what you have in spring or fall. Some perennials should be divided every few years to keep them vigorous. Perennials may also be grown from seed. Most perennials grown from seed do not flower the first year.

- When to clean up the perennial bed depends on the health of the plants and personal taste. If the plants were diseased or infested with insects, clean up the bed as needed throughout the growing season. In fall, cut back plant material that has been killed by frosts and remove stems, seedheads, dead leaves, and other debris. However, if the plants were healthy and they have winter interest, such as attractive seedheads that double as a source of food for birds, you can wait until late winter or early spring to clean up the beds.

- In spring, when perennials start to leaf out, apply an all-purpose granular fertilizer according to label directions or ring the plants with compost. Compost can also be added again in fall when putting the garden to bed for the winter.

- Don't be afraid to change things around. If a plant is too big or requires too much maintenance, move it or pull it out.

- Finally, remember that above all else, gardening, even with perennials, should be fun!

Achillea
Achillea spp.

People either love achillea or hate it. Those who dislike it complain that it falls over. Those who love achillea cherish its long bloom cycle and its use as a cut flower in vases or everlasting arrangments. Many achillea species have an attractive grey-green ferny foliage. This is a trouble-free perennial that is seldom bothered by pests or diseases. It has long had the reputation for having healing powers and is often classified as an herb instead of as a perennial. Its flowers and leaves are fragrant, and its foliage adds nice texture to the perennial bed. In France, achillea is called "carpenter's herb" because it was used to heal cuts on carpenters' hands.

Other Common Name
Yarrow

Bloom Period and Seasonal Color
Summer blooms in yellow, crimson, orange, and white.

Mature Height × Spread
2 to 5 ft. × 3 ft.

When, Where, and How to Plant
Transplants may be planted or divided in the fall or in spring as soon as the soil can be worked. They may also be transplanted in summer if given adequate water. Well-drained, average soil is best. Plant achillea in holes dug three times as wide as the container they were growing in previously, at the same depth they were growing in the container (or slightly higher). Space plants 18 to 24 inches apart. Water them well. Mulch if desired or spread a layer of compost around the plant.

Growing Tips
Once established, yarrow tolerates drought, although it does best when watered regularly. Apply an all-purpose granular fertilizer around the plant in spring when new growth appears or spread a layer of compost in spring and fall.

Care and Maintenance
Achillea is fairly low maintenance. After it flowers, cut back the stems, and it may flower again in late summer or early fall. The foliage is nearly evergreen and is usually visible all winter. Too much fertilizer or organic matter may cause achillea stems to weaken and fall over. Achillea can be grown from seed, though it may not flower the first year. Some *Achillea* species are more aggressive growers than others. To control achillea's floppiness, cut it back by half in spring to create a shorter plant with more, albeit smaller, flowers. Achillea is usually not bothered by pests or disease.

Companion Planting and Design
Taller varieties should be planted in the middle or at the back of a flower border. If you are not bothered by achillea's floppiness, the plants look great in front of the border, too.

We Recommend
The tallest achilleas are *Achillea filipendulina*. Popular named varieties are 'Gold Plate', which may have 6-inch heads; 'Coronation Gold', which grows about 3 feet tall; and 'Moonshine', which grows about 18 to 24 inches tall. Common yarrow, *Achillea millefolium*, rarely grows taller than 3 feet. Popular varieties are 'Paprika', 'Cerise Queen', 'Summer Pastels', 'Anthea', and 'Galaxy Hybrids'.

When, Where, and How to Plant

Plant container-grown transplants in spring as soon as the soil can be worked. Agastache does fine in average, well-drained soil. Sow seeds indoors six to eight weeks before the last frost. The seeds are small. In pots, gently press them into the surface of a moistened soilless mix. Don't cover the seeds because they need light to germinate. Place the pots in a clear plastic bag and keep the soil moist, but not wet. Place in a bright area out of direct sunlight where the temperature is about 55 to 60 degrees Fahrenheit. Germination may take up to four weeks. Remove them from the plastic bag when the seeds sprout. Transplant outdoors when they are 3 or 4 inches tall.

Growing Tips

Agastache is fairly drought tolerant but benefits from a good soaking if dry conditions are prolonged. Apply an all-purpose granular fertilizer according to label directions or ring the plants with compost in midsummer. Fertilize according to instructions in chapter introduction.

Care and Maintenance

Agastache has few pests.

Companion Planting and Design

'Blue Fortune' can be used en masse or clustered in the perennial bed. It mixes well with other plants that attract butterflies and hummingbirds. 'Blue Fortune' looks particularly nice when massed with yellow tickseed (*Coreopsis*), which is discussed in this chapter.

We Recommend

'Golden Jubilee' is a recent All-America Selection with gold leaves and lavender blue flowers. Other good ones are 'Alba' and 'White Spike' with white flowers. *Agastache rupestris* 'Sunset' or 'Apache Sunset', also called hummingbird or licorice mint, is an upright perennial with spikes of apricot or pinkish-orange trumpet-shaped flowers from midsummer to fall. It gets about 2 feet tall and is also drought tolerant. It has a delicate bluish-gray-green foliage. *Agastache mexicana* 'Red Fortune' also has foliage that smells like licorice. This 2-foot-tall plant has red flowers and is hardy in Zone 6 but might also survive in Zone 5.

This upright, bushy, woody perennial has 4-inch long fluffy blue spike flowers that bloom all summer and into fall. It is a cross between the native Agastache foeniculum *and* A. rugosa *from Asia. The hairy leaves have an anise-mint scent that can be used in drinks or cooking. Some agastache self-sows, but seedlings can easily be pulled from the ground. 'Blue Fortune', rated as one of the best new perennials in the last few years, is a fine substitute for* Veronica 'Sunny Border Blue', *which has a terrible problem with powdery mildew, a fungal disease. Agastache's fuzzy, blue flowers attract many pollinating insects.*

Other Common Names

Giant Blue Hyssop, Anise Hyssop

Bloom Period and Seasonal Color

Lavender blue flowers in summer.

Mature Height × Spread

3 ft. × 2 ft.

Amsonia
Amsonia spp.

Amsonia is a gorgeous, willowy, slightly woody plant with light blue, star-shaped flowers that cluster along the stems of this 30-inch-tall perennial in late spring and early summer. After that, the green foliage works as a worthy backdrop for other summer plants. In fall, the foliage turns a spectacular yellow or gold, extending amsonia's usefulness in the garden to three seasons. There are two types of amsonia—one with ferny foliage (A. hubrectii) and one with lance-shaped foliage (A.tabernaemontana). This under-used plant is native to the eastern United States and develops a large clump that, at maturity, serves as a summer shrub. It dies back to the ground in winter.

Other Common Names
Blue Star, Blue Willow, Arkansas Amsonia

Bloom Period and Seasonal Color
Blue flowers in early summer.

Mature Height × Spread
2 to 3 ft. × 2 to 3 ft.

When, Where, and How to Plant
Transplant container-grown plants in spring as soon as the soil can be worked. Amsonias do best in well-drained, average to rich, moist soil. The less sun, the more open the plant will be. Plant in holes dug three times as wide as the rootball or container they came in. Plant them the same depth they were growing in the container, or slightly higher. (See chapter introduction for more planting details.) Some people may have an allergic reaction to amsonia so consider wearing gloves and long sleeves when working with the plant. Growing amsonia from seed can be difficult, so opt for container-grown transplants.

Growing Tips
Amsonia does best in soil that is more moist than dry, although it tolerates the latter. Give it a good soaking during extended dry periods. However, if amsonia is grown in a soil that is too rich in organic matter or with a lot of fertilizer, it will get floppy. Poor to average soil is best for this plant. Fertilize according to instructions in chapter introduction.

Care and Maintenance
Amsonia can be divided in spring or fall. The plant may be cut to the ground in fall or late winter. Amsonia may re-bloom if its beanlike seedheads are removed. The lance-leaf variety may get a bit floppy after it blooms. Use hedge shears or snips and shape the plant in a rounded mound. The threadleaf amsonia probably won't need shaping. Amsonia is fairly free of pest and disease.

Companion Planting and Design
Amsonia's blue blooms make the plant a wonderful companion to more brightly colored flowers. Even when not in flower, amsonia's foliage serves as a nice backdrop to companion plants throughout the season. It works well with ornamental shrubs or larger perennials. Use in the middle or front of the bed.

We Recommend
The species of *Amsonia* is the most readily available. 'Blue Ice', believed to be a cross between *A. tabernaemontana* and an unknown *Amsonia*, gets about 14 inches tall.

When, Where, and How to Plant

Anemone does best when planted in spring as soon as the soil can be worked. A moist, well-drained spot is best, but anemone tolerates average soil. Japanese anemone will do best in light shade, though it tolerates full sun if given plenty of water. Plant anemone in holes dug three times as wide as the container it came in and at the same depth they were growing in the container. Space 12 to 24 inches apart. (See chapter introduction for more about planting.)

Growing Tips

Apply an all-purpose granular fertilizer around the plant in spring when new growth appears or spread a layer of compost around the plant in spring and fall. Water as needed, but anemone is not too picky, wet or dry.

Care and Maintenance

Japanese anemone may be aggressive and may multiply rapidly. It spreads by stolons but is very easy to pull up to be transplanted, given away, or composted. The pink varieties seem to be slightly more winter hardy; we suggest mulching white anemones with a light layer of leaves. Remove the layer as soon as new growth appears in spring. The seedheads turn into "cotton balls on sticks" that dangle above the ground all winter. Cut back to the ground in late winter or early spring.

Companion Planting and Design

Plant in the middle or at the back of the flower garden, or mix them in a bed of daffodils and daylilies for four seasons of interest.

We Recommend

'Alba' and 'Honorine Jobert' have single white flowers; 'September Charm', 'Bressingham Glow', 'Queen Charlotte', and 'Hadspen Abundance' have single pink or rose flowers; 'Prinz Heinrich' and 'Margarete' have double or semi-double rose or pink flowers. *Anemone tomentosa* (sometimes called *Anemone vitifolia* 'Robustissima') is one of the more aggressive types. This is a very hardy plant. *Anemone blanda* are often called Grecian windflowers. These are spring-flowering plants that grow from corms that are treated like bulbs.

Japanese anemone is a long-lasting flower that comes into bloom in late summer or early fall. For weeks, the single or double flowers float on spindly branches well above dark-green, maple-like foliage. Eventually the pink or white flower petals fall away, leaving the seedheads—brown balls which offer late fall interest. In winter, the seedheads turn white and look like cotton balls dangling on wiry stems. Anemone sometimes struggles to take hold, but once established in the garden it requires little care. Anemone is an aggressive grower, spreading by stolons; however, unwanted plants are easy to pull out if they get too rambunctious. Most anemones are planted from transplants or from corms which eventually develop a fibrous root system.

Other Common Name
Japanese Anemone

Bloom Period and Seasonal Color
Pink or white flowers from midsummer to fall.

Mature Height × Spread
3 ft. × 3 ft.

Aster

Aster spp.

The aster is another late bloomer that is indispensable in the perennial garden. Some varieties take on an almost shrub-like quality and are literally covered with daisy-like flowers that bloom for weeks. Flowers are 1 to 2½ inches in diameter. Aster is an easy-to-grow native plant, and it makes an excellent cut flower for indoor arrangements. Newer varieties are shorter and more resistant to mildew. Aster is a must in the late summer garden for butterflies and other nectar loving critters. Aster does best when planted or divided in spring, although it frequently is sold in fall with mums. If you purchase it in the fall, plant it in the ground as soon as possible and don't cut it back until the following spring when new growth sprouts from the base of the plant.

Other Common Names
Michaelmas Daisy, New England Aster, New York Aster

Bloom Period and Seasonal Color
White, violet, pink, or red flowers from late summer to fall.

Mature Height × Spread
2 to 7 ft. × 2 to 5 ft.

When, Where, and How to Plant
Aster is best planted or divided in spring as soon as the soil can be worked. It may be divided in early summer, too. Aster prefers well-drained soil; wet soil may cause the plant to rot. Plant aster in full sun or part shade locations. Space 12 to 24 inches apart. (See chapter introduction for more planting details.)

Growing Tips
Once established, aster tolerates drought but does better with regular watering. Apply an all-purpose granular fertilizer around the plant in spring when new growth appears or add a layer of compost to the bed in spring and fall.

Care and Maintenance
Aster can be pinched to keep it compact and to delay flowering. Stop pinching around July 4. Tall varieties may need to be staked. Dividing plants every two or three years will keep them vigorous. Because it is susceptible to mildew, provide good air circulation. Powdery mildew causes the lower leaves to turn white, then yellow-brown, before falling off.

Companion Planting and Design
Most asters are fairly tall, so plant them in the middle or the back of the perennial border. Some varieties may also be used as late-flowering shrubs in a shrub border. They mix well with other late bloomers, including Japanese anemone and sedum.

We Recommend
For *Aster novae-angliae* (New England aster), consider the following. 'Alma Potschke' grows about 3 feet tall and has salmon-pink flowers; 'Purple Dome' grows about 2 feet tall and has purple flowers; 'Harrington's Pink' is about 4 feet tall with pink flowers; 'September Ruby' is about 4 feet tall with pink-rose flowers; and 'Autumn Snow' has white flowers. For *Aster novi-belgii* (New York aster), consider: 'Crimson Brocade' grows about 4 feet tall and has semi-double, dark-red flowers; 'Professor Kippenburg' grows about 12 inches tall and has lavender-blue flowers. *Aster × frikartii* is a hybrid that is bushier and blooms longer than other asters, but it may be killed by winter in Zone 5. If you wait until spring to cut back the plant, it may winter over more successfully.

Black-Eyed Susan

Rudbeckia fulgida 'Goldsturm'

When, Where, and How to Plant

Transplant or divide in the fall or in spring as soon as the soil can be worked. *Rudbeckia* does best in well-drained soil in full sun. It tolerates light shade. Space 18 to 24 inches apart. Follow planting instructions as given in the chapter introduction.

Growing Tips

Apply an all-purpose granular fertilizer in spring when new growth appears or spread a layer of compost around the plant in spring and fall. Once established, black-eyed Susans can tolerate drought; however, the plant will appreciate an occasional, good soaking during long, dry spells.

Care and Maintenance

Spent flowers may be cut off to encourage more flowers, or they may be left on the plant to feed the birds and provide winter interest. If you are worried about the plants self-sowing, cut off the seedheads. Divide black-eyed Susan every three or four years.

Companion Planting and Design

This is a good plant for the middle of a perennial border. Some of these larger varieties may be too big and rough for small gardens. 'Goldsturm' planted with ornamental grasses and sedums makes a spectacular fall combo with great color, texture, and movement. The yellow also compliments the blue flowers on the shrub *Caryopteris*.

We Recommend

Besides 'Goldsturm', you might consider *Rudbeckia laciniata* and *R. speciosa*, called cutleaf coneflowers. These grow 6 feet tall and have slender yellow flower petals. 'Golden Glow' is a named variety that grows 6 to 8 feet tall. *Rudbeckia nitida* grows 2 to 3 feet tall with reflexed petals, more like the native coneflowers. 'Herbsonne' (also called 'Autumn Sun'), 'Goldquelle' and 'Gold Drop' have double flowers and range from 4 to 6 feet tall.

Black-eyed Susan and yellow coneflower are common names given to these yellow daisy-like flowers with dark centers. Some black-eyed Susans are annuals, and others are perennials. Rudbeckia fulgida 'Goldsturm' is a selection of the native plant often seen along highways, on the fringes of woods, and in meadows. This hybrid is very easy to grow and will frequently self-sow. Goldfinches and other birds like to sit on the cones and eat the seeds. The leaves are dark green, and the flowers get about 3 inches wide. Some seed varieties may have color variance. Most Rudbeckia bloom from July through September. 'Goldsturm' is one of the more compact black-eyed Susans.

Other Common Names

Yellow Coneflower, Brown-eyed Susan

Bloom Period and Seasonal Color

Yellow flowers from midsummer into fall.

Mature Height × Spread

2 ft. × 3 ft.

Blanket Flower
Gaillardia × grandifolia

Blanket flower has a daisy-like blossom that is usually bicolored but is sometimes all one color. It gets its name from its resemblance to the colorful blankets of Native Americans. This is a steady bloomer in the garden, especially when deadheaded, but birds do like to munch on the seedheads. Blanket flower makes excellent long-lasting cut flowers for indoor arrangements. There are annual Gaillardia plants, too. Annual or perennial, blanket flower is a must-have in butterfly and hummingbird gardens. Gaillardia is one of the plants in the fast lane. Because it is such a prolific bloomer, it tends to die after a few years if it's not divided.

Bloom Period and Seasonal Color
Red, yellow, or bronze flowers in summer.

Mature Height × Spread
1 to 3 ft. × 1 to 3 ft.

When, Where, and How to Plant
Transplants may be planted in the fall or in the spring as soon as the soil can be worked. Plants may be divided at these times, too. Blanket flower does best in well-drained soil in full sun. (Follow basic planting instructions in the chapter introduction.)

Growing Tips
Apply an all-purpose granular fertilizer in spring when new growth appears or spread a layer of compost around the plants in spring and fall. Blanket flowers are drought tolerant, so don't overwater them.

Care
Mulching is not recommended because blanket flower may develop mildew or rot at the crown. Clumps tend to die out in the center after a couple of years. Dig up the plant, chop off the side shoots and plant those that are growing vigorously, and discard the center. Sometimes plants may be killed by winter, especially if they are in wet soil. Lightly mulching plants in well-drained soil during the winter may be helpful. Blanket flowers are easy to start from seed, frequently blooming the first year.

Companion Planting and Design
Depending on the variety and size, it can be planted in the front or middle of the flower border. Blanket flower is a staple in the butterfly garden and for cut flowers. Its colors play nicely paired with the *Agastache* 'Blue Fortune'.

We Recommend
'Goblin' grows about 12 inches tall and has red flowers with yellow edges; 'Burgundy' has wine-red flowers; 'Yellow Queen' has yellow flowers. *Gaillardia aristata* is a native perennial variety. 'Monarch Strain', with variegated colors, is a good seed variety. *Gaillardia pulchella* is an annual blanket flower.

When, Where, and How to Plant

Plant in spring as soon as the soil can be worked. Boltonia does best in organically rich, well-drained soil. Boltonia prefers a sunny location. It tolerates light shade, but too much shade will make it leggy and cause fewer flowers. Space at least 3 feet apart. Water well and mulch, keeping mulch away from the crown. (See chapter introduction for more planting instructions.)

Growing Tips

Apply an all-purpose granular fertilizer in early spring when new growth appears or spread a layer of compost around the plant in spring and fall. Boltonia is drought tolerant; however, it will benefit from a good soaking in extended dry periods.

Care and Maintenance

Boltonia tends to be tall and a bit leggy, and some varieties will fall over later in the season from the weight of the flowers. To encourage bushiness, boltonia may be cut back by about $1/3$ to $1/2$ of its original height in late spring or early summer. Boltonia should be divided every three or four years to keep clumps a reasonable size. Division is best done in the spring. The plant grows as a clump and spreads quickly but is rarely invasive. Cut back to the ground when the plant is done blooming. It is fairly free of disease and pests.

Companion Planting and Design

Boltonia works well planted at the back of a perennial border or used as a specimen mixed with shrubs. Boltonia looks fabulous with Russian sage and late blooming perennials, including sedums, anemones, asters, and ornamental grasses. It also is a good companion to goldenrods (*Solidago*), especially 'Fireworks' which has gold flowers that play nicely off boltonia's yellow centers.

We Recommend

Boltonia asteroides 'Snowbank' is a good choice and is readily available. It grows 4 to 5 feet tall, has white flowers, and will bloom into October. 'Pink Beauty' grows 3 to 4 feet tall and has pink flowers. *Boltonia latisquama* is about 3 feet tall and has lavender flowers. 'Nana' is about $2^1/2$ feet tall and has pink flowers.

A lot of people mistake this plant for a Michaelmas daisy because the flowers are similar. Both are native plants, and they bloom about the same time in late summer. But boltonia's flowers are slightly smaller than those of most asters, sometimes only 1 inch in diameter. Boltonia is an easy-to-grow but under-used perennial that deserves a spot in most landscapes. White, pink, or lavender flowers literally cover the plant and last for several weeks in late summer into fall. It also is a long lasting cut flower for indoor arrangements. The popular and readily available cultivar 'Snowbank' was introduced by the New England Wildflower Society.

Other Common Name
False Aster

Bloom Period and Seasonal Color
White, pink, or lavender flowers in late summer and fall.

Mature Height × Spread
2 to 7 ft. × 2 to 7 ft.

Chrysanthemum

Chrysanthemum × morifolium

Chrysanthemum is a confusing, beautiful family of plants that used to include the summer-flowering Shasta daisy and the fall-flowering mum (C. morifolium). Plant experts have been trying to group them together in better ways, which is why Chrysanthemum is frequently listed under several different names, including Pyrethrum, Matricaria, Tanacetum, and Dendranthema. The garden mum category (C. × morifolium and Dendranthema × grandiflorum) includes hardy fall-blooming varieties and the florist types. Mums are at their peak in late summer through early fall when they form cushions of button- or daisy-like flowers that last through a frost or two. They make excellent cut flowers.

Other Common Names
Garden Mum, Hardy Mum

Bloom Period and Seasonal Color
Various colors from late summer into fall.

Mature Height × Spread
2 to 4 ft. × 2 to 4 ft.

When, Where, and How to Plant
The best time to plant fall-flowering garden mums is in spring. Plant mums in well-drained, fertile soil. If used in the perennial border, they should be planted toward the front. Space 1 to 3 feet apart and water them well and mulch. Most garden mums are sold in the fall, but they can be slow to establish roots at this time, as they are putting their energy into flowering. For best results, plant them as early as possible and keep them well watered into winter until the ground freezes. Potted, spring-blooming mums may re-bloom in the fall; however, these varieties are not reliably hardy in Indiana.

Growing Tips
Apply an all-purpose granular fertilizer in spring and summer or spread a layer of compost around the plants in spring or fall. Keep mums well watered but not wet. Mums are "photoperiod sensitive" plants and can be programmed to bloom just about any time of the year.

Care and Maintenance
Very tall varieties may need staking, but most can be pinched to a compact size. Pinch mums back to 6 to 8 inches tall at least twice before the middle of July to keep plants compact and full flowered. Pinching also delays flowering. Mums survive Indiana winters better if the spent flowers and stems are not cut back until early spring when new growth appears. The stems hold tiny bits of leaves and other debris which act as an insulator against the cold.

Companion Planting and Design
Mums provide the best show when planted in drifts or clusters of three or more. They also look lovely in the front of the perennial bed where their fall color can be seen and appreciated. Mums also mix nicely with other late blooming perennials, including boltonias and asters.

We Recommend
'Prophet' series hybrids are excellent fall bloomers, holding their flowers for several weeks. 'Cheyenne' hybrids have good cold tolerance. Other fall-blooming types are the free-flowering daisy-like *C. rubellum* 'Clara Curtis', with pink flowers and 'Mary Stoker', with cream-colored flowers.

Columbine

Aquilegia × *hybrida*

When, Where, and How to Plant
Container-grown transplants may be planted any time throughout the growing season as long as they are well watered. Columbine is usually transplanted or divided in the fall or in early spring as soon as the soil can be worked. Columbine prefers a well-drained, moist spot with average to better-than-average soil. Is does best with a bit of shade but will tolerate full sun. Space hybrids about 1 foot apart and water well. Mulch lightly if desired. Columbine is fairly easy to start from seeds but will only grow leaves the first year, blooming the second.

Growing Tips
Apply an all-purpose granular fertilizer in early spring when new growth appears or spread a layer of compost around the plants in spring and fall. Water when the top 2 inches of soil feels dry.

Care and Maintenance
Cut off spent flower stems to keep the plant looking tidy and to reduce the number of volunteers. Cut the plant to the ground in fall to reduce insects or disease. Columbine should be divided every two or three years to keep the plant vigorous. If it is not divided, it will become woody and have fewer flowers. Leafminers, aphids, and mildew can be bothersome to columbine, which is why good cultural habits are necessary. Some varieties will have a second flush of flowers in fall.

Companion Planting and Design
Columbine makes a good companion to many spring bulbs that bloom in late April and May. It is best in the middle of the border where other perennials can camouflage the sparseness at the base of the plant, and in rock gardens.

We Recommend
Named hybrids include 'McKana Giants', 'Spring Song', 'Nora Barlow', and 'Biedermeyer Strain'. *A. canadensis* is a native plant in eastern North America. It has red and yellow flowers and grows up to 30 inches tall. Although a bit rangy, it seems to mix well with other perennials that can hide its wildness. It also does very well at the edges of woody areas or in rock gardens.

Columbine has some of the most exquisite, incredibly detailed flowers you can imagine. Many have three or more colors or shadings, inch-long spurs, and double flowers. The botanical name Aquilegia means "like an eagle" and refers to the flower's spurs, which are said to resemble talons. If it has a drawback, it is that many of these flowers are short-lived, even the native A. canadensis. It can, however, survive in many gardens by self-sowing, sometimes where it is not wanted. It is easy to dig up and transplant, give away, or compost. Because it blooms in late spring and early summer, it is a good companion for bulbs that bloom then, too. Columbine is a cool-weather perennial that stops flowering when it gets hot.

Bloom Period and Seasonal Color
Various colors in spring and early summer.

Mature Height × Spread
2 to 4 ft. × 2 ft.

Coneflower
Echinacea purpurea

There are lots of reasons to like purple coneflower. It is very easy to grow and blooms for several weeks. It is an excellent cut flower, lasting a long time in the vase. It attracts butterflies, bees, and hummingbirds as well as American goldfinches, which feast on the seedheads, or cones, that rise from the center of this perennial. Purple coneflower is native to the eastern United States. Its foliage is a bit rough and a little hairy, but its dark-green color makes it an attractive foil in the perennial border. Its dried seedheads offer interest in the winter and provide food for birds. The flowers are 2 to 3 inches wide. Echinacea is thought to have curative powers and is frequently included in herb books. We like it so much we put it on the book cover!

Other Common Name
Purple Coneflower

Bloom Period and Seasonal Color
Pink or white blooms in midsummer.

Mature Height × Spread
2 to 3 ft. × 2 ft.

When, Where, and How to Plant
Container-grown transplants and divisions can be planted in the fall or in spring as soon as the soil can be worked. Plants may be divided at these times, too. Purple coneflower does well in well-drained, average soil. Its natural habitat is prairie and meadowland. Space about 2 feet apart and water well. Mulching is not necessary. It is easy to grow from seed, but it may not bloom the first two years. (See introduction for more on planting.)

Growing Tips
Purple coneflower may be a bit slow to come out of the ground in spring. When new growth appears, apply an all-purpose granular fertilizer or spread a layer of compost around the plant in spring and fall. Purple coneflower is fairly drought tolerant once established.

Care and Maintenance
You can cut the plant back in fall or wait until late winter or early spring. It spreads quickly but is not invasive. Purple coneflower is relatively free of pests or diseases.

Companion Planting and Design
Plant coneflower en masse or in the middle of the perennial border. The 2003 Artful Garden™ Design Selections, an education program of the Horticultural Society at the Indianapolis Museum of Art, recommended purple coneflower planted with the native ornamental grass, *Panicum* 'Heavy Metal', 'Dallas Blues', or 'Prairie Sky'. The Society rounds out the selection with Russian sage (*Perovskia*) and a mat of leadwort (*Ceratostigma plumbaginoides*) at the base for a particularly striking combination for late summer.

We Recommend
At about 3 feet tall, 'Bravado' or 'Magnus', a recent Perennial Plant of the Year, or the 2-foot tall 'Kim's Knee High' are good choices. 'Bright Star', a readily available variety, has lavender-purple flowers; 'White Swan' and 'White Lustre' have white petals, though they too are called *Echinacea purpurea*. *Echinacea pallida* is about 4 feet tall and native to Indiana. Its flowers are about the same size, but the petals are narrower and more delicate.

Coral Bells

Heuchera hybrids

When, Where, and How to Plant

Transplant container-grown plants in the fall or in spring as soon as the soil can be worked. Plants may be divided at those times, too. Coral bells requires well-drained soil. It is fairly easy to start from seed but will not bloom the first year or two. Coral bells tolerates full sun but does much better when protected from afternoon and west sun. (See chapter introduction for more on planting.)

Growing Tips

Apply an all-purpose granular fertilizer in spring when new growth appears or spread a layer of compost around the plants in spring and fall. Coral bells doesn't like it too wet (they will rot) or too dry. Err more on the dry side.

Care and Maintenance

The cold winter soil may heave them from the ground. If that happens, just press the plant back into the ground as soon as you can in spring. Coral bells also develops the doughnut effect, where the center of the plant dies out and all of the new growth is ringed around the edges. Lift the plant and cut off the new growth to transplant. Discard the center of the plant. Coral bells is almost an evergreen, frequently retaining its foliage throughout winter. Trim off winter damaged leaves in spring. It is relatively free of pests and diseases.

Companion Planting and Design

The heucheras with purple foliage are excellent planted en masse as a ground cover, or they work well toward the middle of the garden bed, where the flowers can dangle above other perennials.

We Recommend

Select for foliage and flower color. 'Geisha Fan', 'Cherries Jubilee', and ''Chocolate Ruffles' are standouts. The species has the traditional coral bells. *Heucherella* is a cross between *Heuchera* and foam flower (*Tiarella*). The flowers are fuzzy like foam flowers, but the plants are so new that their winter hardiness has not been fully tested.

Hybridizers don't think we have enough purple-leaved coral bells, and many of them are developing more and more cultivars each year. Unfortunately, although many of the newer cultivars have breathtaking foliage, they lack the showy flowers that give coral bells its name. However, their foliage is fantastic in the garden, blending nicely with other perennials and annuals. Whichever cultivars you select, coral bells will reward you with many weeks of delicate stalks filled with blooms held above the scalloped foliage. The flowers also last a very long time when used for indoor arrangements. Most of the time, the foliage holds its color throughout winter, adding to the attributes of this garden-worthy plant.

Bloom Period and Seasonal Color

Red, white, green, or pink flowers in spring through summer.

Mature Height × Spread

2 ft. × 1 ft.

Daylily
Hemerocallis spp. and hybrids

Daylilies may be the easiest perennial to grow. They burst forth in flower from June through early August, depending on the variety and the amount of light. The medium-green strap-like leaves appear first, followed by stalks, called scapes, with flowers at the top. Each trumpet-like flower lasts only a day, thus the name. Other flowers on the stalk will bloom for days after. Some of the newer varieties, such as 'Stella de Oro', bloom intermittently throughout the summer. Daylilies grow from rhizomes. They are not the same plant as lilies (Lilium), which are bulbs (see the Bulbs chapter). Daylilies come in many colors, and several are fragrant. The flowers can be simple, ruffled, or fringed; the 1- to 3-inch-long blossoms are edible.

Bloom Period and Seasonal Color
Various colors in summer.

Mature Height × Spread
1 to 5 ft. × 3 ft.

When, Where, and How to Plant
Daylilies can be planted almost any time during the growing season. Most are transplanted or divided in the fall or in spring as soon as the soil can be worked. Daylilies will bloom in considerable shade, but the flowers will be smaller and there will be fewer of them. Daylilies do well in a wide range of soil conditions. Once established, they will tolerate drought. Space them about 2 feet apart—more for larger varieties. Water well and spread a thin layer of mulch. They seem to thrive in any soil and condition, except in those that are too wet. (See chapter introduction for more on planting.)

Growing Tips
Apply an all-purpose granular fertilizer in spring when new growth breaks ground or spread a layer of compost around the plants in spring and fall. Daylilies benefit from regularly watering, but it is not necessary. They are tough plants and can take it fairly dry without any problem.

Care and Maintenance
Cut back stems and leaves when the plants start to look spotted or brown. They have few, if any, pests. Daylilies can be left undisturbed for years, though the number of flowers may decline. Divide every four to six years to keep them vigorous. Daylilies spread fairly rapidly but are not invasive.

Companion Planting and Design
Plant daylilies in the perennial border according to their size or set them apart in their own bed for a spectacular show. Daylilies make excellent cut flowers. For arrangements, cut stems that have several buds—some close to opening and some just showing color. Snipping the spent flowers off the stem will keep the daylily flowering in the vase. Daylilies are excellent companions for spring flowering bulbs. As the daylilies grow, they camouflage bulbs' ripening foliage.

We Recommend
Choose varieties according to height, color, when they flower, and for how long. All-America Daylily Selections are excellent choices, especially for beginners. *Hemerocallis lilio-asphodelus* and *H. fulva* are the old-fashioned daylilies frequently found growing by roadsides or in clumps on the old family farm.

Foam Flower
Tiarella spp.

When, Where, and How to Plant
Container-grown transplants may be planted in the fall or in early spring as soon as the ground can be worked. Plants may be divided at those times, too. Space foam flower about 12 inches apart. Water well. Mulch lightly with chopped leaves or shredded bark. Once the plants are established, mulching won't be necessary. (See chapter introduction for more on planting.)

Growing Tips
Apply an all-purpose granular fertilizer in early spring when new growth begins or spread a layer of compost or other organic material such as chopped leaves around the plants in spring and fall. Water as needed to keep the soil moist. Foam flower will go dormant in hot weather, especially if not kept moist.

Care and Maintenance
Dead flowers can be removed, called deadheading, to make the plants look tidy, or they can be left to weather naturally. If planted in partial sun, the leaves of foam flower may turn a bronzy or reddish purple, especially in fall. Foam flower is relatively free of pests and diseases.

Companion Planting and Design
Foam flower is a woodland plant, so it does best in moist, humusy soil. It can be planted around the bases of trees or shrubs, or in a shady moist spot in the front of the flower border. *Tiarella cordifolia* spreads by stolons. Its roots are at ground level or slightly below ground level and quickly form a mat, or colony, of plants. *Tiarella wherryi* is more of a clump grower and is considered less aggressive. Its flowers have pinkish tips. Foam flowers are excellent companions with spring flowering bulbs.

We Recommend
'Ninja', 'Brandywine', 'Martha Oliver', or 'Tiger Stripe' are all winners.

This is a charming, little plant that looks more fragile than it is and makes an excellent deciduous flowering ground cover for moist, woodsy areas. Foam flower has maple-like leaves and spikes of star-like white or purple-pink flowers. Some foam flowers spread by surface (or just-below-surface) stolons, or runners, and others grow in clumps. Foam flower is not used nearly enough in the Hoosier landscape. Good moisture will keep foam flower from going dormant in the summer heat. Plant breeders have been improving its ability to withstand summer temperatures. They also have developed many cultivars with attractive foliage and reddish or chocolate colored veins. Its low growth habit makes it an excellent companion with spring flowering bulbs.

Bloom Period and Seasonal Color
White or pink flowers in mid- to late spring.

Mature Height × Spread
6 to 12 in. × 12 in.

Fringed Bleeding Heart
Dicentra eximia

This bleeding heart is native to the eastern United States with flowers in the shape of hearts that look like they are bleeding. It is not nearly as gruesome as it sounds. In fact, the flowers are beautiful, and they will bloom almost all summer, unlike its larger, more showy cousin, the old-fashioned bleeding heart (Dicentra spectabilis). D. spectabilis comes from Asia and has much larger flowers, but it goes dormant by midsummer. D. formosa is native to the Western United States. Most Dicentra species have gray-green foliage that is attractive regardless of the flowers. Fringed bleeding heart self-sows a bit but is easy to dig out for transplants, to give away, or to toss into the compost pile. It also is deer resistant.

Other Common Name
Turkey Corn

Bloom Period and Seasonal Color
Pink or white flowers in spring through fall.

Mature Height × Spread
1 ft. × 1 ft.

When, Where, and How to Plant
Transplant container-grown plants in spring as soon as the ground can be worked. Fringed bleeding heart can be divided then, too. Plant in a moist, well-drained area protected from hot sun from noon on. It can be started with seed sown directly in the soil outdoors in late summer. (See chapter introduction for more about planting.)

Growing Tips
Apply an all-purpose granular fertilizer in spring when the leaves break ground or ring the plant with compost in spring and fall. Don't let fringed bleeding heart dry out; water as needed to keep the soil moist. If it dries out, it will go dormant but should return the following spring.

Care and Maintenance
Fringed bleeding heart has few pests and is a very low maintenance plant. Cut it back to the ground in winter when the tops have been killed by frosts. Sometimes fringed bleeding heart is semi-ever-green, keeping its gray-green foliage in winter if the weather is not too severe.

Companion Planting and Design
Fringed bleeding heart works well as a ground cover, interplanted with spring flowering bulbs. It also is a great companion plant for *Hosta*, lung-wort, and other bold-leaf, shade-loving plants.

We Recommend
Try the species, or 'Luxuriant', which is believed to be a cross between *D. eximia* and *D. formosa*. 'King of Hearts' is a new introduction that is a cross between *D. eximia* and *D. spectabilis*. The plant gets closer to 2 feet tall, and the flowers are larger and redder than the native. 'Adrian Bloom' also is garden worthy. *D. spectabilis* is wonderful in the spring garden. It has pink flowers and gets about 3 feet tall and wide. 'Alba' is a white-flowering version.

When, Where, and How to Plant

Plant transplants or divide hardy begonia in spring as soon as the ground can be worked. It prefers a moist, well-drained spot in part shade. Protect the plant from south and west sun. Hardy begonia is fairly shallow rooted, and the fleshy stems will break easily, so locate the plant where it won't be trampled. It can be planted toward the front of the perennial border or under deciduous or evergreen shrubs. More planting information can be found in the chapter introduction.

Growing Tips

Apply an all-purpose granular fertilizer in spring when the leaves break ground or ring the plant with compost in spring and fall. Because it blooms in the shade, supplemental watering may not be necessary in the fall when soil moisture is more consistent. If hardy begonia gets too wet, it will rot. Water when the top two inches of soil feels dry to the touch.

Care and Maintenance

Hardy begonia is a very low maintenance plant. Cut it back to the ground when foliage is killed by frost. It is fairly free of insects or diseases; however, soil that is too wet will cause the plant to rot.

Companion Planting and Design

Hardy begonia is beautiful planted beneath dogwoods, which turn a bronzy red in fall. The back of the begonia's wing-shaped foliage is more beautiful than the front because of the red veins, so place the plant where you can appreciate them or where the leaves will be backlit by the sun.

We Recommend

Try the species and the white flowering 'Alba'.

The first time I saw this plant was in the shade garden at the Indianapolis Museum of Art. It was late summer, and the hardy begonias were in full bloom with dozens of pink flowers dangling above spectacular pale green foliage marked by maroon veins on the undersides. The gardeners at the IMA said they do nothing special to this delicate looking plants—no extra mulching or babying—and they come back every year. They've been in my garden for more than five years. With each season they become larger and more beautiful. These flowers have a long bloom period, giving you more time to enjoy them outdoors, but don't forget to cut some for indoor arrangements. —J.E.M.S

Bloom Period and Seasonal Color
Pink and white flowers in late summer.

Mature Height × Spread
2 ft. × 2 ft.

Hardy Geranium

Geranium spp.

This is the true geranium. The geranium we use as a summer-flowering annual or houseplant is called Pelargonium *and is discussed in the Annuals chapter of this book. The true* Geranium *noted here is a hardy perennial that flowers in early spring and summer with flushes of color into fall, depending on the variety. This is a rewarding, easy-to-grow but under-used plant that requires minimal care. It gets its name from the long, beak-like seeds (shaped like a cranesbill) that develop after the flowers fade. The flowers are about 1 inch wide; some varieties are double. Most geraniums grow in mounds, but some have a sprawling habit. The foliage frequently turns red, bronze, or dark pink in fall. All these attributes make the hardy geranium a fine candidate for an unusual ground cover.*

Other Common Names
Cranesbill, Big Root Geranium

Bloom Period and Seasonal Color
Various colors in spring and summer.

Mature Height × Spread
12 to 15 in. × 1 to 2 ft.

When, Where, and How to Plant
Container-grown transplants may be planted in the fall or in spring as soon as the soil can be worked. Plants may be divided in spring, too. Plant geraniums in rich, well-drained soil. They do best when shaded from afternoon sun. Space them 18 to 24 inches apart, depending on the variety. Water them well. Mulch lightly if desired. (See chapter introduction for more on planting.)

Growing Tips
Apply an all-purpose granular fertilizer in early spring when new growth appears or spread a layer of compost around the plants in spring and fall. Hardy geraniums prefer an evenly moist, well-drained soil, but once established, they are tolerant of dry spots.

Care and Maintenance
Cut back hardy geraniums after their first bloom to make the plants more compact, to tidy them up, and to encourage flowers later. Cranesbill geranium seldom has to be divided, though doing so is an easy way to get more plants. Geranium is almost evergreen, frequently retaining its foliage through winter. Trim off winter damaged foliage in spring. Hardy geraniums are relatively free of pest and disease.

Companion Planting and Design
Even when it's not flowering, geranium foliage is attractive in the front of the flower border. Many cultivars turn red or purple in fall. Hardy geraniums work well with spring-flowering bulbs, too. The foliage camouflages the ripening leaves of the bulbs.

We Recommend
Select for color and bloom time. *G. himalayense* × *G. pratense* 'Johnson's Blue' forms a 12-inch-tall clump that blooms with violet-blue flowers; 'Plenum' grows 2 feet tall and has large blue-violet flowers. *G. macrorrhizum*, or big-root geranium, is a low-growing plant that can be used as a ground cover for dry, shady spots. The native *G. maculatum* is a trailing type with blue flowers. *G. sanguineum* is called bloody cranesbill. It has pink or magenta flowers. *G. endressii* 'Wargrave Pink' grows up to 18 inches tall and 30 inches wide, blooming with blush-pink flowers during summer to fall.

Hosta
Hosta spp.

When, Where, and How to Plant

Container-grown transplants may be planted in spring or in fall. Hosta prefers well-drained, rich organic soil in shady or semi-shady locations. Hostas with gold leaves need more sun for intense color. Place *Hosta* according to the space requirements of the variety. Keep mulch away from the crown of the plant. (See chapter introduction for more on planting.)

Growing Tips

It's not necessary to divide hosta, but dividing will provide more plants. Apply an all-purpose granular fertilizer in spring when new growth appears or spread a layer of compost around the plants in spring and fall. Watering *Hosta* is more important the first two or three years, or until the plant gets established. Once established, water when the top 2 or 3 inches of soil feels dry to the touch.

Care and Maintenance

Hosta is a slug's favorite treat. Many gardeners prefer not to use wood mulch around hostas because it increases the presence of slugs. Your local garden center or Extension Agent should be able to suggest controls—there are many. Cut back hosta after it's been killed by frost. Plants can be divided any time as long as they are kept well watered. Flower stalks may be cut back after the blooms fade.

Companion Planting and Design

Hosta is best planted in clusters or masses; however, some are excellent specimens for perennial border, especially those that have unusual colors or leaves. Plant fragrant ones where you will smell them, day or night.

We Recommend

There are thousands of *Hosta* cultivars, and new ones are being introduced all the time. Select according to size, foliage color or texture, flowering period and color, or fragrance. Hosta leaves range from the size of your thumb to 4 feet wide or more. Hostas also have different shapes. Some are mound growers and others have a vase, or upright, shape. Hostas are early, mid-, and late season bloomers. August-blooming hostas are among the most fragrant plants in the garden. Among the best in that group are species *H. plantaginea* 'Aphrodite', 'Honeybells', and 'Royal Standard'.

Hosta is an easy-to-grow perennial that was made for flowering in a shady summer garden. Small trumpet-like flowers form along stalks, called scapes, that dangle above the plant, which is primarily grown for its foliage. Some gardeners don't care for the flowers at all, and they quickly cut them off. Many hostas are fragrant, however, especially H. plantaginea, which makes a nice addition to a cutflower arrangement. Hosta is a clump-growing plant that comes in hundreds of varieties. The leaves can be broad or narrow, solid-colored to bi- and tricolored, wrinkled or smooth. The plant tends to be wider than it is tall.

Other Common Names
Funkia, Plantain Lily

Bloom Period and Seasonal Color
White or lavender flowers in summer.

Mature Height × Spread
$1/4$ to 4 ft. × $1/2$ to 5 ft.

Indian Pink

Spigelia marilandica

Indian Pink is a show stopper when it blooms in early summer. Hardly anyone believes it is a native plant because it is so beautiful and unusual. Its foliage is dark, glossy green. Indian pink usually has its greatest flush of flowers in June, with intermittent blooms the rest of summer. The 2-inch-long tubular, star-shaped flowers are red with yellow inserts, and they appear along the stems of the plant. The flowers earn it high marks in attracting butterflies. Native Americans used the root in ceremonies and rituals and to treat for worms. It is a little slow to break ground in spring. The plant may be hard to find in garden centers; however, specialists in native plants, including many mail-order nurseries, carry Indian pink.

Other Common Names
Pinkroot, Wormgrass

Bloom Period and Seasonal Color
Red and yellow flowers in early summer.

Mature Height × Spread
2 ft. × 2 ft.

When, Where, and How to Plant

Plant transplants or divide in spring as soon as the soil can be worked. Indian pink is a woodland plant, so it prefers a moist, rich, organic bed with good drainage. Its size, leaf shape, and cultural requirements make it a nice companion with hostas, lungwort, and other shade-loving perennials. It is a little late to break ground in spring, so be patient. More planting instructions can be found in the chapter introduction.

Growing Tips

Apply an all-purpose granular fertilizer in spring when the leaves break ground or ring the plant with compost in spring and fall. Water as needed to keep the soil moist.

Care and Maintenance

Indian pink requires minimal care. Although it's easy to start from seed, gathering it can be a bit of a challenge, which is one of the reasons Indian pink is uncommon in the garden. It is hard to detect when seedpods have matured. When they're ripe, the pods explode, sending seeds several feet away. It is relatively free of pests and diseases. Cut it back to the ground in fall.

Companion Planting and Design

Indian pink is at home in the perennial bed, usually in the middle or toward the front. The colors compliment the native columbine (*Aquilegia canadensis*) but also blend nicely with other early summer blooming perennials, such as lady's mantle (*Achemilla mollis*), salvias, and geraniums.

We Recommend

Only the species is available.

When, Where, and How to Plant

Container-grown transplants may be planted in spring or fall. Iris does best in full sun with afternoon shade. Japanese iris tolerates more shade and may need more protection in winter. Siberian iris also tolerates some shade and is very hardy. Japanese and Siberian iris prefer wetter soil and can be used in damp places in the landscape or around the margins of ponds. However, bearded iris needs well-drained soil that is more dry than wet. Iris rhizomes grow in one direction, so place the green leafy part the way you want them to grow. Barely cover with soil. The rhizomes should grow right along the soil surface. If planted too deep, they will rot. Space 10 to 24 inches apart.

Growing Tips

Apply an all-purpose granular fertilizer in spring when new growth appears or spread a layer of compost around the plants in spring and fall. Water as needed according to the type of iris planted. Ask your local garden center about the needs of your *Iris* choice.

Care and Maintenance

Deadhead Japanese iris for continued bloom. Bearded iris are susceptible to iris borers or fungal infections, so watch for wilting plants or leaves with streaks. Keeping the bearded iris bed clean of debris is an important control. Trim iris to the ground in late summer or fall and discard the leaves. Divide bearded iris in spring or fall. Siberian and Japanese iris should be divided every three or four years.

Companion Planting and Design

Bearded iris often does best when planted in its own bed without other types of plants. Japanese and Siberian irises are clump growers, and they work much better in perennial beds.

We Recommend

There are many varieties of each type from which to choose. Select according to color, height, and time of bloom. *Iris cristata* is a native dwarf crested iris that grows about 8 inches tall and has a 2-foot spread. It is a good woodland plant. Other irises we like include *Iris reticulata* (see the Bulbs chapter) and *Iris virginica* (see the Water Gardens chapter).

Three different kinds of plants are discussed here under the botanical name Iris, and each is worthy of inclusion in the garden. The most common iris has the most names: flags, bearded iris, and German iris are the familiar, old-fashion plants with blue-green sword leaves and stalks of flowers. Their flowers have an upright portion called the standard and a lower part called the fall, or beard. Most of these irises bloom in late spring and early summer, but some rebloom in fall. Iris ensata is the Japanese iris. It has flat-topped flowers that bloom in early to midsummer, and it grows in a clump. Iris sibirica is the Siberian iris, which has a flower even more delicate than that of the Japanese varieties. It also grows in a clump and blooms in late spring and early summer.

Other Common Name
Flag

Bloom Period and Seasonal Color
Various colors in spring and summer.

Mature Height × Spread
2 ft. × 2 ft., but varies according to type

Lady's Mantle
Alchemilla mollis

Lady's mantle is an under-used plant that is very easy to grow and serves many purposes in the garden. The flowers on this mound-shaped plant are chartreuse, blooming in spring just in time to complement flowering bulbs. The foliage is a medium green with scalloped edges and is shaped like a lady's mantle. The leaves are hairy and collect droplets of water that glisten like jewels in the morning light. This plant is rich in folklore. One legend is that garden fairies like to drink the water from the leaves. Another has it that the droplets hold the secrets to eternal youth. Still another says the leaves were used to adorn the Virgin Mary. It's not folklore that this plant is a worthy addition to the Hoosier garden.

Bloom Period and Seasonal Color
Chartreuse flowers in spring and early summer.

Mature Height × Spread
18 in. × 24 in.

When, Where, and How to Plant
Transplant or divide lady's mantle in the fall or in spring as soon as the ground can be worked. Lady's mantle prefers rich, well-drained, moist soil in part sun or shade. It tolerates average soil. If the soil gets too dry in summer, the plants may turn brown and go dormant until cooler temperatures arrive in fall.

Growing Tips
Apply an all-purpose granular fertilizer in spring when new growth appears or ring the plant with compost in spring and fall. Once established, lady's mantle tolerates drought but will benefit from a good soaking during extended dry periods.

Care and Maintenance
Lady's mantle can self-sow but not so bad that it would be considered invasive. Transplant the seedlings, give them away, or toss them into the compost heap. If the plant starts to look bad in late summer, cut it back. Cutting too close to the crown may kill the plant. The plant will likely send up new leaves, which will be almost semi-evergreen, persisting into fall, if the weather is not too severe. Flowers can be cut for indoor arrangements or dried for everlastings.

Companion Planting and Design
Lady's mantle is a worthy companion to spring-flowering bulbs, especially red tulips and blue hyacinths. In early summer, pair lady's mantle with blue flowering Siberian iris. In summer, the foliage blends nicely in the perennial bed. Plant toward the front of the perennial border where the flowers form a froth of chartreuse above the lovely scalloped foliage.

We Recommend
We like the species, or try 'Thriller' with its gray-green leaves and star-shaped flowers. 'Auslese' is about 18 inches tall and is a bit tidier than the species.

When, Where, and How to Plant

Transplant from containers or divide lungwort in the fall or in spring as soon as the soil can be worked. Lungwort prefers a well-drained spot that is rich in organic matter. It tolerates average soil. If it stays too wet, it will rot. (See chapter introduction for more about planting.)

Growing Tips

Apply an all-purpose granular fertilizer in spring when new growth appears or ring the plant with compost in spring and fall. Water as needed to keep the soil moist. If the soil gets too dry, the plant will wither and possibly go dormant.

Care and Maintenance

Lungwort used to have a problem with powdery mildew; however, many of the newer cultivars are resistant to the fungus. Many are semi-evergreen in Indiana, retaining their foliage through winter if not too severe. Cut back to the ground when the plant starts to look bad. Remove winter damaged foliage in spring.

Companion Planting and Design

Lungwort is prized for its early blooming flowers and for its ornamental foliage that stays in the garden all summer. Lungwort can be planted en masse, or it can edge the front of a perennial bed in the shade. It can be planted with hostas, ferns, or bleeding hearts, or under evergreen or deciduous shrubs.

We Recommend

Select for pattern of foliage, flower color, and resistance to mildew. 'Trevi Fountain' has cobalt blue flowers in spring and spotted foliage that looks great all summer with no mildew. The Chicago Botanic Garden trialed *Pulmonaria* a few years ago and here are the top winners: 'Mrs. Moon', 'Benediction', 'Glacier', 'Little Star', 'Merlin', 'Mrs. Kittle', 'Paul Arden', 'Pierre's Pure Pink', 'Roy Davidson', 'Sissinghurst White', 'Smoky Blue', 'Tim's Silver', 'Blaues Meer', 'Bertram Anderson', 'White Wings', 'Bowles Red', 'Bielefeld Pink', and 'Dora Bielefeld'.

The name lungwort may not sound very attractive, but the plant is. The foliage rivals Hosta when it comes to the shade garden, although lungwort's flowers are not as showy. However, lungwort is usually not bothered by slugs, which love hostas. Lungwort foliage also brings silver to the garden, a great light-catching and corner-brightening color. The hairy leaves may be solid green, silvery green, or splotched or dotted with silver, depending on the cultivar. There's variability in the size and shape of the leaves, too, although none are very large. Some are long and narrow, while others are more rounded with pointed tips. Lungwort provides a long bloom period in a handful of colors.

Bloom Period and Seasonal Color

Blues, pinks, violets, and white in spring.

Mature Height × Spread

12 in. × 12 in.

135

Peony
Paeonia lactiflora

Peony's ability to tolerate a wide variety of soils and still produce a beautiful fragrant flower proves why it was chosen the State Flower of Indiana, despite coming from Asia. The large, luscious flowers grown in most gardens were developed for the cut-flower trade, which is why it tends to be top heavy and fall over. Newer varieties, however, are more garden worthy, with stronger stems and smaller (but just as showy) fragrant flowers. Peony's propensity for attracting small red ants is well known, to the point that some believe there have to be ants present in order for the flowers to open, which is not true. Ants come to enjoy sweet honeydew or sap, left by aphids or other insects. Peony is a fine, fragrant cut flower, ants or no.

Bloom Period and Seasonal Color
Various flowers in late spring to early summer.

Mature Height × Spread
30 in. × 30 in.

When, Where, and How to Plant
Plant container-grown plants in spring. Transplant peony in the garden in late summer or early fall; peonies divided in spring will not flower that year. A well-drained rich spot is best, but peony tolerates average soil. Check the crown of the peony for next year's buds—bright red nubs called "eyes." When planting the woody peony crowns, dig a hole approximately 12 inches wide and deep. Mix the original soil with at least $1/3$ organic matter before refilling the hole to within 2 inches of the top. Plant so the eyes are no deeper than 2 inches below the surface. If planted too deep, the peony may never bloom.

Growing Tips
Apply an all-purpose granular fertilizer in spring when the leaves break ground or ring the plants with compost in spring and fall. Once established, peonies are fairly drought tolerant.

Care and Maintenance
When stems are about 6 inches tall, stake the peonies with a plant ring, bamboo stakes, a basket, or other support. As the buds begin to swell, the flower stems become top-heavy and easily fall over. If peonies are in full bloom and a storm is brewing, quickly cut as many as you can, as rain will flatten the stems. Deadhead spent flowers. As peonies age, most of the flower stems are produced on the edge of a circular ring with small amounts of foliage (or no foliage) in the center. When the clumps get to this stage, divide them in late September or early October.

Companion Planting and Design
Plant them in the middle to the rear of the garden so that their aging foliage will be hidden by other plants. Because of their huge blossoms and short flowering period, many gardeners give peonies their own flower bed.

We Recommend
Two good choices are 'Festiva Maxima', which has double white petals with good fragrance, and 'Sarah Bernhardt', which has large double pink blossoms. 'Cheddar Charm' is white with a large yellow center; 'Cameleon' is a showy pink single; and 'Circus Circus' is a pretty pink semi-double.

When, Where, and How to Plant

The best time to plant garden phlox is in early fall so the roots will have a chance to establish themselves. The second-best time is in early spring before the leaves emerge on the trees. Garden phlox grows best in full sun in moist but well-drained soil that has been enriched with organic matter. (See chapter introduction for more about planting.)

Growing Tips

Apply an all-purpose granular fertilizer in spring and lightly scrape the soil to work it in, or ring the plant with a layer of compost in spring and fall. Water deeply once a week, keeping the leaves as dry as possible. Keep the plant well mulched.

Care and Maintenance

Garden phlox is slightly more demanding than many perennials. As the new foliage begins to grow, thin each clump by removing all but four to six of the sturdiest stems. This will encourage larger flowers, and more importantly, it will improve air circulation. Good circulation discourages powdery mildew, which can completely defoliate plants by the end of summer. Divide phlox every two or three years. Use a sharp spade or shovel to slice through the crown, creating clumps of four to six stems. Keep the dead flowers pruned to encourage more blooms. If mildew plagues your *Phlox paniculata*, it is best to replace it with a mildew-resistant variety of *Phlox maculata* such as 'Miss Lingard'.

Companion Planting and Design

Phlox is at home in the cutting garden or a mixed border. *Phlox subulata*, or creeping phlox, is the low-growing spring-blooming species that has brilliant flowers of white, pink, or lavender. These are excellent for a sunny bank or rock garden and are found everywhere in country gardens. If you have a shadier location, plant woodland phlox, *Phlox divaricata*.

We Recommend

'David' is a mildew-resistant white phlox that was named the Perennial Plant of the Year in 2002. 'Katherine' rated well in trials at the Chicago Botanic Garden. Others with high marks in the trials are 'Bright Eyes' and 'Franz Schubert'—one of the finest white phlox around.

'Phlox' describes many popular garden flowers, including woodland phlox (Phlox divaricata), creeping phlox (Phlox subulata), annual phlox (Phlox drummondii), and garden phlox (Phlox paniculata). Native to North America, garden phlox is an old-fashioned mainstay of the perennial border. Garden phlox grows in spreading clumps with many upright stems. Prized for its fragrant cloud-like blooms, the clusters of tubular flowers at the tips of three-foot stems are a favorite of hummingbirds. It is among the earliest to grow in the spring. Although somewhat finicky and susceptible to powdery mildew, the extra effort required to care for this plant is worth it.

Other Common Names
Garden Phlox, Summer Phlox

Bloom Period and Seasonal Color
Various colors in summer.

Mature Height × Spread
3 ft. × 2 ft.

Pincushion Flower

Scabiosa caucasica

The tightly packed stamens in the center of the round Scabiosa flowers resemble pins in a pincushion and give this plant its common name. Long, blue, fringed petals surround the "pins" and help make up the "cushion." Dark-green leaves are quick to come back each spring, and by summer, pincushion flower sends forth numerous wiry stalks tipped with flowers in shades of blue or white. The original species bloomed a deep shade of blue, almost purple, and because of the dark color was called 'Mournful Widow'. Modern versions of pincushion flower are anything but mournful. When deadheaded, its cheery blooms repeat all summer long, and the fresh blossoms make excellent cut flowers. We've seen this plant bloom from April until November.

Other Common Name
Scabiosa

Bloom Period and Seasonal Color
Blue flowers from spring to fall.

Mature Height × Spread
18 in. × 18 in.

When, Where, and How to Plant

Transplant pincushion flower in early spring as soon as the soil can be worked. The second-best time to plant or transplant is in late summer or early fall. It grows best in moist, well-drained, rich soil. It will produce more flowers in full sun, but it does fine in very light shade.

Growing Tips

Apply an all-purpose granular fertilizer in spring when new growth appears or ring the plant with compost in spring and fall. Water as needed to keep the soil moist. However, too much water will cause the plant to rot, which is why drainage is key.

Care and Maintenance

Pincushion flower is virtually maintenance free when it has good drainage. Deadhead the flowers to encourage a long season of blooms. Divide it every three or four years, or it will gradually decline. Using a sharp spade or shovel, slice through the crown of each plant early in the spring in two or three sections, and transplant. Pincushion flower is not a long-lived perennial and usually dies in three or four years if not divided.

Companion Planting and Design

These blooms are not as dense as those of other perennials, so plant pincushion flowers in groups of three for greater impact. Overall, pincushion flower is a short plant that looks best when planted in the front of the flower garden as an edger. It looks especially attractive near plants that have silver, white, and blue hues. For an excellent combination, plant pincushion flower near Russian sage, agastache, dusty miller, or dwarf fountain grass.

We Recommend

'Butterfly Blue' was named the Perennial Plant of the Year in 2000. Other good ones are 'Blue Perfection', a profuse bloomer with fringed petals and grows to 2 feet; 'Bressingham White' has large flowers on stems up to 3 feet tall; 'House Hybrids' have numerous blooms of blue and white, all on the same plant.

Dianthus gratianopolitanus 'Bath's Pink'

When, Where, and How to Plant
Plant transplants in the fall or in spring as soon as the soil can be worked. Select a spot that has good drainage. Don't plant pinks too deep. They actually seem to survive barely touching the soil. Loosen the soil in the planting area, make a shallow indentation, and place the transplant in the ground, gently pushing the soil to the edge of the plant. This plant looks a lot more delicate than it is. It's toughness makes it an ideal candidate for hot, sunny, dry spots in the landscape.

Growing Tips
Apply an all-purpose granular fertilizer around 'Bath's Pink' when new growth begins in spring, or ring the plant with compost in spring and fall. 'Bath's Pink' is fairly drought tolerant once established.

Care and Maintenance
Removing the spent flowers, called deadheading, prolongs the bloom period. Pinks will develop crown rot if planted where the drainage is poor or the soil stays too wet, especially in winter. If it gets too large, break off portions of the plant and transplant elsewhere.

Companion Planting and Design
'Bath's Pink' works well in the front of the garden bed or to soften a hard corner in the landscape. It blooms in late spring to early summer, so it can be used with spring-flowering bulbs. Because it is fragrant, plant it where the scent can be enjoyed. Pinks also work well in rock gardens or along pathways, where it can creep around stepping stones.

We Recommend
Besides 'Bath's Pink', consider 'Firewitch', 'Oakington', 'Spotty', or 'Tiny Rubies'.

From its spicy flowers in spring to its evergreen mat in winter, 'Bath's Pink' can't be beat for a four-season perennial. This is an under-used plant that is very easy to grow. Inch-wide pink, fragrant, 8-inch tall flowers dance above a dense mat of fine, blue-green foliage that stays on the plant all year. From a tiny transplant, 'Bath's Pink' will grow easily to 2 feet or more. It has the potential of swallowing up everything in sight, but it's not considered invasive. Pinks get their name not from the color of their flower but for the petals' edges, which look like they've been trimmed with pinking shears. This cultivar is named for Bath, England. The nectar-filled flowers attract the large, night-flying moths.

Other Common Names
Cheddar Pinks, Dianthus

Bloom Period and Seasonal Color
Pink from spring to early summer.

Mature Height × Spread
1 ft. × 2 ft.

Russian Sage
Perovskia atriplicifolia

A Perennial Plant of the Year winner and considered one of the finest perennials around, Russian sage provides outstanding blooms from June through frost. The light-blue flowers are produced in thin, wispy spikes at the tips of light-gray stems. The leaves are a light silvery green and have a heavy sage aroma when crushed. The number of blooms and the blue color intensifies as the summer progresses, until Russian sage is at its peak in September. Although it is slow to grow new leaves in the spring, the plant quickly makes up for that by producing numerous spiky stems that collectively give the plant a mound-like shape. Cut the blooms any time to add a delicate but fragrant touch to your garden bouquets.

Bloom Period and Seasonal Color
Blue flowers from summer into fall.

Mature Height × **Spread**
3 ft. × 3 ft.

When, Where, and How to Plant
Transplant Russian sage in early spring as soon as the soil can be worked. It also can be transplanted in late summer or early fall. Russian sage is the perfect plant for hot, dry locations, but it is relatively intolerant of poorly drained or wet soils. It also is a perfect rock garden plant. (See chapter introduction for more planting information.)

Growing Tips
Apply an all-purpose granular fertilizer in spring when new grown appears or ring the plant with compost in spring and fall. Russian sage is very drought tolerant once established.

Care and Maintenance
Russian sage is one of the most care-free plants around, requiring mostly neglect. As a rule, it has woodier stems than most perennials and does not always die back completely to the ground. Leave the foliage alone in the fall and wait until growth becomes apparent in the spring. Then remove the branches that are not producing any new foliage. Sometimes the new buds are hard to identify; if in doubt, cut the whole plant back to about 8 inches. Although Russian sage produces masses of new foliage each season, it doesn't grow a large enough root system to divide. This plant is virtually pest free.

Companion Planting and Design
Plant Russian sage in groups of three or more for the best effect, in front of ornamental grasses, purple coneflower, or butterfly bush. Plant one in the middle of the perennial border where it can grow up and through a shrub rose or small ornamental shrub. The blue is beautiful next to the fall color of many *Viburnum* species, too. A favorite, breath-taking fall combination is *Boltonia* 'Snowbank', *Perovska atriplicifolia*, and *Aster* × *frikartii*.

We Also Recommend
The species, or 'Blue Haze', has lighter blue flowers; 'Blue Spire' has very finely cut, delicate leaves. 'Little Sprite' gets about 18 inches tall. For more design alternatives, see 'Panicum', 'Echinacea', or *Ceratostigma plumbaginoides*.

Salvia 'May Night'

Salvia × superba 'May Night'

When, Where, and How to Plant
Transplant 'May Night' and other perennial salvias in early spring as soon as the soil can be worked or in late summer. Salvias prefer moist, well-drained soil in full sun. They will get leggy in too much shade. (See chapter introduction for more planting instructions.)

Growing Tips
Apply an all-purpose granular fertilizer in spring when new growth appears or ring the plant with compost in spring and fall. Once established, salvia is fairly drought tolerant; however, it will benefit from a good soaking during extended dry periods.

Care and Maintenance
If deadheaded, 'May Night' and other perennial salvias will continue to flower throughout the summer until frost. It is bothered by little, other than too much moisture. It's easy to kill this plant with too much attention. If it starts to sprawl, it's time to divide the plant. Early the following spring, take a sharp spade or shovel and slice down vertically into the crown about 8 inches deep. Cut back dead flowers and leaves by half after blooming to encourage a second flush of flowers and a tidier plant. Be sure to do this early in the year because salvia "greens up" early. Transplant the divisions and water well.

Companion Planting and Design
Salvia is beautiful planted among other spring bloomers like the hardy geranium, columbine, or pinks. Late spring flowering bulbs also look nice with salvia. Plant 'May Night' at the front of the flower border among plants that have a mounded or round shape. 'May Night' looks especially good near the 'Silver Mound' *Artemesia* or 'Moonshine' yarrow. All three have leaves with a silver hue, but the flowers compliment each other to an outstanding degree.

We Recommend
Besides 'May Night', consider 'East Friesland', which has deep-purple blooms on short 18-inch plants; its short stature keeps it from sprawling. 'Rose Queen' has rose-pink spikes and grows to 20 inches tall. *S. nemerosa* 'Blue Hill' is about 18 inches tall with sky-blue flowers.

Salvia is among the most diverse and useful groups of garden flowers, having more than 700 different species. Grown as annuals or perennials, salvia's common attribute is a flower with numerous tubular to cup-shaped blooms attached tightly to a spike. Rising above the leaves, the flowers provide a vertical accent in the garden. 'May Night' produces masses of deep-blue spikes above gray-green leaves in May and June. 'May Night' establishes itself quickly in the garden, growing into an irregular mound shape. Many salvias flop in the middle, but not this one. The Chicago Botanic Garden ranked the cultivar high for its long lasting flowers and ability to hold together in a mound through the growing season. It was the 1997 Perennial Plant of the Year.

Other Common Names
Purple Sage, Meadow Sage

Bloom Period and Seasonal Color
Blue flowers in summer.

Mature Height × Spread
20 in. × 24 in.

Sedum 'Autumn Joy'

Sedum 'Autumn Joy'

'Autumn Joy' sedum is one of the outstanding fall flowers for a perennial garden. More commonly known as "Live Forever," it gets this name for its ability to thrive in hot, dry soils where nothing else will grow. Sedum, with thick, fleshy leaves, is a succulent that closely resembles the popular jade plant we grow indoors. It begins to show masses of light-green flower buds as early as July. The flowers turn pink to russet and persist through winter. It's not uncommon to see goldfinches or other small birds nibble on sedum's tender leaves in spring and early summer. Not all Sedum are tall like 'Autumn Joy'. Some are short and are ideal for ground covers for poor, dry soil.

Other Common Names
Sedum, Stonecrop, Live Forever

Bloom Period and Seasonal Color
Pink, white, or mauve flowers from mid- to late summer into fall.

Mature Height × Spread
2 ft. × 2 ft.

When, Where, and How to Plant
Transplant or divide 'Autumn Joy' and other sedums in early spring as soon as the soil can be worked. Sedum is the perfect plant for hot, dry, sandy soils in full sun to light shade. Prepare the garden as described in the introduction to this chapter. Dig a hole up to three times the width of the rootball or container and about 12 inches deep. Plant it the same depth it was growing or slightly higher.

Growing Tips
'Autumn Joy' prefers soil more dry than wet; however, it would be beneficial to give it a good soaking. Fertilizer is not necessary.

Care and Maintenance
'Autumn Joy' and most sedums are easily propagated after a few years by slicing through the crown of the plant in early spring with a sharp spade or shovel. Pinch tips back in June to keep it shorter and to prevent floppiness. It has no serious pests in our climate. If you don't like the erect stems of brown seedheads in the winter, cut the flower stalks back to 4 inches after the first hard frost. If you like them, cut the stalks back in late winter before signs of new growth.

Companion Planting and Design
Plant them en masse for the best effect. Sedum can be the backbone of a rock garden. 'Autumn Joy' is especially known for its ability to stand tall throughout most of the winter, with the brown seedheads on top of the dead stalks providing good winter interest. For a fantastic display winter, plant 'Autumn Joy' with dwarf fountain grass, *Rudbeckia fulgida* 'Goldsturm' (black-eyed Susan), and winterberry holly.

We Recommend
Sedum 'Ruby Glow' grows to 12 inches and has sprawling stems topped with deep rosy-red flowers in mid- to late summer. 'Vera Jameson' has larger flowers on shorter plants. *Sedum spectabile* 'Meteor', 'Brilliant', and 'Stardust' are upright like 'Autumn Joy' and have deep-pink flowers, and white flowers, respectively. *Sedum kamtschaticum* 'Variegatum' grows to 6 inches tall and has leaves edged in white and flashy yellow flowers in early summer. *A. tataricus* is another long bloomer with lilac flowers but is hardier.

Tickseed
Coreopsis verticillata 'Moonbeam'

When, Where, and How to Plant
Transplant or divide tickseed in the spring as soon as the ground can be worked. It thrives in full sun in a well-drained soil with plenty of organic matter. It tolerates dry locations and makes a good addition to the rock garden. (See chapter introduction for more planting information.)

Growing Tips
Too much fertilizer will reduce the number of flowers. Apply a light sprinkling of all-purpose granular fertilizer in spring when new growth appears or ring the plants with compost in spring and fall. Once established, tickseed is fairly drought tolerant. However, it will benefit from a good periodic soaking during long, dry periods.

Care and Maintenance
Tickseed is a virtually pest-free and low-maintenance plant. As one cycle fades, the next one can be encouraged by shearing the plant about 1 inch below the dead blooms. Trim back to the ground in winter when tops are killed by frost.

Companion Planting and Design
For an excellent contrast, plant 'Moonbeam' in the front of the perennial garden, combined with agastache or salvia. The yellow is also just right for breaking up sections of the garden with color without overwhelming nearby plants.

We Recommend
Besides 'Moonbeam', consider 'Zagreb' (*C. verticillata*), a shorter version with darker gold flowers. *C. rosea* is a threadleaf type that has light-pink, daisy-like petals with yellow centers; 'Sweet Dreams', is a major improvement on *C. rosea*, with a yummy raspberry center and pale pink petals. *C. lanceolata*, or lanceleaf coreopsis, has wide, toothed petals at the end of 18-inch-long stems. It will reseed itself throughout the garden. 'Early Sunrise' is a lanceleaf type with double flowers also. It grows to 12 inches tall and blooms off and on all summer after a fantastic display in June. 'Early Sunrise' grows easily from seed and should be started indoors in February. It dies out after a few years.

A native of the prairies of the Midwest, lanceleaf coreopsis, or tickseed, is the standard older species in this genus of more than 100 known selections. 'Moonbeam', a variety of threadleaf coreopsis, has many of the characteristics of the native that make it widely adaptable to Hoosier gardens. Its cheerful lemon-yellow, daisy-like flowers cover the tips of its needle-like leaves. Like the native tickseed, 'Moonbeam' will tolerate poor, dry soils and neglect. Its ability to bloom day after day throughout the summer, right up until frost, earned it the prestigious Perennial Plant of the Year Award for outstanding character a few years ago.

Other Common Name
Threadleaf Coreopsis

Bloom Period and Seasonal Color
Lemon yellow flowers in summer.

Mature Height × Spread
12 in. × 18 in.

Roses *for Indiana*

We seek for beauty on the height afar;

But on the earth it glimmers all the while:

'Tis in the garden where the roses are;

'Tis in the glory of a mother's smile.

—*E. W. Mason*

My earliest memories of roses are the rectangular rose beds scattered about my grandmother's compact and tidy backyard in *Rose*dale, New York. I can't help but reminisce when I think about their fat, round buds, the soft, thick petals that felt cool to the touch, and, of course, their heady perfume. Although I was too young to ask its name or even realize it *had* a name, I am sure my favorite rose was 'Peace'. (It is still one of my favorite roses—light yellow blushed with pink.) Having lived through several wars and celebrated the safe return of thousands of servicemen and women, including her son from World War II, it is logical that my grandmother would have planted this popular cultivar. Smuggled from France just before the Nazi occupation, its name couldn't be more symbolic today, over fifty years later. While most roses don't bear the weight of world peace on their "shoulders," or canes, I am sure other plant lovers grew to love gardening because of roses in their grandparents' yards. After all, roses have been one of our most popular flowers across the millennia. They have been the subject of more painting, more photography, and more writing than perhaps any other flower. The rose has been our national flower since 1986.

—*T. T.*

Rose Types and Selection

Selecting the right *type* and *cultivar* can make the difference between great success—lavish and fragrant flowers on lush plants all season—or sickly, scrawny, bug-ridden failures by midsummer. Rose experts group roses into many different categories depending on the number and size of flowers or the growth habit of the plant itself. The classifications are complicated and somewhat confusing. We've taken the liberty of grouping many, many separate classes of roses into eight types. Each selection is among the best cultivars based on pest resistance, flower, fragrance, and its ability to "repeat bloom," that is, flower off and on all season long. To learn more about roses and rose classifications, pick up a good rose book, join your local rose society and attend meetings and rose shows, or visit the American Rose Society (ARS) website at http://www.ars.org.

Site and Soil Preparation

Plan to grow roses in full sun or very light shade. Roses growing in less sun will have spindly canes and produce fewer flowers. Full sun in the morning followed by light shade in midafternoon will help dry the dew on leaves and help suppress blackspot and other diseases. Prepare the soil well to ensure greater success. Most roses thrive in soil that drains well. When planting more than a couple of rose plants, prepare a rose *bed* rather than digging separate holes for each plant. Dig the bed to a depth of at least eighteen inches—two feet deep is even better. Digging to this depth will reward your hard work with seasons of good roses. Take soil from the planting location and completely mix one part organic matter with every two parts of soil. Return the soil to the bed and plant accordingly.

A better way to improve drainage and to grow roses is in raised beds. Build a raised rose bed eight to twelve inches above grade using block or landscape timbers or other available environmentally sound materials. A good soil mix for a raised rose bed consists of one-third soil, one-third sand, and one-third organic matter such as compost. This drains water away, brings oxygen to the roots, and holds moisture during the dry periods. Rich, well-drained soil will grow healthier roses better able to withstand the stress of disease and insects and hot Indiana summers.

Planting Roses

Buy bare-root roses for best growth, especially the first year. Plant them in early spring, just as the forsythia begin to bloom. Remove the wrapping from around the roots and soak the entire bush in a bucket of water for two to three hours. In the meantime, dig a planting hole in the prepared bed eighteen inches wide and two feet deep. Add a few inches of compost to the bottom of the hole. Mix one-half cup of fertilizer and one part compost to two parts removed soil and mix well. Continue refilling the hole, making a mound with the soil as it approaches the top. Spread the roots over the mound so that the bud union, or graft, is level with the ground. Plant container-grown roses in much the same way as the bare-root types but without the mound. Gently remove the root ball from the container to minimize breaking the roots. Cut the pot with sharp snips or scissors if necessary and tease the roots apart. Place in the hole and fill, as above.

Space hybrid teas, grandifloras, or miniature roses two feet apart in the rose bed. Plant old garden

Hybrid Tea Rose
'Double Delight'

roses, polyanthas, shrubs, or climbers four to five feet apart. To plant individual roses, dig a hole eighteen inches wide and slightly deeper than the roots and plant accordingly using the mound or container method. Always backfill the hole with the original soil, amended with one part compost to two parts soil.

Care and Maintenance

Roses grow healthier and bloom better after regular fertilizing. Choose a good rose food, organic fertilizer, or complete fertilizer like 5-10-5 or 12-12-12. Add one tablespoon per plant in the early spring. Continue to fertilize with a tablespoon per plant per month until August 15.

With the exception of the lower-maintenance shrub and landscape types, roses don't grow well in dry soils typical of Indiana summers. Water the equivalent of one to one-and-one-half inches of water per week. Use a soaker hose and avoid splashing water on the leaves to prevent the spread of rose diseases.

Bush and Climbing Roses

Keep two to three inches of organic mulch around the roots at all times. This helps keep the roots cool and damp and prevents weeds.

Roses are most susceptible to blackspot and powdery mildew, two common diseases in Indiana gardens. Without the protection of regular fungicide sprays, most susceptible cultivars lose their leaves to the irksome blackspot. To control it, spray a fungicide with the active ingredient triforine every ten to fourteen days starting when the leaves emerge. For a less toxic spray, mix two to two-and-one-half tablespoons of ultrafine horticultural oil and one heaping tablespoon of sodium bicarbonate (baking soda) with one gallon of water, keep agitated, and spray on the upper and lower surfaces of the leaves. Other fungicides may also work.

Most roses are Sunday dinner for voracious Japanese beetles which appear in late June or early July. Vigilant hand picking or regular sprays of carbaryl are necessary to control this hungry pest. Roses are also favorites of aphids, rose midges, rose slugs, and other pests. Always identify the pest before applying any pesticide and follow the directions listed on the label. For good diagnosis and control, contact the local office of the Cooperative Extension Service or your local rosarian.

Pruning

Pruning at the correct time of year will encourage more canes and better flowers. As a rule, prune in the spring as you see the buds begin to swell. Cut away blackened or dead canes and damaged wood. On bush roses like hybrid teas, grandifloras, or floribundas, cut healthy canes back to green wood. Prune bush type roses like hybrid teas and grandi-floras into an open and vase-like shape, removing all canes from the center of the bush. This will help improve air circulation and reduce disease. Always cut the canes back to an outward-facing bud to encourage

Polyantha Roses

an open growth habit. Using sharp pruners, remove dying flowers from all types as soon as they start to fade; this will encourage new blooms. Seal cut canes thicker than a pencil with white glue to prevent rose cane borers. More specific pruning information is described in the discussion for each plant.

Winter Protection

Roses need different types of winter protection. Protect the bud union of grafted roses such as hybrid teas and grandifloras by tying the canes together with twine or other string after the first hard freeze. Then, slip a commercial rose collar over the canes so that it encircles the base of the plant. (You can make a homemade collar using four sheets of newspaper stapled end-to-end to form a circle. Alternatively, use chicken wire or other sturdy wire.) Set the collar on the ground around the base of the rose, forming a cylinder. It should be between eight and twelve inches tall. Mound four to six inches of soil over the crown of the plant to protect the bud union and the base of the canes. Fill the collar to the brim with chopped leaves or straw. Remove the leaves and collars in the spring when the buds begin to swell.

Climbing Rose

Rosa 'America'

Climbing roses stir memories of split-rail fences thick with bright-red blooms. Rose-laden pergolas and gazebos appear in our garden fantasies. With recent breeding for winter hardiness and repeat flowers, climbing roses offer Hoosiers many more options than what were once relegated to the fence by the road in the "old days." Climbers still grow on long canes that need the support of a fence, deck rail, or trellis; however, their recurrent flowers and heavenly fragrance demand a more prestigious place in the landscape—tied to a pillar on the front porch or fastened to a trellis used as a screen for the patio. Their flowers are smaller than hybrid teas and grow singly or in clusters. 'America' has a salmon-pink flower with a spicy clove fragrance. According to rose experts, it is one of the best all-around climbers for Indiana.

Bloom Period and Seasonal Color
Late May through June and intermittently through fall, with flowers in red, yellow, white, pink, orange, or bi-colored.

Mature Height × Spread
6 to 12 ft. × 6 to 12 ft. depending on the cultivar

When, Where, and How to Plant
Plant climbers like 'America' where they will receive at least six hours of full sun each day. Like most roses, they prefer moist but well-drained soils amended with compost. Prepare a planting bed the previous fall or at least six weeks before planting, according to the instructions in the chapter introduction. Then, dig an individual hole 2 feet deep and at least 18 inches wide. Space climbers 4 to 5 feet apart. Trim off damaged canes or excessively long roots with sharp hand pruners and plant accordingly.

Growing Tips
Keep 2 to 3 inches of organic mulch over the roots at all times. Water deeply especially during dry spells in summer. Fertilize monthly with rose food for maximum bloom.

Care and Maintenance
Use appropriate fungicides regularly to prevent blackspot, powdery mildew, and other foliar diseases. Vigilant hand picking or an application of carbaryl will help reduce Japanese beetle infestations. Remove new, spindly growth in spring. Train four or five canes to grow up a trellis or pergola. Snip off dead blooms. Winterize 'America' with 12 inches of soil mounded around the base of the canes to protect the graft union. Gather the canes in a bundle and fasten them to the ground with wire or wood stakes. Cover the canes with 6 inches of mulch and 6 inches of soil to protect them from sub-zero temperatures. Remove protective mulch and soil in the spring as new growth begins. Prune climbers in a fan shape with many lateral canes to encourage the maximum number of blooms.

We Recommend
Other excellent climbers include 'New Dawn' (light pink), 'Clair Matin' (a short, fragrant pink), 'Altissimo' (red), 'Don Juan' (red), and 'Fourth of July' (red and white). Classified as shrubs, these roses get so big they function as climbers. 'William Baffin' (watermelon-pink), 'John Davis' (light pink), and 'John Cabot' (deep pink) are so cold-hardy they don't require winter protection.

Floribunda Rose

Rosa 'Nicole'

When, Where, and How to Plant

Plant bare-root floribundas in early spring as the leaves emerge on the trees. Soak them in a bucket of water for two to three hours to rehydrate. Site the rose bed in full sun and prepare both the bed and individual holes as described in the introduction. Add a few inches of compost or peat moss to the bottom of the hole. Add $1/2$ cup of rose food or balanced fertilizer like 12-12-12 along with 1 part compost to 2 parts displaced soil and mix well. Return the soil mix to the hole forming a mound towards the top. The bud union should be even with or slightly below ground level after planting. Spread the roots over the mound, finish backfilling, and water deeply.

Growing Tips

Keep 2 to 3 inches of organic mulch over the roots at all times. Water deeply especially during dry spells in summer. Fertilize with 1 tablespoon of 12-12-12 or rose food per plant starting after the first bloom. Do this monthly until August 15.

Care and Maintenance

Remove dead, damaged, or diseased canes each spring. Cut back $1/3$ the length of the healthy canes to an outward facing bud. This will encourage vigorous regrowth. Deadhead old flowers to encourage more blooms. 'Nicole' and other floribundas are very disease tolerant, but you can spray for blackspot, powdery mildew, or other pests as needed. Handpick Japanese beetles or spray with carbaryl as needed. Follow label directions when applying any pesticide. Mulch crowns with 4 to 6 inches of chopped leaves or bark after the first hard freeze for protection in winter.

Companion Planting and Design

Floribundas make excellent additions to the landscape when planted in groups. Mass them together to create "drifts" with season-long color. They make great additions to cottage gardens, perennial borders, or mixed with ornamental grasses.

We Recommend

Other floribundas for Hoosier rose gardens include 'Sunsprite', which is a fragrant yellow; 'Showbiz' and 'Europeana', which are excellent red cultivars; 'First Edition' and 'Dicky', which are orange pink; and 'Sexy Rexy', which has pink blooms.

Floribundas are the result of crosses between the large-flowered and fragrant hybrid teas and the petite-flowered but floriferous and sprawling polyantha roses. The result is disease resistant and shrubby plants with many sprays of smaller flowers through most of the year. They are tougher and less fussy than hybrid teas and grandifloras and work wonderfully in home gardens and landscapes. 'Nicole' has stunning white petals edged in pink. According to rose experts, it is one of the best floribundas ever. In Indiana it has very good disease resistance and rewards gardeners with blooms even in August when the rest of the garden seems to wane. An added benefit is its sweet but subtle fragrance that perfumes the air.

Bloom Period and Seasonal Color
June through fall; white with pink edges; other cultivars in yellow, pink, red, white, orange, and more.

Mature Height × Spread
2 to 4 ft. × 2 to 3 ft.

Hybrid Tea Rose
Rosa 'Touch of Class'

No other flower is as beloved or as sought after as the red rose. Whether given out of love and romance or for comfort during grief, a red hybrid tea is considered royalty—the standard by which other flowers are judged. Hybrid teas are made for the gardener who likes to pamper. A well-tended hybrid tea will reward the attentive owner with regal flowers. Though not a red, 'Touch of Class' is an exception to the notion that hybrid teas are fraught with disease. This sweetly fragrant, disease-resistant, orange-pink has a classic bush form with lovely pointed buds on long stems. The American Rose Society gave 'Touch of Class' one if its highest ratings ever, and Indiana rose experts agree.

Other Common Name
Grandiflora Rose

Bloom Period and Seasonal Color
June and early July repeating blooms, with more in September, in red yellow, orange, pink, white, blends, and bi-colors.

Mature Height × Spread
3 to 6 ft. × 2 to 3 ft.

When, Where, and How to Plant
Plant hybrid teas in full sun in early spring, according to the instructions in the chapter introduction. Prepare planting beds and position multiple bushes 2 feet apart. Plant so that the graft union is even with or slightly below the ground around it. Tamp the soil lightly and water deeply.

Growing Tips
Keep 2 to 3 inches of mulch around the roots at all times. Water deeply in summer, especially during dry spells. After the first bloom in June, fertilize each rose plant with 1 tablespoon of rose food or a balanced fertilizer like 12-12-12. Fertilize monthly until August 15.

Care and Maintenance
Cut dead canes back to green tissue in spring. Keep older canes facing upward and outward. Remove inward facing or crossing canes to improve air circulation. For cut flowers indoors, cut the stems just above a leaf with five leaflets to encourage more blooms. Despite disease-free claims, 'Touch of Class' and others will benefit from regular applications of fungicides. See the introduction for recommendations. The graft union needs winter protection. Place a rose collar around each plant after the first hard freeze to protect the bud union. Remove it in the spring as the buds begin to swell.

Companion Planting and Design
Hybrid teas and grandiflora types don't mix well with other landscape plants. Plant them in rose beds. Try underplanting pansies and violas in spring and fall or lavender and other herbs as perennials. Be careful, however, not to disturb the root system of the roses when digging.

We Recommend
'Olympiad' is an excellent red. 'Dolly Parton' is orange-red. 'Helene Naude' and 'Moonstone' are white. 'Marijke Koopman' (pink), 'St. Patrick' (yellow), 'Dainty Bess' (single pink), and 'Double Delight' (white and red bicolor) bloom throughout the summer. Grandifloras are slightly larger hybrid teas. 'Gold Medal' (yellow), 'Queen Elizabeth' and 'Tournament of Roses' (both pinks) are excellent grandiflora types.

Miniature Rose

Rosa 'Jean Keneally'

When, Where and How to Plant

Plant 'Jean Keneally' and other minis or mini-floras in the spring in gardens that get six hours of full sun per day. Plant in slightly acidic soils that drain well. Soak bare-root plants in water for two to three hours before planting. Prepare rose beds and planting holes as described in the introduction. Backfill the holes with amended soil per the instructions, tamp lightly, and water deeply.

Growing Tips

Keep 2 to 3 inches of mulch over the roots at all times. Water deeply during dry spells in summer. Grow potted minis in containers that are 12 to 18 inches in diameter. Plant in commercial soilless potting mix or make your own blend. Overwinter potted minis in south-facing windows or under fluorescent lights, or allow them to go dormant in cool, dark basements or attached garages. Water every six weeks; acclimate them to the outdoor weather in spring, around the last frost date in your area. Repot every two to three years. Fertilize each spring with a teaspoon of rose food or balanced fertilizer and repeat monthly until August 15. For potted plants, use a liquid houseplant fertilizer.

Care and Maintenance

Keep soil moist in summer. Miniatures like 'Jean Keneally' will only need winter protection the first year. In following years, a few inches of mulch or shredded fall leaves will suffice. In early spring, prune the branches by $1/3$ to $1/2$ their original length. Minis are mostly disease free. Control Japanese beetles accordingly (see chapter introduction).

Companion Planting and Design

Plant them in the foreground of the rose garden or perennial beds. On the patio or deck, group pots together for the popular look of a containerized rose garden.

We Recommend

Excellent minis include a wonderful yellow blend called 'Party Girl' named for an Indianapolis rosarian. 'Minnie Pearl' is a pink blend. 'Hot Tamale' has yellow-orange flowers that fade to pink. 'Miss Flippins' is a red. 'Jeanne Lajoie' is a climbing pink miniature. Try 'Autumn Spendor' (orange-red), 'Gentlemen's Agreement' (red), or 'Tiffany Lynn' (white and pink) mini-floras.

When you need ever-blooming roses for tiny spaces, miniature roses are the answer. Modern miniatures come in different heights, but the flowers and leaves are all smaller than 2 inches. Some grow on single stems similar to hybrid teas, while others bloom in clusters or sprays. The tiniest miniatures will grow in pots as small as a jelly jar! They come in a range of colors except the elusive blue, and virtually all bloom continuously. Minifloras, a new class of small roses, have larger blooms on smaller plants. With regular watering, minis and minifloras grow well as container plants and are excellent for summer decks or patios. 'Jean Keneally', one of the highest rated rose varieties ever, is a medium-sized miniature that blooms throughout the summer. Its tea-like flowers open to a lush apricot color.

Bloom Period and Seasonal Color

Continuous bloom May through fall in white, pink, red, yellow, orange, and bi-colors.

Mature Height × Spread

$1^1/2$ to 2 ft. × $1^1/2$ to 2 ft.

Old Garden Rose
Rosa 'Souvenir de la Malmaison'

Old garden roses include all roses cultivated prior to 1867. They make a complex collection, but all are forerunners of the popular roses we have today. After the development of 'Peace' and other early hybrid teas, these older roses fell out of favor. Fortunately, they have experienced resurgence and are popular once again. 'Souvenir de la Malmaison' is a classic "Bourbon-type" with large pale-pink, sweetly scented blooms with over fifty petals per flower. The flowers repeat bloom throughout the summer and fall. 'Souvenir de la Malmaison' was released in 1843 in honor of La Malmaison, the rose garden of Empress Josephine I. Her garden was home to the 250 named varieties of the time. Her passion for growing them helped popularize roses throughout the world.

Other Common Names
Bourbons, Noisettes, Centifolias, Albas, Damasks

Bloom Period and Seasonal Color
June to July, repeating throughout the summer and fall depending on cultivar, in shades of mauve, pink, white, and red.

Mature Height × Spread
3 to 5 ft. × 3 to 5 ft.

When, Where, and How to Plant
Plant old garden roses in the spring in slightly acidic but well-drained soil. Prepare a planting bed as described in the introduction, then soak the bare-root plant in water for two to three hours. Dig planting holes 2 feet deep and 18 inches wide. Add a few inches of compost or peat moss to the bottom of the hole while mixing $1/2$ cup of balanced rose fertilizer to the displaced soil. Return the amended soil to the planting hole, making a mound towards the top of the hole. Plant the rose by spreading the roots over the mounded soil. Backfill the hole so that the crown is even with the ground around it; tamp lightly and water deeply.

Growing Tips
Keep 2 to 3 inches of organic mulch over the root zone at all times. Water in summer, especially during dry spells. Fertilize after the first bloom in spring with 1 tablespoon of balanced fertilizer like 12-12-12 or rose food.

Care and Maintenance
'Souvenir de la Malmaison' is somewhat resistant to blackspot and mildew. To ensure disease-free plants, however, follow a regular spray schedule using recommended fungicides. Prune to remove dead or damaged canes each spring. Cut healthy canes to half their original height to stimulate new and vigorous growth. Winterize 'Souvenir de la Malmaison' by tying up the canes, placing a rose collar around the plant, and filling the collar to the brim with chopped leaves.

Companion Planting and Design
Plant fragrant roses like 'Souvenir de la Malmaison' where you can enjoy their sweet scent as often as possible; next to a doorway or open window is ideal. Combine with annuals, perennials, and herbs. They make excellent additions to cottage-style gardens.

We Recommend
Bourbon is an old garden rose class known for its heady fragrance. 'Marchesa Bocella' is fragrant light pink and repeats. 'Sombreuil' is a disease-resistant white climber from 1850. 'Salet' and 'Baronne Prevost' are medium pink and repeat. 'Reine des Violettes' is mauve with heavy fragrance. 'Rose de Rescht' is also deep pink and repeats very well.

Old Shrub Rose

Rosa rugosa 'Frau Dagmar Hastrup'

When, Where, and How to Plant

Plant rugosas in early spring in moist, slightly acidic but well-drained soils. They are well-known to tolerate tougher conditions, too. Soak bare-root rugosas in water for two hours. In the meantime, prepare a planting bed as described in the introduction. Dig a planting hole up to 2 feet deep and 18 inches wide. Add a few inches of compost to the bottom of the hole, then add 1/2 cup of balanced fertilizer and 1 part compost to 2 parts soil and mix well. Return the amended soil to the planting hole, forming a mound toward the top of the hole. Spread the roots of the plant over the mound, finish filling the hole, and water deeply.

Growing Tips

Keep 2 to 3 inches of bark mulch over the root zone at all times. Fertilize sparingly as rugosas may be sensitive and drop their leaves. Water deeply, especially during dry spells in summer.

Care and Maintenance

Protect yourself with heavy gloves and long sleeves for pruning dead wood in the spring. Remove thick, older canes every two or three years to encourage new growth. Japanese beetles may feed on the blooms and the leaves. Pick them by hand when they appear in small numbers. Follow label directions and apply an insecticide containing carbaryl. Rugosas may turn yellow after heavy sprays. Test a small area first before spraying. They are very winter hardy and do not require winter protection. Rugosas spread by suckering.

Companion Planting and Design

Plant rugosas on banks and slopes or as a hedge along the driveway or sidewalk. To make a hedge, space plants 2 1/2 feet apart. Pair with the native bearberry and ornamental grasses or mix among annual and perennial beds.

We Recommend

'Jens Munk' has light-pink semi-double flowers. 'Blanc Double de Coubert' is a white rugosa with all the attributes of 'Frau Dagmar Hastrup' except for the showy hips. 'F. J. Grootendorst' is a tall red. Try rugosa hips to make jam or take advantage of their high concentration of Vitamin C.

Known for their vigorous growth habit and ability to thrive in poor conditions, rugosas are among the toughest roses available. Rugosas seem programmed for gardeners who have neither the time nor the patience to care for their finicky cousins, the hybrid teas. Some rugosas grow 8 to 10 feet tall and wide, while others, such as 'Frau Dagmar Hastrup', are more diminutive. Their flowers seem fragile with one to three rows of petals that open wide to show off bright yellow centers. Rugosas have lush, dark green leaves with an upright, bushy, slightly mounded growth habit and very thorny stems. For this reason they make a good "living fence." 'Frau Dagmar Hastrup' repeat-blooms all summer with very fragrant, deep-pink flowers. After flowering, many rugosas produce bright orange-red fruit, called "hips," which begin turning color in July and last through late fall.

Other Common Names

Hedge Rose, Shrub Rose

Bloom Period and Seasonal Color

June, July, and intermittently through fall; red, pink, and white flowers and orange hips depending on cultivar.

Mature Height × Spread

4 to 10 ft. × 4 to 10 ft.

Polyantha Rose
Rosa 'The Fairy'

Polyanthas are older roses with small, fine-textured leaves usually covered with sprays of dainty pink or white flowers. The plants grow low to the ground, spreading wider than they are tall. Only a few pure polyanthas are common today; most were replaced by the floribundas, which have a wider color range and more generous fragrance. Introduced in 1932, one selection has survived the fall from glory—and for good reason. 'The Fairy' must have been named for its magical effect in the garden. It blooms all season long with full sprays of small, light pink flowers. Bothered by few diseases or insects, 'The Fairy' is virtually maintenance free, making it a superb choice for the beginner or weekend gardener.

Bloom Period and Seasonal Color
June through fall; clusters and sprays of pink or white flowers.

Mature Height × Spread
3 ft. × 3 ft. or more

When, Where, and How to Plant
Plant bare-root polyanthas in early spring as the leaves emerge on the trees. Soak them in a bucket of water for two to three hours to rehydrate. Site the rose bed in full sun and prepare both the bed and individual holes as described in the introduction and plant accordingly.

Growing Tips
Keep 2 to 3 inches of organic mulch over the root zone. Water deeply in summer, especially during dry periods. 'The Fairy' grows well in average soil. It usually grows adequately without preparing special rose beds. Fertilize with 1 tablespoon of 12-12-12 or rose food per plant starting after the first bloom. Continue this monthly until August 15.

Care and Maintenance
Remove dead, damaged, or diseased canes each spring. Cut back healthy canes by $1/3$ their length to an outward facing bud. This will encourage vigorous regrowth. Deadhead old flowers to encourage more blooms. 'The Fairy' and other polyanthas are very disease tolerant. Spray for blackspot, powdery mildew, or other pests only as needed. Handpick Japanese beetles or spray with carbaryl as needed. 'The Fairy' may be bothered by spider mites, especially in dry weather. To test for spider mites, hold a white sheet of paper under a branch and tap hard. The pinhead-sized mites will fall onto the paper. Hose the leaves off with water daily or treat with an appropriate miticide. Always read and follow the label directions when applying any pesticide. Mulch crowns with 4 to 6 inches of chopped leaves or bark after the first hard freeze for protection in winter.

Companion Planting and Design
Their sprawling nature makes polyantha ideal for low walls, walkways, and sunny banks. 'The Fairy's light pink combines well with the blue and lavender flowers of perennials such as scabiosa and Russian sage, or annual vinca and blue salvia.

We Recommend
'Orange Morsdag' is an orange blend. 'Marie Pavie' has continuous white flowers and strong fragrance. 'Cecile Brunner' is also light pink. 'Phyllis Bide' is a yellow blend that climbs.

Shrub Rose
Rosa 'Carefree Wonder'

When, Where, and How to Plant
Plant bare-root or container-grown shrub roses in early spring as the leaves emerge on the trees. Soak bare-root specimens in a bucket of water for two to three hours to rehydrate. Modern shrub roses such as 'Carefree Wonder' tolerate harsher growing environments; therefore, rose beds won't be necessary. Plant in full to part sun in soil that is moist but well-drained and amended with 1 part compost to 2 parts soil. Plant according to directions in the introduction to this chapter.

Growing Tips
Keep 2 to 3 inches of mulch around the root zone at all times. Though slightly drought tolerant, water deeply in summer, especially during dry periods. Even though it is less finicky than hybrid teas, it will benefit from occasional fertilizing.

Care and Maintenance
As its name implies, 'Carefree Wonder' and other modern shrubs are just that: carefree. Prune dead or damaged canes in spring. Cut good canes back by 1/3 their length every two or three years. They are mostly disease free, needing minimal to no spraying to control pests. They are extremely winter hardy and don't require winter protection.

Companion Planting and Design
Plant modern shrub roses in places you forget about—along a hill or bank or out by the road. Mix with ornamental grasses such as switch grass or maiden grass. Plant in front of arborvitae or yew—two dark green backgrounds sure to help show off their flowers.

We Recommend
'Carefree Delight' has single pink flowers with yellow centers. The red, pink, or white Meideland series roses are excellent, disease-free, low maintenance roses. 'Golden Wings' has petite single light yellow flowers on a large shrubby plant with few thorns. A good repeating David Austin rose is 'Belle Story', a fragrant dusky pink. Plant it where you'll enjoy the spicy scent. 'Mayflower' is a small plant with rose pink flowers similar to old garden roses. 'Prospero' is a fragrant dark red. 'Carefree Beauty', 'Aunt Honey', and 'Earth Song' are cold-hardy Griffith Buck series roses.

The modern shrub rose is a catch-all class that groups new roses with a sprawling habit more suitable for landscaping purposes. For the most part, they are disease resistant and rebloom throughout summer. As a group they are not as fragrant as others. Popular types include David Austin Roses® bred for old-fashioned flowers and fragrance, and the cold-hardy Griffith Bucks series. Austins and Bucks are more upright and sprawling. Meidelands are excellent lower-growing landscape roses. 'Carefree Wonder' is a modern shrub in a class of its own. Mildly sweet double pink flowers bloom singly and in clusters on its sprawling canes. It is a workhorse in the garden, blooming non-stop with disease-free leaves. An added bonus is the dainty red-orange hips that form in late summer.

Other Common Name
Landscape Rose

Bloom Period and Seasonal Color
June through fall in pinks, white, reds, yellows, oranges, and blends.

Mature Height × Spread
4 ft. × 4 ft.

Shrubs *for Indiana*

For many gardeners, shrubs are just another chore to add to the list of weekend yard activities—the green "meatballs" they have to clip throughout the season. But a carefully chosen shrub will give a special gift with each passing season: springtime flowers, the glossy green leaves of summer that become fall's scarlet red, and brilliant berries or peeling bark in winter.

Whether planted alone or in calculated designs, shrubs make up the "walls" of our landscapes, much as trees form the "ceilings." Their shorter stature helps to enclose the garden, giving it shape and feeling. They also serve as living fences, screening off unsightly views and creating privacy. Shrubs provide essential food and cover for wildlife and make excellent backgrounds for flower gardens. When planted strategically, they can make small buildings look larger and help to soften harsh views.

Shrubs come in all shapes, sizes, colors, and textures. However, the most important thing to consider when selecting a shrub is its appropriateness for the planting site. Consider the amount of sun the site receives, whether it gets morning or afternoon light, the soil drainage and type. There are many tough shrubs that adapt to difficult growing conditions, but they are more likely to *thrive* in the environment best suited for their needs. When selecting a shrub, take into account its size when full grown. Don't forget outdoor views through windows or potential root restricting sidewalks, underground utility lines, or driveways. Finally, select a plant that gives you the most enjoyment for a reasonable price: clean and disease-free foliage, sweet fragrance, interesting bark, enticing flowers, brilliant color in fall, luscious fruit in winter. Most of the shrubs chosen for this chapter fit these criteria and, we hope, give the most bang for the buck.

Hydrangea 'Annabelle'

Redosier Dogwood

Purchase shrubs as either container-grown, balled-and-burlapped, or bare-root plants. All three types grow equally well when handled correctly. Finally, be realistic about how much time you can spend tending to your landscape. Many shrubs in this chapter are low-maintenance plants, but most require pruning, watering, or some other care, especially when they are less than five years old.

Preparing to Plant

Mail-order plant companies frequently send bare-root specimens, especially in early spring or late fall. Plant them as soon as possible after they arrive. Store them in cool temperatures if you can't get to it immediately, since they will begin to deteriorate after more than a few days. Before planting, remove the protective root covering and soak the roots in water for two or three hours. Note the shrubs estimated mature height and spread and plant them close enough so that when full grown the branches will overlap. Shrubs planted for screening purposes or as a hedge can be planted slightly closer together. Place at least six feet from the house since the eves will block water. Excessive amounts of water will pour onto the plants if planted too close to a house with no gutters. Consult your local nursery operator, garden center staff, or the Purdue Cooperative Extension Service for more detailed information.

Dig In

Soil preparation procedures are the same regardless of shrub species. First, dig a hole that is up to three times the width of the rootball or container. Most of the roots grow outward from the plant rather than downward, so it is important to loosen the soil as far out as possible. Dig deep enough that the plant will be at the same depth it was growing in the field or container. Don't dig too deeply because you can't return soft soil to the bottom of the hole. If you do this, the soil will settle and the plant may end up below grade and drown. In fact, we advise planting one to two inches above grade in clay soils to improve drainage.

For container-grown specimens, unravel any roots growing in concentric circles around the bottom of the pot. Gently tease them apart, or in severe cases, use a pruning knife to score the roots with four or five vertical cuts. Spread the roots out in the hole and knead some soil around them. Remove any twine or wire wrapped around the stems of balled-and-burlapped shrubs; if left in place, this could eventually girdle the stem. Remove synthetic burlap from around the roots and dispose. We recommend cutting away at least half of any natural burlap. Leave the rest in the hole as it will eventually decompose. For shrubs that arrive with wire baskets, we suggest following the planting instructions above but cutting away at least half, if not all, of the basket after you place it in the hole.

When planting bare-root types, look for the soil line, visible on the trunk just above the roots. You will plant the shrub to this depth. Backfill the planting holes with the original soil. It is not necessary to amend the displaced soil with organic matter before returning it to the hole. However, if you are planting containerized shrubs grown in an organic soil mix like fine bark or peat, there may be some benefit to incorporating two to three inches of compost in the entire planting bed if it's heavy clay. In heavy clay, if you add organic matter only to the planting hole, the shrub might eventually drown. Loosen the soil before returning it to the hole by pulverizing with a shovel or hoe. Water deeply and spread two to three inches of organic mulch over the entire planting area. Mulch will help the shrubs establish better and grow more quickly by keeping the roots moist and cool and preventing weed growth. During the first five years after planting, it is important to water with the equivalent of 1 to $1^1/2$ inches of rain per week. Adequate soil moisture is most important during the hot, dry days of summer. Plant pest diagnosticians frequently trace borer attack and reduced flowering to dry weather the previous summer.

Care and Maintenance

Pruning is a regular maintenance chore needed to keep shrubs the appropriate size. It also stimulates growth and helps keep the plant healthy. If the right plant has been selected for the right place, however, pruning is rarely needed. Pruning methods depend on how the plant functions in the landscape. It's best to start by knowing the shrub's natural growth habit and shape. Whenever possible, maintain the natural shape of the plant when pruning. The green meatball shape, while popular, is rarely found in nature! We've included more detailed information about pruning on pages 239–240.

Plants acquire nutrients and water from the soil and energy from the sun. A regular soil test is like checking your blood pressure or heart rate. Knowing basic pH and fertility levels helps avoid the guessing game and enables you to supply the nutrients that are in shortest supply. Adjust the soil pH with lime or sulfur according to test results. Nitrogen is the nutrient most often in shortest supply. Soil tests recommend fertilizing based on the need to supply the right amount of nitrogen. (See main introduction for soil testing details.)

In the absence of a soil test, fertilize shrubs based on supplying up to four pounds of nitrogen per 1000 square feet of root area, per year. To figure the root area, calculate twice the diameter of a shrub for

individual specimens or an entire planting bed for multiple plants. Use the following chart based on recommendations from Purdue Cooperative Extension Service scientists, according to the type of fertilizer you have. Split the application in two and apply the first half in early spring (late March through April) and the second half in early fall (late September through October). Don't fertilize newly planted shrubs in the first year. Instead, wait until the second year after planting to begin a fertilizing program, then fertilize at the higher rate. Fertilize mature shrubs and conifers like yews, spruce, fir, and arborvitae at the lower rate. Contact your local office of the Purdue Cooperative Extension Service to learn how to obtain a soil test.

Amount of Nitrogen Fertilizers Needed to Supply 4, 2, and 1 Pound of Actual Nitrogen per 1000 Square Feet of Root Zone.

Fertilizer	Pounds of Nitrogen Per 1,000 Square Feet		
	4	2	1
	Pounds of Fertilizer		
Urea (45-0-0)	8	4	2
Ammonium Nitrate (33-0-0)	12	6	4
Ammonium Sulfate (21-0-0)	20	10	5
10-10-10	40	20	10
12-12-12	32	16	8
18-6-12	22	11	5.5
Calcium Nitrate (15-0-0)*	26	13	6.5

*avoid using in high pH soils

American Cranberry Bush
Viburnum trilobum

Native to Canada, the upper Midwest, and northern plains states, the name "cranberry bush" might lead one to believe that this plant is responsible for the ruby-red gelatinous mass served alongside holiday turkeys. Fortunately, this is not the case. The American cranberry bush is suitable for modern landscapes while the Thanksgiving Day mainstay is not. Its lacecap bloom is a sophisticated collection of showy hydrangea-like florets that surround smaller fertile flowers. Together they form a flat, circular mound reminiscent of a lace doily. It is stunning set against the background of the maple-like lush green leaves. The inner flowers produce ample bright red berries in late summer that persist well into fall and early winter. The fruit shrivel after several hard freezes but cling to the branch tips all winter. Covered in snow, even the withered berries are charming.

Bloom Period and Seasonal Color
White flowers open in May; yellow-red leaves in fall.

Mature Height × Spread
8 to 12 ft. × 8 to 12 ft.

When, Where, and How to Plant
Plant American cranberry bush just about any time of the year the ground is dry. It is very adaptable but grows more compact and bushy and produces more flowers and fruit in full sun. The soil should be moist and well-drained, and either acidic or alkaline. Prepare a planting hole three times the width of the rootball. Dig deep enough so that, after planting, the top of the rootball is level with the ground around it. Backfill the hole with the original soil, tamp lightly, and water deeply. They are known to grow in wet marshy soils in nature and may adapt well to similar conditions in home landscapes.

Growing Tips
Keep a 2- to 3-inch layer of organic mulch around the root zone. Water when dry, especially in summer. An early November application of fertilizer will encourage better growth.

Care and Maintenance
American cranberry bush will thrive with little care. After blooming, prune large branches all the way to the ground to allow for better light penetration to the inside of the shrub. This will help prevent "legginess," which is typical. This plant has no regular pest problems.

Companion Planting and Design
Mass plant for a screen or as food for wildlife. Mix with ornamental grasses whose straw color matches their yellow leaves in fall and gives the fruit a fire engine red glow. Use the fruit for jams and jellies.

We Recommend
The cultivar 'Compactum' is the most popular form in the nursery trade. It only grows to 5 or 6 feet tall but has all the attributes of the taller species. The native arrowood viburnum, *Viburnum dentatum*, grows quickly to 15 feet tall. Its dark blue-black fall berries make an excellent food source for the birds. Look for Autumn Jazz®, Northern Burgundy®, and Chicago Lustre®, cultivars from the Chicagoland Grows program. The fruit is edible after cooking. Other excellent viburnum species for fall fruit and color are the coarser-leaved Linden and Wright viburnums, *Viburnum. dilatatum* (especially 'Erie') and *Viburnum wrightii*.

When, Where, and How to Plant

Plant elderberry in spring when danger of frost is past. Plant in either acid or alkaline soils that are moist and well-drained. Mix copious amounts of rotted organic matter such as compost into the planting bed. Wet sites and roadside ditches that fill with rainwater are also ideal. Dig a planting hole that is three times the width of the rootball. Dig deep enough so that, after planting, the top of the rootball is level with the ground around it. Backfill the hole with the original soil, tamp lightly, and water deeply.

Growing Tips

Keep a 2 to 3 inch layer of organic mulch around the root zone. Shredded bark or leaves work well. Water deeply each week in summer, especially during dry periods. Elderberry grows so prolifically that fertilizing is unnecessary.

Care and Maintenance

Elderberry gets too big and top heavy if left unpruned. Once established, tame it by cutting it to the ground every year or every other year. Alternatively, cut back and remove 1/3 to 1/2 of the stems each year. Carefully remove root suckers from the base to contain this aggressive shrub, but don't dispose of them—share with your friends. Elderberry has no serious pests.

Companion Planting and Design

If trees are the backbone, elderberry certainly helps form the arms and legs of a native garden. Mix it with other natives such as ornamental grasses whose straw color in late summer will contrast nicely with the fruit. It also blends well with river birch, which also likes wet soils.

We Recommend

A shorter and less rangy cultivar with feathery leaves is 'Acutiloba', sometimes listed as 'Laciniata'. 'Aurea' has golden-yellow leaves all year with bright red fruit. If you want to grow elderberry for large and productive fruit, plant 'Adams', 'Kent', or 'York'. The European red elder, *Sambucus racemosa*, produces an outstanding cut-leaved cultivar, much like Japanese maples or ferns, that also has golden-yellow leaves. Named 'Plumosa Aurea', it is more common in Europe. Common elder, *Sambucus nigra*, produces several cultivars with deep purple leaves such as 'Black Beauty' or 'Purpurea'.

If you live in the country you will recognize this selection. This shrub is native to all parts of Indiana, though the types that are natural appear a little unkempt and rangy. The newer types, some of which we list below, are more refined and suitable for tidier landscapes. The fine-textured compound leaves emanate from fast growing stems of multiple heights. Flowers open in early summer to reveal white, rounded, flat-topped blossoms 6 to 10 inches across. American elderberry suckers profusely, giving it an irregular but mounded shape. The stems often bend from the weight of the blue-black berries. The berries are a welcome staple of jams, jellies, pies, and wine. Use stems in late summer flower arrangements for something different but beware of stains from elderberry juice! Note that the raw berries and other plant parts are poisonous.

Bloom Period and Seasonal Color

June to July; blue-black fruit in August to September.

Mature Height × Spread

5 to 12 ft. × 8 to 12 ft.

Arborvitae
Thuja occidentalis

The story going around in junior high school was that if you went to the local golf course late at night, you could see the silhouettes of hooded monks praying in the moonlight. Never mind that the golf course was closed at night; the monks were reported to stand perfectly still, like statues. I'm sure the "monks" were actually arborvitae shrubs; however, I never went to the golf course to verify this. They do resemble human figures at night—if you use your imagination. In some circles, their upright, formal shape earned them the moniker "toy soldier." Their fan-shaped, evergreen leaves and vertical habit make them excellent screens, hedges, or accent plants, providing an exclamation point in an otherwise dull landscape. Though they can grow to 30 feet tall, they rarely exceed the height of a tall shrub. Dwarf types are available. —T.T.

Bloom Period and Seasonal Color
Evergreen scale-type needles all year; tiny brown cones at end of summer.

Mature Height × Spread
20 to 30 ft. × 10 to 15 ft.

When, Where, and How to Plant
Plant arborvitae in spring in moist but well-drained soils with high organic matter content. In full sun, it will grow dense and provide excellent screening. (See chapter intro for more planting instructions.)

Growing Tips
If you have a wet site, plant the shrub 1 to 2 inches above grade to improve drainage. Water regularly during dry spells, especially in the first year. Like most evergreens, it does not require additional fertilizer.

Care and Maintenance
Keep 2 to 3 inches of mulch over the root zone. Arborvitae grows slowly and rarely reaches its full 30 feet. It should not require regular pruning unless you need a specific sized hedge; in this case, prune in the early spring. Prevent snow from piling on the branches. Bagworms eat the needles and spin brown cocoon-like "bags" for protection. Control with *Bacillus thurengiensis* (Bt) in June when the larvae are young, or pull the bags off by hand in early August before they adhere to the branches too tightly. This plant naturally sheds its inner needles in the fall.

Companion Planting and Design
Its dark green color is a wonderful background for the mixed-flower border; it also makes an excellent accent plant because of its unique shape. Use it as a screen to block unsightly views such as air conditioners, trash bins, and sheds. If deer visit your yard regularly, we suggest an alternate plant.

We Recommend
Common arborvitae turns an ugly brownish-yellow during the winter. When planting new shrubs, don't be afraid to be selective. Choose shorter "shrub-sized" cultivars known to retain their dark-green color throughout winter. 'Techny' (also known as 'Mission') and 'Emerald Green' grow 15 feet tall and stay dark-green in winter. 'Globosa' is a perfect globe shape, growing 6 feet high and turning light green in winter. 'Hetz Midget' stays green all winter and slowly grows to a mature height of 4 feet. *Thuja heterophylla*, the western arborvitae, is reported to be deer resistant. Try 'Spring Grove' or 'Green Giant' for their fast growth rate and dark green winter color.

When, Where, and How to Plant

Transplant bayberry in spring after soil dries. Bayberry is not fussy. Plant in full sun to part shade in moist, slightly acidic clay or sandy soil. Dig a planting hole three times the width of the pot or rootball. Dig only deep enough so that, after planting, the top of the rootball is level with the ground around it. Backfill the hole with the original soil, tamp lightly, and water deeply.

Growing Tips

Keep 2 to 3 inches of organic mulch over the roots at all times. Water during dry periods in summer. If leaves yellow, get a soil test and adjust pH accordingly (see main intoduction regarding testing). Bayberry tolerates such poor planting sites that supplemental fertilizing is not necessary.

Care and Maintenance

Bayberry suckers readily and forms a colony of plants. Prune in late winter when you can easily see its branch structure. Never shear this shrub. Instead, always prune it to retain its informal and billowy shape. Prune taller branches all the way to the ground to reduce the overall height. If necessary, cut side branches back to the next largest branch. Remove the small root suckers that will begin to sprout around the base of the plant when it is a few years old. It has few to no known serious pests.

Companion Planting and Design

Bayberry are excellent for massing on slopes, hillsides, and in tough urban locations. Plant in front of evergreens such as arborvitae to better appreciate the berries. Underplant with early blooming crocus or hellebores. Cut branches with berries make excellent additions to holiday arrangements.

We Recommend

Bayberry needs both male and female plants to produce a good crop of berries. The female plant produces the berries, so plant one or two male plants for every five female plants to ensure good pollination. 'Morton' is a more compact clone with silvery green leaves. Wax collected from the berries is used to make bayberry-scented candles.

I remember bayberry from childhood vacations on the eastern seashore where it grows wild and scrubby and helps to stabilize beach dunes. Bayberry's unique ability to tolerate salt and high winds enables it to thrive in such locations. Since we never spent much time at the beach during winter, I never noticed the berries, which are light-gray, almost chalky white, and which cling tightly to their stems from fall until about February. After the first hard freezes of October or November, bayberry leaves give way to light gray upright stems packed full of these summer survivors. The berries make this shrub a must for the winter garden. And who can help but think of bayberry-scented candles when conjuring up images of this fine shrub? Its leathery green leaves are semievergreen in southern Indiana but completely deciduous in northern parts of the state. —T.T.

Bloom Period and Seasonal Color

Insignificant blooms in spring; purple-bronze leaves in fall and winter; chalky white fruit in fall and winter.

Mature Height × Spread

6 to 12 ft. × 6 to 12 ft.

Bluebeard

Caryopteris × clandonensis

When summer begins to wane and the garden passes its peak, 'Bluebeard' is a welcome relief, brightening the gardens of late summer and fall. At almost 3 feet tall and round, this plant will be a veil of blue from the ground up. In a manner rare for shrubs, the small clusters of dainty medium-blue flowers bloom at the base of the outermost leaves. With its flowers and silvery-green leaves, it's obvious why we sometimes call it "blue-mist shrub." Both the flowers and the leaves have a light, sweet fragrance. Bluebeard grows in a mound and rarely reaches over 3 feet tall. Its branches die to the ground each winter. Bluebeard is a maintenance-free landscape plant, an excellent choice for the weekend gardener.

Other Common Names
Caryopteris, Blue Mist, Blue Spirea

Bloom Period and Seasonal Color
Light green leaves spring through fall; flowers from July through September.

Mature Height × Spread
3 ft. × 3 ft.

When, Where, and How to Plant
Transplant bluebeard in the early spring, around the time the leaves emerge on the trees. Plant in full sun for maximum flower production. It grows in most soils but does best in sites with good drainage and plenty of organic matter. Prepare a planting hole that is three times the width of the rootball. Dig only deep enough so that, after planting, the top of the rootball will be level with the ground around it. Gently tap the side of the pot on a hard surface to loosen the rootball from the pot. Tease any roots that are growing in a circular fashion away from the rest of the root mass. Backfill the hole with the original soil. Tamp the soil lightly and water deeply.

Growing Tips
Spread a 2- to 3-inch layer of organic mulch over the entire planting area. Keep watered during dry spells in summer, especially the first year. Fertilize with a balanced fertilizer each spring. Be careful not to overfeed, or bluebeard will grow more leaves at the expense of flowers.

Care and Maintenance
Sheer dead flowers from the shrub in late fall to keep it neat. Cut bluebeard almost to the ground in late winter. Bluebeard has no serious pests.

Companion Planting and Design
Plant these late-summer beauties along a walkway or in a mixed flower garden. Bluebeard attracts bees and other insects in great supply. Their uniform growth makes them suitable for a low hedge or border plant. They die to the ground each winter and are usually treated as a perennial. Good combinations include annuals and perennials in blue, purple and white such as the salvias and boltonias for fall, or ornamental grasses such as *Pennisetum*.

We Recommend
'Blue Mist' is the most common variety and has light powder-blue flowers that are slightly fringed around the edges. 'Dark Knight' is a deep purple-blue variety with good fragrance. 'Worcester Gold' has yellow foliage to brighten a shadier spot.

Bottlebrush Buckeye
Aesculus parviflora

When, Where, and How to Plant
Transplant in the early spring just before or after the leaves emerge on the trees. Bottlebrush is very adaptable, growing in full sun or full shade. It prefers acid or alkaline soils that stay moist and have plenty of organic matter. Prepare the planting site by digging a hole three times the width of the pot. Dig deep enough so that when placed in the hole, the top of the pot is level with the ground around it. Carefully remove the plant from the pot and tease out any roots growing in a circular pattern around the sides. Backfill the hole with the original soil, tamp lightly, and water deeply.

Growing Tips
Keep 2 to 3 inches of organic mulch around the base of the plant at all times. Broadcast a balanced fertilizer around the root zone in early spring. The more organic matter is worked into the soil, the quicker and farther bottlebrush will spread.

Care and Maintenance
This native is virtually pest free. Remove $1/3$ of the branches each year for three years (see back of book for pruning information). Each year, prune the largest and most overgrown branches. This will keep it at a manageable size all the time.

Companion Planting and Design
Bottlebrush buckeye makes nice corner plantings but needs to be kept in check. When massed together, they make a good screen. It grows well in woodland gardens, blooming profusely despite the shade. Combine with *Hydrangea arborescens* or *Hydrangea quercifolia*, which also like shade.

We Recommend
There are a few improved varieties but they may be difficult to locate. 'Rogers' has large blooms that open a few weeks later than the original but tends to bend over because of their length. The red buckeye, *Aesculus pavia*, is a small tree that grows to 25 feet, native to the southeast. Its large erect red blooms open earlier in the spring and are quite a sight.

With a name like 'Bottlebrush', it is a small wonder that this shrub makes it into contemporary landscapes. The name does not do it justice, for this is one of our most beautiful native shrubs. Indigenous to the southeastern United States, it makes an excellent addition if there is ample room for it to spread. It reaches a maximum height of only 12 to 15 feet but spreads at least that wide by sending up root suckers. Bottlebrush is related to the Ohio buckeye and horse chestnut, but its large palm-like leaves are not bothered by the foliar diseases that afflict its relatives. Showy bristle-like blooms cover the shrub in late June and July, growing 4 inches wide and 1 foot long. After the rush of spring-blooming plants when larger shrubs and trees have ceased flowering, bottlebrush buckeye is a glorious sight.

Bloom Period and Seasonal Color
White blooms in late June to July; yellow leaves in fall.

Mature Height × Spread
8 to 15 ft. × 15 ft.

Carolina Allspice
Calycanthus floridus

Allspice has sweet fragrant flowers that open in late spring and early summer. The name "allspice" fits it well—leaves, stems, and flowers all carry fragrances likened to strawberry, pineapple, grapefruit, and banana, as well as cider and cinnamon! The unusual but dainty dark-maroon to brown blooms are subtly beautiful, nothing like the loud hydrangea or ubiquitous lilac. Its light-green leaves set off the darker flowers like a picture frame and help them to stand out. Its fragrance is light but sweet, unlike the spicier viburnums. The fragrance varies from plant to plant, so crush a leaf or flower or scrape the stem to compare. Buy plants that are in bloom to assure yourself that you have one of the more aromatic specimens. Enjoy it all year by using dried allspice blooms in flower arrangements.

Other Common Name
Sweetshrub

Bloom Period and Seasonal Color
Maroon-brown blooms from late June lasting through July; yellow fall color.

Mature Height × Spread
6 to 9 ft. × 6 to 12 ft.

When, Where, and How to Plant
Carolina allspice is a hardy plant that can be planted any time the soil is dry. It grows in full sun or shade, placing it near bottlebrush buckeye in versatility. Native to the southeastern United States, it thrives in both wet and dry soils that are either acid or alkaline. Add ample compost to the planting area since it likes organic matter. Though allspice has a medium growth rate, it grows faster if the soil is well prepared. Start by digging a hole three times the width of the rootball. Dig deep enough so that, after planting, the top of the rootball is level with the ground around it. Backfill the hole with the original soil and water deeply.

Growing Tips
Keep a 2- to 3-inch layer of organic mulch around the root zone to hold moisture. This will also encourage it to sprout suckers which help it thicken and spread. It will grow shorter and denser with more sun. Allspice will benefit from occasional applications of fertilizer. Sprinkle a balanced fertilizer around the root zone in early spring for best results.

Care and Maintenance
Allspice is a care-free plant. This shrub will benefit from having the roots damp but not wet. Allspice will not require regular pruning since it grows slowly. Prune out the root suckers to keep it from spreading too wide; do this shortly after blooming in the early weeks of summer. Allspice is virtually pest-free.

Companion Planting and Design
Plant allspice in a shrub border, near a patio or walkway where brushing up against it will release its scent, or as a background plant in a shady or woodland garden.

We Recommend
It is not completely clear whether allspice is native to Indiana. Nevertheless, it is in the Eastern U.S. and a favorite American shrub and quite common in the South. 'Edith Wilder', Michael Lindsey', and 'Urbana' are favorite cultivars that are extremely fragrant. Flowers are more red than brown. 'Athens' is more compact and has yellow flowers.

Doublefile Viburnum

Viburnum plicatum var. *tomentosum*

When, Where, and How to Plant

Transplant balled-and-burlapped specimens in early spring or late fall. Plant in soils that are moist but well drained with plenty of organic matter. Full sun will encourage the maximum number of flowers possible, but double-file viburnum also grows well in partial shade. Prepare the planting site by digging a hole three times the diameter of the rootball. Dig deep enough so that the top of the rootball is level with the ground around it after planting. Backfill the hole with the original soil, tamp lightly, and water deeply.

Growing Tips

Keep a 2- to 3-inch layer of organic mulch around the entire planting area to help hold moisture and keep weeds down. Otherwise, it's not a fussy plant. Fertilize in early spring or late fall.

Care and Maintenance

Water doublefile viburnums during periods of drought in summer. Prune overly long branches that throw the plant out of balance shortly after the flowers fade. When pruning, be careful not to remove the lower branches that grow close to the ground. *Do not* sheer with hedge clippers as this would destroy its natural shape. Work *with* the shrub to accentuate the parallel layers of branches. This plant has no serious pest problems.

Companion Planting and Design

Use as an accent plant in a partly shaded corner or on the edge of a woodland garden. Combine with plants with red leaves to complement the red berries and red pedicels that remain after the birds devour the fruit. Make sure you give it plenty of room so that it reaches its full potential. The leaves turn a rich wine-red in the fall. With few pests and outstanding year-round character, we consider doublefile viburnum one of the best all-around shrubs for the landscape. It may experience branch dieback from winterkill in severe weather, especially in northern Indiana.

We Recommend

Among the best varieties is 'Mariesii', which has much larger flowers and fruit and strong horizontal branches. 'Shasta', grows only 6 to 8 feet high but spreads twice that far. It has huge, 6-inch flowers and is best suited to southern Indiana. Both have excellent burgundy red leaves in fall.

Doublefile viburnum is an exquisite shrub that is underutilized. Its shape is unique, growing long horizontal branches in layers, or rows, up to 12 feet long. Its elegant white, upright flowers rise just above the leaves and line the branches. They are round and flat like small lacecap hydrangeas. The inner flowers produce bright red berries in July and August and turn black shortly afterward if the birds don't get them first. Doublefile viburnum has easily identifiable leaves with many parallel and furrowed veins. They turn a rich wine red in fall. Many horticulturists say that this plant is sensitive to drought. We have both transplanted this shrub in the heat of summer (against conventional wisdom) and found that it bounced back better than ever in subsequent years. Doublefile viburnum experiences occasional dieback from cold in Zone 5b, in northern Indiana.

Bloom Period and Seasonal Color

White flowers in May, leaves like burgundy leather in fall.

Mature Height × Spread

8 to 12 ft. × 10 to 12 ft.

Dwarf Alberta Spruce
Picea glauca 'Conica'

A cultivar of white spruce, the dwarf Alberta spruce represents a favorite group of novelty plants called "dwarf conifers." These are slow growing, shorter versions of their tree-sized cousins and are popular among hobbyists and patient gardeners. They usually do not mix well in shrub or flower gardens, so plant these novelties as accents or in rock gardens where they easily stand out. Hobbyists add them to gardens reserved just for dwarf conifers. Their diminutive size also makes them a good choice for small spaces. Dwarf Alberta spruce grows in a perfect cone shape with short, soft, light-green needles. Its dense foliage and symmetric shape is perfect for a formal garden setting or for those gardeners who like their plants "neat and tidy."

Bloom Period and Seasonal Color
Evergreen; best types do not discolor in winter.

Mature Height × Spread
12 ft. × 4 ft., *very* slow growing.

When, Where, and How to Plant
Transplant dwarf conifers in early spring, as soon as the ground is dry. Soil should be slightly acid or alkaline and moist but well-drained with ample organic matter. Many dwarf conifers also tolerate sandy soil; however, heavy wet clay soils will drown them. Plant in full sun for best growth. Dig a planting hole three times the size of the container. Dig deep enough so that the top of the rootball is level with the ground after planting. Backfill the hole with the original soil, tamp lightly, and water deeply.

Growing Tips
Keep a 2- to 3-inch layer of organic mulch spread over the root zone. Water in summer during dry spells and again in fall to prepare it for winter. Avoid planting near walkways as this encourages spider mites.

Care and Maintenance
These are slow-growing shrubs, so pruning will not be necessary. Hot and dry weather in the summer predispose the dwarf Alberta spruce to spider mites. To check for spider mites, hold a white sheet of paper under one of the branches and tap it hard. Pinhead-sized mites will begin moving around on the paper. Depending on the time of the year, treatment may include a dormant or summer weight oil or a traditional miticide.

Companion Planting and Design
Plant as specimens, accents, or in large containers. Keep the rootball of potted conifers from freezing by piling straw bales around it; move the pot up against a building for warmth or over-winter the rootball by burying the pot.

We Recommend
Most conifers, including pine, fir, arborvitae, and hemlock, have some short or irregularly shaped variants considered dwarf. *Pinus mugo* 'Compacta', the dwarf form of mugo pine, has a more rounded mound shape and longer and stiffer pine-type needles. Beware of pine needle scale, however. *Chamaecyparis pisifera*, the Threadleaf Japanese False Cypress, has many dwarf cultivars including the 'Filifera Nana', the golden-leaved 'Gold Spangle', and a blue-gray called 'Boulevard'. Hinoki False Cypress, *Chamaecyparis obtusa*, produces needles in fan shapes that look like green coral. 'Nana Gracilis' is excellent.

Dwarf Fothergilla
Fothergilla gardenii

When, Where, and How to Plant
Plant dwarf fothergilla in the early spring or late fall in moist but well-drained slightly acidic soils high in organic matter. It blooms more heavily when it receives at least four to six hours of full sun per day. Prepare the planting site by digging a hole three times as wide as the rootball. Dig only deep enough so that, after planting, the top of the rootball will be level with the ground around it. Backfill the hole with the original soil, tamp lightly, and water deeply.

Growing Tips
Keep a 2- to 3-inch layer of organic mulch over the entire planting area. Fothergilla grows slowly but will speed up with extra care. Broadcast fertilizer around the root zone in early spring or early fall and amend the soil with organic matter.

Care and Maintenance
It rarely needs pruning since it barely grows taller than 3 feet. Like all spring-blooming shrubs, *Fothergilla* develops flower buds for the next year during the previous summer. If necessary, prune it shortly after blooming to avoid removing future flowers. Let it spread by suckering at the roots. Dig the outer suckers, keeping roots intact, and share with friends. Leaves may turn yellow (chlorotic) if the soil pH is too high. Have the soil tested to be sure. Fothergilla has no serious pests.

Companion Planting and Design
Dwarf fothergilla is wonderful in the foreground of a shrub border, as foundation plantings, or mixed with late-blooming daffodils. Mix with hellebores in partly shaded sites. Enjoy the slightly twisting stems in winter. Dwarf fothergilla is a plant for all seasons.

We Recommend
'Epstein Form' is a dwarf with excellent fall color. 'Blue Mist' grows to 3 feet tall. Large fothergilla, *Fothergilla major*, has similar flowers and bloom times but grows to 10 feet tall and almost as wide. *F. major* 'Mt. Airy' survives extreme cold and continues blooming. It is widely popular, growing to 5 or 6 feet tall and suckering heavily.

Fothergilla flowers float in the air like tiny white bottlebrushes that send out a mildly sweet perfume when in bloom. Opening before there are any leaves on its branches, the flowers resemble short white candles atop a candelabra made of twigs. When the flowers fade and give way to summer, the shrub takes on a mound shape suitable for foundation planting. The blue-green leaves have prominent veins with a slightly scalloped edge. They turn bright yellow-orange and rival the burning bush for most brilliant in the fall. This is a pest-free, slow growing shrub. Since it is native to the Southeast, dwarf fothergilla may not be hardy in northern Indiana, except around the lake where it stays warmer. Fothergilla was named after an English horticulturist, John Fothergill, who lived in the eighteenth century and claimed the largest collection of American plants anywhere.

Other Common Name
Witchalder

Bloom Period and Seasonal Color
White blooms in early spring; brilliant yellow-orange leaves in October.

Mature Height × Spread
2 to 5 ft. × 3 to 5 ft., with a suckering habit

Hydrangea

Hydrangea arborescens 'Annabelle'

The difficulty in choosing one hydrangea for this book bespeaks the variety and adaptability of this collection of plants. Hydrangea blooms from late spring through fall, depending on the type. Its flowers range from mop-head or snowball types, to lacecaps, and others in between. Annabelle is a shrubby, lower-growing, mop-head type with large dark green leaves. Its 8-inch white flowers make a lush, bold statement when they open in June, lasting up to eight weeks. It dies back to the ground each year. The peegee hydrangea, Hydrangea paniculata *'Grandiflora', was among the most common of all landscape shrubs but is now described as "old-fashioned." The faded flowers are extremely popular for cutting and in dried arrangements, wreaths, and garlands. The oakleaf hydrangea,* Hydrangea quercifolia, *has year-round interest, blooming in June with excellent fall color and cinnamon-colored papery bark in winter.*

Bloom Period and Seasonal Color
White blooms in June to August; yellow leaves in fall.

Mature Height × Spread
4 ft. × 4 ft.

When, Where, and How to Plant
Plant 'Annabelle' in early spring in moist soils filled with organic matter. It is adapted to many light conditions, growing naturally in partial shade. It also blooms profusely in full sun. Part-sun to part-shade is ideal. Dig a planting hole three times the width of the rootball. Dig only deep enough so that, after planting, the top of the rootball is level with the ground around it. Backfill the hole with the original soil, tamp lightly, and water deeply.

Growing tips
Keep a 2- to 3-inch layer of organic matter around the root zone. 'Annabelle' may wilt in the heat of summer in dry soils. Water deeply and regularly to avoid this. It adapts well to periodic flooding. An interesting side note: Bigleaf hydrangea, *Hydrangea macrophylla*, produces blue flowers in acidic soils and pink flowers in alkaline soils. Because of its intolerance of cold, however, it only blooms reliably in extreme southern parts of the state.

Care and Maintenance
Hydrangea has few pest problems. Prune 'Annabelle' to the ground each spring. It may require occasional staking since the large flowers sometimes cause the stems to flop over. (Consult a Master Gardener or an Extension professional for the right time to prune other hydrangea types.)

Companion Planting and Design
Plant 'Annabelle' in a shrub border with *Fothergilla* or *Caryopteris* in the foreground, or as an accent plant. It stands out even more with fine-textured evergreens, such as arborvitae, in the background. Mix oakleaf hydrangea with other shade tolerant natives like bottlebrush buckeye.

We Recommend
Hydrangea paniculata 'Tardiva' is an excellent late summer and fall blooming cultivar. It also tolerates partially shaded sites. Large-flowered oakleaf cultivars include 'Alice', 'Snow Queen', and 'Snowflake'. 'Pee Wee' is a dwarf oakleaf type. A new cultivar of *Hydrangea macrophylla*, called 'Endless Summer', will be available in 2004. Its blue and pink blooms open reliably every year, regardless of your location.

Inkberry Holly
Ilex glabra

When, Where, and How to Plant
Plant inkberry in early spring in moist but well-drained soil with plenty of organic matter. It will grow thicker when planted in full sun. It prefers slightly acidic soils. Spread sulfur according to soil test directions to help acidify (see main introduction regarding soil testing). It grows naturally in swampy areas, so poorly drained sites with abundant moisture suit it well. Plant according to instructions in chapter introduction.

Growing Tips
Maintain 2 to 3 inches of organic mulch over the root zone, especially as the plant prepares for the cold in fall. Broadleaf evergreens frequently suffer winterburn if not properly mulched. Water weekly especially during dry spells in summer. Fertilize lightly according to instructions in the chapter introduction.

Care and Maintenance
Remove dead or broken branches in the spring with sharp pruning shears. When left alone, inkberry grows open and airy and frequently loses its lower leaves. To renew its vigor and density, cut it to the ground in the spring. Winter temperatures below -10 degrees Fahrenheit may kill some of the leaves or branches. Chlorotic yellow leaves may form if the soil is too alkaline. Acidify the soil with sulfur if needed.

Companion Planting and Design
Use inkberry as a screen or background plant for the mixed-flower border or trim it into a hedge. Inkberry needs both male and female plants to set fruit well. Plant at least one male for every five females.

We Recommend
'Compacta' only reaches 4 to 6 feet. 'Nordic' is a dwarf that tolerates temperatures below -20 degrees Fahrenheit. 'Shamrock' holds its lower leaves well. Broadleaf evergreen hollies with traditional bright red berries reliable in Indiana are the meserve hybrids, *Ilex × meserveae*. Good cultivars include 'China Girl' and its pollinator, 'China Boy', and 'Blue Princess' and 'Blue Prince.' They grow 8 to 10 feet, have lustrous, dark blue-green, traditionally spiny leaves and bright-red fruit. Prune to shape the meserves if they get out of hand.

Mention the word "holly" and images of bright-red berries and spine-tipped leaves come to mind. Though it lacks these attributes common to its popular cousins, it is one of the few broadleaf hollies that regularly survives Indiana's harsh winters. What it lacks in red fruit in December, it more than makes up for in fine leaf texture the remainder of the year. Its small and narrow, slightly pointed, dark-green leaves are a welcome relief from the common yew and juniper. The leaves have a few "teeth" at the tips, but they do not jab like other hollies. When present, the berries are a dark blue-black. These attributes differ enough from traditional holly that many a rookie horticulturist has mistaken it for a different plant. This is a tough evergreen shrub that tolerates salt, air pollution, and other conditions found in urban areas.

Other Common Name
Gallberry

Bloom Period and Seasonal Color
Insignificant spring flowers; blue-black fruit in fall.

Mature Height × Spread
6 to 8 ft. × 8 to 10 ft.

Japanese Kerria
Kerria japonica

Nothing beats Japanese kerria for pure brightness of color in early spring. This vase-shaped shrub spreads its branches like a fountain in the middle of a pond, sprawling as if it has many legs. It is a hardy substitute for forsythia whose buds are regularly killed by cold in the deep of winter. A relative of the rose, apple, and cherry the five-petaled flowers line the stems like large buttercups in late winter. They bloom off and on through summer. The dark green arching stems provide relief in winter and harken of warm days ahead. Few shrubs tolerate shade so well and then bloom so profusely.

Other Common Name
Japanese Rose

Bloom Period and Seasonal Color
March to April; interesting green stems in winter.

Mature Height × Spread
3 to 6 ft. × 6 to 9 ft.

When, Where, and How to Plant
Plant Japanese kerria in early spring or late fall in moist, slightly acidic but well-drained soils. Although it grows in full sun, it performs best in part sun or shade. The full sun and exposure causes the flowers to bleach and then fade more quickly. Filtered light or the northeast side of the house is ideal. Dig a planting hole up to three times the width of the rootball. Dig only deep enough so that, after planting, the top of the rootball is level with the ground around it. Backfill with the original soil, tamp lightly, and water deeply.

Growing Tips
Keep 2 to 3 inches of organic mulch such as shredded bark over the root zone at all times. Water deeply on a weekly basis during dry spells in summer. Fertilize in early spring or late fall. Avoid over-fertilizing as it may encourage abundant but spindly growth at the expense of flowers.

Care and Maintenance
Prune approximately $1/3$ of the oldest and largest stems back to the ground each year to keep the center of the plant open. This helps the plant show off its naturally fountain-like growth habit. If overgrown, kerria will withstand pruning to the ground to rejuvenate. Train regrowth by selecting the strongest stems and cutting away spindlier ones. This plant has no serious pests.

Companion Planting and Design
Japanese kerria beckons woodland walkers if planted along a path. An evergreen background helps set off the yellow flowers, and the contrasting green stems and foliage provide visual interest. Let it sprawl around the edge of a path or down a slight slope.

We Recommend
Kerria boasts single and double flower types. 'Golden Guinea' is a large-flowered single yellow that blooms over a long period. 'Albescens' is a light, creamy yellow that appears almost white in full sun. 'Pleniflora' is a double-flowered type with blooms up to 2 inches across, reminiscent of strawflowers.

Japanese Spirea
Spirea japonica 'Shirobana'

When, Where, and How to Plant
Plant 'Shirobana' and other spireas in spring or fall when the ground is dry in any soil that is well drained. Spirea languishes in wet, poorly drained soils. It produces more flowers in full sun. Dig planting holes three times the width of the rootball or container. Dig only deep enough so that, after planting, the top of the rootball is level with the ground around it. Lightly tap the side of the container on a hard surface to loosen the root mass. Carefully remove the rootball from the container, place in hole, spread the roots, and backfill. Tamp lightly and water deeply.

Growing Tips
Spirea may get pot bound before planting. If so, don't be afraid to make three or four vertical cuts in the root mass and then spread the roots apart while planting. Keep a 2- to 3-inch layer of organic mulch over the root zone and water during dry spells. Fertilize in early spring or early fall to encourage growth.

Care and Maintenance
When overgrown or spindly, spirea will rejuvenate nicely if cut to the ground every few years. Alternatively, prune out 1/3 of the oldest and largest branches each year in spring. Pinch off dead or fading flowers to encourage intermittent blooming throughout the rest of the summer and to keep it tidy.

Companion Planting and Design
Spirea grows best as a foundation plant or as a low-growing edging in the shrub and perennial border. It will gently cascade over a low wall and mixes well in rock gardens. Brilliantly colored gold-leaved varieties serve well as accent plants.

We Recommend
Spirea × *bumalda* 'Anthony Waterer' is a hybrid that grows 4 feet tall. Its deep-pink flowers bloom prolifically against a background of blue-green foliage. 'Goldflame' and 'Limemound' have brilliant yellow and yellow-green foliage with red tips in the spring. 'Alpina', 'Golden Elf', and 'Magic Carpet' are dwarfs that are used more like groundcovers. *Spirea* × *cinerea* 'Grefsheim' is a great replacement for bridal veil spirea. Its delicate leaves emerge after blooming alongside spring bulbs.

For those of us who can't make up our minds, this is the perfect shrub. With flowers of white, pink, and magenta all on the same plant, gardeners get three plants for the cost of one. This species and related hybrids such as Spirea × bumalda burst forth just when the perennial garden peaks in early summer. Its flat-topped, circular clusters of flowers cover the entire plant and remind us of pale, fuzzy mums. Depending on the cultivar, the soft and narrow but sharply pointed leaves often emerge light-green with pink, red, or golden tips. 'Shirobana', 'Little Princess', and others will bloom off and on throughout the summer, especially if you pinch off the old blooms. Spireas are easy, low-maintenance, fast-growing plants that are seldom bothered by serious pests.

Other Common Name
Bumald Spirea

Bloom Period and Seasonal Color
White, pink, and red blooms in June and July and sporadically throughout summer; bronze-purple leaves in fall.

Mature Height × Spread
2 to 3 ft. × 2 to 3 ft.

Judd Viburnum
Viburnum × juddii

The sweet smell of viburnum in April is a sure sign that spring has arrived. There are earlier blooming shrubs than viburnum, but their fragrance pales by comparison. Reminiscent of lilac in shear aromatic "punch," plant them near a window to let the sweet, fresh spring air in. Judd viburnums have round clusters (cymes) of swollen pink buds that open to reveal white flowers. The flowers are a little larger than the related burkwood or Korean-spice viburnums. The leaves that follow are soft and a pale to medium green. The shrub forms a rounded mound when left alone and blends into the landscape in summer; however, it makes a comeback in fall when the leaves turn deep copper red.

Bloom Period and Seasonal Color
Early spring pink buds open to white flowers; burgundy red color in fall.

Mature Height × Spread
6 to 8 ft. × 6 to 8 ft.

When, Where, and How to Plant
Judd viburnum is a versatile shrub that tolerates planting any time the soil is dry, but early spring is best. Plant in slightly acid or alkaline soil that is moist but well drained. For best flower display, plant it where it will receive six hours of full sun per day. It blooms less in shadier locations. Dig a hole three times the width of the rootball and deep enough so that, after planting, the top of the rootball is level with the ground around it. Backfill the hole with the original soil, tamp lightly forming a 'bowl' to collect moisture, and water deeply.

Growing Tips
Keep a 2 to 3-inch layer of mulch around the roots to keep them moist. Water regularly, especially after planting and in summer when it starts to develop flower buds for the next spring. Fertilize lightly in early spring or early fall.

Care and Maintenance
Prune shortly after it blooms in the spring. *Don't shear* the shrub into a ball; instead, remove select branches to retain the natural shape. If it becomes overgrown, remove 1/3 of the largest stems back to the ground each year for three years. Leaf spots are common but rarely cause serious problems.

Companion Planting and Design
Plant judd and other fragrant viburnums near a common walk or door and revel in their spicy perfume. Underplant with spring bulbs like daffodils. In southern Indiana, other viburnums like burkwoods remain partially evergreen.

We Recommend
The burkwood viburnum, *Viburnum × burkwoodii,* is a similar species that grows slightly larger and is semievergreen. 'Mohawk' develops larger, swollen red flower buds that open very slowly and extend the effective bloom period by several weeks. The Koreanspice viburnum, *Viburnum carlesii,* has a fragrance perhaps stronger than the judd's or burkwood's and is more widely grown. Nevertheless, judd and burkwood are superior types. Ask your nursery supplier for one if they are difficult to find.

Leatherleaf Viburnum
Viburnum rhytidophyllum

When, Where, and How to Plant
Transplant leatherleaf in early spring after the ground dries. Planting in late fall may subject it to additional winter leaf scorch. Like many viburnums, leatherleaf is not picky about soil type; however, it does best in moist, well-drained locations with plenty of organic matter. Leatherleaf grows well in shade and is ideal on the north side of a building. It likes sun but should be protected from exposed and windy locations, especially in the winter. In fact, leatherleaf is considered a semi-evergreen in the northern reaches of the state. Prepare a planting hole that is three times the width of the rootball. Dig only deep enough so that after planting the top of the rootball is level with the ground around it. Backfill the hole with the original soil, tamp lightly, and water deeply.

Growing Tips
Keep a 2- to 3-inch layer of organic matter over the entire planting area. Water weekly in summer. Mulch again in fall to reduce winterburn. Broadcast fertilizer around the root zone in early spring to encourage growth.

Care and Maintenance
In severe winters, leatherleaf may suffer extensive leaf dieback if it is not protected from the sun and wind or if it is planted where there is poor drainage. Prune any dead or broken branches after blooming in late May or early June. If overgrown, leatherleaf survives severe rejuvenation pruning. Leatherleaf is seldom bothered by pests.

Companion Planting and Design
Though not as refined as other broadleaf evergreens, leatherleaf has its place in the southern Indiana landscape. It makes an excellent screen or background for the shrub and flower border. The coarse foliage contrasts well with fine-needled evergreens such as spruce, fir, and hemlock.

We Recommend
Viburnum × rhytidophylloides, lantanaphyllum viburnum, has smoother leaves and is hardier than the species leatherleaf, especially in northern Indiana. Leaf dieback will not be nearly as severe with this cultivar. The varieties 'Willowood' and 'Alleghany' repeat their bloom in late summer.

As its name suggests, the leaves of this viburnum are as rugged as they come. The thick, rough, wrinkled upper surface complements the softer fuzzy underside. From a distance, the leatherleaf resembles rhododendron, but it's not nearly as finicky about soil. In southern Indiana, the creamy-white flowers open in early May in flat but circular clusters consisting of many smaller flowers, sometimes reaching 8 inches in diameter. The flowers are followed by bright red fruit in late summer that fade to black (if birds don't gobble them up first!). It blooms intermittently again in late summer. Leatherleaf grows 15 feet tall in a rounded shape and is very useful when set against a brick or concrete building.

Bloom Period and Seasonal Color
Creamy white blooms in May; red berries in fall.

Mature Height × Spread
8 to 12 ft. × 8 to 12 ft.

175

Lilac

Syringa vulgaris

Lilacs have no equal when it comes to captivating fragrance. For many gardeners, the strongly perfumed blooms bring back childhood memories of grandmother's house. In today's modern landscapes, lilac is often planted for nostalgic purposes. Growing up Catholic, my earliest memories of lilacs are of picking them from yards, where I wasn't supposed to be, to honor the Virgin Mary during the month of May. More than 1,600 species and varieties of lilac exist today. Of the types adapted to Indiana, the flowers are pink, blue, purple, or white and come in double- and single-petaled versions. The smallest bouquet will fill your home with their heady perfume and your spirit with joy. —T.T.

Bloom Period and Seasonal Color
Pink, blue, purple, and white flowers in April; no fall color.

Mature Height × Spread
6 to 12 ft. × 8 ft.

When, Where, and How to plant
Plant lilac in full sun in early spring or late fall in moist but well-drained soil. It grows best in soils with a neutral or alkaline pH with plenty of organic matter. Prepare a planting hole three times the width of the rootball. Dig the hole only deep enough so that the top of the rootball is level with the ground around it after planting. Backfill the hole with the original soil, tamp lightly, and water deeply.

Growing Tips
Keep a 2- to 3-inch layer of organic mulch like shredded bark around the entire root zone. Water in summer during dry spells.

Care and Maintenance
Lilac flowers are formed on growth from the previous season. Prune shortly after blooming to encourage maximum flower bud formation. To prune, first "deadhead" the fading flowers by snipping them off at the base. Then, choose $1/3$ of the largest and oldest stems and prune them all the way to the ground, encouraging a few sprouting suckers to grow as their replacements each year. To share with friends, dig the outermost suckers, keeping roots intact. Rejuvenate overgrown lilacs by cutting them to the ground. It may take three years before they bloom again. Lilac borers "drill" into canes causing dieback. Lilac is susceptible to a disease called powdery mildew. This common fungus turns the leaves a chalky white color by late summer. Controls are not practical or recommended.

Companion Planting and Design
Because it tends to thin at the bottom, plant lilac as a background in the shrub border or as a screen. Plant where you can enjoy its spicy bouquet!

We Recommend
There are hundreds of lilac cultivars and hybrids. Check with your nursery supplier for availability. 'President Grevy' (blue) and 'Belle de Nancy' (pink) are old-time double-flowered types. *Syringa* 'Betsy Ross' is a shorter but wider, shrubby, white hybrid with mildew resistance, as reported from the National Arboretum. Korean lilacs, such as 'Miss Kim', are shorter and work well in smaller yards. They are resistant to mildew.

Purple Beautyberry
Callicarpa dichotoma

When, Where, and How to Plant
Plant in full sun to part sun in well-drained soil amended with plenty of organic matter. Dig a hole that is up to three times the diameter of the root-ball. Dig so that, after planting, the top of the rootball will be even with the ground around it. Backfill the hole with the original soil, tamp lightly, and water deeply.

Growing Tips
Mulch with 2 to 3 inches of shredded bark around the root zone. Water regularly, especially during periods of drought in summer. This will help it reach its maximum height for the year, especially if it is growing in the northern part of the state where it usually dies back to the ground each year. Fertilize lightly according to chapter introduction.

Care and Maintenance
It blooms on new growth each year, so prune in early spring as soon as you notice buds swelling. Cut away deadwood with sharp hand pruners. This may require pruning all the way to the ground, depending on how cold the weather was in winter. (See the back of the book regarding pruning.) Beautyberry may get a little rangy and overgrown in southern Indiana, where the stems are more likely to survive the winter onslaught. Cut out about ⅓ of the oldest branches each year, maintaining its natural, cascading shape. Beautyberry is rarely bothered by pests. It may die back to the ground in Zone 5; use it in that zone like a large perennial.

Companion Planting and Design
Beautyberry makes an excellent background shrub, especially if planted in front of evergreen screens. Their cascading stems beckon walkers along a woodland path in filtered light. Planted in a circle at their base, fall crocus make a natural altar around this deserving specimen.

We Recommend
'Early Amethyst' is a shorter cultivar. Though not as vigorous, 'Albifructus' has white fruit as its name suggests. The native *Callicarpa americana*, the American beautyberry, grows taller and has larger fruit, like big lavender mulberries. It is more rangy and is best planted in a native garden. It is only reliable in extreme southern Indiana.

A subtle shrub most of the year, purple beautyberry sneaks up on us. Its upright and arching stems grow so quickly each year that gardeners hardly notice it dies back to the ground most winters. It has medium green leaves, similar to forsythia, that blend with most shrubs until late summer. The petite and pale-pink fuzzy flowers, hidden in the axils of the leaves, almost go unnoticed throughout the summer. Tight clusters of blushing pink berries follow in September. They reach their full glory, a glossy lavender, later in the month. They cling tightly to the branches during fall color change (a vivid yellow) in October and last well into November. Few plants pack such a powerful punch this late in the year. Owners of this spectacular fall shrub had better be prepared to answer the question "What's that?!"

Other Common Name
Beautyberry

Bloom Period and Seasonal Color
Lavender-pink flowers in July and August; lavender fruit September to November.

Mature Height × Spread
4 to 6 ft. × 6 to 8 ft.

Red Chokeberry
Aronia arbutifolia 'Brilliantissima'

The red chokeberry is another shrub for all seasons. A close relative of the native black chokeberry, it blooms in May throughout most of the state—earlier around Evansville. The subtle apple blossom-like white blooms are tinged with pink. In fall, chokeberry leaves turn a brilliant red, rivaling any burning bush. Its fruit turns wine-red in the fall and lasts all winter. The 1/4-inch berries are stunning at their peak and resemble misplaced cherries. The fruit finally shrivels in late winter. The shrub gets its name from the berries' bitter taste. It is strong enough to choke human and beast! This explains why fruit can still be found clinging to the branches as late as March—local wildlife tend to avoid it.

Bloom Period and Seasonal Color
White flowers in late April; wine-red berries in early fall through winter.

Mature Height × Spread
6 to 10 ft. × 5 ft.

When, Where, and How to Plant
Plant chokeberries in the early spring or late fall after the leaves drop. For best flower and fruit production, plant in full sun. They grow well in partial sun but produce fewer berries. Chokeberries prefer moist, well-drained soil rich in organic matter. They also tolerate harsh growing conditions such as very wet or very dry soil. Dig the planting hole three times the width of the rootball. Dig deep enough so that, after planting, the top of the rootball is level with the ground around it. Backfill with the original soil, tamp lightly, and water deeply.

Growing Tips
Keep 2 to 3 inches of organic mulch over the root zone. Water deeply on a weekly basis in summer. Encourage growth by broadcasting fertilizer around the root zone in early spring or late fall.

Care and Maintenance
If they get leggy, prune to promote denser growth by cutting from 1/3 to 1/2 of the oldest stems to the ground. This will allow more light to reach the center of the plant and encourage bushier growth with more flowers. Try cutting back a few overly long stems to sturdy buds to encourage branching. Overgrown and spindly specimens rejuvenate quickly if cut to the ground. (See the back of this book for more on pruning.) Chokeberries are not regularly bothered by any pests.

Companion Planting and Design
Plant as a screen or mass planting to enjoy the tremendous fall color and fruit display. It suckers freely, so give it room to spread The berries look especially beautiful when mixed with ornamental grasses that turn straw colored in the fall. Mass plantings of fruiting red chokeberry will turn the head, especially after the leaves drop.

We Recommend
'Brilliantissima' is the best known cultivar, with larger, glossier leaves turning scarlet in fall. Some say it rivals burning bush. It also has larger and glossier red fruit. The black chokeberry, *Aronia melanocarpa*, is similar to the red except for its black berries. Plant it in wet, native gardens and wetlands. Iroquois Beauty™ is a dwarf.

Red Twig Dogwood
Cornus alba

When, Where, and How to Plant

Transplant red twig in the spring in moist but well-drained soils with plenty of organic matter. Native to swampy and boggy areas, it tolerates wet soils better than most shrubs. Grow it in full sun or part shade where it has room to spread. Stem color will be brighter with more sun. (See chapter introduction for more planting instructions.)

Growing Tips

Keep 2 to 3 inches of mulch over the roots. Share suckers with friends or root the branch tips by bending to the ground and covering with mulch. You can use a shovelful of soil and place it over the tip at about 8 inches down, leaving the tip or uppermost 8 inches exposed. It will root (over time) where the leaves attach to the stem (the node). Fertilize lightly (see chapter introduction).

Care and Maintenance

Rejuvenate red twig dogwood and encourage more intense stem coloration by pruning it to the ground with loppers every year in early spring before leaves start to emerge. As vigorous new growth emerges, cut some shoots back to nodes about halfway to encourage branching. A stem canker disease, though rarely fatal, causes random branch dieback during the growing season. Cut infected branches at the base to improve its appearance.

Companion Planting and Design

Tall, evergreen backgrounds such as 'Hicks Yew' and arborvitae help frame the stems in winter. Mix with tall ornamental grasses or chokeberries for a great effect. When cut, the stems make excellent additions to holiday greenery and other arrangements.

We Recommend

'Bloodgood' has brilliant red stems. 'Variegata' and 'Argenteo-marginata' have white to creamy-white green leaves. 'Bailhalo' also has variegated leaves but is more compact and refined. *Cornus sericea* is similar in form but may be more susceptible to stem canker. 'Cardinal' is an excellent cultivar. 'Flaviramea' has golden-yellow stems. 'Silver and Gold' is shorter, with leaves edged in white and yellow stems. The native pagoda dogwood, *Cornus alternifolia*, is a large shrub or small tree. Its branches grow in whorls, causing a remarkable layered effect.

One glance at this favorite in December snow and you'll understand why it is so popular. The stems look like they were dipped in bright red paint and stuck in the garden. In the winter, you can pick out its native cousin growing in the ditches and fence rows along I-65 south of Indianapolis. It sends forth creamy white, round but flat-topped blooms in May and June, followed by dull-white berries that are immediately eaten by birds. For the rest of the summer, this dogwood makes a nice background shrub, and its variegated cultivars help keep it interesting. With the onset of cold weather, the twigs begin to turn red. The color reaches its peak as the foliage drops in fall. The stems stay red all winter and fade to green again with the arrival of spring.

Other Common Name

Tatarian Dogwood, Redosier Dogwood

Bloom Period and Seasonal Color

Creamy white blooms in spring; red stems in fall and winter.

Mature Height × Spread

8 to 10 ft. × 5 to 10 ft.

Summersweet
Clethra alnifolia

A highly adaptable shrub, summersweet is well named for the fragrance its flowers exude during the height of summer, when most other shrubs have "shut down." Summersweet's flowers are as loved by bees and other pollinators as they are by their owners. In July, numerous small white or pink blooms open in fuzzy, 6-inch-long spikes on the tips of arching branches. It continues to bloom for most of the rest of summer. The dried seeds cling all winter. The leaves are a thick, shiny, dark green that turn light yellow in the fall. Summersweet develops root suckers that help give it a rounded mound shape often wider than it is tall.

Other Common Name
Sweet Pepper Bush

Bloom Period and Seasonal Color
White or pink blooms in early summer; yellow leaves in fall.

Mature Height × Spread
4 to 8 ft. × 4 to 6 ft.

When, Where, and How to Plant
Transplant summersweet in early spring or late fall. It adapts easily to sun or shade but may not bloom as prolifically in shade. Summersweet grows best in moist soil that has plenty of organic matter. It prefers slightly acidic soils but also grows in alkaline sites. Prepare the planting site by digging a hole three times the width of the container or rootball. Dig the hole only deep enough so that, after planting, the top of the rootball is level with the ground around it. Backfill the hole with the original soil, tamp lightly, and water deeply.

Growing Tips
Keep a 2- to 3-inch layer of mulch around the root zone at all times. Water deeply during dry periods. Fertilize in early spring or late fall to encourage growth.

Care and Maintenance
Summersweet blooms on the current season's growth, so prune it in early spring to shape it or to remove dead or broken branches. (See back of book for more on pruning.) Spider mites might cause stippling of leaves in dry years. Otherwise, summersweet has few pests. It is highly tolerant of salt conditions and grows naturally near the seashore on the East Coast. It's tolerant of the salt spray used on roads and sidewalks here during the winter. In moist sites it spreads by sending up root suckers that help give it a rounder shape. Gently remove these, keeping the soil intact, and share them with friends or family.

Companion Planting and Design
With its dense green leaves giving way to summer blooms, summersweet makes an excellent background shrub for the flower border. Place shorter cultivars in the foreground or use as foundation plants where you can enjoy their sweet smell.

We Recommend
'Hummingbird' won a Gold Medal from the prestigious Pennsylvania Horticultural Society for its outstanding character and numerous and large lovely white blooms. It grows 4 feet tall. 'Ruby Spice' and 'Pink Spires' have medium-pink blooms and hold their color well.

Vernal Witchhazel

Hamamelis vernalis

When, Where, and How to Plant

For best results, transplant vernal witchhazel in early spring into moist soil with plenty of organic matter. Though native to shadier stream banks, it will produce more blooms when planted in full sun. Wet soils with poor drainage may also prove to be good sites. Dig planting holes three times the width of the rootball. Dig only deep enough so that, after planting, the top of the rootball is level with the ground around it. Backfill with the original soil, tamp lightly, and water deeply.

Growing Tips

Keep 2 to 3 inches of organic mulch around the root zone at all times. Water when dry in summer. Broadcast fertilizer around the root zone in early spring or early fall.

Care and Maintenance

Prune to remove dead or broken branches after blooming. Make pruning cuts to encourage its natural and wide-spreading horizontal branch habit when mature. Pests rarely affect witchhazel, but native wasps cause unsightly nipple-like galls on the leaves. These galls do not cause any long-term damage.

Companion Planting and Design

Vernal witchhazel's mound shape helps soften the corners of buildings. Since flowers are small, plant in front of an evergreen background to frame it. Plant near an entryway to the house or office, where you will enjoy it the most.

We Recommend

'Carnea' has deep red-pink flowers. 'Autumn Embers' has orange flowers and outstanding red-purple fall color. The common witchhazel, *Hamamelis virginiana*, blooms in the fall and grows tall enough to be considered a small tree. Its inner bark produces an extract used as an astrigent and for other medicinal purposes. The hybrid witchhazels, *Hamamelis × intermedia* have showier flowers but are only partially hardy in Zone 5. Plant 'Jelena' (fragrant copper color), 'Diana' (crimson) or 'Arnold Promise' (bright yellow).

If you can't get to Florida each winter, you can always look forward to the witchhazel blooming! A true harbinger of spring, vernal witchhazel is easily our earliest-blooming shrub, with short, yellow fringe-like flowers that cling to the branches like redbud. Flowers open as early as January, revealing strap-like petals that unfurl on warm days and curl up when the weather turns chilly. This enables the blooms to last up to four weeks. It grows into a multi-stemmed shrub with thick green scallop-edged leaves that turn brilliant yellow in the fall. When mature, the branches are more horizontal than vertical, making it wider than it is tall. Cut some branches to force indoors during January and reward yourself with their sweet fragrance to help you out of the winter doldrums.

Bloom Period and Seasonal Color

Golden yellow blooms in January; yellow leaves in fall.

Mature Height × Spread

6 to 10 ft. × 8 to 12 ft.

White Fringetree
Chionanthus virginicus

Sometimes the names we give plants make perfect sense. This is true for the native fringetree—its simple name describes its flower perfectly. Think of the soft fringe of a bedspread or pillow, and you've just pictured this flower. These unusual soft, white, strap-like petals appear in late spring in clusters up to 8 inches long. The flowers seem to peek out from behind the thick, light-green leaves. Fringetree is one of our best native plants and can be found growing in moist stream banks and ponds in the Southeast. Its slow growth rate probably explains its scarcity in Hoosier landscapes. In its native environment, fringetree grows into a small tree. As a cultivated landscape plant, it grows into a rounded open shrub. The blooms of white fringetree have a scent that some gardeners enjoy, while others do not.

Other Common Name
Old Man's Beard

Bloom Period and Seasonal Color
White blooms in late spring; dark blue fruit in summer; yellow leaves in fall.

Mature Height × Spread
6 to 10 ft. × 6 to 10 ft.

When, Where, and How to Plant
Plant specimens of white fringetree in early spring, in moist but well-drained soils in full sun. Tolerant of tough sites, it also does well in urban conditions or along a roadside. Prepare a planting hole three times as wide as the rootball. Dig the hole deep enough so that, after planting, the top of the rootball will be even with the ground around it. Backfill with the original soil, tamp lightly, and water deeply.

Growing Tips
Spread a 2- to 3-inch layer of organic mulch over the entire planting area to conserve moisture. Water deeply during dry periods in summer. Broadcast fertilizer around the root system in early spring or early fall. (See the chapter introduction for more on fertilizing.)

Care and Maintenance
Prune dead and broken branches as needed or shape it into a small tree by removing lower branches. Tame its "shrubbiness" with regular pruning to keep it tidier. (See the back of the book for more on pruning.) It may turn yellow in soils with a higher pH. Adjust according to soil test results if this happens. Fringetree has no serious pests.

Companion Planting and Design
Plant it as a specimen shrub or small tree, or as a screen or background in the shrub border. Plant near streams or ponds to help mimic its native habitat along stream banks. Plant some earlier blooming shrubs like dwarf fothergilla, American cranberry, and dogwood to stagger the blooming in your landscape and to prolong your enjoyment. Fringetree is reported to be tolerant of air pollution and grows well in an urban environment, provided other conditions are adequate.

We Recommend
Use both male and female plants for best fruiting. You may have to purchase them in summer to tell them apart, when the female develops its olive-like berry. The Chinese fringetree, *Chionanthus retusus*, is a slow growing, but magnificent small tree for those who wait. Because it's hardy in southern Indiana, you will love its cloud-like blooms in spring, its thick, leathery, dark green leaves in summer and striped bark in winter.

Winterberry Holly
Ilex verticillata

When, Where, and How to Plant
Transplant winterberry in early spring or late fall in deep, moist, organic soils typical of those found in and around a "wetland." It thrives in wet, boggy soils that flood or that drain poorly. It prefers slightly acidic soils and will develop yellow leaves if the pH goes much above neutral. In the home landscape, winterberry will grow in both wet and dry sites. Dig a planting hole three times the width of the rootball. Dig the hole only deep enough so that, after planting, the top of the rootball is level with the ground around it. Backfill the hole with the original soil after pulverizing with your shovel. Tamp lightly and water deeply.

Growing Tips
Be sure the nursery provides you with the right pollinator for the variety you choose; you must buy winterberry in pairs to insure heavy fruiting. Broadcast fertilizer around the root zone in early spring or early fall. (See chapter introduction for fertilizing information.) Keep a 2- to 3-inch layer of mulch over the root zone. Water generously during drought to keep this shrub growing vigorously.

Care and Maintenance
Winterberry is low maintenance. Prune large spindly branches to the ground so they don't become top heavy. If overgrown, it can be cut to the ground to rejuvenate. This plant has no serious pests.

Companion Planting and Design
Plant winterberry where you can enjoy the berries the most, such as near an entryway or against an evergreen background like spruce or yew. Mix with ornamental grasses for added effect. Use in native wetland reclamation projects or in low, poorly drained areas in the garden.

We Recommend
Plant one male plant of the appropriate cultivar for every three to five females. The short, compact 'Red Sprite' grows only 4 feet tall and is pollinated by 'Jim Dandy' or 'Apollo'. 'Red Sprite' has larger fruit than most. *Ilex* 'Sparkleberry' is a taller hybrid that is laden with berries. It is pollinated by 'Apollo' as well.

Native to Indiana, winterberry is an absolute must for winter landscapes. Its brilliant red berries brighten the overcast days of late fall and winter, finally withering or falling in spring. Obscure white flowers open in June, followed by pea-sized lime green fruit. Both flowers and fruit are hidden by winterberry holly's dark-green spineless leaves. By late summer, the berries turn pink then fire engine red when the leaves drop in October. They cling tightly to the branches and are sought by commercial florists for fresh holiday flower arrangements. There is nothing as exquisite as winterberry holly branches under a fresh coating of snow. Plant it with other natives like river birch or with some ornamental grass, and you'll forget how cold it is outside.

Other Common Name
Michigan Holly

Bloom Period and Seasonal Color
Insignificant white flowers in spring; bright red berries October through February.

Mature Height × Spread
6 to 10 ft. × 6 to 10 ft.

Wintergreen Korean Boxwood

Buxus microphylla var. *koreana* 'Wintergreen'

Vacations to Mount Vernon, Colonial Williamsburg, and other historical sites have helped to popularize this evergreen favorite. The common boxwood, Buxus sempervirens, *is a shrub we prune into formal hedges, topiaries, and sheared edgings around herb and rose gardens. Common boxwood, however, is not hardy here in Indiana. The hardier Korean boxwood closely resembles it but grows only a few feet tall with slightly smaller leaves. Like yew, Korean boxwood is a favorite evergreen for pruning into the popular "meatball" shape. Its small, thick, pointed leaves make it a good background plant for low growing bulbs or perennials as well as for edging around the garden. Common boxwood had multiple uses in Colonial times. Not-so-reputable physicians used boxwood for "unmentionable" illnesses. A legitimate leaf extract was a common sedative and narcotic during WWII.*

Other Common Name
Box

Bloom Period and Seasonal Color
Non-showy blooms in early spring; evergreen.

Mature Height × Spread
3 to 4 ft. × 3 to 4 ft.

When, Where, and How to Plant
Plant this cold hardy boxwood in early spring in moist but well-drained soil with plenty of organic matter. Good drainage is extremely important and will help prevent root rot. Plant in partially protected sites with full sun or part shade. Windy and exposed sites may cause the branch tips to brown and die during the winter. Prepare a planting hole that is three times the width of the rootball. Dig only deep enough so that the top of the rootball is level with the ground around it after planting. Backfill the hole with the original soil, tamp lightly, and water deeply.

Growing Tips
Keep a 2- to 3-inch layer of organic mulch around the root zone. Continue deep watering on a weekly basis throughout the summer. Fertilize according to instructions in the chapter introduction.

Care and Maintenance
If using as a formal hedge, boxwood requires annual pruning. It grows more slowly than yew, however, and will not require shearing as often. Trim hedges so that the base of the plant is wider than the top. Shear in early spring before the buds break. If overgrown, Korean box will tolerate severe pruning, but they may take a few years to grow back. Boxwood is also very susceptible to salt damage. Don't use salt on walkways and driveways near boxwood. Keep your eye out for boxwood leaf minors and psyllids, which cause the leaves to brown and/or shrivel. Consult your local office of the Purdue Cooperative Extension Service for control recommendations.

Companion Planting and Design
Korean boxwood makes a perfect low edging around a rose or herb garden. It is also an excellent low-growing hedge or foundation plant.

We Recommend
All boxwoods are not equal. Look for cultivars that are hardy and stay green in winter. Many will turn a yellow-bronze color which is less desirable. 'Wintergreen' is hardy in all parts of the state and is probably the best Korean boxwood for Indiana. 'Green Velvet' and 'Green Ice' and Chicagoland Green® are hybrids with glossy green leaves all year.

Yew

Taxus spp.

When, Where, and How to Plant

Transplant yew in the spring into a rich loamy soil with plenty of organic matter. Yew must have good drainage or it will die. Poor soil preparation, along with poor drainage, kills many newly planted yews each year. Prepare the planting site by digging a hole three times the width of the rootball. Dig only deep enough so that the top of the rootball will be level with the ground around it. Planting the yew too deep could "drown" it or cause root rot. In heavy clay, plant it an inch or two higher than the soil level. Backfill with the original soil, tamp lightly, and water deeply.

Growing Tips

Spread a 2- to 3-inch layer of organic mulch around the planting site and water in summer. No fertilizer is needed.

Care and Maintenance

Prune yews once a year just before buds break in spring. Remove dead or broken branches with sharp hand pruners. Where sheared hedges or specific shapes and sizes are desired, prune them at least twice a year. Always shear so that the bottom is wider than the top to prevent shading and the eventual thinning of the lower branches. We recommend annual pruning for productive, healthy growth. Mulch yew again in fall and water deeply if rain is scarce; this will help reduce winterkill of younger and more tender branches. Black vine weevil may be a problem. Consult the Purdue Cooperative Extension Service for controls.

Companion Planting and Design

Though it grows well in sun, it's the perfect evergreen for the north side of a home. It makes an excellent background screen or sheared hedge.

We Recommend

Both *Taxus cuspidata* and *Taxus × media* produce excellent cultivars. Among these are 'Hicksii', which has an upright and columnar shape and is excellent for use as a screen. 'Capitata' has a conical shape, while 'Nana' and 'Intermedia' are shorter with a rounded habit. At maturity, 'Wardii' and 'Densiformis' are both much wider than they are tall. 'Emerald Spreader' grows 2¹/₂ feet tall but 20 feet wide, making it a great filler plant.

Affectionately known as the "meatball" plant, yews are synonymous with the word evergreen. They are possibly the most widely planted shrub in Indiana, dotting the foundations of homes from Ft. Wayne to Evansville. There is good reason for their popularity. Yews are true "workhorses" in the landscape, filling voids and providing year-round help to otherwise bleak views. Combine this with their ability to withstand partly shady locations, and the widespread use of yew is easy to understand. Yews are sold in a variety of shapes and sizes, from dwarf and spreading to upright and columnar. The soft new spring leaves are a light green that turn darker when they mature. Scientists have used "taxol," extracted from the leaves and bark of yew, to help fight cancer. Also, according to legend, Robin Hood used the wood from yews to make his bows.

Other Common Names

Anglojap Yew, Japanese Yew

Bloom Period and Seasonal color

Evergreen; fleshy red berries in fall.

Mature Height × Spread

2 to 40 ft. × 40 ft., depending on the cultivar

Trees *for Indiana*

A drive through a new subdivision always begs the question: What would the world be like if there were no trees? The thought is incomprehensible! We also recall the very destructive Hurricane Hugo, which decimated parts of the Carolina coast in 1989. Residents interviewed after this catastrophe said that more than anything else, they missed the trees.

Trees make invaluable contributions to our daily lives that many of us take for granted. They are nature's air conditioners, shading buildings in summer and giving us a cool place to rest when the temperatures soar. In winter, they serve as windbreaks and help keep heating costs down. Trees absorb water and reduce runoff and erosion. They clean the air by removing carbon dioxide and other impurities in the city as well as in the country. Trees also serve as shelter for birds and other wildlife. They keep us closer to nature and replenish the human spirit.

Selecting and Planting Trees

No amount of soil preparation or coddling by attentive gardeners can make up for planting a tree where it doesn't belong. Select the appropriate tree species for your planting site and it will thrive. Design planting schemes with the mature height and spread of the tree in mind. Trees planted too close to the house may become hazards in the future. Young trees planted under power lines, though small at first,

Kousa Dogwood

Redbud

grow tall and can entangle the wires over time. In today's fast-paced life, everyone wants an instant landscape. Our plants, especially our shade trees, grow more slowly and may not reach their full size during our lifetimes. However, if we don't plant them, who will?

Remember this important fact when selecting new trees or caring for existing trees in your landscape: When unimpeded by sidewalks and streets, at least two-thirds of a tree's root system is in the top two feet of soil when the tree is full grown. The roots grow two to three times the width of the drip line. The dripline is the point where the shade ends, farthest from the trunk, if the sun is shining directly overhead. The goal is to spend most of your energy caring for the roots, which are vast, not to mention hidden below ground.

Planting

Each tree we suggest has planting and care instructions in this chapter. Cross reference with our planting and maintenance recommendations here for best results. For faster establishment, dig a hole that is three times the width of the rootball or pot. Gently slope the sides of the hole outward from the bottom and up to ground level, like a shallow bowl. Dig the hole only deep enough so that when the rootball is sitting at the bottom of the hole, the top of the rootball is even, or one to two inches above, the surrounding grade. Don't dig too deep and don't add pulverized soil to the bottom of the hole before planting. The soil will settle, and the tree will sink. Make sure the root flare is exposed and slighly above grade before filling the hole.

Whether planting balled-and-burlapped or container-grown trees, handle them by the rootball. Never move trees by grabbing the trunk even though it is tempting. Don't let trees drop from your hands or off the back end of a pickup truck. For container-grown trees, place them in the hole and cut away the plastic pot with sharp wire cutters or snips. Pull the pot away from the rootball and gently tease long roots from the natural mold of the container. This is especially important if you notice that they are potbound (growing in concentric circles around the sides of the pot). If so, gently pull them apart.

Nursery workers must sever more than ninety percent of a tree's roots at digging time in order to wrap the rootball in burlap and remove it from the field. If we care for them well enough during planting and the years that follow, they will re-grow the lost root mass. When planting balled-and-burlapped trees, place the rootball in the bottom of the hole and cut away all rope or twine wrapped around the trunk. Cut away two-thirds of the wire and burlap around the rootball, or as much as you can see. If the nursery wrapped the roots in synthetic burlap, remove all of it. At the same time, remove any tags used to identify the tree. Surprisingly, these pieces of wire or twine can eventually girdle the trunk or branches and cause problems later on.

Only bare-root trees, trees in high pedestrian zones, or container-grown trees on windy sites usually need staking. Always cover any wire wrapped around the trunk for staking purposes with plastic or rubber tubing. Old garden hose cut in small pieces works well.

It is not necessary to fertilize at planting time. Don't add organic matter before backfilling the hole either, unless you're planting in very sandy soil or unless you're planting trees grown in containers with mostly bark or soilless mix and then planting them in clay. In this case, mix a cubic foot of compost or soil conditioner with every two cubic feet of soil and backfill the hole. Pulverize the soil with a shovel or hoe before backfilling. Make a small ridge or saucer with the backfill at the edge of the planting hole to help catch water. Water deeply after planting. This means, water the equivalent of one to one-and-one-half inches of rain water. Alternatively, fill a five-gallon bucket twice and pour into the your homemade "saucer." Spread organic bark mulch to a depth of two or three inches out to the drip line of the tree.

Care and Maintenance

Fertilize young trees on an annual basis based on results from soil tests. Fertilizer helps young trees recover from planting. Fertilize young trees as you would fertilize shrubs. Follow instructions and application rates as discussed in the introduction to the Shrubs chapter. Mature trees don't need fertilization.

Keep two to three inches of organic mulch around the critical root zone to keep it moist and cool and to prevent weeds. Add 1 to 2 inches of compost to the critical root zone of mature or stressed trees each year. The critical root zone is measured by multiplying the trunk diameter at chest height (in inches) by 1 to $1^1/2$ feet. A tree with a trunk diameter of 10 inches should have compost and mulch in a 10 to 15 foot radius from the trunk. Well mulched trees grow faster with more extensive root systems than when they have to compete with grass or weeds for moisture and nutrients. Don't mound the mulch "volcanoes" despite what you may see in others' landscapes. Keep the mulch from touching the bark at the base of the trunk and spread it out to the drip line on new trees. Never cover the rootflare with mulch. As the trees grow, gradually extend the mulch to keep up with the critical root zone. Besides protecting the roots, mulch is a visual barrier and helps prevent lawn mower and weed whacker blight—that is, cuts and bruises on the bark at the base of the tree.

Continue watering deeply once a week through the first growing season, especially during the height of summer. Avoid watering for short periods every day in the evenings after you come home from work because this promotes shallow root growth. Use a "soaker hose," which lets the water seep into the ground. Water the entire root zone of older or mature trees. Leave the hose on until the top eight to ten inches of soil is moist.

Green Ash

Pruning

Trees need regular pruning to remove dead, diseased, or broken branches and to maintain good vigor. They need corrective pruning to help them develop stronger and safer branch structure. It is part art and part science and best left to professionals, especially on large or mature trees. For more detailed information, see the section in the back on pruning.

Threats to Your Trees

Environmental or "people-pressure" factors such as compacted soil, cold injury, drought stress, salt toxicity, wind damage, injury to the root system, or poor planting procedures cause about seventy-five percent of all tree problems. Diagnosing tree problems is not an easy task. Misdiagnoses are costly to both the homeowner and the environment, so consult a professional arborist if in doubt. Visit www.isa.org to find a certified arborist in your area. Follow the routine maintenance recommendations in this chapter to help keep your trees pest and problem free.

Learning about insect pests and routine disease will help your diagnosis. Many pests are seasonal or short-lived and only cause cosmetic damage. Examples include leaf diseases such as maple, sycamore, or ash anthracnose. Even though they may cause significant leaf drop in the spring, they rarely cause long-term problems. Some insects and mites lay eggs inside a leaf, which cause abnormal growths called "galls." Galls are unsightly but rarely jeopardize the tree's health. Use pesticides to control insects or diseases only after you've identified the culprit and exhausted other and more environmentally sound control options. Consult your local office of the Purdue Cooperative Extension Service or a certified arborist for help identifying pests.

American Beech
Fagus grandifolia

American beech is one of our most beloved native trees. Its upward and arching branches develop into a broad but slightly pyramidal outline that casts heavy shade on its roots. Beware the gardener who tries to grow grass beneath this dense canopy! Its glossy green leaves emerge from very sharp and pointed buds on branches that have a slight zigzag shape. They turn brilliant yellow then brown in fall but cling tightly all winter, especially on the lower branches of young trees. Unimpeded, beech trees generally have short trunks in the landscape. For years, perhaps centuries, couples have expressed their undying love for each other by carving their initials in its smooth, silvery-gray but thin bark. We know you'll be compelled to express your undying love for beech trees once you see them in all their glory.

Bloom Period and Seasonal Color
Dark glossy green leaves; yellow then brown fall color.

Mature Height × Spread
50 to 70 ft. × 50 to 70 ft.

When, Where, and How to Plant
Plant beech in spring into moist but, well-drained soil with high organic matter content. Like most other nut trees, they do not tolerate fall planting. Beech roots grow much closer to the surface so protect the root zone with mulch. Slightly acid soil is best. Dig a hole three times the width of the rootball. Dig only deep enough so that, after planting, the top of the rootball is level with the ground around it. Handle carefully and cut away any burlap, wire, or twine to half the height of the rootball. Backfill the hole with the original soil, tamp lightly, and water deeply.

Growing Tips
Beech have shallow roots that need mulch for added moisture and protection. Keep a 2- to 3-inch layer of mulch around the root zone. Water deeply each week in summer to prevent drought stress. Broadcast fertilizer around the root zone of young trees in early spring or early fall.

Care and Maintenance
Beech trees "bleed" (drip excessive sap) when pruned. Prune any time after June to avoid this. Pests are not a recurring problem with beech.

Companion Planting and Design
Plant beech in full to part sun where they will have plenty of room to grow: in large lawns, golf courses, and parks. In naturalized areas, beech will sucker from the roots and establish a small stand of trees over time. Beech are among the slowest growing landscape trees; we must plant them for the next generation. Show your *undying love* for beech trees by resisting the temptation to carve your initials in their trunks. *Plant* a beech tree for your beloved, instead.

We Recommend
Similar to the American beech, the European beech, *Fagus sylvatica,* is more tolerant of poor soils and urban conditions. The brilliant leaves of the purple beech, *Fagus sylvatica* 'Purpurea', or 'Riversii' make them perfect specimen trees. The color of late afternoon sun backlighting young leaves in early spring is unforgettable. *Fagus sylvatica* 'Tricolor' is a popular purple-leaved variety with rosy-white edges. Unfortunately, in Indiana the leaf edges turn brown in midsummer.

American Hornbeam

Carpinus caroliniana

When, Where, and How to Plant

Hornbeam is one of the few plants that grow as well in sun as in shade. Plant in spring into slightly acidic or alkaline, moist but well-drained soils. Hornbeam is perfect along stream banks that occasionally flood or in poorly drained areas. Dig a planting hole three times the width of the rootball. Dig only deep enough so that, after planting, the top of the rootball is level with the ground around it. Backfill the hole with the original soil, tamp lightly, and water deeply.

Growing Tips

Sites with less sun produce trees that have thinner and more irregular-shaped canopies. Keep 2 to 3 inches of organic mulch over the root zone at all times. Water deeply especially during dry spells in summer. Fertilize in early spring or early fall and keep the roots moist to try to speed up its growth rate.

Care and Maintenance

This is a low maintenance care-free tree that tolerates tough growing conditions. Prune in late winter or early spring. Remove dead, dying, broken, or diseased branches. As a general rule they are slow growers. Leaf spots, canker diseases, and scale insects are occasional problems. Contact your local office of the Purdue Cooperative Extension Service if you encounter any pests.

Companion Planting and Design

Use in native landscapes or woodland gardens. Along a stream, underplant with Japanese Hokone Grass. In drier sites, combine with native wildflowers such as woodland phlox, *Phlox divaricata*, or Virginia bluebells, *Mertensia virginica*, or ferns.

We Recommend

Plant cultivars of the European Hornbeam, *Carpinus betulus*, in urban and suburban landscapes. The cultivar 'Fastigiata' grows as a very shrubby, teardrop- to oval-shaped small tree. It has many branches and no dominant leader or trunk. The cultivar 'Columnaris' has a strong central leader. Both cultivars are useful in formal gardens, confined spaces, or as accent plants. They are lovely when sheared into tall hedges as is commonly done in Europe.

A native understory tree, hornbeam often goes unnoticed until its papery and pendulous bracts start to mature in summer. Lesser known than other natives like tuliptrees and oaks, hornbeam leaves many tree-lovers scratching their heads in wonder as they walk through the woods. Nicknamed "musclewood," one glance at the trunk and branches of older trees will show you why. The thin blue-gray bark resembles the taut muscles of your arms and legs. Its sinuous, undulating, and fluted character is easy to identify even in winter. In full sun it takes on a more upright, rounded, and full canopy shape. In shade, however, it is more open and irregular, sometimes even flat-topped. The dark green leaves have sharp serrations and resemble beech but are narrower. In fall, the leaves turn bright yellow or warm orange-red. Hornbeams are essential in native or woodland landscapes.

Other Common Names
Musclewood, Ironwood, Blue Beech

Bloom Period and Seasonal Color
Papery and pendulous subtle flowers hidden by leaves in early summer; yellow or orange-red leaves in fall; sinewy bark in winter.

Mature Height × Spread
20 to 30 ft. × 20 to 30 ft. or more

Bald Cypress
Taxodium distichum

A visit to the Okeefenokee Swamp or the Florida Everglades, and you'll remember this outstanding native tree. We usually think of it next to ponds and wetlands where it sends up knobby growths called "knees." When growing above the water-line, the knees impart an eerie or haunted look. Bald cypress is a deciduous conifer with short, flat, feathery, needle-like leaves. Emerging light-green in spring, they turn darker as summer passes and then coppery-brown before they drop to the ground. They are so fine they disappear into the lawn or ground cover and rarely need raking. When young, the tree has a more formal, pyramidal shape. As it ages, it develops a broad and open cylindrical shape with a flat top. The branches bend slightly at the tips, giving it an unmatched gracefulness.

Bloom Period and Seasonal Color
Light green feathery needles in spring; copper-brown fall color.

Mature Height × Spread
50 to 70 ft. × 20 to 30 ft.

When, Where, and How to Plant
Plant bald cypress in spring, preferably when the soil is dry enough to crumble in your hand. Plant in full sun in deep and well-drained sandy soil with plenty of organic matter. It thrives in wet soils, along stream or pond banks, and tolerates flooding. Slightly acidic soils are best. Dig a hole three times as wide as the rootball. Place the tree in the hole so that the top of the rootball is level with the ground around it. Backfill the hole with the original soil, tamp lightly, and water deeply.

Growing Tips
Keep 2 to 3 inches of organic mulch like shredded bark over the root zone. Though tolerant of drought, water generously especially in summer. Fertilize young trees around the root zone in early spring or early fall, especially during the first five to ten years after transplanting.

Care and Maintenance
Prune to remove dead, dying, broken, or diseased branches. For faster growth, keep watered throughout the year, especially when young. Mites may cause the inner needles to yellow. Harmless galls sometimes form in the leaves of the branch tips.

Companion Planting and Design
It makes an excellent specimen tree but also provides a nice fine-textured background for smaller trees with coarse texture. Plant it next to streams or ponds and enjoy the knees that will emerge from the water. Bald cypress has one of the hardest and most rot-resistant woods and is often used as mulch for landscaping purposes for this reason.

We Recommend
There are very few exceptional cultivars on the market. 'Monarch of Illinois' has branches that may spread 65 feet, so plant it with enough room to grow. 'Shawnee Brave' is narrower and more columnar; use it where space is tighter. A tree frequently mistaken for bald cypress is dawn redwood, *Metasequoia glyptostroboides*. Known as the "fossil tree," at one time dawn redwoods were believed to be extinct. Though wider than bald cypress, they are fast growing and elegant but shorter than their cousin, the giant sequoia.

Bur Oak

Quercus macrocarpa

When, Where, and How to Plant

Bur oak is notoriously difficult to transplant but is well worth the trouble. Plant in the spring in full sun, after the soil dries. Oaks planted in fall frequently die—not having enough time to adapt. Bur oak tolerates a wide range of soil conditions and growing environments, including pollution and other urban ills. It grows well in heavy clay or sandy loam but does best on deep prairie-type soils with good drainage. It tolerates both an acidic and alkaline pH range. Handle the tree carefully so as not to cause the soil to break away from the roots. Dig a planting hole three times the width of the rootball. Dig the hole only deep enough so that, after planting, the top of the rootball is level with the ground around it. Carefully remove all twine, wire, and burlap from around the rootball and trunk. Backfill the hole with the original soil, tamp lightly, and water deeply.

Growing Tips

Keep a 2- to 3-inch layer of organic mulch over the root zone. Water deeply, especially during dry periods in summer, when it's young. Fertilize young trees in early spring or early fall to encourage growth, especially when it's young.

Care and Maintenance

Prune out any deadwood. Bur oak has no serious pests. Leaf galls occasionally grow on leaves but are mostly harmless.

Companion Planting and Design

Fall color on most oaks can vary greatly because of the many possible genetic crosses. Plant bur oak in open spaces where it will have plenty of room to grow. It grows very slowly, but don't despair; you are planting a tree for your grandchildren to enjoy.

We Recommend

The swamp white oak, *Quercus bicolor*, transplants easily. As its name suggests, swamp white oak tolerates damp soils. The red oak, *Quercus rubra*, is one of the fastest growing oaks, but it sometimes yellows in Indiana's alkaline soils. Plant it where soils are more acidic. *Quercus shumardii*, the shumard oak, is similar to red oak and is drought tolerant.

There is no larger, statelier, or more rugged tree in Indiana than the bur oak. Its massive trunk and sturdy limbs dwarf most others around it. The trunk's deep furrows and the twigs' cork-like ridges gives it a rough and gnarled appearance. The silhouette of a bur oak during a winter sunset along an Indiana country road is quite a sight. Bur oak leaves are dark green with deep, round-edged, irregular lobes. It has a large acorn almost completely enveloped by a fibrous "cap" which gives it the name "bur oak." They turn yellow-green then dull brown in fall. A tough tree, it tolerates wind and cold extremes and grows naturally in open fields. Though their rugged nature helps them withstand city conditions, even a bur oak cannot survive heavy root damage.

Bloom Period and Seasonal Color

Dark green leaves turning yellow-green to brown in fall.

Mature Height × Spread

70 to 80 ft. × 70 to 80 ft.

Flowering Crabapple

Malus spp.

Blooming in shades of red, pink, or white, it's easy to understand why this tree has become so popular. There is no tree more spectacular in spring than the flowering crabapple. Billowy clouds of cotton-candy-like blooms along city streets, in yards, parks, church lots, and other green spaces announce that spring is here. In fall, children like to use the large fruit of the older crabs as ammunition during neighborhood "battles." Fortunately, new hybrids with smaller and more colorful fruit are replacing the old varieties. The cherry-like fruits range from yellow to red and cling to the branches for weeks or months, depending on the type (or the bird population)! Our feathered friends are especially fond of them, so plant the trees close to the house to better watch their feeding frenzies.

Bloom Period and Seasonal Color
Flowers in April; yellow to red leaves in fall; yellow to red fruit display from August to January.

Mature Height × Spread
6 to 20 ft. × 15 to 20 ft.

When, Where, and How to Plant
Plant crabapple after the soil dries in spring in well-drained and slightly acidic or alkaline soils. Plant in full sun to ensure maximum bloom. Dig a planting hole three times the width of the rootball. Dig deep enough so that, after planting, the top of the rootball is level with the ground around it. Backfill the hole with the original soil, tamp lightly, and water deeply.

Growing Tips
Keep a 2- to 3-inch layer of organic mulch around the planting area. Water deeply during dry spells, especially in summer. Fertilize in early spring and early fall for fastest growth.

Care and Maintenance
Young sprouts, called "suckers," often proliferate from the roots and the base of the trunk. Prune them away at any time of the year. Prune excessive growth from branches, called water sprouts, to open the canopy. Crabapple is prone to several diseases in Indiana including scab, rust, and leaf spot. Scab causes yellow spots followed by gray-black scabs on the leaves and fruit. By midsummer, many of the leaves drop off. Japanese beetles also feed heavily on the leaves. The most reliable way to control these problems is to plant resistant cultivars.

Companion Planting and Design
Plant crabapple along the street and under power lines where larger specimens would grow too tall, or near the front door. Avoid patios and walkways because dropping fruit may cause a mess.

We Recommend
To avoid pest problems, it is very important to plant a recommended cultivar. *Malus* 'Bob White' (white flowers with golden yellow fruit), 'Louisa' (pink with yellow-red fruit), 'Prairiefire' (red with cherry red fruit), 'White Angel' (white with red fruit), and 'Red Jewel' (white with cherry red fruit) have been listed as highly resistant to scab and Japanese beetles in Indiana. *Malus* 'Ann E.' is also pest resistant and grows to 10 by 10 with a weeping habit. *Malus sargentii*, the Sargent Crab, grows only 6 to 10 feet tall and spreads to 12 to 15 feet wide. It makes an excellent low growing screen.

Flowering Pear
Pyrus calleryana

When, Where, and How to Plant

Flowering pear recovers slowly after transplanting. Plant in early spring to give it the longest growing season possible during the first year. It prefers soils that are slightly acid or alkaline, well-drained, and in full sun. Dig planting holes three times the width of the rootball. Dig only deep enough so that, after planting, the top of the rootball is level with the ground around it. Backfill the hole with the original soil, tamp lightly, and water deeply.

Growing Tips

Keep 2 to 3 inches of organic mulch over the root zone. Water regularly, especially during dry spells in summer. Fertilize young trees in early fall only.

Care and Maintenance

Prune in spring immediately after bloom. Prune carefully and leave the branches with the widest crotch angle. Some flowering pear cultivars such as 'Bradford' are notorious for weak branches due to narrow crotch angles. If pruned correctly starting when young, even they can be satisfactory. Fire blight is a disease that causes branches to dieback at random throughout the tree. Carefully remove dead branches with sharp pruning tools. Disinfect the pruners after each cut to avoid spreading the disease. To discourage this disease, fertilize in early fall only. Select disease resistant cultivars whenever possible. Contact your County Extension Office for proper fire blight control techniques.

Companion Planting and Design

This tree has been synonymous with the word "subdivision" for many years. It grows well in confined spaces, like tree lawns and boxes along the street, or in raised areas such as berms.

We Recommend

'Chanticleer', also known as 'Cleveland Select', is probably the best. It has sturdy limbs, and its leaves color much earlier than 'Bradford Pear' in the fall. As far as it is known, it also has the best resistance to fire blight. 'Earlyred' and 'Whitehouse' may also be somewhat resistant. The cultivar 'Bradford' was over-planted by nurseries and the gardening public starting in the 1970s. After Bradfords turn twenty or thirty years old, their branches break, especially during storms. Avoid using 'Bradford Pear' because of its weak branch angles—and for safety's sake!

Flowering pear is one of our earliest and most beautiful spring blooming trees. Unlike other rangy or more open trees, the flowering pear grows in a formal, pyramidal shape. The branches turn white with flowers in late March and very early April. When the pears are blooming, be sure to visit the American Legion Mall in Indianapolis at sunrise for a real treat. Glossy green heart-shaped leaves with wavy edges follow the blooms and last well into fall. They turn scarlet red in October and November and are one of the last trees to shed their leaves. Its fruit, which rarely exceeds $1/2$-inch in diameter, turns a dull brown in late summer. Choose non-fruiting types and avoid any mess!

Bloom Period and Seasonal Color

White flowers in early April; scarlet leaves in late fall.

Mature Height × Spread

30 to 50 ft. × 20 to 35 ft.

Ginkgo

Ginkgo biloba

Ginkgo is one of the most trouble-free and exotic-looking trees for Hoosier landscapes. Grow it for the shade it provides in summer as well as its spectacular fall color. It tolerates confined spaces, pollution, and other stresses of city life extremely well and is often the preferred tree for dense urban centers. Its ability to thrive in difficult planting sites also makes it perfect for suburban or rural areas, too. In the fall, ginkgo leaves will change quickly, turning from a thick, medium green to a bright and dramatic yellow. They usually drop from the tree within a few days. Ginkgo is one of the oldest and most primitive cultivated trees; ginkgo fossils millions of years old have been found in North America. Ginkgo extract has recently been promoted for health reasons, but consult your physician before taking it.

Other Common Name
Maidenhair Tree

Bloom Period and Seasonal Color
Bright yellow leaves in fall.

Mature Height × Spread
50 to 80 ft. × 30 to 40 ft.

When, Where, and How to Plant

Plant ginkgo in spring or fall in full sun, when the soil is dry and crumbly. It grows best in well-drained acid or alkaline soil. Dig a hole three times the diameter of the rootball. Dig only deep enough so that, after planting, the top of the rootball is even with the ground around it. Backfill the hole with the original soil, tamp lightly, and water deeply.

Growing Tips

Keep a 2- to 3- inch layer of organic mulch around the root zone to conserve moisture and keep the weeds down. Water deeply each week in summer, especially during dry spells. Fertilize young trees in early spring or early fall, especially during the first ten to twenty years after transplanting.

Care and Maintenance

Ginkgo takes several years to recover after transplanting. Even after recovery it still has a medium to slow growth rate; this is a tree we plant for future generations. Ginkgo will develop more rapidly if you provide it with extra care. Prune the tree when it's young to help stimulate lateral branches. Shape the tree to encourage the ginkgo's strong central leader. (See the back of this book for more information about pruning.)

Companion Planting and Design

When young, before side branches have begun to fill out the canopy, ginkgos appear thin and spindly. The mature ginkgo has fork-like limbs that spread forty feet wide and easily shade the hot pavement in summer. Plant for shade in large lawn areas, golf courses, and parks. This tree grows well despite pollution and heavy use of road salt.

We Recommend

Ginkgo has male and female trees. The female tree develops tan- to yellow-colored fruit about the size of a cherry in the fall. A soft flesh, well-known for its malodorous effect, covers the ginkgo seed inside the fruit. In fact, they smell so bad that even the birds won't eat them! For this reason, be sure to plant the seedless and more acceptable male specimens. 'Autumn Gold' is seedless and grows in a symmetric shape with outstanding yellow leaves in fall. 'Princeton Sentry' and 'Fastigiata', also seedless, grow like very narrow or columnar pyramids. They are excellent choices for confined spaces.

Green Ash
Fraxinus pennsylvanica

When, Where, and How to Plant
Plant green ash just about any time the soil is dry in spring, summer, or fall. It thrives in part- to full sun and moist but well-drained acid or alkaline soils. It is flexible about soil quality. Dig a planting hole at least three times the width of the rootball. Dig only deep enough so that, after planting, the top of the rootball is level with the ground around it. Backfill the hole with the original soil, tamp lightly, and water deeply.

Growing Tips
Green ash is a tough tree and requires little attention, but it will grow more rapidly if you keep the soil moist. Maintain a 2- to 3-inch layer of organic mulch over the roots. We have seen these trees wilt in the height of summer droughts; therefore, water deeply on a weekly basis. Fertilize young trees in early spring or early fall.

Care and Maintenance
Green ash has weak wood and narrow crotch angles causing limbs to break easily. Prune at a young age to develop a solid branching pattern. Ash borers will attack when it is under stress from drought or other environmental conditions. A spring foliar disease called anthracnose causes brown blotches on the leaf margins and near the veins. Temporary leaf drop may result, but the tree will recover.

Companion Planting and Design
Plant green ash where fast shade is desired. Give the tree some room to spread, as the crown can reach 30 feet wide or more. Rows of green ash create a nice avenue effect when planted along a street or driveway.

We Recommend
Green ash produces prolific amounts of seed which sprout in the yard and become a nuisance. Choose seedless cultivars to reduce maintenance. 'Marshall's Seedless', 'Patmore', and 'Summit' are all excellent seedless types. 'Cimmzam', or cimmaron ash, has strong branch angles and develops purplish-bronze fall color instead of the typical yellow. Use white ash, *Fraxinus americana*, in moist areas of native landscapes. 'Autumn Blaze' and Autumn Purple®, have wonderful bronze-purple fall color.

There is hardly a more adaptable or faster growing tree than the green ash. It easily grows 2 to 3 feet per year and, in this age of instant gratification, makes a good choice for instant shade. Green ash is suitable for any Hoosier landscape and is widely used. Like its cousin the white ash, the green ash is a native tree in Indiana. In its natural habitat, it grows near streams and rivers and other bottomland locations. In cultivation, green ash adapts to just about any growing condition including confined and urban areas. It develops a broadly spreading, rounded canopy; its glossy compound leaves emerge late in the spring and turn a bright yellow tinged with purple in the fall. When mature, the green ash's bark is deeply fissured and forms irregular diamond shapes that help to identify it.

Bloom Period and Seasonal Color
Yellow to purple leaves in fall.

Mature Height × Spread
50 to 60 ft. × 25 to 30 ft.

Hemlock

Tsuga canadensis

Native to southern portions of Indiana, hemlock is a popular evergreen. The silvery-white stripes on the underside of their short, flat needles and the diminutive cones make them easy to identify. In spring, new growth emerges as light green and gives the branch tips a feathery appearance. Left alone, it grows into a medium to large tree that provides some light screening. Hemlocks make excellent hedges and dense screens if properly sheered. When mature, their graceful and slightly pendulous branches create a dark green background for smaller flowering trees. They are one of the few evergreens that grow well in shady locations. In contrast to other evergreens, especially pines, hemlock needles are small enough to disappear into the lawn. Deer love to browse on hemlock branches, so if deer are a problem in your area we suggest planting another tree.

Bloom Period and Seasonal Color
Evergreen.

Mature Height × Spread
40 to 70 ft. × 25 to 35 ft.

When, Where, and How to Plant
Plant in spring or early fall in moist, slightly acid, well-drained soil with high organic matter content. They dislike dry and/or waterlogged soils. Hemlock is one of the few conifers that grows well in shade, but it becomes more dense in full sun. Don't plant it in windy or exposed sites. Dig a hole three times the width of the rootball and deep enough so that the top of the rootball is level with the ground after planting. In heavy soils where drainage is poor, plant it 2 inches higher than the soil around it. Backfill the hole with the original soil, tamp lightly, and water deeply.

Growing Tips
Maintain a 2- to 3-inch layer of organic mulch around the root zone. Water deeply on a weekly basis, especially during dry spells in summer for up to ten years after planting. Evergreens do not require supplemental fertilization.

Care and Maintenance
Apply sulfur to the root zone according to soil test results to keep the soil slightly acidic. (See book introduction for more on soil testing.) Remove dead branches each spring. Shear regularly starting in early spring if growing as a hedge. Mites and hemlock woolly adelgids, an imported insect, can be severe problems. Controlling these pests is important—contact your local Purdue Cooperative Extension Service for information, and monitor hemlock regularly. Hemlock continuously sheds some needles, but they are small enough to be disguised by the turf.

Companion Planting and Design
As hedges, they provide an excellent and formal background for a perennial flower bed. Plant as understory trees for moderate screening.

We Recommend
There are many dwarf cultivars to use as accent plants or for dwarf conifer gardens. 'Sargentii' is a weeping form that grows 30 feet wide and 15 feet tall with pendulous branches. It is an outstanding specimen plant. *Tsuga heterophylla*, the western hemlock, resists the woolly adelgid and may be a good substitute in Zone 6 in southern Indiana. *Tsuga diversifolia*, the northern Japanese hemlock, is a smaller, shrubbier tree that is also resistant to the adelgid.

Japanese Maple
Acer palmatum

When, Where, and How to Plant

Plant the Japanese maple in either late spring or early fall when the ground is dry. Plant in slightly acidic soil with ample organic matter and good drainage. It grows best where it avoids midday sun; a partially sheltered location with dappled shade, or a courtyard is ideal. Since Japanese maples require extra watering in the heat of Indiana summers, plant them where you can reach them with the hose. Dig holes three times the width of the rootball. Dig only deep enough so that, after planting, the top of the rootball is level with the ground around the hole. Pulverize and backfill the hole with the original soil, tamp lightly, and water deeply.

Growing Tips

Keep 2 to 3 inches of organic mulch around the root zone at all times. Water deeply, especially during dry spells in summer. Fertilize in early spring or early fall.

Care and Maintenance

Prune out dead or broken branches. Keep mulch from piling up around the trunk of the tree. Japanese beetles occasionally chew the leaves. Plant these maples according to directions, and they will have few other pest problems.

Companion Planting and Design

Plant as a specimen tree to enjoy the beautiful leaves which gradually change color throughout the season. Leaf color will change according to sun exposure. Purple-leafed cultivars are more purple in sun and more green in shade. Japanese maples also work well in mixed-flower borders as an accent plant or background screen.

We Recommend

Select only cultivars that are hardy in your region since many are not hardy in Zone 5a. 'Bloodgood' has typical Japanese maple foliage with deep-red leaves and is one of the best selections for Indiana gardens. 'Burgundy Lace' has finely dissected crimson-colored leaves. 'Crimson Queen' and 'Ornatum' have cascading and mound-like growth habits and are excellent along pathways, in rock gardens, or next to a water feature. *Acer japonicum*, the full moon maple, grows slightly taller and has larger leaves. Its fall color is spectacular, with leaves that look like they are on fire.

The Japanese maple is the "queen" of small trees in the garden. Its slender, pointed, lacy leaves in a wide variety of shapes and colors make it hugely popular. The fine texture of its leaves lends interest to the garden at a time in the season when perennials and shrubs seem to take a break from blooming. As its name suggests, this maple is native to Japan and Korea, where breeders have developed hundreds of different varieties which differ in height and growth habit, such as spreading branches vs. weeping, leaf color, and the degree to which the leaves are naturally pointed or greatly "dissected." Some cultivars have brilliant red fall color. For the patient and meticulous gardener, Japanese maples are good to try as bonsai. There are Japanese maple bonsai specimens at the National Arboretum in Washington, D.C. that are hundreds of years old.

Bloom Period and Seasonal Color
Colorful leaves and fruit change throughout the season.

Mature Height × Spread
6 to 25 ft. × 15 to 25 ft. or more

Japanese Tree Lilac
Syringa reticulata

Landscape architects create "rooms" in the landscape just as building architects create rooms in a house. In this scenario, tree lilacs function as the "walls." Their thick dark-green elliptic leaves closely resemble those of their cousin, the common lilac, but are not quite so heart-shaped. Their strong, vertical, multi-stemmed trunks with smooth, dark cinnamon-brown bark are speckled with horizontal lenticels and look outstanding, especially in winter. Tree lilacs grow more graceful with age as their branches arch outward toward the tips. Opening in late May, their large, bold, creamy-white panicles grow wide at the base and taper to a point. Their fragrance is different from the common lilac and is described as closer to privet. Tree lilacs have a medium growth rate.

Bloom Period and Seasonal Color
Late May to early June, with dark green leaves and creamy white fragrant blooms.

Mature Height × Spread
20 to 30 ft. × 15 to 20 ft.

When, Where, and How to Plant
Plant tree lilac in either spring or fall, when the ground is dry. It tolerates wide ranges of pH and should grow well in just about any Indiana soil as long as it is well-drained. The more sun it receives, the greater the number of flowers it will produce. Dig the planting hole three times the width of the rootball. Dig only deep enough so that, after planting, the top of the rootball is level with the ground around it. Backfill the hole with the original soil, tamp lightly, and water deeply.

Growing Tips
Keep 2 to 3 inches of mulch around the root zone at all times. Water deeply especially during dry spells in summer. Fertilize in early spring or early fall, especially during the first ten years after transplanting.

Care and Maintenance
Japanese tree lilacs are low maintenance trees. Remove dead flowers after they fade in June to encourage more blooms the following year. Remove any dead branches or prune to shape immediately after flowering as well. Prune or shape into multi-stemmed forms for greater architectural interest. Japanese tree lilac is not bothered by the powdery mildew that plagues the common lilac. Borers only occasionally bother it. Contact Purdue Cooperative Extension for control options.

Companion Planting and Design
Plant as a background screen in the flower border or around the corners of buildings to help soften the edges. Tree lilacs make excellent street trees; some cities promote them for this purpose since they are tough and won't grow into overhead power lines. Plant around patios or where you can observe the bark in winter, especially from indoors.

We Recommend
'Ivory Silk' grows to 20 or 25 feet but produces more flowers than other cultivars. 'Summer Snow' grows shorter and more slowly. 'Regent' is a fast growing cultivar.

Katsura Tree
Cercidiphyllum japonicum

When, Where, and How to Plant

Plant in early spring in slightly acidic or alkaline, moist but well-drained soil. Katsura trees grow in most soil-types but dislike hot and dry sites in full sun. Light shade during the heat of a summer afternoon is ideal. Dig a planting hole three times the width of the rootball. Dig only deep enough so that, after planting, the top of the rootball is even with the ground around it. Backfill with the original soil, tamp lightly, and water deeply.

Growing Tips

Keep 2 to 3 inches of organic bark mulch over the root zone at all times. Water deeply, especially during hot dry spells in summer. Fertilize in early spring or early fall according to directions. (See chapter introduction on fertilizing.)

Care and Maintenance

Prune dead, diseased, or broken branches in spring. Katsura tree has a tendency to develop multiple trunks. The trunks and branches of this type have a propensity to break more frequently as they get older. Katsura tree's height and width are more variable than most trees. Multi-trunked specimens tend to grow wider, too. Train into a single-trunked specimen when young by cutting out competing stems, favoring the largest and most vertical trunk. This style is more elegant and sophisticated. There are no regular insect or disease pests that bother katsura trees. In the right site, it takes care of itself.

Companion Planting and Design

Its pyramid shape makes it a good accent tree when young. Grow it as a specimen in the front or backyard. Though larger than most patio trees, it doesn't drop litter all year and will provide good shade if given ample root space. Single-trunk katsura tree also makes a good specimen in tree lawns if you can irrigate in summer.

We Recommend

'Aureum' has lighter green foliage and bright yellow leaves in fall. 'Pendulum' has a stunning weeping habit. 'Tidal Wave' and 'Amazing Grace' are also weepers that make excellent specimen trees. 'Ruby' grows to 30 feet and has bluish-purple leaves.

As the leaves of the katsura tree turn color in the fall, it gives off a remarkable smell similar to burnt sugar and cinnamon, and not unlike cotton candy. Katsura tree's heart-shaped leaves resemble redbud, only smaller and with scalloped edges. They start out faintly red-purple in spring, are medium green in summer, and turn apricot yellow in the fall. The leaves are slightly cupped at the vein, too, not unlike redbud in that regard either. They shimmer slightly in the wind, like aspen. Katsura trees are elegant and graceful. Their pest-free and speedy growth rate makes us wonder why we don't see more of these beauties.

Bloom Period and Seasonal Color

Green leaves in summer; apricot-yellow in fall.

Mature Height × Spread

40 to 60 ft. × 30 to 60 ft. or more

Kousa Dogwood
Cornus kousa

Kousa dogwood is often overlooked in favor of its more popular cousin, the native flowering dogwood (Cornus kousa). But Kousa is just as beautiful in bloom and has many other positive attributes as well. The flowers open after the native dogwood in late spring and after it sprouts new leaves. The flowers last up to six weeks, perhaps twice that of the native flowering dogwood. Each Kousa dogwood flower has four pointed bracts; the leaves resemble the native flowering types and turn a dull, bronzy red in the fall. As the plant matures, it develops elegant horizontal branches and sometimes grows as wide as it is tall. The gray outer bark peels to reveal inner bark that is light gray or tan giving it winter interest. In late summer, it produces an unusual fruit that resembles a large raspberry on a long stem.

Other Common Names
Korean Dogwood, Chinese Dogwood

Bloom Period and Seasonal Color
Mid-May to early June; red fruit in fall; burgundy leaves in October.

Mature Height × Spread
20 to 30 ft. × 20 to 30 ft.

When, Where, and How to Plant
Plant Kousa dogwood in spring or fall, when the ground is dry. Kousa prefers moist but slightly acidic well-drained soil. It blooms more heavily when growing in more sun; however, give it light shade in midafternoon to preserve the bloom. Dig the planting hole three times the size of the width of the rootball. Dig the hole only deep enough so that, when sitting on the bottom of the hole, the top of the rootball is level with the ground around it. Backfill the hole with the original soil, tamp lightly, and water deeply.

Growing Tips
Keep a 2- to 3-inch layer of organic mulch around the root zone. Water deeply during dry spells, especially during summer. Fertilize young trees in early spring or early fall especially during the first five to ten years after transplanting.

Care and Maintenance
Remove dead branches or prune to shape after the tree finishes blooming in late spring. This will ensure maximum flower production for the following year. Remove branches selectively to show off the layered branch habit. As the tree matures, prune lower branches to display the peeling character of the older bark. Kousa dogwood is mostly trouble-free. It is more reliable than the native type, which is often bothered by leaf diseases, dogwood borer, and site or exposure problems.

Companion Planting and Design
Use this tree to break up vertical lines at the corners of buildings. For heaviest fruit production in the fall, plant at least two specimens. Plant them as background plants in the shrub or flower border, or in corners where nothing else seems to work.

We Recommend
Plant kousa instead of our native flowering dogwood to avoid anthracnose, a disease that started killing dogwood stands in the forest in the mid-1990s. 'China Girl' and 'Milky Way' are excellent white cultivars. 'Satomi' has light pink bracts while 'Beni Fuji' is darkest pink of all. 'Gold Star' has variegated gold-and-green leaves with white bracts. 'Summer Stars', a white flowered type, retains its bracts until midsummer.

Littleleaf Linden
Tilia cordata

When, Where, and How to Plant
Plant littleleaf linden in moist but well-drained soil with plenty of organic matter. It tolerates compact soil and confined spaces with no preference regarding pH. Cities use it regularly for street trees since it tolerates pollution and other urban ills. Dig a planting hole three times the width of the rootball. Dig only deep enough so that, after planting, the top of the rootball is level with the ground around it. Backfill the hole with the original soil, tamp lightly, and water deeply.

Growing Tips
Keep a 2- to 3-inch layer of organic mulch around the root zone at all times. Water deeply during dry spells, especially in summer. Regular fertilization will help lindens grow more rapidly. Fertilize young trees in early spring or early fall, especially during the first five to ten years after transplanting.

Care and Maintenance
Remove dead or broken branches in early spring; corrective pruning is not normally necessary. Littleleaf linden is a favorite food for voracious Japanese beetles. They sometimes chew off half the leaves by the end of June. Beetle feeding causes cosmetic damage, but the long-term health of the tree is rarely jeopardized. Contact your county extension office for control options.

Companion Planting and Design
Plant an avenue of lindens along the driveway or to screen views. Its symmetric shape makes it a good specimen tree also. Use for heavy shade near a patio and to enjoy the intoxicating fragrance. Littleleaf linden adapts well to heavy shearing and makes an excellent tree for hedges in formal gardens. It is very hardy and makes a good container tree for very large raised planters.

We Recommend
The most common variety of littleleaf linden is 'Greenspire', but it is very susceptible to Japanese beetles. 'June Bride' is covered in flowers. 'Prestige' and 'Baileyi' grow quickly, while 'Rancho' shows some resistance to pesky beetles. *Tilia tomentosa*, the silverleaf linden, is an outstanding pyramid-shaped street tree. Though not as fragrant, it makes a good substitute because it resists Japanese beetles. Use the native *Tilia americana* in woodland settings.

This tree is an unusual exception to the rule that shade trees don't have interesting flowers. Lush, dark green, glossy, heart-shaped leaves emerge in spring. Huge clusters of pendulous flowers send a sweet scent into the air and follow suit in June. The blooms themselves, a rather dull yellow-green, are no match for a dogwood or crabapple; however, what they lack in flash they easily make up for in fragrance. Littleleaf linden makes an excellent shade tree. Its dense, symmetric and pyramidal canopy casts heavy shade on the ground around it. The littleleaf linden is a smaller European relative of the American linden, or basswood, Tilia americana. The basswood can reach heights of over 100 feet, so the fragrance is usually lost to the wind — all the more reason to plant its smaller cousin, the littleleaf linden.

Bloom Period and Seasonal Color
Flowers in June; yellow leaves in fall.

Mature Height × Spread
60 to 70 ft. × 30 to 35 ft.

Paperbark Maple
Acer griseum

Though lesser-known, the paperbark maple has many qualities that make it preferable to its favored cousin, the Japanese maple. The paperbark counts itself among the tri-foliate maples. That is, its small leaves appear in groups of three leaflets with branches forming an open rounded canopy. They are deep blue-green on the surface and light silver-green on the undersides. Its red droopy spring flower in spring precedes the developing fruit, called a samara. Given many a nickname such as "helicopters," they don't reseed everywhere like some maple seeds. In fall, the leaves turn deep scarlet red. Despite its attractive foliage, paperbark maple is one of our finest trees for the winter landscape. Its spectacular cinnamon-colored bark peels in papery sheets all year. Like fine wine and good people, it improves with age.

Bloom Period and Seasonal Color
Green leaves in summer; scarlet-red fall color; cinnamon-colored bark all year.

Mature Height × Spread
20 to 30 ft. × 15 to 30 ft.

When, Where, and How to Plant
Plant paperbark maple into moist, slightly acidic (up to a pH of 7.0), well-drained soil. Dig a planting hole three times the width of the rootball. Dig only deep enough so that the top of the rootball is even with the ground around it after planting. It transplants easily but try not to loosen any soil from around the roots. Backfill with the original soil, tamp lightly, and water deeply.

Growing Tips
Keep a 2- to 3- inch layer of mulch over the root system at all times. Water deeply at least once per week, especially during dry spells in summer and during the first one to five years after planting. Fertilize young trees in early spring or early fall, especially during the first five to ten years.

Care and Maintenance
Prune lower branches to reveal the papery bark. Allow the canopy to spread and open as it naturally does, with time. Few pests bother paperbark maple on a regular basis.

Companion Planting and Design
Combine with coarse or big-leaved plants such as hydrangea to contrast with the fine leaves. Plant spring blooming bulbs like crocus and daffodils at the base to bring attention to the peeling trunk. Alternatively, use decorative stone such as river rock to frame the stem. Combine with red-leaved or red-flowered shrubs such as American cranberry bush, American elderberry 'Black Beauty', or winterberry holly. This is an excellent small tree for an enclosed patio or courtyard garden.

We Recommend
An excellent short-statured maple is the amur maple, *Acer ginnala* ssp. *tataricum*. Its sharp pointed leaves turn brilliant in fall. Its samaras turn fiery red by midsummer and give the appearance that it is flowering. As its name suggests, the hedge maple, *Acer campestre*, makes an excellent formal hedge if properly pruned. The less common three-flower maple, *Acer triflorum*, is similar to paperbark with ash-brown peeling bark and more orange-red leaves in fall.

Redbud

Cercis canadensis

When, Where, and How to Plant

Plant redbud in spring or fall in moist but well-drained soils with ample organic matter. They grow well in either acid or alkaline sites but prefer full sun to light shade. Dig a planting hole three times the width of the rootball. Dig only deep enough so that, after planting, the top of the rootball is level with the ground around it. Backfill the hole with the original soil, tamp lightly, and water deeply.

Growing Tips

Keep 2 to 3 inches of organic mulch around the root zone at all times. Water deeply, especially during dry periods in summer. Redbuds do not tolerate overly dry or overly wet soils. Avoid planting in these sites if possible. Fertilize young trees in early spring or early fall for faster growth.

Care and Maintenance

Redbuds grow in multi-stemmed or clump forms with two or three trunks growing on the same root system. Prune to encourage this natural growth habit. Prune away dead branches or prune correctively in spring, right after the blooms fade. Redbuds occasionally suffer from a wilt or a canker-causing disease which causes sudden death of scattered branches. Over the years, this can be fatal. However, redbud usually overcomes it by sprouting new stems from the same root system which are wilt and canker-free. There is no effective treatment to relieve the canker or wilt problem.

Companion Planting and Design

Though they grow best in their natural setting, they also tolerate urban conditions well. Many a Hoosier gardener has brought seedling trees back from the farm or a country cabin to suburbia for planting.

We Recommend

If planting a redbud, why not go for "royalty?" If you live in Zone 6 in southern Indiana, plant the cultivar 'Forest Pansy'. Marginally hardy in Zone 5, its leaves emerge bright purple after it blooms. It only gradually fades to a dark green with purple tinge over the summer. 'Flame' has double flowers and is a vigorous grower. 'Royal White' and 'Alba' are both white cultivars; the former has larger flowers than 'Alba' and blooms longer.

The purple buds and rose-pink flowers of our beloved redbuds are sometimes overshadowed by the bodacious crabapples and dogwoods. Redbuds, however, are equally brilliant—blooming at the edge of a woods or in the tiniest patio garden. Branches grow upright and spreading and flatten with age into a classic vase shape. In early April, the deep-red, almost purple buds open to reveal rose-pink flowers held tightly to the branches. The branches seem to reach skyward, like rosy fingers. A close-up view of the flowers through a window is breathtaking. The flowers are edible, so pull some of the blooms from the branches to brighten an otherwise dull salad. The heart-shaped leaves can reach 5 to 6 inches in length and give the tree a more rounded appearance. Leaves turn bright yellow in fall.

Bloom Period and Seasonal Color
Rose-pink flowers in early April; yellow leaves in October.

Mature Height × Spread
20 to 30 ft. × 25 to 35 ft.

Red Maple
Acer rubrum

Native to Indiana, the red maple grows well in most soils, even tolerating the stress of urban areas. Red maple has an oval shape when mature and occasionally grows to over 100 feet tall in its native habitat. Its leaves emerge from crimson red buds that swell in late winter and then drop to the ground. Initially, leaves are tinged with red and have usually three but sometimes five lobes, or points. The leaves stay a dark, glossy green throughout the summer. The red buds, red petioles (which attach the leaf to the stem), and red twigs of new growth helps distinguish the red maple from other maples. The red fall color can be outstanding. Purchase maples grown from seedlings in Zones 5 or 6. Trees purchased from southerly locations may not be hardy in Indiana, even though they are called red maples.

Bloom Period and Seasonal Color
Fat red buds in early spring; reddish orange to bright red leaves in October.

Mature Height × Spread
40 to 60 ft. × 30 to 40 ft.

When, Where, and How to Plant
Plant in early spring or late fall, after the leaves drop, in moist but well-drained soils with a neutral to slightly acid pH. Red maples turn chlorotic (yellow-green) in soils that are too alkaline. They tolerate heavy, wet soil and adapt well to low spots in the landscape. In partial to full sun, dig a planting hole three times the width of the rootball. Dig deep enough so that, after planting, the top of the rootball is level with the ground around it. Backfill the hole with the original soil, tamp lightly, and water deeply.

Growing Tips
Keep 2 to 3 inches of organic mulch around the root zone at all times. Water deeply, especially during dry spells in summer. Fertilize young trees in early spring or early fall. The red maple has a medium to fast growth rate.

Care and Maintenance
Remove dead branches any time, but prune to shape the tree in midsummer or late fall. Like other maples, red maples are "bleeders" and drip excessive sap from pruning cuts made in spring. Young red maples frequently suffer from sunscald which causes bark to crack following warm sunny days in winter. Leaves sometimes scorch during dry summers. Keep soils moist to avoid this. Pests aren't usually a problem for red maple.

Companion Planting and Design
Red maple is an excellent medium-to-fast-growing specimen shade tree. Plant it in the front yard or as a row along the driveway. Though shallow rooted, red maple is excellent for planting along the street.

We Recommend
To ensure spectacular and reliable coloration, plant select cultivars. Excellent choices for color include 'Red Sunset', 'October Glory', and 'Autumn Flame'. 'Brandywine', 'Somerset', and 'Sun Valley' are seedless and hold their colorful leaves for extended periods. Avoid planting silver maple, *Acer saccharinum*, an over-planted, fast-growing, and weak-wooded tree with a shallow root system that invades drain tiles and septics. Instead plant silver maple in its native wetland or in swampy areas, away from drain pipes, sidewalks, cars, or the house.

River Birch

Betula nigra 'Heritage'

When, Where, and How to Plant

Plant river birch in spring in moist soils that hold a lot of water. Wet sites that occasionally flood are ideal. River birch grows best in slightly acid soil; it sometimes develops chlorosis in alkaline soils. Dig a planting hole three times the width of the root ball. Dig so that the top of the rootball can be placed evenly with the ground around it. Backfill the hole with the original soil, tamp lightly, and water deeply.

Growing Tips

River birch is a solution for the gardener who has to have a fast-growing tree. Keep 2 to 3 inches of organic mulch around the root zone. As the river birch moniker implies, it likes water. Their inner leaves will turn yellow and fall off in summer if you let them dry out. Water deeply on a weekly basis to keep their roots moist. Fertilize young trees in early spring or early fall.

Care and Maintenance

Like maples, river birch "bleeds" excessive sap if pruned in mid-spring. Wait until midsummer for corrective pruning or to remove dead and broken branches. It is resistant to the bronze birch borer which kills countless white birch trees each year. Aphids, a type of insect, suck the juice from leaves. Leafminers chew the tissue between the upper and lower surfaces of the leaves, causing them to turn brown. Contact the Purdue Cooperative Extension Service for control options.

Companion Planting and Design

Plant this tree with an evergreen background and clumps of daffodils at the base for an exquisite effect in early spring. River birch makes a good patio tree or even screen. Plant it near a window so you can enjoy its winter character.

We Recommend

River birch grows as a single stem or multi-stem, clump-forming specimen. The multi-stem form is far more interesting and multiplies your enjoyment. Dura-Heat® has smaller but glossier and darker green leaves that are resistant to aphids and leafminers. It is an outstanding tree. We do NOT recommend the popular white birch, *Betula papyrifera*, which usually succumbs to borers after about ten years.

River birch is a plant lover's tree; each season it changes character to reveal its multiple personalities. 'Heritage' is the industry standard and grows up to 3 feet per year. Its bark peels in shades of light tan, cream, white, and salmon. In late winter the wispy and sponge-like male flowers, called "catkins," hang at least two inches from the branch tips. Glossy light-green triangular leaves with large "teeth" around the edges emerge in April. Their color deepens as summer approaches but turns bright yellow in the fall. In winter, the trunk and branches are clothed in beige-colored sheets of papery bark. The outer layers peel away to reveal lighter, creamier inner bark that sometimes takes on pink tones. On older trees, the bark tears off in large curly sheets, like paper. For speed of growth and architectural effect, river birch is ideal.

Bloom Period and Seasonal Color
Catkins in March-April; yellow leaves in fall.

Mature Height × Spread
40 to 70 ft. × 40 to 60 ft.

Serbian Spruce
Picea omorika

Though not as widely known as the popular Norway or Colorado spruces, the Serbian spruce is superior to both for Indiana. All spruce are native to more northerly climates so it is surprising that any of them tolerate our hot and humid summers. The Serbian spruce grows in a graceful and narrow pyramid shape that illustrates the words "Christmas tree." It can reach 50 or 60 feet tall while the base only spreads to 25 feet wide. The upper surface of the needles is dark green; two whitish-blue stripes run the length of the underside. Its branches swoop down and outward from the trunk. Other spruce are regularly bothered by bagworms, mites, and needle-cast disease, but Serbian spruce avoids these. In fact, it has few difficulties with our growing conditions. It is an elegant and effective evergreen screen.

Bloom Period and Seasonal Color
Evergreen; brown cones in fall.

Mature Height × Spread
50 to 60 ft. × 20 to 25 ft.

When, Where, and How to Plant
Plant the Serbian spruce in moist but well-drained organic soil. Unlike most evergreens which prefer acidic soil, the Serbian spruce also grows well under alkaline conditions. Plant it in full sun but avoid open and exposed areas where it must endure strong winter winds. It tolerates pollution well and makes an excellent evergreen for urban areas. Dig a planting hole three times the width of the rootball. Dig only deep enough so that, after planting, the top of the rootball is level with the ground. Backfill the hole with the original soil, tamp lightly, and water deeply.

Growing Tips
Keep a 2- to 3-inch layer of organic mulch around the root zone. Water deeply on a weekly basis in summer, especially if dry. Fertilizer is not needed—it fends for itself better than its deciduous counterparts.

Care and Maintenance
Serbian spruce is almost maintenance free. Prune to remove dead or dying branches. The branches are very pendulous, so don't shear Serbian spruce (especially when young) as some people do with other spruces. Enjoy it for its natural shape. In winter evergreens lose water through their needles when the temperature is above45 degrees. It needs a steady supply of water in the soil so it can replace what is lost; otherwise it may suffer tip burn during the winter. Re-mulching the root zone in fall will help.

Companion Planting and Design
Plant Serbian spruce near the corner of a house to soften the edges or as a group at the edge of the yard. Because of its color, blue spruce screams for attention if planted near the house, and Norway spruce grows far too wide for this location. Serbian is a more versatile choice.

We Recommend
'Pendula' is a shorter cultivar with a weeping habit. The Norway spruce, *Picea abies*, and the Colorado blue spruce, *Picea pungens*, are other good evergreens but are more prone to pests. The Norway spruce is a good windbreak in open areas. Blue spruce makes an excellent specimen or focal point. Choose 'Hoopsii' or 'Thompsenii' which are dense and an intense bluish-white.

Serviceberry
Amelanchier × grandiflora

When, Where, and How to Plant
Plant serviceberry in spring in moist but well-drained soil with plenty of organic matter. Serviceberry prefers soils with an acidic pH but also tolerates slightly alkaline soils. It blooms even in a partly shaded environment. Windy and exposed sites are not recommended. Dig a planting hole three times the width of the rootball. Dig the hole only deep enough so that, after planting, the top of the rootball is level with the ground around it. Backfill the hole with the original soil, tamp lightly, and water deeply.

Growing Tips
Keep 2 to 3 inches of organic mulch around the root zone. Water deeply, especially during dry spells in summer. Fertilize in early spring or early fall, especially during the first five to ten years after transplanting.

Care
A yearly application of sulfur after Thanksgiving will help keep the pH in the acidic range. Test the soil to check for recommended rates (refer to main introduction). Prune any deadwood and shape into the more interesting and valuable multi-stemmed or clump form. The hybrid, *Amelanchier × grandiflora*, is more resistant to common native serviceberry diseases such as rust, fire blight, leaf spots, or mites. Beware of Japanese beetles which enjoy serviceberry. Knock them into a pot of boiling hot water or vegetable oil to reduce damage.

Companion Planting and Design
Plant serviceberry near the house to enjoy the smooth gray bark in winter; hang a feeder to enjoy both the birds and the bark. Serviceberry makes an excellent small patio tree, so plant it around your outdoor sitting area.

We Recommend
'Autumn Brilliance', 'Cole's Select', and 'Princess Diana' all have spectacular fall color. 'Robin Hill' blooms before any other serviceberry. Its pink buds open to white flowers. *Amelanchier laevis* 'Cumulus' is a fast grower with upright form that makes a nice screen or background for the flower or shrub border. Its natural tendency to grow as a single trunk makes it useful as a street tree. 'Snowcloud' has large white flowers and blue-green leaves.

Serviceberry is a tree for year-round enjoyment. Its large clusters of dainty white flowers are among the first to open in spring, along with the early daffodils. The native serviceberry is easily recognized blooming at the edge of woods and helps break the monotony of the winter landscape. The plentiful cherry-red fruit follows in June and makes wonderful pies and preserves. The berries finally turn blue-black if the birds don't gobble them up first. The small and smooth, shiny green leaves cast a touch of elegance on the garden as they shimmer in summer breezes. Their fall display, a brilliant orange-red, is a precursor to winter. The smooth light gray bark is an asset in any winter garden. Amelanchier × grandiflora is a hybrid of two native species, A. arborea and A. laevis.

Other Common Names
Shadblow, Juneberry

Bloom Period and Seasonal Color
White flowers in late March and early April, and red fruit turning blue-black in June; orange-red leaves in October.

Mature Height × Spread
15 to 25 ft. × 15 to 20 ft.

Shingle Oak

Quercus imbricaria

Shingle oak, like other oaks and large shade trees, forms the foundation or "backbone" of the landscape. The shade cast by its massive canopy helps cool nearby buildings in summer, while the bare branches and massive trunk serve as windbreaks in winter. The shingle oak's glossy-green, narrow leaves more closely resemble willow leaves than they do the heavily-lobed shapes of other oaks. The leaves turn a golden yellow in fall, then brown, and persist on the branches for many months. The rustling of leaves on windy days brings some relief during the bitter cold of dead winter. Shingle oak is a native tree in Indiana, and early settlers used the wood for roofing tiles. The Latin word imbrex *means "tile," hence its botanical name,* Quercus imbricaria.

Other Common Name
Laurel Oak

Bloom Period and Seasonal Color
Yellow-brown leaves in fall.

Mature Height × Spread
50 to 60 ft. × 40 to 60 ft.

When, Where, and How to Plant
Plant shingle oak in spring in moist but well-drained, acidic or alkaline soil. Though easier to transplant than other oaks, avoid planting this (and other oaks) in the fall. Dig a planting hole three times the width of the rootball. Plant the shingle oak only deep enough that, after planting, the top of the rootball is level with the ground. With all oak species, be especially careful not to let the soil break away from the roots during planting. Backfill the hole with the original soil, tamp lightly, and water deeply.

Growing Tips
Keep 2 to 3 inches of organic mulch over the root zone. Water deeply in summer, especially during dry spells. Fertilize in early spring or early fall, especially during the first ten to twenty years after transplanting.

Care and Maintenance
Prune dead or broken branches in late winter. Galls sometimes form on the leaves and twigs. When the tree is young and the galls are easy to reach, remove the twig galls with hand pruners or loppers. Larger trees might be more of a challenge. Fortunately, the galls cause no long-term damage.

Companion Planting and Design
Plant shingle oak as a screen or windbreak in wide open areas like parks or golf courses. It also makes a good tree for street planting and tolerates city conditions well. Shear shingle oak for a nice formal hedge.

We Recommend
There are no improved varieties of shingle oak available. Landscapers frequently pass over shingle oak in favor of the over-planted pin oak, *Quercus palustris*. Shingle oak's pyramid shape and lower hanging branches even resemble pin oaks, especially when young. With age however, the popular pin oak becomes extremely sensitive to alkaline soil conditions and will develop yellow leaves. Pin oaks may die because of high soil pH. Shingle oak is an excellent substitute for pin oak and should be used in all situations where soil pH is over 7.0. Use the pin oak in acidic soils only.

When, Where, and How to Plant

Plant in spring into moist but well-drained soils. Sumac is a tough plant known to withstand poor, dry growing conditions but not wet soils. Staghorn will also tolerate tough conditions, so plant it where nothing else seems to grow such as urban sites where with heavy air pollution. Dig a planting hole three times the width of the rootball. Dig only deep enough so that the top of the rootball is level with the ground around it. Backfill with the original soil, tamp lightly, and water deeply.

Growing Tips

Keep 2 to 3 inches of organic mulch around the root zone at all times. Water deeply in summer, especially during dry spells. Once established, this tree should not require fertilizer.

Care and Maintenance

Staghorn sumac requires very little care. Remove any deadwood down to the ground each spring. In smaller planting areas, you may have to keep the suckers in check with regular pruning. Staghorn sumac is prone to a canker disease that causes some stems to die back each year; however, it quickly produces new canes to replace the dead ones.

Companion Planting and Design

This is a wonderful small tree for native gardens, steep banks, or hillsides where it will sucker freely with ample space. Combine with other natives like elderberry, winterberry, and ornamental grasses. The fuzzy red fruit is attractive both on and off the plant and works wonderfully in dried flower arrangements with a Victorian feel. Their red color makes them a perfect addition to holiday trees, wreaths, or garlands.

We Recommend

'Laciniata' and 'Dissecta' are outstanding shorter specimens with highly dissected leaves and yellow-orange-red fall color. *Rhus glabra* is closely related to *R. typhina* and differs only by having smooth rather than velvety bark. *Rhus aromatica* 'Gro-Low', or fragrant sumac, is a ground cover that grows to 2 feet tall and 5 feet wide. It has leaves appearing in threes which turn a bright orange-red in fall.

Staghorn sumac gets its name from the thick, velvety, upright branches that resemble deer antlers after the leaves drop. The flowers open in an erect, tightly packed, light-green panicle that turns deep red when it matures. The bristly red fruit will last until early spring and provide great winter interest in the bleak Indiana landscape. The compound leaves of the staghorn sumac have leaflets 8 inches long. They resemble a walnut leaf from a distance but are much smaller and more delicate. Staghorn sumac's greatest attribute is the spectacular fiery red color of its leaves in fall. In its natural environment, it grows in large colonies that "light up" a hillside or bank. The deep-red fuzzy berries stand tall above the "flames." In today's fast-paced society, the staghorn sumac fills the need for a fast-growing tree.

Bloom Period and Seasonal Color

Red fruit in August, persisting through winter; fiery red leaves in fall.

Mature Height × Spread

15 to 25 ft. × 15 to 25 ft.

Sugar Maple
Acer saccharum

When most people think of sugar maple, visions of church steeples rising above brilliantly colored leaves in small New England towns come to mind. Oh, the sugar maple in fall! Hordes of tourists return to New England and Canada each year like pilgrims to view the turning of the maple leaves. The reds, oranges, and yellows look like balls of fire covering the mountainsides. The rustling of the leaves as children walk by on their way home from school is an unforgettable memory. This beloved tree is the state tree for four states and is the national symbol of Canada. Whether for the fiery colors of fall, the sweet syrup we pour over pancakes, or the dense shade cast over hot homes in summer, we owe a great debt to this landscape stalwart.

Other Common Name
Hard Maple

Bloom Period and Seasonal Color
Red-orange-yellow leaves in fall.

Mature Height × Spread
60 to 75 ft. × 40 to 60 ft.

When, Where, and How to Plant
Plant sugar maple in moist but well-drained, slightly acidic or alkaline soils. Unlike red maple, sugar maple dislikes heavy or compact soil. It does not tolerate salt accumulation, so plant it far from the street if salt trucks are frequent in winter. Dig the planting hole three times the width of the rootball. Dig so that, after planting, the top of the rootball is even with the ground around it. Backfill the hole with the original soil, tamp lightly, and water deeply.

Growing Tips
Keep 2 to 3 inches of organic mulch over the root zone. Be sure to water deeply, especially in summer as sugar maple will scorch around the leaf margins during the long, hot dry spells of summer. Fertilize in early spring and early fall.

Care and Maintenance
Provide sugar maple with extra care for faster growth. Prune dead branches or prune to shape in June or late fall. Pruning in the spring causes excessive amounts of sap to "bleed" from the cut. This does not hurt the tree, but the extra sap flow is surprising and unsightly. Aphids suck the juice from leaves in summer. Though not a threat to the tree, the aphid excrement, called "honeydew," will drip on cars parked below.

Companion Planting and Design
Plant in large lawns or in the backyard for shade. Plant groundcover like pachysandra or English ivy beneath the canopy. Grass rarely thrives under the canopy of sugar maples.

We Recommend
'Green Mountain' resists scorch from hot and dry weather; however, 'Legacy' and 'Commemoration' tolerate the heat better. 'Legacy' has deep dark glossy green thick leaves while 'Commemoration' grows faster and turns color earlier than most. For smaller planting sites, 'Goldspire' is an excellent choice for its narrow canopy, scorch resistance, and beautiful golden leaves. Norway Maple, *Acer platanoides* (including 'Crimson King'), is a popular shade tree, but it is invasive in natural areas and displaces native species; therefore, we don't recommend it.

Sweet Bay Magnolia

Magnolia virginiana

When, Where, and How to Plant

Plant in early spring in slightly moist and well-drained soil. Plant sweet bay magnolia where it will get plenty of moisture. It dislikes dry sites and will not grow well there. Poorly drained, swampy sites are preferable. Sweet bay magnolia must have a slightly acidic soil and will yellow in alkaline sites. If the soil pH is above 7.0, adjust by adding sulfur according to soil test results (refer to introduction). Magnolia prefers full sun but also grows well in partly shaded sites. Dig a planting hole three times as wide as the rootball, digging only deep enough that the top of the rootball is even with the ground after planting. Backfill the hole with the original soil, tamp lightly, and water deeply.

Growing Tips

Keep 2 to 3 inches of mulch over the root zone at all times. Water deeply in summer, especially during dry spells, and spread 2 to 3 inches of organic mulch around the planting site. Fertilize according to instructions in chapter introduction.

Care and Maintenance

Sweet bay magnolia is a low maintenance plant and has few pest problems. Prune dead branches as necessary. Train into a multi-stemmed specimen for more interest. It may be partially evergreen in southern locations such as Evansville. In the coldest regions of northern Indiana, it may get winterburn or suffer winter damage.

Companion Planting and Design

Plant near patios and decks or the front door to enjoy the sweet fragrance. Plant it with shrub roses and ornamental grasses to combine colors and contrast textures.

We Recommend

'Henry Hicks' stays evergreen at temperatures well below zero. 'Milton', 'Ravenswood', and 'Wilson' are also evergreen and hardy. *Magnolia stellata*, the star magnolia, and *Magnolia* × *soulangiana*, the saucer magnolia, are more popular species in this area. However, their flowers are routinely killed by late spring freezes; as a result, the flowers become brown mush two out of every three years on average. The sweet bay magnolia is a much better selection.

A primary structural component of beaver dams, this native small to medium-sized tree was sometimes called "Beaverwood." Sweet bay more aptly describes its use around home landscapes. Opening after the "spring rush" of early flowering trees like redbud and crabapple, its quiet blossoms lack the gaudiness of its cousins, the star and saucer magnolias. The light green leaves also help to conceal the creamy white blooms giving it a softer appearance. It blooms off and on all summer, though not as heavily as in the spring. Its sweet fragrance will calm you after a bad day at the office and bring a smile to your face. With ample moisture it grows quickly, a bonus for the impatient gardener. Plant the native sweet bay magnolia near a patio, deck, or window so you can enjoy the wonderful fragrance. Sweet bay magnolia is partially evergreen in Southern Indiana.

Other Common Name
Swamp Magnolia

Bloom Period and Seasonal Color
Creamy white fragrant flowers from June to July.

Mature Height × Spread
10 to 20 ft. × 10 to 20 ft.

White Fir
Abies concolor

White fir's erect and formal shape and pale blue needles resembles the popular Colorado blue spruce. Closer examination will reveal that its needles are longer, softer, and a paler blue. The feathery new growth in spring curves inward and upward toward the tips and forms a v-shape, which is much different than the shorter spruce needles that prick your skin if you get too close. Its adaptability to heat, cold, and drought as well as its pest-free nature make it an outstanding specimen for Hoosier landscapes. Enjoy the citrusy fragrance it releases when you brush up against them. Its dense branches grow thick with needles, making it a good nesting site for birds. In the west, its wood is desirable for lumber. It's also a popular Christmas tree.

Bloom Period and Seasonal Color
Light blue-green needles all year; brown cones in fall.

Mature Height × Spread
30 to 50 ft. × 15 to 30 ft.

When, Where, and How to Plant
The best time to plant is early spring before the flush of new growth. The second best time is early fall when the soil is still warm. When planting in the fall, water deeply once a week until the time the ground freezes. This will help keep it from drying out in cold, dry weather. Plant in soils that stay moist but drain well; they do not grow well in heavy clay soils that stay wet. In its native habitat out west, it grows in shallow granite and rocky soils. Here in the Midwest, it tolerates drier and sandier sites better than most other evergreens. It grows best in sunny sites but also does well in partial shade. Dig a planting hole three times as wide as the rootball. Dig only deep enough so that, after planting, the top of the rootball is level with the ground around it. Backfill the hole with the original soil, tamp lightly, and water deeply.

Growing Tips
Keep 2 to 3 inches of organic mulch around the root zone at all times. Water deeply during dry spells of summer and mulch again in fall. Conifers don't require additional fertilizer.

Care and Maintenance
White fir is practically care-free after planting. It doesn't require regular pruning. Remove dead or broken branches as needed. It suffers occasional bagworms. Carefully pull or snip the brown bags from the branch tips in winter.

Companion Planting and Design
Plant as an accent or specimen at the corner of the house. Use in groups as a screen or as a background for small trees and shrubs with winter interest such as paperbark maple, witchhazels, crabapples, and the Winter King hawthorn. Its narrow spread makes it much more useful in smaller landscapes than Norway spruce.

We Recommend
The cultivar 'Candicans' has eye-catching silver-blue needles. 'Compacta' is dwarf with good blue needles. 'Conica' is a semi-dwarf with a very narrow spread. Though difficult to locate, these cultivars are worth the search.

Winter King Hawthorn

Crataegus viridis 'Winter King'

When, Where, and How to Plant

Plant hawthorn in moist but well-drained acidic or alkaline soil, in early spring. It grows best in full sun to part sun but seems to tolerate poor, compact soils and confined root areas, such as on city streets, very well. Dig a planting hole three times the width of the rootball. Dig only deep enough so that, after planting, the top of the rootball is even with the ground around it. Backfill the hole with the original soil, tamp lightly, and water deeply.

Growing Tips

Keep 2 to 3 inches of organic mulch over the root zone at all times. Keep moist, especially during dry spells in summer. Fertilize young trees in early spring or early fall for faster growth.

Care and Maintenance

Winter king hawthorn is a tough plant for tough places. Prune right after flowering in spring. Remove dead and broken branches then shape to keep the natural upright, spreading, horizontal branches and open canopy. Be careful of occasional thorns, which can be fierce. Cedar hawthorn rust causes leaf spot, deformed fruit, and occasional twig dieback. This is much less of a problem on 'Winter King' hawthorn than on Washington, green, or other hawthorns. After the leaves drop in fall, prune out the branch tips that are swollen with the dark brown cankers that harbor this fungus.

Companion Planting and Design

Plant near patios and decks or the edge of the house. Underplant with small ornamental grasses or spreading yews to help frame the tree in winter. Use tall evergreens such as Serbian spruce or white fir in the background for contrast. The haws make festive additions to wreaths and other holiday decorations.

We Recommend

Crataegus phaenopyrum, the Washington hawthorn, has slightly smaller fruit but is more prone to rust than winter king. *C. phaenopyrum* 'Fastigiata' has a columnar growth habit. 'Princeton Sentry' is shaped like a narrow pyramid and is practically thorn-free.

Few can match the bang for the buck Winter King gives us each season of the year. A "native Hoosier," this cultivar was selected from a group of green hawthorns in the Simpson Nursery in Vincennes, Indiana. Glossy green leaves are followed by clusters of creamy white, apple-like flowers in May. In late summer, the $1/4$-inch developing berries, called "haws," turn bright red. Leaves turn a warm orange-red and finally drop in late October. It bares its royal soul all winter as the haws persist on its silver-gray branches well into February. When blanketed in snow, the combination of red haws and gray bark is truly stunning. On older specimens, the naturally open canopy helps to expose the peeling bark that reveals a creamy-orange inner bark. It is a gift that keeps on giving.

Other Common Name

Green Hawthorn

Bloom Period and Seasonal Color

Creamy white blooms in May; orange-red leaves in fall; bright red berries all winter.

Mature Height × Spread

20 to 25 ft. × 25 to 35 ft.

Vines *for Indiana*

> A physician can bury his mistakes, but the architect
> can only advise his clients to plant vines.
> —*Frank Lloyd Wright, architect*

Indeed, vines cover a multitude of sins in the landscape as they climb, cling, mound, or ramble. They also add beauty to the garden through color, texture, foliage, bark, flowers, seedheads, and fruit. Fast-growing annual or perennial vines form summer screens that shade or provide privacy for a porch. A vine mounding over a stump in the yard provides an interesting contour of foliage or flowers. Vines also bring vertical interest in the landscape when allowed to grow up a tower or trellis in the middle of the garden. They can climb up shrubs, such as viburnum or roses, or they can scamper along the ground, popping up among other perennials or annuals.

Some vines are natural climbers, and others are trailers. How they climb or trail can also vary. Clematis leaf stems must twine around a structure and climb, so it would never make it up a smooth surface, such as a lamppost, without some help from string bridges or other aid. However, many of the ivies can easily grow up a smooth surface because they sends out little rootlets that cling onto a surface with suction-like tendrils that help them climb.

Climbers and trailers may require some training. Weave them through fences or provide string bridges to get them started; this will train the vines to cover further surfaces horizontally and vertically.

Mandevilla

Because they can be heavy and have a natural tendency to fall away from the trellis or wall, it may sometimes be necessary to tie vines to a support. Jute, cotton twine, or nylon stockings are excellent for this task. Make a loose figure eight with the string or stocking around the support to the plants so that their growth is not restricted.

Use caution when allowing vines to climb wood or masonry houses, fences, or other structures. At best, the plants may mar or stain the surfaces; at worst, the vines could weaken already damaged mortar joints. Plant vines several inches from the support or wall on which they are to grow. There may be large clumps of concrete around fence posts, lampposts, and mailboxes that make digging there difficult. Move a foot or so away from the post and train the vine with a string bridge, wire, or wooden stakes angling toward the structure.

Unless you are growing a lightweight annual vine, such as a climbing black-eyed Susan, invest in a sturdy support. Perennial vines can get quite woody, heavy, and large. Make sure that the trellis, fence, arbor, or other support is sturdy and securely mounted so it won't fall down or collapse from the weight of a vine.

Some perennial vines, including a few natives, can be rampant growers and easily swallow up or strangle nearby plants. Vigorous growers will need to be kept in check by pruning them back as needed. When selecting vines, consider those that have long bloom periods, such as honeysuckle, and those that have winter interest, such as clematis, for added benefits in the landscape. Depending on where it is located and its growth habit, a vine can look a bit scraggly at its base. Consider planting annuals, perennials, or low growing shrubs, or cluster some containers and pots of plants there.

Vines may need pruning to give them shape, to stimulate growth or to keep them in check, so don't be afraid to cut them back. Prune out large branches down to the vine's base every few years to keep the plant's growth balanced. If you trim back only the top, growth will be focused there and the bottom will become sparse. Vines that bloom on new growth should be pruned in late winter or early spring, while those that bloom on year-old growth should be pruned immediately after they flower. Plant container-grown stock the same depth it was growing, unless otherwise noted. When preparing a large area to plant, add a two- to four-inch layer of compost or other organic matter and work that into the soil six to eight inches deep. Sow seeds according to packet instructions. Vines planted under eaves, trees, or other areas sheltered from the rain will benefit from an occasional supplemental soaking.

Boston Ivy

Parthenocissus tricuspidata

This is the plant that gave Ivy League colleges the name. Boston ivy forms disk-like root clusters that help it climb and cling to masonry. Its flowers are insignificant and occur only on mature growth. The flowers may be followed by dark-blue berries. The three-lobed leaves are shiny green, and they form a dense screen when growing on a wall. Each leaf has three points, hence the species name tricuspidata. The leaves turn red or bright orange in fall before they drop to the ground, revealing a woody vine. Despite its Boston moniker, this plant is from Asia. It is related to Virginia creeper, which is a native plant of North America. Boston ivy is good for urban settings because it tolerates pollution, shade, and average soil.

Bloom Period and Seasonal Color
Shiny green foliage in spring and summer, turning to bright orange or red in fall.

Mature Length
40 to 60 ft.

When, Where, and How to Plant
Container-grown transplants may be planted in early spring as soon as the soil can be worked. Plants usually come in small peat pots, which can be planted pot and all. If transplants come in plastic, remove the pot before planting. Boston ivy seems to prefer a northern or eastern exposure. These plants are not fussy, so a lot of bed preparation is not necessary. It tolerates average soil, but it does best in a well-drained, moist spot that has been amended with compost or organic material. The planting hole should be slightly wider than the transplant. Water well, supplementing rainfall, so that new plants get about 1 inch of water every week or ten days.

Growing Tips
Once established, the ivy will not need watering unless it becomes very dry. Apply an all-purpose granular fertilizer according to label instructions in late fall or winter or add a thin layer of compost around the base of the plants in spring and fall.

Care and Maintenance
Pruning usually isn't necessary except to keep the plant under control and away from windows, doors, gutters, and downspouts. Some of the foliage or parts of the vine may suffer winterkill, but Boston ivy usually recovers without any effort on the gardener's part. The leaves may be hit by mildew or Japanese beetles, but neither is fatal and usually does not require treatment. Good air circulation and environmental controls, such as raking up fallen leaves, should help with the mildew problem.

Companion Planting and Design
Boston ivy looks fine by itself. It is such a woody and vigorous grower that it would likely overtake other plants. As it ages, the shape of the shiny green leaves may change.

We Recommend
Parthenocissus tricuspidata 'Lowii', or 'Low's' Japanese creeper, has smaller leaves; 'Veitchii' turns purple in fall; 'Robusta' is considered very hardy.

Clematis

Clematis spp. and hybrids

When, Where and How to Plant

Plant container-grown transplants in early spring as soon as you can work the soil. Plant in a sunny, well-drained spot that is moderately moist but not wet. Dig a hole about 1 foot deep and 1 foot wide. Amend the planting spot with compost and a couple of handfuls of sand, peat moss, finely chopped leaves, or other organic material. Dig a hole about twice the width of the pot and place soil in the hole so that the plant's crown will be 2 to 3 inches below ground level. (This is deeper than it was growing in its container.) Space plants about 18 inches apart. Water well and add mulch.

Growing Tips

As a basic rule, clematis likes hot heads and cool feet—full sun for the top and a shaded, well-mulched, moist area for the roots. Apply an all-purpose granular fertilizer when new growth appears in spring or spread a layer of compost around the plants in the spring and fall. Water as needed during the blooming period.

Care and Maintenance

The bloom period of clematis determines when you should prune it. Pests are not an issue with clematis.

Companion Planting and Design

Many clematis varieties blend nicely with shrubs, including viburnum, roses, and forsythia. Because they tend to be bare at the bottom, round annuals, perennials or smaller shrubs, such as spirea, look nice growing at the base of clematis. The companion plants also shade the vine's roots.

We Recommend

The fragrant, sweet autumn clematis (*C. maximowicziana, C. terniflora*) is a wonderful plant that quickly covers fences with star-shaped white flowers from late July through fall. *Clematis tangutica*, or golden clematis, has yellow, lantern-like flowers that bloom on new growth in early summer; in the fall it produces silky seedpods. *Clematis integrifolia* is not a climbing plant but one that rambles in the perennial bed, poking its beautiful dark blue, bell-shaped flowers through other plants.

The long-lasting flowers of clematis (pronounced CLEM-a-tis or Cle-MA-tis) make this woody, perennial vine a worthy addition to any landscape. Clematis climbs posts, twists up trees, or spreads along the soil to make an unusual ground cover. You can cut the flowers (some are fragrant) for indoor arrangements or leave them to dry on the vine, where they develop spidery seedheads that persist through winter. Clematis has two basic types of flowers: small and large, with the latter the most popular. Within the two types, however, are dozens of classifications and varieties, all of which seem to have different pruning requirements. A good reference guide will be helpful to eliminate confusion, or check with a local garden center or the Purdue Cooperative Extension Service for instructions. Clematis is beautiful, delightful, and worth the effort.

Bloom Period and Seasonal Color

Spring through fall in a range of colors, depending on variety.

Mature Length

4 to 40 ft.

Climbing Black-Eyed Susan
Thunbergia alata

A tender perennial native to Africa, the climbing black-eyed Susan is grown as a charming summer annual in the Midwest. The most common varieties have orange, yellow, or cream-colored trumpet-like 1¼-inch-wide flowers with dark throats. Its small flowers are never ostentatious. This plant does well in containers mixed with other annuals, including windowboxes or hanging baskets. In cottage gardens, it's allowed to scamper along the ground or trained to go up a trellis in the middle of the bed. The pointed green leaves are soft and a bit hairy. Thunbergia alata is named for Carl Peter Thunberg, a Swedish botanical author.

Other Common Name
Clockvine

Bloom Period and Seasonal Color
Orange, yellow, or cream in summer.

Mature Length
6 ft.

When, Where, and How to Plant
Plant transplants in the spring after the danger of frost has passed. If you are planting seeds, start them in March or April and follow the seed packet instructions. Sow two or three seeds about ¼ inch deep in 3-inch peat pots that are filled with soilless mix. Water gently and place indoors in a warm, bright spot out of direct sunlight. For best results, grow them under fluorescent lights until they are large enough for transplanting. Germination may take up to three weeks. Snip off the weakest seedling and transplant the remaining seedling, peat pot and all, breaking off any of the pot that sticks out above the ground. Plant climbing black-eyed Susan in full sun or dappled shade in well-drained, moist soil. If it gets too hot, climbing black-eyed Susan may slow down or stop flowering, so a little protection from afternoon sun would be best. Plant about 12 inches apart and water well.

Growing Tips
During the growing season, apply a slow-release, water-soluble fertilizer or compost tea about every two weeks. Water to keep the soil moist but not wet.

Care and Maintenance
Pruning is not required. Black-eyed Susan vines are relatively pest and disease free.

Companion Planting and Design
Climbing black-eyed Susan can be used as a summer ground cover, in a hanging basket or pot, or it can be trained to cover a fence. It also looks good in rock gardens, where it scampers along without overtaking companion plants.

We Recommend
T. alata 'Suzy Mixed' has yellow, orange, and white flowers. *T. fragrans* 'Angel Wings' has 2-inch-wide white flowers that bloom sixteen weeks after the seed is sown. The vine may reach a length of 8 feet, but despite the plants botanical name, the flowers are only mildly fragrant.

Climbing Hydrangea
Hydrangea anomala ssp. *petiolaris*

When, Where, and How to Plant

Plant container-grown transplants in the spring as soon as you can work the soil. Climbing hydrangea is one of our most adaptable vines, thriving in both full sun and full shade and growing best with eastern or northern exposure. Allow plenty of room to climb or wander. Choose well-drained soil. Dig a hole that is as deep as the container the plant has been growing in and twice as wide. Amend the soil with organic material. Place the specimen, fill the hole, and firm the soil around the plant. Water it well, and apply mulch.

Growing Tips

Climbing hydrangea is slow to establish, taking three or more years before blooming. This is a woody plant that can get quite large and heavy, so be sure it has adequate support from a fence, trellis, or other structure. Apply an all-purpose granular fertilizer in the spring when new growth appears, and then again in fall; or spread a layer of compost around the base of the plant in spring and fall. Water when the soil feels dry to the touch.

Care and Maintenance

Pruning is usually not necessary, but if you need to keep the plant looking tidy, prune it after it blooms. Pests are not a concern with climbing hydrangea.

Companion Planting and Design

Climbing hydrangea is best planted by itself; however, smaller, rounded plants such as hosta at the base of the vine shade the roots and provide a more complete look in the landscape.

We Recommend

There is only the species of *Hydrangea anomala* ssp. *petiolaris*. A similar plant, *H. anomala*, hardy in Zone 6, has small flowers, longer, more pointed leaves and is attractive in June and July. The Japanese climbing hydrangea (*Schizophragma hydrangeoides*) is another under-used woody vine similar to climbing hydrangea. It has silvery, heart-shaped, blue-green foliage and clusters of white, lacecap flowers.

Yes, hydrangea is a shrub with large white, blue, pink, or green flowers, but this variety is a beautiful woody vine that is not used nearly enough. The leaves are glossy, dark green, and heart shaped. Airy clusters of white flowers bloom for two to four weeks in June before turning a warm, light brown. These flowers remain on the vine until Christmas or beyond, and its peeling cinnamon or reddish-brown bark adds winter interest to the landscape. Climbing hydrangea readily clings to flat surfaces or can be used as a groundcover. This plant does not usually damage masonry or wood. It was formerly known as Hydrangea petiolaris.

Bloom Period and Seasonal Color
White flowers in early summer.

Mature Length
50 to 60 ft.

Cup-and-Saucer Vine
Cobaea scandens

Cup-and-saucer vine has been grown in conservatories and greenhouses for more than one hundred years. This plant is named for Father Cobo, a seventeenth-century Jesuit missionary and naturalist from Spain who lived and worked in Central America for almost forty years until his death in 1659. Cup-and-saucer vine grows as a rambling perennial in Central America, but in Indiana it is an annual vine that offers a very unusual flower for a trellis, arbor, or other support. The name "cup-and-saucer" describes the flowers, which start as pale-green buds that turn purple as they open into 2-inch-long "cups" and eventually form greenish "saucers." The leaves are pointed and grow almost 4 inches in length. The plant uses tendrils from branch tips to hold onto its support.

Bloom Period and Seasonal Color
Pale green to purple in summer.

Mature Length
15 ft.

When, Where, and How to Plant
Plant container-grown transplants in the spring after the danger of frost has passed. Place 24 to 30 inches apart and water well. Start seeds indoors six or eight weeks before the last frost. Nick seeds with a knife before sowing. Place two or three seeds in 3-inch peat pots that are filled with soilless potting mix. Barely cover the seeds. Moisten and place pots in a warm spot out of direct sunlight. For best results indoors, grow cup-and-saucer vine under fluorescent or grow lights until large enough to transplant. Germination may take a month. Snip off the weakest seedlings with scissors then plant the vine, pot and all. Plant cup-and-saucer vine in full sun or light shade. Choose well-drained soil and amend it with compost or other organic material. Water it well.

Growing Tips
Cup-and-saucer vine prefers moist soil, so water when the soil feels dry to the touch. Apply a water-soluble fertilizer or compost tea regularly throughout the growing season. Cup-and-saucer vine's flowers smell bad when they first appear and may attract flies. Once they open, however, the flowers acquire a more pleasant smell and may attract bees. Bats also pollinate the plants.

Care and Maintenance
If you protect it from the afternoon sun, you will prolong its blooms. You may pinch it for branching and shape. There are no pest concerns for this vine.

Companion Planting and Design
This is a subtle vine, so it is best planted on a support such as an arbor or trellis where it has a chance to show off its unusual flowers. Smaller annuals or perennials planted at the base of the vine rounds out the picture.

We Recommend
A newer cultivar is 'Royal Plum', which has deep purple flowers. Another new one, 'Key Lime' has pale green bell-shaped flowers. 'Flore Albo', or 'Alba', has white.

Cypress Vine
Ipomoea quamoclit

When, Where, and How to Plant

I. quamoclit does not transplant well, so sow seeds directly in the soil in spring as soon as all threat of frost has passed. For best results, nick seeds with a knife or scrape them with a file and soak them overnight before sowing. Sow outside directly, about $1/2$ inch deep in moistened soil. For flowers earlier in the season, sow seeds indoors four to six weeks before the last frost in biodegradable pots, such as those made out of newspaper or peat. Cypress vine needs support, such as a fence or trellis. It also can ramble as a seasonal ground cover. Sow seeds according to seed packet instructions in full sun in a well-drained, loamy soil that has been amended with compost or other organic material. Cypress vine also can be sown directly and grown in hanging baskets or other containers.

Growing Tips

Too much water and nitrogen fertilizer will cause more foliage than flowers. Once established, cypress vine can be grown in a drier environment. Usually fertilizer is not necessary, and it is relatively free of pests and diseases.

Care and Maintenance

Cypress vine is considered care free.

Companion Planting and Design

Avoid planting cypress vine where it can climb, take over, or strangle nearby plantings. Because it attracts hummingbirds, locate the vine where you can watch these tiny birds. It is not a heavy vine, so it will do well on a lightweight trellis or on a fence. It grows well with other *Ipomoeas*.

We Recommend

The species is the showiest. 'Alba' has white flowers. Cypress vine is very similar to another annual cardinal climber *Ipomoea × multifidi* whose red flower resembles the shape of the Chrysler® Corporation logo. The foliage is finely cut and arrow-shaped. *Ipomoea coccinea*, also known as starflower, has heart-shaped leaves. The trumpet-shaped flowers are red with a yellow throat. All of these attract hummingbirds.

Cypress vine has the same growing habit as morning glories, but the foliage is very feathery. The $1^{1}/_{2}$-inch long flowers are red and trumpet-shaped, a form that brings in the hummingbirds. Every once in a while, a flower will be white. Ipomoea comes from the Greek meaning "worm-like," which refers to its vining habit. The Greek word quamoclit means "dwarf kidney bean." Almost all Ipomoea, including morning glories, bloom fairly late in the season, usually not revving up until late July or early August. It makes up for lost time by blooming heavily until hard frosts.

Other Common Name
Cardinal flower

Bloom Period and Seasonal Color
Red flowers appearing in August to October.

Mature Length
12 ft.

Honeysuckle

Lonicera spp.

There's nothing like the fragrant honey or lemon scent of honeysuckle in early summer. Even unscented varieties of this vine may attract hummingbirds. Though most honeysuckle varieties lose their leaves in the fall, some plants are almost semi-evergreen, keeping their leaves well into winter. Lonicera × heckrotti 'Goldflame' is an everblooming honeysuckle that may be semi-evergreen, depending on the severity of winter. The fragrant flowers bloom May to November or December. Lonicera sempervirens, or trumpet honeysuckle, has orange-red flowers that are yellow inside. The beautiful flowers are not fragrant, but they attract hummingbirds. Lonicera japonica 'Halliana' is readily available at garden centers and through mail-order catalogs but is not recommended because it is extremely invasive.

Bloom Period and Seasonal Color
Pink, orange, red, and yellow blooms in summer; some are winter-blooming.

Mature Length
10 to 40 ft.

When, Where, and How to Plant
Plant container-grown transplants in a well-drained location as soon as you can work the soil in spring. Space at least 24 inches apart. Honeysuckle is not picky about soil quality, but if you want it to last a long time, amend the planting hole with organic material. Water well and mulch lightly.

Growing Tips
Too much nitrogen fertilizer with cause more foliage than flowers and may bring on an attack of aphids. Apply an all-purpose granular fertilizer in the spring when new growth begins or spread a layer of compost around the base of the plant in the spring and fall.

Care and Maintenance
Prune two-year-old honeysuckle stems to the ground within a month after its first strong flush of flowers. If you wait too long to prune, you will cut off the branches that will form next year's flowers. Many honeysuckle varieties will continue to bloom throughout the summer and into fall. 'Goldflame' may bloom until December, depending on the weather. Prune after it flowers to shape up the plant. Watch for aphids in the tips of new growth. Some honeysuckles get powdery mildew, which is unattractive but not deadly. Sulfur products control powdery mildew, but when and how it is applied can be a bit tricky. Read and follow label directions.

Companion Planting and Design
Honeysuckle will climb fences, trellises, and other supports, or it can be left to ramble along the ground. If your specimen is fragrant, plant it where you can enjoy the smell. Because it attracts hummingbirds, locate it where you can see the action. Some vines are sparse close to the ground, so round out the look by planting a few annuals or perennials to camouflage the base of the vines when growing up a trellis, or cluster some flower-filled pots there.

We Recommend
'Goldflame'and 'Dropmore Scarlet'. The latter blooms all summer and is one of the best honeysuckles available. The orange flowers are not fragrant but attract hummingbirds.

When, Where, and How to Plant

Hyacinth bean does not transplant well, so you may not be able to buy container-grown plants. Instead, sow seeds directly in the garden after the last frost. For best results, soak the seeds in water for a day before sowing. Sow seed 1/2 to 1 inch deep. Sow in loamy, moist, well-drained soil in full sun or light shade, where there is a support for hyacinth bean to climb, such as near a trellis or fence. Water well after planting. For earlier blooms, soak seeds and sow indoors six to eight weeks before the last frost in the spring in biodegradable pots, such as peat or pots made with newspaper. Follow seed packet instructions.

Growing Tips

Hyacinth bean does best when watered regularly, but it also tolerates drought conditions. Hyacinth bean loves hot weather and thrives in the humid weather of southern Indiana. Frost will kill the vine. Apply an all-purpose granular fertilizer around the base of the plants once hyacinth beans are about 6 or 8 inches tall, and again about a month later. Add a thin layer of compost on top of the soil at planting time.

Care and Maintenance

Once you plant a hyacinth bean, you'll be rewarded year after year since the seed is easily saved. Harvest dried and shriveled seed pods from the vine and store in a cool, dry place until the following spring. No pruning is needed, and the vine is relatively pest and disease free.

Companion Planting and Design

This is a showy plant that is best appreciated on a trellis or fence where you can see the flowers and colorful seed pods. A few annuals or perennials at the base will soften the look.

We Recommend

'Darkness' has purple flowers; 'Daylight' has white. 'Ruby Moon' has purple-ish leaves. Sometimes hyacinth bean is listed as *Lablab purpureus*.

Hyacinth bean, a tropical plant native to North America, is a woody annual vine that quickly twines up a trellis or fence to make a dense, green summer screen. It has 6-inch, heart-shaped, purplish-green leaves. The fragrant flowers are purple or white and resemble sweet peas; they are 1 inch long and stand 6 inches from the foliage. The flowers are followed by decorative, purple seedpods that grow 2 to 2 1/2 inches long. The pod is eaten in the tropics. Dolichos is a Greek word for "bean."

Other Common Names
Lablab, Indian Bean

Bloom Period and Seasonal Color
Pinkish-purple flowers followed by purple seed pods in mid- to late summer.

Mature Length
15 to 20 ft.

Mandevilla

Mandevilla × amabilis

Mandevilla vine is a popular tropical that can be found on patios and porches at some of the best dressed Hoosier homes. This tender perennial has a dark green glossy, ridged foliage and 2- to 4-inch, trumpet-shaped flowers. The vine grows fairly quickly once summer heats up, unfurling satiny pink, white, or yellow flowers. Mandevilla is usually purchased in the spring growing in a container with a trellis at garden centers. It also can be purchased through mail-order catalogs in early spring. In Indiana, this woody plant is best grown as an annual in a container. It can be taken inside during winter, but prune it back to a manageable size and give it plenty of light. Indoors, water when the soil feels dry to the first knuckle and fertilize according to package instructions when the plant is blooming.

Bloom Period and Seasonal Color
Pink, white, and yellow flowers in summer.

Mature Length
6 ft.

When, Where, and How to Plant
Mandevilla is usually purchased already growing in a container. If desired, transplant to a 10-inch or larger decorative container with drainage holes. Use a soilless planting mix and plant the same depth the mandevilla was growing in the original container. If indoors, place the pot in a bright window but out of direct sun. Move outdoors when all threat of frost has passed.

Growing Tips
Water so that the soil is kept moist but not wet. Use a bloom-booster water-soluble fertilizer or compost tea every two weeks throughout the growing season. Do not let the plant dry out.

Care and Maintenance
Although it likes it hot, mandevilla does best when protected from harsh southern or western sun. Mandevilla is very susceptible to frost. Fifty degrees is about as chilly as it can handle, so keep an eye on night temperatures early in the season and toward the end of summer. The plant can be overwintered indoors, but it will need a lot of light. Mandevilla is relatively pest and disease free, but sometimes mites, mealybugs, or whitefly may attack. Read and follow pesticide label directions.

Companion Planting and Design
Cluster Mandevilla with other containers of annuals or summer bulbs on the deck, patio, porch, or balcony. Because it is fragrant and attracts hummingbirds, place mandevilla where you can enjoy those attributes, too.

We Recommend
'Alice duPont,' which has pink flowers; 'Ruby Star' has dark red. There's also 'Yellow Delight' and 'White Delight'.

When, Where, and How to Plant

Morning glories don't like being transplanted, so they probably won't be available from garden centers. You can start them from seeds in spring after all danger of frost has past. Nick the seeds with a knife or scrape them with a file and soak them overnight. Sow them about $1/2$ inch deep in moistened soil directly where they will grow outdoors. Plant in full sun in a well-drained, loamy soil that has been amended with compost or other organic material. For flowers earlier in the season, sow seeds indoors four to six weeks before the last frost in biodegradable pots, such as those made out of newspaper or peat. Plants grown in biodegradable pots do not need to be removed from the container before planting. They are plopped in the ground, pot and all. Follow the instructions on the seed packets.

Growing Tips

Water at planting time, but too much water and nitrogen fertilizer will cause more foliage than flowers. Morning glories are fairly drought tolerant.

Care and Maintenance

Morning glories are generally maintenance and pest free.

Companion Planting and Design

You can allow morning glory to ramble over a woodpile, a stump, or any other structure in the landscape as a summer ground cover. To grow vertically, a morning glory vine needs some support such as a fence or trellis. It can also be grown in hanging baskets or other containers. Avoid planting where it can climb, take over, or strangle nearby plantings. Morning glory readily self-sows, a habit that may make it invasive in some gardens. To keep it under control, remove the flowers as they wilt and dry but before they can release their seeds.

We Recommend

'Heavenly Blue' has 4-inch-diameter flowers; 'Scarlet O'Hara' has wine-red 4-inch flowers; 'Pearly Gates' has 4-inch white flowers. The latter two are All-America Selections. *I. batatas* is the popular, annual sweet potato vine, a wonderful ground cover or addition to summer containers. It is grown for its purple or chartreuse leaves.

This vining annual has historic roots in the American landscape as a symbol of home, covering fence posts and porches as pioneers moved west. These are late bloomers, not living up to their name until mid- to late summer when blue, pink, white, red, or bi-colored trumpet-shaped flowers appear. They are a welcome addition to the garden at a time when there isn't a lot else going on. Morning glories bloom in the morning, closing by afternoon. Many of the newer varieties will stay open on cloudy days. Morning glories are native to tropical North America. Calonyction aculeatum, or moonflower, is sometimes confused with Ipomoea alba. Grown the same way as morning glory, moonflower has 6-inch, white satiny blooms that unfurl at night to release their sweet scent and attract night moths.

Other Common Name

Cardinal Cimber

Bloom Period and Seasonal Color

Various colors including blue, red, white, pink, and bi-colored in mid- to late summer.

Mature Length

8 to 20 ft.

Trumpet Vine
Campsis radicans

Trumpet vine is native to the eastern United States and will climb up or creep over whatever is in its path. As it is an aggressive grower, give it something to climb on but do not let it attach itself to your house or it could do damage. Trumpet vine produces clusters of six or more reddish-orange, trumpet-shaped, 3-inch-long flowers from June through September. The colors may vary from plant to plant, but that doesn't matter to hummingbirds, who love trumpet vine. It climbs by aerial roots, but the stems also twist and turn with reckless abandon. It has dark-green, serrated leaves that may not appear until mid- to late May. The vine retains its woody seedpods into cold weather, giving it an interesting appearance in winter.

Other Common Names
Trumpet Creeper, Hummingbird Vine

Bloom Period and Seasonal Color
Reddish-orange flowers in summer.

Mature Height
40 ft.

When, Where, and How to Plant
Plant container-grown transplants in the spring as soon as you can work the soil. This vine grows aggressively. Give it something to climb on besides your house, such as a fence or trellis. The vine can creep into downspouts, gutters, windows, or any other crack or crevice. Trumpet vine does best in full sun but will tolerate partial shade. It is not picky about soil but does best when you start them out in a well-prepared site. Dig the hole the same depth as the container the plant is growing in and about twice as wide. Amend the soil with organic material. Space plants 2 feet or more apart. Firm soil around the plant, water well, and mulch lightly.

Growing Tips
Apply a water-soluble fertilizer or compost tea throughout the growing season for the first year or two. Later, apply an all-purpose granular fertilizer in early spring and late fall or spread a layer of compost around the base of the plant in the spring and fall. New plantings will benefit from 1 inch of water or rainfall every week or ten days. Once established, no water is needed.

Care and Maintenance
Cut back to shorten stems or thin the plant as needed. It has the potential to strangle other plants if not carefully pruned. Growth tips can be pinched out during the summer to help shape the plant and fill in gaps. Trumpet vine is relatively pest and disease free.

Companion Planting and Design
Trim back about $^1/_3$ of the plant's branches to the ground each year, especially if there is little growth at the bottom. This will keep the flowers low enough so that you can see the hummingbirds. Trumpet vine also can be shaped into a shrub-like plant along a fence row. Trumpet vine needs to be kept in check and given substantial support.

We Recommend
'Flava' has yellow or orange-yellow flowers. 'Crimson Trumpet' has red flowers. 'Praecox' has red flowers that appear earlier in the season. 'Madam Galen' (*Campsis tagliabuana*) is a showy hybrid that may be less reliably hardy in Zone 5; it should be fine in Zone 6.

Virginia Creeper
Parthenocissus quinquefolia

When, Where, and How to Plant
Plant container-grown transplants in the spring as soon as you can work the soil. Virginia creeper can also be planted in the fall. This is a vigorous grower, so it will do better on a fence away from the house. Because this vine grows so quickly, consider using it as a seasonal screen or cover for an unsightly aspect in the landscape, such as a pile of debris or stump. Plant in average, well-drained soil, but it will tolerate poor soil. Virginia creeper is flexible about growing in sun or shade. Prepare a hole that is as deep and twice as wide as the container the vine was growing in; add organic material. Don't plant Virginia creeper any deeper than it was growing in its container. Fill the hole, firm the soil around the plant, and water well.

Growing Tips
Apply an all-purpose granular fertilizer when new growth appears in the spring or spread a layer of compost around the plant in spring and fall. Supplemental watering usually isn't necessary once the plant is established.

Care and Maintenance
Pruning usually isn't necessary but may be done in early spring if desired. Little care is needed, except keeping it in check so it doesn't wander where it's not wanted. Once planted, Virginia creeper is hard to get rid of. It is relatively pest and disease free.

Companion Planting and Design
It's best if Virginia creeper is trained to climb along fences. Otherwise it will smother anything it its path.

We Recommend
Only the species is available. *Parthenocissus quinquefolia* var. *englemannii* has smaller leaves that are denser and more leathery than *P. quinquefolia*. *P. quinquefolia* var. *saint-paulli's* leaves are also smaller, and the vine may cling better.

Virginia creeper is a relative of Boston ivy (Partheno-cissus tricuspidata) that often decorates the ivy-covered walls of colleges and universities. Virginia creeper is native to the eastern United States and is grown for its foliage, which is reddish when new and dark green in the summer. It turns brilliant purple or crimson in autumn before falling to the ground and revealing 1/4- to 1/2-inch-wide blue-black fruit. This deciduous vine is a woody climber that needs strong support. It can be shaped into a hedge or allowed to grow along the ground. It will also climb trees. Virginia creeper has an open growth pattern; you can see the structure or wall on which it is growing. This plant is sometimes confused with poison ivy, since they seem to grow in the same habitat. Virginia creeper has five leaflets however, while poison ivy has only three.

Other Common Name
Woodbine

Bloom Period and Seasonal Color
Green leaves in summer; bright to deep red in fall.

Mature Height
50 ft.

Water Gardens *for Indiana*

Water can be more than an element of the garden. It can be the garden. Water gardening adds another aspect of nature to the landscape with looks and sounds that create a calming, relaxing mood. A water garden attracts birds and other wildlife and provides a chance to grow and enjoy fish and a whole new group of plants.

Water gardening is a fast growing landscaping trend, and you don't need a lake in the backyard to dive in. Those without their own natural or man-made body of water can buy manufactured kits to create them. The kits may be as simple as a half-whiskey barrel or as complex as a concrete pond complete with streams, waterfalls, or fountains.

The kits come with instructions; however, if you are considering a large in-ground installation or are inexperienced at working with electrical wiring, it would probably be best to work with a contractor. There are many resources to help you with your project, including books, video tapes, CD-ROMs, and other instructional materials at local libraries, internet sites, county extension offices, bookstores, and home improvement centers. These aids will be useful regardless of whether you do it yourself or hire a contractor for your water garden.

Before you begin, check with local officials and your neighborhood association about ordinances or covenants that may regulate water gardens. For instance, an ordinance may require a fence or other barrier around ponds of a certain depth or size, or a covenant may limit the location of a water feature in your yard. Also, check with your local water utility about any restrictions on the amount of water you can use. If needed, there are commercial suppliers who will fill ponds and pools without drawing on your water supply.

Yellow Flag Irises and Water Lilies

There are several ways to bring water into the garden. The ones listed below are the most popular.

- Containers: such as ceramic urns or whiskey barrels, which are used above ground. A sealant or flexible liner may be needed for the inside of the container to make sure it doesn't leak. Containers are particularly attractive in small gardens or on patios and decks.

- Pre-formed ponds: which come in a variety of shapes and sizes. These are rigid and are usually made of plastic or fiberglass. Pre-formed ponds are usually installed in-ground, although some may work in an above-ground application.

- A flexible liner: can create a pond in any shape. The heavy-duty liner is developed specifically for water garden use.

- A fountain: powered by a recirculating pump, it is easy to install in above- and in-ground water gardens. Fountains, misters, or sprays have the added benefit of sound.

- A waterfall: brings sound to the landscape, and it, too, depends on a recirculating pump. A landscape that is naturally sloped lends itself to a waterfall, or one can be constructed.

- A stream or a dry creek: may be created where water runs naturally or where it rushes during a rain storm.

When designing or selecting your water garden, forget the adage to start small. Of course, you have to keep it in the right proportion for your landscape, but go for as big as the site will accommodate and the budget will bear. A common refrain from experienced gardeners is they wished their water garden were twice the size.

Where Do I Put It?

When deciding where to locate a water garden, keep several factors in mind.

- The site should have four to six hours of full sun a day. Landscapes that slope naturally lend themselves to waterfalls. A pond—whether above ground or in ground—may be the perfect solution in the landscape where it has been difficult to grow plants.

  If an in-ground water garden is planned, it should be located on high ground. If sited in a low area, run off, silt, and other matter will run into the pond. The run-off can muddy up the pond, flood it, or, if contaminated with lawn chemicals, may kill the fish and water garden plants. Run-off will not likely be a problem for an above-ground water garden, such as a whiskey barrel or ceramic pot.

- The site should have access to water and electricity. The pond will have to be filled, and many pumps and filtration systems require electricity to operate.

- Check for any underground utilities before installing a pond. Avoid locations, such as under trees, where debris will fall into the pond.

- For the best enjoyment, the water garden should be visible from the house, deck, or patio. However, make sure a deck, balcony, or other suspended structure will support the weight of people, furniture, other pots of plants, or whatever else might be housed there, as well as a container filled with water.

Planting

Water gardens in containers, pre-formed units, or flexible liners are filled only with water. No soil is placed on the bottom or the sides of these gardens. Almost all plants are grown in their own pots, which are then placed in the water. A few water garden plants float along the surface, unrooted in soil. Water garden plants also are grown this way because many specimens are aggressive, so pots keep them under control.

The soil used for planting water garden plants in pots should be heavy, loamy, and free of chemicals. Slow-release fertilizer tablets or granules specially made for water gardens may be mixed with the soil when planting.

Water garden plants (frequently referred to as aquatics) have a specific depth they need to grow. That depth is measured from the plant's crown, or point where growth comes from the soil in a pot, to the top of the water surface. A plant required to grow three inches deep means its growing point is that far below the water surface. Shelves can be made in the ponds from concrete blocks or other materials so plants can be placed at various heights, according to their planting needs and light requirements.

Plants for water gardens consist of oxygenators, marginals, floaters, deep water, or bog lovers. Oxygenators are fast growing and help clean the pond, including removing certain mineral salts that allow algae to thrive. These plants are helpful if fish are in the pond. Marginals live on the edges, or margins, of ponds, usually in shallow water. They provide cover for wildlife, and some varieties may provide oxygen to the water. Deep-water aquatics are planted a foot or more below the water surface, and floaters do just what the name implies—they float on the water's surface. There also are bog- and moisture-loving plants that thrive near the edges of ponds or in very wet areas but usually not directly in the water. However, many marginal and bog plants may survive in each other's environment, so it's all right to experiment.

Winter Care

Special care is needed for water gardens in winter. In general, if the container is made of porous material and there is danger the water garden will freeze solid, it's best to drain it. Water gardens made with flexible liners or pre-formed units do not have to be drained. A pump or heater in the water also keeps it from freezing, depending on the depth of the water garden, but it may be expensive to operate. Placing balls, logs, or other material on the pond in fall helps to keep the pressure from building up when the water freezes.

Many aquatics are winter hardy in Indiana, but that assumes their crowns grow or can be sunk to about thirty inches below the ice that will form on the pond. Cut back the foliage to the crown and sink the pots, plants and all. Smaller container gardens and ponds are apt to freeze solid, killing any plants that remain, which is why most water garden plants are treated as annuals and discarded at the end of the season. Tropicals, such as many water lilies, are tender and not winter hardy in Indiana. These are also treated as annuals.

If you have the space, plants can be wintered over out of the water. Pull the pots from the water garden and cut back the plants to their crown. Store the plants in their pots in an area that is cool (not freezing) and dark. The plants should stay moist. Many water garden enthusiasts store the pots in trash bags packed with wet newspapers to accomplish this.

There are dozens of water gardens plants to choose from. Here are seven plants that are readily available and easy to grow, but don't be afraid to try others.

Arrow Arum *Peltandra virginica, P. undulata*

A native North American plant, arrow arum has rich, green, heavily veined leaves that grow 1 to 6 feet tall in 2-foot clumps near the edge of water. The flower in early summer, called a spathe, is small and insignificant, but bronze-black berries develop along the stalk as the growing season continues. The berries contain seeds. Native Americans harvested the roots, steamed them to get rid of poisonous materials, dried them, and ground them into meal. Wood ducks love the fruit, too, which accounts for one of its nicknames, duck corn. Another common name is tuckahoe.

Arrow arum, which provides shelter and food for wildlife, prefers full sun but will tolerate light shade, especially from noon on. In spring, plant arrow arum in pots along the margins, or edges, of ponds. Plant in a large, deep container. Depending on the selection, place the base of the plant 3 inches to 4 feet below the water surface.

If left outdoors, arrow arum must spend the winter below the pond's anticipated ice level. If your water garden is small and/or shallow, either bring the plant indoors during the winter or treat it as an annual and discard. If you choose to bring it indoors, do so before the first frost. Arrow arum is easy to divide. It is sometimes confused with arrowhead (*Sagittaria latifolia*), which forms stands but not clumps. You can divide arrow arum in the spring.

Because the plant is a climber, it can be used as a wave break or fish cover without becoming an impenetrable thicket like arrowhead. Use with other marginal water plants and perennials such as *Pontederia* or *Decodon*. *Peltandra sagittaefolia* is native from the Carolinas to Mississippi, where it is called spoon or white arum. Its flower is edged in white, and its berries are red. Favorite cultivars are 'Hudson Valley', which gets about five feet tall and 'Snow Splash', which has variegated foliage.

Arrowhead *Sagittaria latifolia*

Arrowhead grows as a 2 foot by 2 foot clump at the water's edge. It gets its name from the shape of its three-pointed leaves and because it was a food used by many Native American tribes. The tubers, or roots, were harvested in fall then dried and stored for winter. Native Americans boiled the tubers for food; they can also be eaten raw, baked, or roasted. Sometimes called duck potato, they sweeten when cooked; otherwise, they are otherwise fairly bitter. The plant has dark-green leaves that can reach 2 feet. It grows in a cluster, or clump; the stems ooze a white, milky substance when broken. The white flowers in mid- to late summer have yellow centers and grow on stems that shoot from the plant. Arrowhead can be weedy when planted directly in the bottom of a pond, so growing it in a container is recommended.

A native plant, arrowhead provides shelter and food for wildlife. Grow it in a large pot. Place the pot in full to part sun on the edge of a pond, lake, or slow-moving stream. Arrowhead can be planted from March through July and can be divided during that same period. It tolerates shade, especially in the afternoon. *Sagittaria* needs to grow 2 to 5 inches below the water surface. In late fall, sink the container at least 1 foot deep, or well below the ice line that will form during the winter. Return it to its shelf in the spring.

Only the species is available, which is known more for its decorative berries than white flowers. *Sagittaria japonica* has white flowers with yellow centers. *Sagittaria japonica* 'Flora plena' is a slow-spreading plant with double, white flowers, which are small and short-lived.

Blue Flag Iris *Iris virginica, I. versicolor*

Many irises are as at home in dry soil as they are in the margins of ponds. Blue flag iris is a native plant that is hardy from Newfoundland to Virginia, and it adapts readily in various sites, including shallow water and wet soil. The plant has narrow leaves and purple-blue flowers with gold flecks. It forms large, dense clumps at the edges of shallow ponds and is an effective filtration plant. It is more refined than its European sister, *I. pseudacorus*, making it more adaptable to smaller ponds. Native Americans used blue flag for medicinal purposes. It reportedly was a remedy for thyroid growths and for getting rid of tapeworms.

This is the iris called fleur-de-lis, with blue flowers early to midseason. It forms 2 foot by 3 foot clumps and serves as shelter for wildlife. It also attracts bees and can be used as a fragrant cut flower. Plant in spring in full sun or light shade at the edge of the water. *Iris virginica* prefers moist soil but may tolerate drier soil. Plant in a large container and place 2 to 4 inches below the water surface. Favorites are: 'Kermesina', which has plum flowers and green leaves; Japanese water iris, (*I. laevigata*), the species of which has blue flowers; *I. laevigata* 'Colcherensis' has white-and-violet flowers; 'Alba' has white; 'Rose Queen' has pink; 'Snowdrift' blooms white with a streak of yellow and lilac; and 'Midnight' has deep-blue flowers with a yellow stripe. *I. laevigata* 'Variegata' has green-and-white foliage and lilac flowers.

Frogfruit *Phyla lanceolata*

This lovely plant has 2- to 6-inch-tall flowers that bob above serrated leaves. The flowers from July through September are pinkish-white and surround a dark red, purple, or brown pointed center, not unlike a coneflower. The flowers attract bees and butterflies. Its 2 foot by 2 foot mat-forming growth makes it a good anchor plant to help prevent soil erosion. It also tolerates some foot traffic. Ducks and other wildlife eat the seed on this native plant.

Plant frogfruit in full sun or part shade about 4 inches deep along the margins of ponds. Only the species is available for this plant, whose growth habit compliments other marginals by covering the edges of nearby pots or containers.

Pickerel Weed *Pontederia cordata*

Pickerel weed is a native plant that grows along the muddy margins of lakes, ponds, and slow-moving rivers from Minnesota to South Carolina. Native Americans made cereal out of its nut-like seeds or ground them for bread. Pickerel weed, sometimes called wampee, is easy to grow and has beautiful, butterfly-attracting blue, pink, or white flowers on tall stalks from July to September. It gets about 4 feet tall and 2 feet wide but is not considered invasive and is among the hardiest plants for water gardening. Depending on the depth of your water garden, you can sink pickerel weed's container and leave it outdoors during the winter. It has shiny edible olive-green leaves that are sometimes said to resemble an arrowhead or heart. Dragonflies and damselflies lay eggs on plant stems near the water surface. It gets its name—pickerel weed—because fish hide in the plants.

In spring, place pots of pickerel weed on the margins of ponds or water gardens in full sun to part shade. You can also divide it at this time or up to three weeks before the last frost. It must be 3 to 6 inches below water during the growing season but can go as deep as 1 foot.

If left outdoors, pickerel weed must spend the winter below the pond's anticipated ice level. In late fall, place it in the bottom of the pond. Return it to its shelf in the spring. Because it is not invasive and is showy, pickerel weed can be mixed with similar species, such as *P. cordata* var. *lanceolata*, which gets 4 feet tall with lance-shaped leaves and blue flowers. It may be less hardy in Indiana. *P. cordata* 'Alba' has white flowers and may also be less hardy in Indiana. 'Pink Pons' has pink flowers. A favorite cultivar is 'Crown Point', a compact grower with blue blooms that has five times the flower power as the species.

Water Lily *Nymphaea* spp.

Pond lilies, lily pads, and water lilies call to mind fairy tale images of exotic floating flowers and frogs resting on green, rounded leaves. Water lilies are deep-growing plants that send up leaves and flowers from pots placed at the bottom of the pond. Large ones grow from a depth of 3 feet and spread to 5 feet or more; the flowers can achieve widths of 10 inches. Water lilies are frequently the focal point or main feature of a water garden, so selecting the right variety is important. *Nymphaea* species and hybrids come in four types: dwarf, with a water planting depth of 4 to 6 inches; small, at 6 to 18 inches; medium, 2 feet; and vigorous, with a planting depth of 3 feet. Sometimes called alligator bonnet, water lilies are good filtration plants.

Water lilies bloom from June through September. The flower color depends on the cultivar. The long-blooming flowers attract butterflies and bees. Some water lilies are native, and some have fragrant flowers.

You can also divide water lilies in the spring. Do not plant tropical water lilies until the water temperature reaches 70 degrees Fahrenheit. Containers should be at least 6 inches deep and 12 inches wide; large cultivars may need 7- to 30-gallon pots. Set the containers on the bottom of the the pond or water garden. Insert a slow-release tablet of fertilizer into the container— one for every gallon of soil about every three weeks. The deeper the plant needs to be, the wider it will spread;

Water Lily 'St. Louis'

therefore, dwarf and small varieties are recommended for container ponds or other shallow water gardens. Given the right conditions—warm water temperatures, little competition, and sunny days—water lilies can quickly take over, so opt for smaller rather than larger plants.

If the pond is at least 30 inches deep and the water lily is growing below the expected ice or freeze level, it can stay outdoors for the winter. If the pond is shallow, you will need to bring the hardy water lilies indoors and refrigerate. Hardy lilies need a rest period similar to what they would have in nature. There are hardy and tropical water lilies, the latter adding fragrance and night bloomers to the mix. Some hardy water lilies are native to North America, while others come from Asia and Europe, so be sure to check their hardiness rating. Treat tropical water lilies like annuals and discard them at the end of the growing season. Favorite cultivars are: 'Texas Dawn', a good water lily for beginners because it produces many yellow flowers, even when planted in a small pond under less-than-ideal conditions; and 'Laydekeri' hybrids, which are recommended for container gardens and pools. They prefer to be planted a few inches below the water surface but will tolerate depths of 24 inches.

Several water lilies are known as "changeables," including 'Indiana', which has purple-spotted leaves and flowers that turn from peach to copper-orange with red stains. 'Little Sue', 'Sioux', or 'Comanche' has flowers that change from buff to pink to copper.

Tropical water lilies to consider are 'Missouri', a night-bloomer with white flowers, and 'Daubeniana', which has small blue flowers. Tropical water lilies are usually hardy only to Zone 8.

Water Parsnip *Sium suave*

This light and airy plant resembles Queen Anne's lace. Both are in the carrot family and have white umbel (or umbrella-like) flowers. The botanical names come from the Latin: *sion* which means "water parsley" and *suave* which means "sweet." Water parsnip also looks like the mature plant of the highly poisonous (remember Socrates?) hemlock (*Conium maculatum*), which grows along stream beds. Yet another hemlock it can be confused with is water hemlock (*Cicuta maculata*), which is highly poisonous but has a magenta-streaked stem and lanceolate leaflets with sharply-toothed edges. Water parsnip (*Sium suave*) is not poisonous and has toothed lanceolate leaflets. The native plant gets 2 to 6 feet tall and 3 feet wide and is used by wildlife for shelter. It has whitish green flowers in July and August, followed by berries.

In spring, plant pots of water parsnip about 6 inches below the water surface in a marsh or boggy area in full sun to part shade. Its lower leaves usually grow under water. Because of the airy umbrella-like flowers, it makes a nice contrast to the more bold foliage of iris and arum. Only the species is available.

Pruning Trees and Shrubs

Pruning eliminates dead branches, helps shape the tree, and stimulates new growth. It is a routine maintenance practice that will encourage a good growth habit and possibly increase the tree's or shrub's longevity.

Pruning is safe for the overall health of the plant at any time of the year. However, there are more logical times to prune depending on whether or not it blooms. As a rule of thumb, prune spring-blooming trees and shrubs such as dogwood, lilac, or fothergilla shortly after the flowers die. This encourages maximum flower production for the following year. Prune shade trees during late fall or early spring, when the leaves are absent, because it's easier to see the branch structure and shape it properly.

Pruning Trees

Schedule your trees for pruning every three years to remove dead wood and to make sure the crown is strong enough to withstand strong winds. This will greatly increase the health of the tree and the safety of those around it. Trees that are not regularly pruned are the first to drop branches or fall in heavy wind and ice storms.

Thinning Before

Study the natural growth habit of the tree to get a good idea of how much of a branch needs to be removed. Cut the branch all the way back to the collar, but don't actually cut into the collar. The collar is located where the smaller branch attaches itself to a larger branch or trunk. This will leave a small swelling or lump at the point of the pruning cut, which is necessary for proper healing. Never make a pruning cut that is completely flush with the branch or trunk, as these wounds will never heal. Pruning paint or sealants are not recommended for fresh tree or shrub wounds. Never leave stubby branches as is typical of the pruning practice called "topping." This is unhealthy for the tree and will cause an over-abundance of weak-wooded branches called "water sprouts" to grow. Topping is also a huge disservice to a tree's natural growth pattern. If a tree is growing into overhead powerlines, it would be a wise investment to remove it and replace it with a shorter species that will have room to grow to its normal size.

Thinning After

Most homeowners don't have the equipment or knowledge to prune large trees safely. These should be left to Certified Arborists who have the training and experience necessary to do the best job for you and the tree. To find a list of Certified Arborists near you, please visit the website of the International Society of Arboriculture at www.isa-arbor.org.

Limb Removal

Home gardeners are better able to prune young trees or some of the smaller branches of tall trees. For branches you can reach, use the three-cut method to keep the bark from tearing which can later serve as an entry-point for decay organisms. Train young trees by removing thin and spindly branches or branches with weak attachments such as on Bradford pear. Encourage a strong central leader and several scaffold branches.

Pruning Shrubs

Pruning is part art and part science, so don't be afraid to try your hand at this chore that sometimes mystifies even the most seasoned gardener. Experts often disagree over which branches to keep or remove. Start pruning by removing any dead or broken branches all the way down to the next living branch, or all the way to the ground, using sharp bypass loppers or hand pruners. Cut back to the collar or swollen area where the two branches join, leaving a short bump. Thin shrubs by removing tall and overgrown branches all the way down to the ground; however, it's best not to remove more than one-third of the total branches in any one year. Shorten other branches by heading back $1/3$ to $1/2$ their length to a smaller branch or bud. Remove select branches on all sides to maintain a balanced shape and to allow light to reach the center of the plant. This encourages new growth from low points on the branches and keeps it full. Don't leave short stubby branches, as this will cause an abundance of regrowth from just below the cut, similar to trees that have been topped.

When using shrubs for background or a privacy screen (not a hedge), prune once per year. For flowering shrubs, time pruning chores according to when the plant blooms. Prune spring blooming shrubs like viburnums and lilacs immediately after they bloom. Spring bloomers develop flower buds for the next season on the current season's growth. Poor flower production in spring is often the result of having pruned the plant too late in the season the previous year. Summer and fall blooming shrubs develop flowers on the current season's growth. Prune summer and fall bloomers early in the spring, just as new growth begins. Shorten overgrown shrubs, called "renewal pruning," by removing one-third of the tallest and oldest branches each year for three years. Some shrubs, such as spirea, tolerate cutting all the stems to the ground in spring. However, others, such as most needled evergreens, do not. Check the text for specifics.

"Shearing" removes the tips of the branches and is appropriate for formal hedges or when other unnatural shapes, like topiary, are desired. Evergreens like boxwood, yew, and juniper are often sheared to maintain their shape. Shear hedges in the early spring as new growth begins. In both formal and informal hedges, prune so that the bottom of the shrub is wider than the top. This will keep the lower branches green and full. Shrubs that are sheared to be wider at the top will eventually become spindly.

Rejuvenation

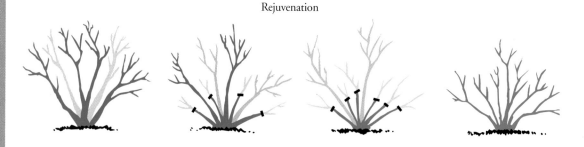

Public Gardens and Horticultural Attractions

Indiana is fortunate to have many public parks and gardens to enjoy and visit for inspiration. Although the following operating schedules are believed to be correct, visitors should call ahead to check schedules, admission fees, special events, and programs.

Cool Creek Park and Nature Center

2000-1 E. 151st Street
Fishers, IN 46038
(317) 848-0576
www.co.hamilton.in.us/gov/parks/coolcreek.asp

A recent addition to the Hamilton County Parks system, the Nature Center at Cool Creek Park in Fishers features a greenhouse with over 1,000 butterflies in various stages of metamorphosis. The butterflies live on more than 50 species of plants and flowers maintained by a dedicated staff of volunteers. Outdoor gardens designed for butterflies surround the greenhouse and are a great way to get ideas to bring home to your yard! The butterfly sanctuary and nature center conducts regularly scheduled activities for families and has group tours by request.

The Display Garden

Allen County Extension Office
4001 Crescent Avenue
Fort Wayne, IN 46815-4590
(260) 481-6826
http://www.ces.purdue.edu/allen

This display garden features more than 13 theme gardens highlighting butterfly and hummingbird plants, herbs, prairie plants, ornamental grasses, woodland plants and wildflowers, vegetables, cottage garden plants, and a children's garden. Maintained by dedicated Master Gardener volunteers, a visit to this garden is an educational opportunity for both beginning and advanced gardeners.

E. G. Hill Memorial Rose Garden

Richmond All-America Rose Garden
Friendship Rose Garden
Glen Miller Park, 828 Promenade
Richmond, IN 47374
(765) 962-1638
www.waynet.org/nonprofit/rosegarden.htm

Three gardens with more than 2,200 roses are open to the public during park hours. The Hill Memorial Garden was founded in 1937 and is the most formal, featuring about 200 plants. The All-America Rose Garden was started in 1987 and has about 2,000 plants. Friendship Garden opened in 1992 and is a sister garden to Richmond's sister city, Zweibruken, Germany. Some of the 120 roses are the same as those that grow in the German garden. The Richmond Parks & Recreation Department takes care of the Hill Memorial Garden; volunteers and the Richmond Rose Garden Board of Directors oversee the other two.

Foellinger-Freimann Botanical Conservatory

1100 S. Calhoun Street

Ft. Wayne, IN 46802

(260) 427-6440

www.botanicalconservatory.org/

Managed by Fort Wayne Parks and Recreation, the Foellinger-Freimann Botanical Conservatory is a natural oasis in the middle of an urban jungle. The three glass-domed conservatories house collections of tropical plants with distinctly different environments. The Showcase area has seasonal displays of flowers for six different occasions throughout the year, including a fall mum show, poinsettia show, spring bulbs, and more. The Tropical House is a jungle of exotic flowering and foliage plants maintained in a humid environment, and includes a wonderful cascading waterfall and sparkling stream. The Desert House is home to plants from dry and desert environments and features the massive saguaro and barrel cactus and many others. The Conservatory is host to numerous lectures, events, and educational programs throughout the year. The Tulip Tree Gift Shop features unique plants and botanical gifts. Group tours are available.

Garfield Park Conservatory and Sunken Gardens

2450 S. Shelby Street

Indianapolis, IN 46203

(317) 327-7184

www.garfieldgardensconservatory.org

Garfield Park is the oldest park in Indianapolis, and the Conservatory and Victorian-era Sunken Gardens have a long botanical history. Having recently completed a full-scale renovation, the Conservatory houses an Amazon River region rainforest environment with extensive displays of bromeliads and numerous other tropical plants in a recreated tropical setting. Self-guided and guided tours are available. Various seasonal floral shows are exhibited in the Conservatory throughout the year, including a fall mum show, holiday poinsettia show, and a spring bulb show. A variety of plants are for sale in the gift shop. The historic Sunken Gardens, which were recently renovated, are just west of the Conservatory and have beautifully patterned brick pathways among the flower beds. A highlight of the gardens is the fountains, which are lighted at night.

Gene Stratton-Porter State Historic Sites

Wildflower Woods

1205 Pleasant Point

Rome City, IN 46784

(260) 854-3790

www.in.gov/ism/HistoricSites/GeneStrattonPorter/historic.asp

and

Limberlost State Historic Site

P.O. Box 356

Geneva, IN 46740

(260) 368-7428

www.in.gov/ism/HistoricSites/Limberlost/Historic.asp

The state has taken over both Noble County homesites of the famous Hoosier writer, Gene Stratton-Porter (1863-1924), author of Girl of the Limberlost and other nature books. The homesites are now being restored, including the swampland at Limberlost and Wildflower Woods. Stratton-Porter grew up near Geneva on about 25,000 acres of swampland that served as a personal laboratory for her interest in natural history and botany. When the land was drained in 1913 she moved to Rome City, bringing with her hundreds of native plants she salvaged from the swamps and woods. Many of the plants she rescued have taken root at Wildflower Woods, where the public gardens are open dusk to dawn. Tours of Stratton-Porter's 16-room cabin are available. The peak time to visit is in late April and early May when hundreds of wildflowers are in bloom. There's also a 1-acre formal garden that includes several plots laid out by Stratton-Porter.

Hayes Regional Arboretum

> 801 Elks Road
> Richmond, IN 47374
> (765) 962-3745
> www.hayesarboretum.org

The Hayes Regional Arboretum sits on 285 acres of land acquired by railroad official and inventor Stanley W. Hayes. As a regional arboretum, plant collections have been deliberately limited to those that are native to the Whitewater Drainage Basin, which encompasses 14 counties in east-central Indiana and west-central Ohio. The arboretum borders U.S. 40 and is located on the eastern edge of Richmond. It can be enjoyed while on foot as well as on a 3.5-mile tour by automobile. Attractions abound, including the Mabelle Hayes Fern Garden, the Native Woody Plant Preserve, the Wildflower Display Garden, and a 40-acre original beech maple forest. Activities and information revolve around the Nature Center, which schedules numerous seasonal programs and events throughout the year. These include, but are not limited to, hosting group tours, summer classes for kids of all ages, an Arbor Day Tree Giveaway, and specially scheduled gardening and environmental workshops. The arboretum is a relaxing and beautiful escape as well as an educational opportunity not to be missed. Admission is free.

Holcomb Gardens and Butler Prairie

> Butler University
> 4600 Sunset Avenue
> Indianapolis, IN 46208
> (317) 940-9413
> www.butler.edu/herbarium/prairie.htm

Holcomb Gardens offers a nice display of annuals and perennials in well-manicured grounds along the Indianapolis Water Company Canal immediately north of the Butler University campus. Rectangular beds of peonies, iris, and daylilies greet the many dog-walkers and strollers who visit the gardens, and are replaced with a good collection of popular annuals later in the season. Holcomb Gardens once boasted a collection of 101 different varieties of lilac, a favorite spring-blooming shrub with heavenly fragrance. Although not as extensive, remnants of those shrubs still bloom today. Scattered throughout the grounds are sitting areas and statuary with pensive quotes from famous American authors and figureheads. Tall-grass prairies covered 15 percent of Indiana before the settlers transformed the land for agricultural use. In an effort to create the original prairie environment found in west central and northwest Indiana, the Butler University Biology Department established the Butler University prairie in 1987. Located west of campus, across the Indianapolis Water Company Canal and adjacent to the Butler playing fields, the several-acre prairie is used as an outdoor laboratory for Biology courses, as a public education resource, and for wildlife living along the nearby White River. The area combines elements of several different prairie types including tall- and short-grass species. More than 30 different plant species were sown to make up the Butler prairie. Only a short 10-minute drive from the heart of downtown, the Butler prairie is a natural hidden treasure in the midst of urban sprawl.

Indianapolis Museum of Art

> 4000 N. Michigan Road
> Indianapolis, IN 46208-4196
> (317) 923-1331
> www.ima-art.org

The Indianapolis Museum of Art includes Oldfields, a 26-acre, American Country-Era Estate landscaped by the Olmsted Brothers of Brookline, Mass. The estate and gardens have been restored in the original style of the 1920s, and are listed on the National Register of Historic Places. Impeccably maintained by a dedicated staff of horticulturists, the IMA's gardens are a wonderful place to escape the hectic pace of city life. There are numerous smaller gardens within the larger grounds, where it is easy to lose oneself exploring the unique collection of plants. Plants are well labeled, and self-guided or guided tours of the grounds are available from staff or volunteers. One of the focal points of the grounds is the Madeline F. Elder Greenhouse, which sells unique tropical, bedding, and perennial plants, as well as other gardening gifts. The museum and grounds are undergoing a $76 million expansion and renovation, set to be completed in Spring 2005. Also in the works is the IMA's Virginia B. Fairbanks Art & Nature Park, set to open in 2004. It will offer both temporary and permanent installations of art as well as recreational experiences for visitors on 100 acres of woodlands, wetlands, lake and meadow. The park is being developed in partnership with Indy Parks Greenways, the Indianapolis Water Company (IWC), Historic Landmarks Foundation of Indiana, and other civic organizations. The grounds are open daily dawn to dusk.

Irwin Gardens

608 Fifth Street
Columbus, IN 47201
(812) 376-3331, Ext. 235
http://columbus.in.us/page.asp?page=Gardens

The home and gardens of the Irwin, Sweeney, and Miller family includes a delightful herb and knot garden. The gardens have an Italian influence and are done in three tiers. The waterfall steps up to a garden house whose only purpose is a lovely view of the landscape. Interesting sculptures include a child and dolphin. Massive plantings of annuals in spring and summer enhance perennials, trees, and shrubs. The gardens are open Saturdays and Sundays, mid-April to the end of October. Admission is free.

Jerry E. Clegg Foundation Botanical Gardens

1782 N. 400 E.
Lafayette, IN 47905

(765) 423-1325

Due east of Lafayette, the Jerry E. Clegg Botanical Garden is a short distance from I-65 and overlooks beautiful Wildcat Creek. After Clegg's death in 1963, his family summer home and grounds were turned into a memorial. Five different trails traverse the sometimes steep and wooded terrain that is home to hundreds of species of woodland wildflowers collected by the Clegg family and their friends. The display of Shooting Star, a native wildflower, is considered one of the finest in the state. There are at least 44 different species of trees that are well labeled in the garden, a favorite for schoolchildren making leaf collections. One of the most popular spots in the garden is Lookout Point, which gives a sweeping, breathtaking view of the Wildcat Valley below. The garden is open from 10 a.m. to sunset daily. Admission is free. Group tours are available by calling the County Naturalist or Garden Manager.

Oakhurst Gardens

1200 N. Minnetrista Parkway
Muncie, IN 47303
(765) 282-4848
(800) CULTURE
www.mccoak.org/gardens.html

Opened in May 1995, the 6.5-acre Oakhurst Gardens is part of the Minnetrista Cultural Center and the former home of George and Frances Ball and their daughter Elisabeth. The mission of Oakhurst is to create awareness, understanding, and appreciation of our natural environment. Built in 1895 and restored with the 1995 opening, Oakhurst includes a sunken garden, formal gardens, and a woodlands wildflower meadow. A visit to Discovery Cabin, a hands-on center, will teach visitors more about nature and its many wonders.

Purdue University Horticulture Gardens

1165 Horticulture Building
Purdue University
W. Lafayette, IN 47907-1165
(765) 494-1296
www.hort.purdue.edu/ext/hort_gardens.html

The Horticulture Gardens are a bright spot on the south end of the Purdue campus, just outside the Horticulture Building on Marstellar Street. The gardens feature a broad, well-maintained collection of herbaceous annuals and some perennials that have been tastefully planted in large curving beds. Visiting the gardens is an educational adventure since most of the plants have won awards or are new varieties for the market. The plants are all well labeled and referenced in a guide that is provided for visitors at the entrance to the garden. The Purdue Horticulture Department and Master Gardeners host the annual Purdue Garden Day in the horticulture gardens in June or July. Check the Web site for the date.

Taltree Arboretum and Gardens

71 N. 500 W. (enter on 100 N.)
Valparaiso, IN 46385
(219) 462-0025

www.taltree.org

Taltree is a 360-acre property that celebrates and preserves a south Lake Michigan environment, complete with hiking trails, an education center, and gardens. The 3-acre Heron Pond is surrounded by a large collection of mostly native herbaceous and woody wetland plants. There are also prairie plantings and gardens created with the pre-settlement landscape in mind. The project was started by the Gabis family in the 1990s. Since then, the Gabis Family Foundation was established as an Indiana not-for-profit corporation to fund and operate Taltree. In 2002, the name changed to the Taltree Arboretum and Gardens Foundation.

T.C. Steele State Historic Site

4220 S. T. C. Steele Road

Nashville, IN 47448

(812) 988-2785

www.in.gov/ism/HistoricSites/TCSteele/Historic.asp

More than 200 acres nestled in the hills of beautiful Brown County, the summer retreat of Hoosier impressionist painter T.C. Steele and his wife, Selma Neubacher Steele, is a nature-lover's paradise. The grounds and natural areas around the estate were often the subject or the inspiration for many of Steele's paintings. Managed by the Indiana Department of Natural Resources, the property has partially restored lily ponds, a formal garden, and hillside and perennial gardens, as well as the 92-acre Selma Steele State Nature Preserve. Dedicated in 1990, the preserve remains a "tribute to natural beauty," as requested by Mrs. Steele, and is crisscrossed by five hiking trails. The nature preserve is a favorite among wildflower lovers and is host to a "Wildflower Foray" each spring. Numerous other events are scheduled every year as well as educational outreach and summer programs.

White River Gardens

1200 W. Washington Street

P.O. Box 22309

Indianapolis, IN 46222-0309

(317) 630-2001

www.whiterivergardens.com

Located in White River State Park, White River Gardens encompass 3.3 acres of exterior display gardens surrounding a 5,000-square-foot glass-enclosed conservatory. Operated by the Indianapolis Zoological Society, the gardens are separate, but situated at the east end of the Indianapolis Zoo and overlooking the White River. The gardens feature intimate spaces where you can relax, be inspired, and gather ideas for your own backyard. Outdoor display areas include a wedding garden, a water garden, a formal garden, and numerous seasonal "theme" gardens, all with practical ideas for visitors to take home. A resource center gives visitors the opportunity to ask questions and have their home gardening problems answered. Accredited as a botanical garden, the existing grounds of the Zoo are already a great "green" escape a short walk across the restored Old Washington Street Bridge from the heart of downtown Indianapolis.

Mail-Order and On-Line Plant Resources

The following listing includes sources for a variety of plant materials suitable for the home gardener. Inclusion in the list should not be considered an endorsement nor should exclusion be viewed as disapproval. Information was deemed correct at the time of publication.

Antique Rose Emporium
9300 Lueckemeyer Road
Brenham, TX 77833
(800) 441-0002
www.antiqueroseemporium.com
Antique and old garden roses

Beaver Creek Nursery
7526 Pelleaux Road
Knoxville, TN 37938
(865) 922-3961
Unusual trees, shrubs, and vines

Bluestone Perennials
7211 Middle Ridge Road
Madison, OH 44057
(800) 852-5243
www.bluestoneperennials.com
Perennial flowers

Brent and Becky's Bulbs
7900 Daffodil Lane
Gloucester, VA 23061
(804) 693-3966
www.brentandbeckysbulbs.com
Hardy and tender bulbs

Caprice Nursery
10944 Mill Creek Road S.E.
Aumsville, OR 97325-9709
(503) 749-1397
www.capricenursery.com
Daylilies, hostas, peonies

Crystal Palace Perennials, Ltd
P.O. Box 154
St John, IN 46373
(219) 374-9419
www.crystalpalaceperennials.com
Aquatics, grasses, rare and variegated perennials

Davidson-Wilson Greenhouses
Rt. 2, Box 168, Dept. 48
Crawfordsville, IN 47933-9426
(877) 723-6834
Scented, novelty pelargoniums

Dutch Gardens
144 Intervale Road
Burlington, VT 05401
(800) 944-2250
www.dutchgardens.com
Hardy and tender bulbs

Earthly Goods Ltd.
P.O. Box 614
New Albany, IN 47151
(812) 944-2903
www.earthlygoods.com
Wildflower plants and seeds, herbs, grasses

Fairweather Gardens
P.O. Box 330
Greenwich, NJ 08323
(856) 451-6261
www.fairweathergardens.com
Unusual trees and shrubs

Forest Farm
990 Tetherow Road
Williams, OR 97544-9599
(541) 846-7269
www.forestfarm.com
Trees, shrubs, perennials

Girard Nurseries
6839 N. Ridge E.
Geneva, OH 44041
(919) 967-5529
www.girardnurseries.com
Trees, shrubs, vines

Glasshouseworks
Church Street
P.O. Box 97
Stewart, OH 45778
(800) 837-2142
www.glasshouseworks.com
Tropicals, annuals and perennials

Heronswood Nursery
7530 N.E. 288th Street
Kingston, WA 98346
(360) 297-4172
www.heronswood.com
Unusual trees, shrubs and perennials

Hortico Nurseries, Inc.
723 Robson Road, R.R. #1,
Waterdown, Ontario LOR2H1
(905) 689-9323
www.Hortico.com
Roses, trees, shrubs

Indiana Division of Forestry
Jasper-Pulaski Nursery
15508 W. 700 N.
Medaryville, IN 47957
(219) 843-4827
Native tree and shrub seedlings for conservation

Indiana Division of Forestry
Vallonia Nursery
2782 W. Co. Road 540 S.
Vallonia, IN 47281
(812) 358-3621
Native tree and shrub seedlings for conservation

Johnny's Selected Seeds
955 Benton Avenue
Winslow, ME 04901
(207) 861-3900
www.johnnyseeds.com
Organic seeds

Kurt Bluemel, Inc.
2740 Greene Lane
Baldwin, MD 21013
(800) 498-1560
www.kurtbluemel.com
Ornamental grasses and sedges

Lilypons Water Gardens
6800 Lilypons Road
Buckeystown, MD 21717
(800) 999-5459
www.lilypons.com
Water garden plants and supplies

Mellinger's
2310 W. South Range Road
North Lima, OH 44452-9731
(800) 321-7444
www.mellingers.com
Perennials, seeds, tropicals, garden supplies

Munchkin Nursery & Gardens
323 Woodside Dr., N.W.
Depauw, IN 47115-9039
(812) 633-4858
www.munchkinnursery.com
*Native and non-native woodland plants; rare and
    unusual perennials*

Nichols Garden Nursery
1190 Old Salem Road N.E.
Albany, OR 97321
(800) 422-3985
Herbs and rare seeds

Nor'East Miniature Roses, Inc.
P.O. Box 307
Rowley, MA 01969
(800) 426-6485
(978) 948-7964
www.noreast-miniroses.com
Miniature roses

Old House Gardens
536 Third Street
Ann Arbor, MI 48103
(734) 995-1486
www.oldhousegardens.com
Specializes in rare, unusual and antique bulbs

Park Seed Company
1 Parkton Avenue
Greenwood, SC 29647-0001
(800) 213-0076
www.parkseed.com
Flower and vegetable seeds, perennial plants

Pinetree Garden Seeds
P.O. Box 300
New Gloucester, ME 04260
(207) 926-3400
www.superseeds.com
Flower, vegetable, and herb seeds

Plant Delights Nursery, Inc.
9241 Sauls Road
Raleigh, NC 27603
(919) 772-4794
www.plantdelights.com
Rare and unusual perennials and tropical plants

Prairie Nursery
P.O. Box 306
Westfield, WI 53964
(800) GRO-WILD
www.prairienursery.com
Wildflowers and native grasses, plants and seed

Renee's Garden
7389 W. Zayante Road
Felton, CA 95018
(888) 880-7228
www.reneesgarden.com
Gourmet vegetables, herbs, and country garden flowers

Seed Saver's Exchange
3076 N. Winn Road
Decorah, IA 52101
www.seedsavers.org
(563) 382-5990
Heirloom vegetable and flower seeds and plants

Seeds of Change
P.O. Box 15700
Sante Fe, NM 87506-5700
(888) 762-7333
Vegetable and flower seeds, organically grown

Shady Oaks Nursery
700 19th Avenue N.E.
Waseca, MN 56093
Shade-loving perennials, trees and shrubs

Shepherd's Garden Seeds
30 Irene Street
Torrington, CT 06790-6658
(860) 482-3638
www.shepherdseeds.com
Flower, vegetable, and herb seeds

Song Sparrow Perennial Farm
13101 E. Rye Road
Avalon, WI 53505
(800) 553-3715
www.songsparrow.com

Spence Restoration Nursery
2220 E. Fuson Road
P.O. Box 546
Muncie IN 47308
(765) 286-7154
www.spencenursery.com
Native plants for prairie, wetland and woodland restoration

Stokes Tropicals
4806 E. Old Spanish Trail
Jeanerette, LA 70544
(800) 624-9706
www.stokestropicals.com
Tropical plants

Thompson and Morgan
P.O. Box 1308
Jackson, NJ 08527-0308
(800) 274-7333
http://seeds.thompson-morgan.com/us
Flower, vegetable, tree, and shrub seeds; exotic seeds

Van Bourgondien Bulbs
P.O. Box 1000
Babylon, New York 11702
(800) 622-9997
www.dutchbulbs.com

W. Atlee Burpee & Co.
300 Park Avenue
Warminster, PA 18974
(800) 888-1447
www.burpee.com
Flower and vegetable seeds; plants

White Flower Farm
P.O. Box 50, Route 63
Litchfield, CT 06759-9988
(800) 503-9624
www.shepherdseeds.com
Perennial flowers, bulbs, shrubs

Glossary

Acid soil: soil with a pH less than 7.0. Many plants thrive in soils with pH between 6.0 and 7, or "slightly acid." Sometimes called "sour" soil.

Alkaline soil: soil with a pH greater than 7.0. It lacks acidity, often because it has limestone in it. Sometimes called "sweet" soil.

All-purpose fertilizer: powdered, liquid, or granular fertilizer with a balanced proportion of the three key nutrients—nitrogen (N), phosphorus (P), and potassium (K). It is suitable for maintenance nutrition for most plants.

Annual: a plant that lives its entire life in one season. It is genetically determined to germinate, grow, flower, set seed, and die the same year.

Aerial root: roots that do not grow in the soil and which form above ground, usually along a stem or leaf. Aerial roots help support plants and absorb moisture and nutrients to a limited extent.

All-America Selection (Winner): an award given to the newest annual flowers, vegetables, and herbs for their outstanding character, such as flower color, length of bloom, pest resistance, etc. New plants are designated as such each year by the All-America Selections committee.

Balled and burlapped: describes a tree or shrub grown in the field whose soil and rootball was wrapped with protective burlap and twine and sometimes wire, when the plant was dug up to be sold or transplanted.

Bare root: describes plants that have been packaged without any soil around their roots. Young shrubs, trees, and perennials purchased through the mail often arrive with their roots covered with only moist sphagnum moss, sawdust, or similar material, and wrapped in plastic. As a rule-of-thumb, soak these plants in water for 6 to 12 hours before planting.

Barrier plant: a plant that has intimidating thorns or spines and is sited purposely to block foot traffic or other access to the home or yard.

Bedding plants: describes annuals used for flowers or foliage that are massed together in large groups or beds.

Beneficial insects: insects or their larvae that prey on pest organisms and their eggs. They may be flying insects, such as ladybugs, parasitic wasps, praying mantids, and soldier bugs, or soil dwellers such as predatory nematodes, spiders, and ants.

Berm: an elongated hill of soil used to screen traffic and noise or for planting trees, shrubs and flowers.

Bienniel: a plant that needs two years to mature. The first year it develops leaves and roots. The second year it produces more leaves, then flowers, sets seed, and dies.

Bract: a modified leaf structure on a plant stem near its flower that resembles a petal. Often it is more colorful and visible than the actual flower, as in dogwood or poinsettia.

Bud union: the place where the top of a more desirable plant was grafted to the rootstock of a less desirable plant, as with many roses.

Bulb: An underground storage structure used by many plants composed of short, fleshy modified leaves and stems, as in tulips and daffodils.

Canopy: the overhead and branching area of a tree, including leaves.

Chlorosis: a term to describe leaves that turn yellow. The veins of leaves with chlorosis usually stay green. Chlorosis is the result of a nutrient deficiency, such as iron, due to high soil pH.

Compost: organic matter such as leaves, grass clippings, hedge trimmings, and kitchen scraps that has undergone progressive decomposition from microbes, earthworms, and other soil organisms until it is reduced to a dark brown material with spongy, fluffy texture. Added to soil of any type, it improves the soil's ability to hold air and water and to drain well. Compost also increases the nutrient supply for plants and is arguably the best thing to add to any garden soil.

Compost tea: a natural liquid fertilizer made by soaking compost in water. Nutrient composition depends on the quality of the compost but is usually higher in nitrogen than other nutrients.

Conifer: a cone bearing plant such as spruce, pine ,and fir.

Corm: an underground storage structure found at the base of some plants such as crocus and gladiolus. It is similar to a bulb but consists of modified stem material.

Critical root zone: describes the most important part of the root system in woody plants, usually trees. The critical root zone is calculated by multiplying 1 to 1.5 feet for every inch of trunk diameter at chest high. The critical root zone of a tree with a trunk diameter of 10 inches at chest high is 10 to 15 feet measured outward from the trunk in all directions.

Crown: the base of a plant at, or just beneath, the surface of the soil where the roots meet the stems.

Cultivar: a CULTIvated VARiety. It is a naturally occurring form of a plant that has been identified as special or superior because of its leaf or flower color, fruit habit, shape, height, pest tolerance, or for many other reasons. Cultivars are purposely selected for propagation and production in the nursery industry.

Deadhead: a pruning technique that removes dead or dying flowers from plants to improve their appearance, prevent seeds from forming, and to stimulate further flowering. It is especially important to deadhead many annuals to encourage continued blooming.

Deciduous plants: these trees, shrubs, vines, and groundcovers shed their leaves in the fall.

Desiccation: drying out of foliage tissues, usually due to drought or wind.

Division: the practice of splitting apart perennial plants to create several smaller-rooted segments. The practice is useful for controlling the plant's size and for sharing plants with friends; it is also essential to the health and continued flowering of certain ones.

Dormant: term used to describe the period, usually the winter, when perennial plants temporarily cease active growth and rest. Some plants, like spring-blooming bulbs, also go dormant in the summer.

Drift: a planting scheme involving large numbers of one type or one color of plant, usually annual flowers or bulbs. Drifts can be formal but are usually informal or natural.

Dripline: The farthest edge from the trunk where rain water would drip from the canopy of a tree. If the sun is directly overhead, the dripline is the outer edge of the shadow cast on the ground from the tree canopy.

Ephemeral: a short-lived plant or flowers such as spring wildflowers, which bloom and then quickly go dormant. Also describes daylily blossoms, which last for only one day.

Established: the point at which a newly planted tree, shrub, or flower overcomes the ill-effects of transplanting and begins to produce new growth, either foliage or stems.

Evergreen: perennial plants that do not lose their leaves annually with the onset of winter. Leaves of needled evergreens, like pine and spruce, or broadleaf evergreens, like viburnum and azalea, persist and continue to function on a plant through one or more winters, aging and dropping gradually in cycles of three or four years or more.

Exfoliating: peeling off in thin layers as with the bark in some trees.

Fertile/fertility: refers to the nutrient content of the soil and/or the need to add nutrients in the form of fertilizers or composts.

Foliar: of or about foliage—usually refers to foliage, or leaves.

Floret: a tiny flower, usually one of many forming a cluster, that comprises a single blossom.

Fungicide: a pesticide used to control fungi that cause plant disease.

Frost-free date: refers to the average date of the last killing frost in spring. This date varies based on where you live in Indiana.

Germinate: to sprout. Germination is a fertile seed's first stage of development.

Graft (union): the point on the stem of a woody plant where a stem (scion) from a more ornamental plant is inserted so that it will join and grow as one on the roots of the original (stock) plant it. Roses are commonly grafted to rose plants with sturdier root systems.

Habit: the natural growth pattern and mature form of a plant, such as upright and spreading, rounded mound, pyramidal, upright, etc.

Harden/harden off: To gradually expose a plant to the natural conditions of a landscape, such as with spring annuals grown in a greenhouse but destined for planting outdoors. Hardening off allows plants to acclimate to the light and temperatures of the existing landscape before planting.

Hardy/hardiness: term used to describe the ability of a plant to survive the winter cold in a particular area. A plant's cold hardiness is measured using the USDA Hardiness Zone Map which depicts average annual minimum temperatures. Indiana is located in Zones 5 and 6 of the hardiness zone map.

Hardscape: the permanent, structural, non-plant part of a landscape, such as walls, sheds, pools, patios, arbors, driveways and walkways.

Herbaceous: plants having fleshy or soft stems that die back with frost, such as annuals and perennials; the opposite of woody, as in trees and shrubs.

Herbicide: a pesticide used to kill unwanted vegetation such as weeds.

Hybrid: the offspring that is the result of intentional or natural cross-pollination between two plants of the same, or similar, genus and species.

Leader: the main stem or trunk of a tree.

Lenticel: a raised and slightly rounded slit in the bark of trees and shrubs. Lenticels are used for gas exchange between plant and the air and can be plentiful or sparse.

Loam: general term describing soils with roughly equal parts of sand, silt and clay particles, and organic materials. Loamy soils are fertile and have lots of air spaces, but hold moisture well, too. They are excellent soils for gardening usually.

Microclimate: smaller pockets in a landscape with different growing conditions as a result of topography, buildings, soil-types, exposure to sun, underground utilities, etc. Courtyards generally have warmer temperatures because of radiant heat from a building and less wind, for example.

Mulch: a layer of material over bare soil to protect it from erosion, to discourage weeds, and to maintain soil moisture. It may be organic (wood chips, bark, pine needles, chopped leaves, straw, etc.) or inorganic (gravel, fabric, rubber, or plastic).

Naturalize: a.) to plant seeds, bulbs, or plants in a random, informal pattern as they would appear in their natural habitat; b.) to adapt to and spread throughout adopted habitats (a tendency of some non-native plants).

Nectar: the sweet fluid produced by glands on flowers that attract pollinators such as hummingbirds and honeybees for whom it is a source of energy.

Organic material, organic matter: any material or debris that is derived from plants. It is carbon-based material capable of undergoing decomposition and decay such as leaves or wood. It may be a derivative of plants as in newspaper or a by-product of livestock such as manure.

Peat moss: organic matter from naturally occurring bogs of peat sedges (United States) or sphagnum mosses (Canada), often used to loosen compact soils and improve drainage. It is a non-renewable resource that has a slight acidifying effect on the soil.

Perennial: a flowering plant that lives over two or more seasons. Many die back with frost, but their roots survive the winter and generate new shoots in the spring.

Perennial Plant of the Year: an award to recognize a perennial's outstanding characteristics such as long bloom period, pest resistance, and ease of growth. It is given by the Perennial Plant Association, a national organization that researches and promotes perennial plants.

pH: a measurement of the relative acidity or alkalinity of soil or water based on a scale of 1 to 14, pH 7 being neutral. Individual plants require soil to be within a certain pH range so that nutrients can dissolve in moisture and be available to them. The only way to know the pH of the soil is to perform a soil test.

Pinch: to remove tender stems, leaves, and/or flower buds by nipping them off with your thumb and forefinger. This pruning technique encourages branching, compactness, and flowering in many plants. You can also deadhead flowers with this technique.

Pruning: the process by which plant growth is encouraged and controlled by selective removal of branches, branch tips, stems, flowers or roots.

Pollen: the yellow, powdery grains in the center of a flower, which are the male sex cells. Pollen grains are transferred to the female plant parts by means of insects, wind, and sometimes animals to fertilize them and create seeds. This process must occur for fruit to develop.

Raceme: describes an arrangement of single stalked flowers along an elongated, unbranched stem. Spike-like.

Repeat bloom: the ability of a plant to re-bloom after its principal bloom period, such as roses or perennials.

Rejuvenation pruning: The removal of older, woody stems to encourage new growth.

Rhizome: a swollen, fleshy, energy-storing stem structure, similar to a bulb, that lies horizontally in the soil, with roots emerging from its lower surface and growth shoots from a growing point at or near its tip, as in bearded iris. Some rhizomes grow and spread very quickly and can be a nuisance or invasive.

Rootbound (or potbound): the condition of a plant that has been confined in a container too long, its roots having been forced to wrap around themselves and even grow out of the container. Successful transplanting or repotting requires untangling and trimming away some of the matted roots.

Root flare: the transition at the base of a tree trunk where the bark tissue begins to differentiate and roots begin to form just before entering the soil. The root flare is identified by its flaring out from the trunk. This area should stay visible and not be covered with soil when planting a tree.

Seedling: a young plant grown from seed as in annuals or vegetables. Tree and shrub seedlings are also grown from seed but are only one to a few years old.

Self-seeding/self-sow: the tendency of some plants to sow their seeds freely around the yard. It creates many seedlings the following season that may or may not be welcome.

Semievergreen: tending to be evergreen in a mild climate but deciduous in a rigorous one. In Indiana, semievergreen plants shed some of their leaves.

Shearing: the pruning technique whereby plant stems and branches are cut uniformly with long-bladed pruning shears (hedge shears) or powered hedge trimmers. It is to keep all growth at a uniform level such as with formal hedges and topiary.

Side-dress: to apply fertilizer or compost away from the crown, but near the roots of plants. Side-dressed fertilizers are usually applied at lower rates about mid-season.

Slow-release fertilizer: fertilizer that releases its nutrients gradually as a function of soil temperature, moisture, and related microbial activity. It is usually granular and may be organic or synthetic.

Soil amendment: anything added to change the texture of soils such as sand or organic matter.

Soilless mix: a mixture of peat, compost, vermiculite, or perlite used to grow plants in pots or containers, or for starting seeds.

Species: usually a morphologically similar group of plants that commonly exist in nature and that produce similar offspring. A species may be subdivided, hybridized or otherwise genetically altered by humans or nature to produce subspecies, varieties, and cultivars that may or may not be able to reproduce, but that are morphologically distinct from the species.

Stolon: a horizontal stem growing along the soil surface and producing roots and shoots at nodes. Also called a runner.

Succulent growth: the sometimes undesirable production of fleshy, water-storing leaves or stems that results from overfertilization.

Sucker: a new growing shoot from the base of a plant. Roots produce suckers to form new stems and spread to form large plantings, or colonies. Usually this type of growth is considered undesirable except in natural settings or areas where the plants have room to spread.

Thatch: an accumulation of dead or dying plant stems and roots at the surface of the soil, such as with turf.

Thinning/thinning out: refers to selective removal of seedling plants so those left in the soil will grow to their mature size. Also refers to selective removal of branches in trees and shrubs to allow better light penetration and air circulation inside the leaf canopy, and to encourage new growth.

Topdress: the application of compost or fertilizer to the surface of the soil around a plant.

Topping: the removal of the primary leader of a tree. The irrational, general, and disfiguring removal of all of a tree's branches to a uniform length to control its size. Topping promotes disease and insect infestation in trees and destroys its natural shape.

Tuber: a type of underground storage structure or specialized root, similar to a bulb. It generates roots below and stems above ground, such as with dahlias.

Variegated: foliage that is streaked, edged, blotched, or mottled with a contrasting color, often green leaves with yellow, cream, or white markings.

Variety: The naturally occurring variant of a plant species found in the wild.

Water sprouts: vigorous upright shoots that develop along tree and shrub branches, usually where they have been pruned or injured. Water sprouts should almost always be removed.

Wings: a.) the corky tissue that forms edges along the twigs of some woody plants such as winged euonymus; b.) the flat, dried extension of tissue on some seeds, such as maple, that catch the wind and help them disseminate.

Winterburn: the yellowing and browning of the leaves of evergreen plants in winter from drying winds, southern exposures, or ice and snow melt used on roads and walkways in winter.

Bibliography

Allison, James. *Water in the Garden*. Salamander Books, 1991.

Archibald, David and Mary Patton. *Firefly Gardener's Guide: Water Gardens*. Firefly Books, 1996.

Armitage, Allan. *Armitage's Garden Perennials: A Color Encyclopedia*, Timber Press, 2000.

Armitage, Allan. *Herbaceous Perennial Plants: A Treatise on Their Identification, Culture, and Garden Attributes*. Varsity Press Inc., 1989.

Armitage, Allan; Maureen Heffernan; Chela Kleiber; and Holly Shimizu. *Burpee Complete Gardener*. Macmillan, Inc., 1995.

Armitage, Allan M. *Armitage's Manual of Annuals, Biennials and Half-Hardy Perennials*. Timber Press, 2001.

Aust, Tracy DiSabato. *The Well-Tended Perennial Garden*. Timber Press, 1998.

Ball, Jeff and Liz. *Flower Garden Problem Solver*. Rodale Press, 1990.

Beard, James B. *Turfgrass Science and Culture*. Prentice Hall, Inc., 1973.

Better Homes and Gardens: Bulbs For All Seasons. Better Homes and Gardens Books, 1994.

Boerner Botanical Gardens. *Rose Gardening*. Pantheon Books, 1995.

Brady, Fern Marshall, editor. *Gardening with Perennials*. Rodale Press, 1996.

Brand, Mark. *University of Connecticut Plant Database of Trees, Shrubs and Vines*. University of Connecticut. 1997–2001. http://www.hort.uconn.edu/plants/about.html

Brickell, Christopher, Elvin McDonald, and Trevor Cole. *The American Horticultural Society Encyclopedia of Gardening*. Dorling Kindersley, 1993.

Bryan, John E. *Hearst Garden Guides: Bulbs*. Hearst Books, 1992.

Burns, Russell M. and Barbara H. Honkala. *Silvics of North America Volume I. Conifers*. U.S. Forest Service, 1990.

Burrell, C. Colston. *Perennial Combinations*. Rodale Press, 1999.

Bush-Brown, Louise and James. *America's Garden Book*. Revised edition by Howard S. Irwin with the assistance of the Brooklyn Botanic Garden. Macmillan Inc., 1996.

Clausen, Ruth Rogers and Nicolas H. Ekstrom. *Perennials for American Gardens*. Random House, Inc., 1989.

Coats, Alice M. *Garden Shrubs and Their Histories*. Simon and Schuster, 1992.

Cox, Jeff. *Perennial All-Stars*. Rodale Press, 1998.

Cox, Jeff and Marilyn. *The Perennial Garden: Color Harmonies Through the Seasons*. Rodale Press, 1985.

Crandall, Chuck and Barbara. *Flowering, Fruiting & Foliage Vines: A Gardener's Guide*. Sterling Publishing Co., 1995.

Cutler, Karan Davis, editor. *A Harrowsmith Gardener's Guide: Vines*. Camden House Publishing, Inc., 1992.

Damrosch, Barbara. *The Garden Primer.* Workman Publishing, 1988.

Dana, Michael N. *Ornamental Grasses for Indiana Landscapes.* Purdue University Department of Horticulture Cooperative Extension Home Yard and Garden Series, 1994.

—. *Cooperative Extension Trees and Landscaping Publications.* Purdue University Department of Horticulture.

Deam, Charles C. *Shrubs of Indiana, Second Edition.* Historic Hoosier Hills Woodland Committee, 1932.

Dirr, Michael A. *Manual of Woody Landscape Plants*, Fourth Edition. Stipes Publishing Co., 1990.

Druse, Ken. *The Natural Garden.* Clarkson N. Potter, Inc., 1989.

Ellis, Barbara W. *Taylor's Guide, Growing North America's Favorite Plants.* Houghton Mifflin Co., 1998.

Ellis, Barbara W. and Fern Marshall Bradley, editors. *The Organic Gardener's Handbook of Natural Insect and Disease Control.* Rodale Press, 1992.

Ernst, Ruth Shaw. *The Naturalist's Garden.* Globe Pequot Press, 1993.

Flint, Harrison. *Landscape Plants for Eastern North America.* John Wiley and Sons, 1997.

Glattstein, Judy. *The American Gardener's World of Bulbs.* Little, Brown and Co., 1994.

Glattstein, Judy. *Waterscaping.* Garden Way Publishing, 1994.

Glimn-Lacy, Janice. *What Flowers When with Hints on Home Landscaping.* The Flower and the Leaf Press, 1995.

Greenlee, John. *The Encyclopedia of Ornamental Grasses.* Michael Friedman Publishing Group, 1992.

Grehold, Lacasse and Wandell. *Street Tree Fact Sheets.* Pennsylvania State University Press, 1993.

Griffiths, Trevor. *The Book of Classic Old Roses.* Michael Joseph Limited, 1987.

Haggard, Ezra. *Perennials for the Lower Midwest.* Indiana University Press, 1996.

Halpin, Anne. *Foolproof Planting.* Rodale Press, 1990.

Harstad, Carolyn. *Go Native: Gardening with Native Plants and Wildflowers in the Lower Midwest.* Indiana University Press, 1999.

Heath, Brent and Becky. *Daffodils for American Gardens.* Elliott & Clark Publishing, 1995.

Hendrickson, Robert. *Ladybugs, Tiger Lilies & Wallflowers: A Gardener's Book of Words.* Prentice-Hall General Reference, 1993.

Heriteau, Jacqueline and Marc Cathey. *The National Arboretum Book of Outstanding Garden Plants.* Simon and Schuster, 1990.

Hessayon, D.G. *The Bulb Expert.* Expert Books, 1995.

Hill, Lewis and Nancy. *Bulbs: Four Seasons of Beautiful Blooms.* Garden Way Publishing, 1994.

—. *Successful Perennial Gardening: A Practical Guide.* Garden Way Publishing, 1988.

Hull, George. *The Language of Gardening: An Informal Dictionary.* World Publishing Co., 1967.

Indianapolis Rose Society. *Successful Rose Growing in Indiana.*

Jacobsen, Arthur Lee. *North American Landscape Trees.* Ten Speed Press, 1996.

Karnok, Keith. *Certified Turfgrass Professional.* University of Georgia and the Georgia Center for Continuing Education, 1994.

Lacy, Allen. *Gardening with Groundcovers and Vines.* Harper Collins, 1993.

Lathrop, Norma Jean. *Herbs: How to Select, Grow and Enjoy.* HP Books, 1981.

Lawn Care Series. Purdue University Department of Agronomy.

Lerner, B. R. *Roses. Purdue Department of Horticulture Home Yard and Garden Series.* Purdue University Press, 1988.

Loewer, Peter. *Rodale's Annual Garden.* Wings Books, 1992.

McClure, Susan. *The Herb Gardener: A Guide for All Seasons.* Garden Way Publishing, 1996.

McDonald, Elvin. *Rose Gardening.* Meredith Books, 1995.

McKeon, Judith. *The Encyclopedia of Roses.* Rodale Press, 1995.

MacCaskey, Michael. Lawns and Ground Covers: How to Select, Grow and Enjoy. HP Books, 1982.

Mathew, Brian and Philip Swindells. *The Complete Book of Bulbs, Corms, Tubers, and Rhizomes.* Reader's Digest Books, 1994.

Morgan, Hal. *The Mail Order Gardener.* Harper and Row, 1988.

Morrisey, Sharon Irwin and F. A. Giles. *Dwarf Flowering Shrubs for the Midwest.* University of Illinois at Urbana-Champaign, College of Agriculture Special Publication 60, 1980.

—. *Large Flowering Shrubs for the Midwest.* University of Illinois at Urbana-Champaign, College of Agriculture Special Publication 74.

Nash, Helen. *The Pond Doctor: Planning & Maintaining a Healthy Water Garden.* Sterling Publishing Co., 1994.

Oakes, A. J. *Ornamental Grasses and Grasslike Plants.* Van Nostrand Reinhold, 1990.

Osborne, Robert and Beth Powning. *Hardy Roses.* Storey Communications, Inc., 1991.

Ottesen, Carole. *Ornamental Grasses, The Amber Wave.* McGraw Hill, 1989.

Phillips, Roger and Martyn Rix. *The Random House Book of Perennials, Vol. 1 and 2.* Random House, 1991.

Poor, Janet M., Editor and Nancy Peterson Brewster. *Plants that Merit Attention: Volume I, Trees.* Timber Press, 1984.

—. *Plants That Merit Attention: Volume II, Shrubs.* Timber Press, 1996.

Powell, Eileen. *From Seed to Bloom.* Garden Way Publishing, 1995.

Reader's Digest Handbooks: Herbs. Reader's Digest, 1990.

Redell, Rayford Clayton. *Rose Bible.*

Rice, Graham. *The Complete Book of Perennials.* Reader's Digest, 1996.

Ritter, Frances, Editor. *Shrubs and Climbers.* DK Publishing, 1996.

Robinson, Peter. *Wayside Gardens Collection: The Water Garden*. Sterling Publishing Co., 1995.

Rodale's Chemical-Free Yard & Garden. Rodale Press, Inc., 1991.

Rose, Peter Q. *Climbers and Wall Plants*. Blandford, 1990.

—. *Ivies*. Blandford, 1990.

Sala, Orietta. *The World's Best Roses*. Prentice Hall, 1990.

Scaniello, Stephen and Tanya Bayard. *Climbing Roses*. Hall, 1994.

Schulz, Warren. *The Chemical Free Lawn*. Rodale Press, 1983.

Scott, O. M. and Sons. *Scotts Information Manual for Lawns*. O. M. Scott and Sons Company, 1979.

Seiler, John R. and John A. Peterson. *Dendrology at Virginia Tech*. Virginia Polytechnic and State University. http://www.cnr.vt.edu/dendro/dendrology/main.htm

Sternberg, Guy and Jim Wilson. *Landscaping With Native Trees*. Chapters Publishing Limited, 1995.

Still, Steven M. *Manual of Herbaceous Ornamental Plants*. Stipes Publishing LLC, 1994.

Stokes, Donald and Lillian. *The Wildflower Book East of the Rockies*. Little, Brown and Co., 1992.

Swindells, Philip. *Planning and Planting Water Gardens*. Ward Lock Books, 1996.

Taylor's Master Guide to Gardening. Houghton Mifflin Co., 1994.

Thomas, Paul A. and Mel P. Garber, Extension Horticulturists. *Growing Ferns*. The University of Georgia College of Agricultural and Environmental Sciences Bulletin 737, http://www.ces.uga.edu/pubcd/B737-w.htm. 1999.

Thomas, R. William. *Trees and Shrubs*. Hearst Books, 1992.

Turgeon, A. J. *Turfgrass Management*. Reston Publishing Company, Inc., 1980.

Wyman, Donald. *Shrubs and Vines for American Gardens*. Macmillan, Inc., 1969.

Photography Credits

William Adams: pages 99, 108, 129, 139, 227, 236

Liz Ball and Rick Ray: pages 11, 15, 16, 24, 40, 49, 56, 62, 63, 72, 79, 86, 89, 124, 127, 132, 143, 163, 170, 171, 180, 181, 190, 191, 192, 193, 195, 196, 199, 206, 210, 215, 221

Cathy Wilkinson Barash: page 200

Laura Coit: page185

Mike Dirr: page 189

Thomas Eltzroth: pages 8, 12, 21, 22, 25, 26, 27, 28, 30, 31, 32, 33, 34, 35, 36, 37, 38, 39, 41, 42, 43, 44, 45, 46, 47, 50, 52, 53, 57, 59, 64, 65, 67, 68, 69, 71, 73, 74, 75, 76, 77, 78, 80, 82, 83, 84, 85, 87, 88, 90, 91, 92, 93, 94, 97, 101, 112, 113, 114, 119, 122, 123, 125, 126, 128, 135, 138, 140, 142, 145, 146, 160, 161, 162, 164, 168, 172, 173, 194, 198, 201, 203, 211, 214, 218, 220, 222, 223, 226, 228, 229, 236 (bottom), 237

Pamela Harper: pages 55, 103, 106, 130, 141, 156, 166, 167, 169, 175, 182, 207, 209, 212, 213, 224

Heirloom Roses, Inc. (www.heirloomroses.com): pages 149, 151

Dency Kane: front cover, pages 17, 100, 118, 121, 148, 150, 152, 155, 183, 184

Peter Loewer: page 102

Robert Lyons: page 104

D. Mackenzie: page 109

Charles Mann: pages 157, 176, 179, 197

Jerry Pavia: pages 23, 28, 29, 51, 54, 60, 61, 70, 81, 105, 107, 110, 111, 115, 116, 120, 131, 133, 136, 137, 147, 153, 154, 159, 174, 177, 178, 186, 187, 202, 204, 205, 208, 225, 230, back cover photos

Carol Reese: page 92

Felder Rushing: page 48, 165

Greg Speichert: pages 233, 234, 235 (bottom), 238

Ralph Snodsmith: page 58

Mark Turner: pages 66, 134, 235 (top)

Andre Viette: pages 20, 98, 117, 216, 217, 219

Plant Index

Featured plant selections are indicated in **boldface**.

Meet the Authors

Jo Ellen Meyers Sharp

Jo Ellen Meyers Sharp has been writing about gardening since 1989 in a weekly column for *The Indianapolis Star.* She also writes a garden column for the *Indianapolis Business Journal's At Home Quarterly.* She teaches and lectures about gardening and is a frequent guest on area television and radio programs.

A regional director of the Garden Writers Association, she also serves as vice president of the Indianapolis Museum of Art Horticultural Society, director of the Friends of Garfield Park, Inc., and president of the board of the Neighborhood Self-Employment Initiative. She is an Advanced Master Gardener and is a member of the Perennial Plant Association, the Indiana Native Plant and Wildflower Society, the Indiana Organic Gardeners Association, and the Indiana Nursery & Landscape Association.

After more than twenty years as a reporter in Louisville, KY, and Indianapolis, IN, she left the newspaper business in 1997 to found a freelance writing and communications firm. An Indianapolis native, she grew up on the city's south side as part of a family of German immigrants who operated greenhouses and florist businesses. She lives in Indianapolis (Zone 5) with her dog, Penn, and cat, Cowgirl, and where she plants in drifts of one in a small urban garden.

Tom Tyler

Tom Tyler was an Extension Agent and Coordinator for Urban Gardening Programs in Indianapolis from 1988-98. For more than four years he was heard on WMYS Radio on Thursday mornings answering lawn and garden call-in questions and was a regular contributor to the news media on gardening subjects. A former Peace Corps Volunteer, he is also past-President of the American Community Gardening Association. In 1998 he received a Distinguished Hoosier Award from Governor Frank O'Bannon for his contributions to community gardening and horticulture in the Capital City.

Tom currently works as an Extension Agent in Arlington, Virginia where he develops sustainable landscape gardening educational programs for residents, Master Gardeners, Tree Stewards, and the green industry. He has hosted Lawn and Garden Chats on USAToday.com and has appeared on National Public Radio with Diane Rehm. He is an adjunct faculty member at The George Washington University where he teaches Woody Plants in the Landscape Design program. Tom is a graduate of Clemson and Purdue Universities and is an ISA Certified Arborist. He lives and gardens with his partner, Chris Bobowski, in Zone 7, in Washington, D.C.